Introducing Archaeology

Third Edition

INTRODUCING ARCHAEOLOGY

Third Edition

ROBERT J. MUCKLE and STACEY L. CAMP

UNIVERSITY OF TORONTO PRESS
Toronto Buffalo London

© University of Toronto Press 2021
Toronto Buffalo London
utorontopress.com
Printed in the U.S.A.

ISBN 978-1-4875-0662-9 (cloth) ISBN 978-1-4875-3453-0 (EPUB)
ISBN 978-1-4875-2445-6 (paper) ISBN 978-1-4875-3452-3 (PDF)

Library and Archives Canada Cataloguing in Publication

Title: Introducing archaeology / Robert J. Muckle and Stacey L. Camp.
Names: Muckle, Robert James, author. | Camp, Stacey Lynn, author.
Description: Third edition. | Includes bibliographical references and index.
Identifiers: Canadiana (print) 20200281518 | Canadiana (ebook) 20200281526 | ISBN 9781487506629 (hardcover) | ISBN 9781487524456 (softcover) | ISBN 9781487534530 (EPUB) | ISBN 9781487534523 (PDF)
Subjects: LCSH: Archaeology – Textbooks. | LCGFT: Textbooks.
Classification: LCC CC165 .M83 2021 | DDC 930.1 – dc23

We welcome comments and suggestions regarding any aspect of our publications – please feel free to contact us at news@utorontopress.com or visit us at utorontopress.com.

Every effort has been made to contact copyright holders; in the event of an error or omission, please notify the publisher.

University of Toronto Press acknowledges the financial assistance to its publishing program of the Canada Council for the Arts and the Ontario Arts Council, an agency of the Government of Ontario.

 Canada Council for the Arts   Conseil des Arts du Canada

 ONTARIO ARTS COUNCIL CONSEIL DES ARTS DE L'ONTARIO an Ontario government agency un organisme du gouvernement de l'Ontario

Funded by the Government of Canada   Financé par le gouvernement du Canada

CONTENTS

List of Figures   IX
List of Tables   XI
List of Text Boxes   XIII
Note to Instructors   XV
Note to Students   XVII
Acknowledgments   XIX
About the Authors   XXI
Preface to the Third Edition   XXIII

PROLOGUE: IT'S MORE THAN VIKING HOARDS, SHIPWRECKS, AND LOVERS
ENTANGLED IN DEATH   I

CHAPTER 1: SITUATING ARCHAEOLOGY   5
Introduction   5
The Allure of Archaeology   5
The Lens of Archaeology   8
Defining Archaeology   9
A Scholarly Endeavor, a Profession, and a Craft   10
Archaeology versus Archeology   11
Contextualizing Archaeology   12
Rationalizing Archaeology   22
Basic Concepts in Archaeology   24
Key Resources and Suggested Reading   26

CHAPTER 2: LOOKING AT ARCHAEOLOGY'S PAST   29
Introduction   29
From the Ancient Philosophers to the End of the Eighteenth Century   29
Archaeology in the Nineteenth Century   34
Archaeology in the Twentieth Century   37

Recent History of Archaeology 46

Key Resources and Suggested Reading 50

CHAPTER 3: MANAGING ARCHAEOLOGY IN THE EARLY TWENTY-FIRST
CENTURY 53

Introduction 53

The Four Major Types of Archaeology 53

Subfields of Archaeology 57

National and International Heritage Management 62

Ethics and Archaeology 72

Career Tracks in Archaeology 76

Sharing Information 76

Key Resources and Suggested Reading 77

CHAPTER 4: COMPREHENDING THE ARCHAEOLOGICAL RECORD 79

Introduction 79

Defining the Archaeological Record and Its Components 79

Creating Archaeological Sites 84

Understanding Bias in the Preservation of Material Remains 90

Site Disturbance 93

Key Resources and Suggested Reading 97

CHAPTER 5: WORKING IN THE FIELD 99

Introduction 99

Designing Archaeological Field Projects 99

Discovering Archaeological Sites 104

Excavation 111

Field Laboratories 115

Ethnoarchaeology and Experimental Archaeology: Research Design
and Field Methods 115

Hazards of Fieldwork 117

Key Resources and Suggested Reading 119

CHAPTER 6: WORKING IN THE LABORATORY 121

Introduction 121

Laboratory Processes 121

Artifact Analysis   123

Ecofact Analysis   130

Analysis of Human Remains   132

Using DNA in Archaeology   138

Key Resources and Suggested Reading   139

CHAPTER 7: RECONSTRUCTING CULTURE HISTORY   141

Introduction   141

Determining Antiquity   141

Conceptualizing Time   150

World Prehistory   153

Ancient Civilizations   161

Key Resources and Suggested Reading   162

CHAPTER 8: RECONSTRUCTING ECOLOGICAL ADAPTATIONS   165

Introduction   165

Reconstructing Paleoenvironments   165

Reconstructing Settlement Patterns   168

Reconstructing Subsistence Strategies   173

Distinguishing Wild Plants and Animals from Domestic   176

Reconstructing Diet   179

Key Resources and Suggested Reading   182

CHAPTER 9: RECONSTRUCTING THE SOCIAL AND IDEOLOGICAL ASPECTS
OF CULTURE   185

Introduction   185

Reconstructing Inequality   186

Reconstructing Types of Societies   187

Reconstructing Identity   191

Reconstructing Ideology   197

Key Resources and Suggested Reading   204

CHAPTER 10: EXPLAINING THINGS OF ARCHAEOLOGICAL INTEREST   207

Introduction   207

Three Levels of Archaeological Research   207

Mechanisms of Culture Change   209

Conceptual Frameworks   211
Explaining the Transition to Food Production   214
Explaining the Collapse of Civilizations   217
Understanding Bias in Archaeological Explanations   219
Evaluating Competing Explanations   221
Key Resources and Suggested Reading   226

CHAPTER 11: THE ARCHAEOLOGY OF YESTERDAY, TODAY, AND
TOMORROW   229
The Current State of Archaeology   229
Archaeologies of the Contemporary   231
Digital Archaeology   246
Archaeology, Climate Change, and Sustainability   248
Predicting the Future of Archaeology   251
Interpreting the Present in the Future   253
Final Comments   255
Key Resources and Suggested Reading   256

Glossary   257
Bibliography   273
Index   289

FIGURES

1.1 The Parthenon on the Acropolis of Athens, Greece   7

1.2 Machu Picchu, Peru   8

1.3 Situating Archaeology in the Early Twenty-First Century   11

1.4 Angkor, Cambodia   15

1.5 Reconstructed Neolithic Houses   16

1.6 Skellig Michael   20

2.1 Rosetta Stone   33

2.2 Howard Carter Examining the Third, Innermost Coffin of King Tut   39

2.3 Louis Leakey: From Archaeologist to Artifact   40

2.4 The Many Interpretive Lenses of Archaeological Theory   47

2.5 Indigenous Women Doing Archaeology   49

3.1 Astronaut on the Moon   60

3.2 Mesa Verde, Colorado   69

3.3 Terra Cotta Warriors, Xi'an   71

3.4 Stonehenge, UK   73

4.1 Carnac, France   81

4.2 Pictographs at Kakadu, Australia   82

4.3 Life History of an Archaeological Site   85

4.4 Pompeii   88

4.5 Collapsed House, Lower Ninth Ward, Louisiana, October 2005   89

5.1 Using a Drone in Archaeology   106

5.2 Looking for Archaeological Sites in a Forest   108

5.3 Finding Archaeological Sites Using a Magnetometer   109

5.4 Archaeological Fieldwork   113

5.5 Excavation and Sifting   114

6.1 Working in the Lab   122

6.2 Lithic Technology   125

6.3 Porcelain Rice/Soup Bowl   128

6.4 Human Skeleton   133

6.5 Cranial Sutures   134

6.6 Male and Female Human Pelvis 136

6.7 A Day in the Life of an Archaeological Laboratory 137

7.1 Stratigraphy: The Story beneath Your Feet 149

7.2 Spear Thrower in Use 158

7.3 Human Expansion across the Globe 159

7.4 Egyptian Pyramid 162

8.1 Turkana Village, Africa 169

8.2 Maasai Village, Africa 171

8.3 Pastoralists in Kenya 175

8.4 Butchery in a Village 178

8.5 Cow Skeleton 180

9.1 Roman Coliseum 191

9.2 Japanese Bottles 193

9.3 Children's Graffiti at Polly Hill Plantation 195

9.4 Mortuary Archaeology 200

9.5 Goddess Figurine from Çatalhöyük 201

9.6 Trepanated Skull 204

10.1 Agriculture in Egypt 215

10.2 Tikal, Guatemala 219

10.3 Hummingbird Glyph on the Nazca Desert, Peru 224

10.4 Statues of Rapa Nui 225

11.1 Activist Archaeology 232

11.2 Guantánamo Bay Detention Camp (GITMO) 236

11.3 The Many Faces of Public Archaeology 240

11.4 The Archaeology of Homelessness 241

11.5 Archaeology of Undocumented Migration 242

11.6 Archaeology Students Sorting Contemporary Trash 246

TABLES

1.1 Branches of Anthropology   13

1.2 Principal Functions of the Heritage Industry   14

2.1 The Unilinear Theory of Cultural Evolution   36

3.1 Archaeological Subfields and Specialties   58

3.2 National and International Heritage Regulations   63

3.3 Selected UNESCO World Heritage Sites   67

3.4 Major Archaeological Associations and Issues Addressed by Their Codes of Ethics   72

4.1 Major Types of Archaeological Sites   80

4.2 Site Formation Processes   86

4.3 Site Disturbance Processes   94

5.1 Basic Stages of Archaeological Research   100

5.2 Methods of Discovering Archaeological Sites   105

5.3 Hazards of Archaeology   118

6.1 Attributes of Various Methods of Chipping Stone   126

6.2 Attributes of Various Methods of Pottery Manufacture   129

7.1 Relative Dating Techniques   142

7.2 Absolute Dating Techniques   145

7.3 Geological Epochs   151

7.4 Major Time Frames in Archaeology   152

8.1 Reasons for Reconstructing Paleoenvironments   166

8.2 Types of Settlement Pattern Studies in Archaeology   168

8.3 Methods to Estimate Population   173

8.4 Major Subsistence Strategies   174

8.5 Criteria for Distinguishing Domestic versus Wild Plants and Animals   177

9.1 Reconstructing Categories of Societies in Archaeology   187

9.2 Reconstructing Identity in Archaeology   192

9.3 Archaeological Indicators of Ritual   198

9.4 Types and Archaeological Indicators of Cannibalism   202

10.1 Three Levels of Archaeological Research   208

10.2 Major Areas of Grand Theoretical Interest in Archaeology 209
10.3 Conceptual Frameworks in Archaeology 212
10.4 Explanations for the Collapse of Civilizations 218
10.5 Major Kinds of Bias in Archaeological Explanations 220
10.6 Criteria for Evaluating Archaeological Explanations 222
11.1 Defining Attributes of Disaster Archaeology 244
11.2 American Trash 245

TEXT BOXES

1.1   Archaeology and Popular Culture   21

1.2   Archaeology and Nuclear Waste   23

2.1   King Tut   41

2.2   Feminist Archaeology   44

3.1   Archaeology and Indigenous Peoples of North America   56

3.2   "To Infinity and Beyond!": The Advent of Space Archaeology   61

4.1   Decay of Human Remains   87

4.2   Preserving the Archaeological Record: Taphonomy after Hurricane Katrina   89

5.1   From Exclusivity to Inclusivity: Making Archaeology an Equitable Profession   103

5.2   Eating a Shrew in the Name of Archaeology   116

6.1   Coprolites   137

6.2   Artifacts in Crisis: Orphaned and Neglected Archaeological Collections   138

7.1   Fire!   156

7.2   Beer!   160

8.1   The Paleodiet and Other Fantasies   179

8.2   Eat Like an Egyptian: Reconstructing Ancient Foodways   182

9.1   Finding Children in the Past: Children's Graffiti at Polly Hill Plantation   195

9.2   Identifying Pirates in the Archaeological Record   196

10.1   Pseudoarchaeology   223

10.2   From Wolf to Fido: The Domestication of Dogs   225

11.1   Archaeology of Undocumented Migration   242

11.2   Fire and Ice: Archaeology and Our Changing Climate   250

NOTE TO INSTRUCTORS

This book is designed as a textbook for introductory archaeology courses as they are taught in most colleges and universities in North America: with the focus on methods. It is deliberately concise, offering the option of combining it with a package of readings or a case study. The concise nature of this text also makes it suitable to be used as one of multiple books in introductory courses that combine methods with world prehistory, archaeology with biological anthropology, or all four branches of anthropology together (archaeology, biological anthropology, cultural anthropology, and linguistics). But the coverage is broad enough that some instructors may wish to use it as the sole required reading for a course.

The development of the book has been guided by the principles of curriculum reform articulated by the Society for American Archaeology (SAA). To bring the teaching of archaeology more into line with the reality of archaeology in the world today, the SAA promotes seven principles for curriculum reform at all levels of college and university education, which revolve around making students explicitly aware of (i) the nonrenewable nature of the archaeological record, (ii) the fact that many other groups besides archaeologists have vested interests in the archaeological record, (iii) the socially relevant contributions of archaeology in the present and future, (iv) the ethical principles that guide archaeologists, (v) the importance for archaeologists to be effective communicators, (vi) the basic cognitive and methodological skills used by archaeologists, and (vii) real-world problem solving by archaeologists.

We don't think it was the intention of the SAA that each principle necessarily guide the formation of every course or text used in archaeology education, but we have incorporated each into this book. The nonrenewable nature of the archaeological record is emphasized through such topics as the rise of cultural resource management, heritage legislation, and the destruction of sites through looting and warfare. Vested interests in the archaeological record by non-archaeologists are covered by examining Indigenous archaeology and the many parts of the heritage industry, including tourism. Making archaeology socially relevant is included in many areas, such as studies of contemporary garbage. Archaeological ethics are made explicit, as is the value of communication, with the sharing of information built into research designs. Real-world problem-solving is explored in such topics as forensics and the involvement of archaeologists in designing markers for nuclear waste sites.

Besides being guided by the SAA principles of curriculum reform, many characteristics of this book set it apart from competitors. It situates archaeology in the contemporary world much more than others do. This includes contextualizing archaeology in academia, industry, global social movements, politics, and popular culture. It places more emphasis on the management of heritage resources and includes sections on legislation and international agreements concerning archaeology. Unlike most textbooks for courses focusing on methods, this book includes a brief section outlining world prehistory and ancient civilizations, providing a frame of reference for students. Most books avoid the disagreements, ambiguities, and gray areas within the discipline, instead presenting information as if there was consensus among archaeologists. This book explicitly identifies these areas, ranging from differences in definitions of archaeology to explanations of the collapse of civilizations.

Introducing Archaeology, third edition, is accompanied by a website for students, including learning objectives, chapter summaries, study questions, exhibits weblinks, and a glossary. Instructor ancillaries for *Introducing Archaeology* include an instructor's manual, PowerPoint slides, and a test bank. To access these materials, visit www.introducingarchaeology.com.

Comments and suggestions for future editions from instructors are welcome and can be directed to Dr. Stacey Camp at campstac@msu.edu.

NOTE TO STUDENTS

Welcome to the world of archaeology. This text provides a broad introduction to archaeology as it is practiced in the twenty-first century. It focuses on the practical aspects of research, such as how projects are designed, what methods are used in field and laboratory work, and how archaeologists make interpretations. It is also about how archaeology is situated in the contemporary world outside colleges and universities, such as in industry, and how it is related to global social movements, politics, popular culture, and real-world problem solving.

One of the purposes of an introductory course is to familiarize students with vocabulary common to the subject. Even though this text is relatively short, you will undoubtedly come across many words you have never seen before or see other words being used in a new way. Such words are included in the Glossary and are identified in bold type the first time they appear in the text.

ACKNOWLEDGMENTS

We are grateful for the support and contributions of many in the creation of this book. This third edition has been built on the shoulders of the first two, and we appreciate all the help in the development of those two editions. We are especially appreciative of the support of Anne Brackenbury, former executive editor at the University of Toronto Press (UTP), who guided the first two editions from initial concept to books in hand, and also was the impetus and guiding hand through the accepted proposal stage of this third edition. Anne's departure from UTP was seamless, however, and we have been well served by Acquisitions Editor Carli Hansen, who has been a pleasure to work with. We further acknowledge the valuable contributions and efficiencies of UTP managing editor Janice Evans and editorial assistant Kiley Venables. as well as Beth McAuley and her team at The Editing Company for the excellent copyedit.

Many others, of course, have been instrumental in the creation of this edition. We are awestruck by the several drawings done for this edition by Katherine Cook. Katherine is an outstanding archaeologist and professor who had been making significant contributions in archaeology, including in the areas of public, digital, and mortuary archaeology, and who also happens to draw on the side. We are extremely pleased with Katherine's ability to conceptualize and visualize illustrations to match our thinking and writing, and then carry through with her sense of color and drawing ability.

All those colleagues, friends, and former students who have provided photographs for this edition are gratefully acknowledged, as are the people identified in the images for allowing their use. We are committed to keeping the book as affordable as possible for students, and the free use of images contributed by these individuals goes a long way to reducing the costs. These people, to which we express sincere gratitude, include Cruz Botello, Jane Baxter, Jeff Burnett, Gillian Crowther, Leah Evans-Janke, Allison Fashing, Mark Galvani, Chad Hill, Ian Hodder, Stacy Kozakavich, Morag Kersel, Shannon Dawdy, Jason De León, Tiana Lewis, Alexa Love, Serena Love, Gabe Moshenska, Autumn Painter, Nadine Ryan, Emma Scott, Amanda Vick, and Larry Zimmerman. We are also grateful to Barry Kass, a colleague, owner of Images of Anthropology, and long-time friend of Bob's who has provided images at a deep discount.

Stacey greatly appreciates the support of her colleagues at Michigan State University, who have provided support and encouragement with this project. Stacey also appreciates students in her Introduction to Archaeology course at Michigan State, who keep her on her toes and continue to make her think about the contemporary relevance of archaeology. She appreciates her hardworking Campus Archaeology staff, who have provided some content for this book. Stacey greatly appreciates her husband, Ben, and children, Lana and Tyson, who were patient and understanding as she finished her portion of this textbook. Her dog, Mimsy, also kept her company during late-night writing sessions. She is thankful for the mentors who have crossed her path as an archaeologist and academic; she is forever grateful to the many people who have given her advice and guidance every step of the way – this includes Bob Muckle, who has been an absolute pleasure to work with. Finally, her parents, Sandra Oviedo and Richard Oviedo, have always been supportive of all the work she has done across the world.

Bob is further grateful for the excellent working environment provided by Capilano University, and is especially indebted to his long-time colleagues in the Department of Anthropology, Maureen Bracewell and Gillian Crowther, who while not archaeologists themselves are very supportive of all his research and writing projects and listen intently while he shares his latest discoveries and thoughts about archaeology. Bob also appreciates the support of family in the writing of this book, especially his wife Victoria. Several years ago he asked her to stop him if he ever agreed to write another book. She sensed he really did enjoy writing, so didn't try to stop him; and he is very grateful for that, as well as all the support offered in a million or more other ways.

ABOUT THE AUTHORS

Dr. Stacey Camp fell in love with archaeology when she was an undergraduate at Occidental College, a small liberal arts college in Los Angeles. While she was an undergraduate, she attended an archaeological field school in Ireland with Dr. Chuck E. Orser, Jr. that showed her how archaeology connects the people living in the present to the past. She continues to be interested in archaeology's relevance to the modern world. She is currently an associate professor of anthropology and director of the Campus Archaeology Program at Michigan State University. Prior to working at Michigan State University, she oversaw one of three archaeological repositories in the state of Idaho at the University of Idaho. Her book, *The Archaeology of Citizenship* (2013, University Press of Florida), explores how immigrants living in the late nineteenth and early twentieth century United States envisioned citizenship and national belonging. She has conducted archaeological and ethnographic research in the Midwest and Western United States, Ireland, and China.

Robert (Bob) Muckle began his studies at a community college, with no idea that he would even take an archaeology class, let alone have a career in it. He simply enrolled in an archaeology class at community college because it fit his schedule, was hooked by that introductory class, and subsequently completed his undergraduate and graduate degrees in archaeology at Simon Fraser University in British Columbia, Canada. He has experience in consulting archaeology, Indigenous archaeology, and academic archaeology, including fieldwork in Canada, Egypt, and the United States. He is a professor in the Department of Anthropology at Capilano University in North Vancouver, British Columbia, where he teaches several courses and has an active research program involving field and laboratory work. Other books he has authored include *Through the Lens of Anthropology: An Introduction to Human Evolution and Culture*, second edition (with Laura Gonzalez, 2019), and *Indigenous Peoples of North America* (2012), both with University of Toronto Press. He is excited about all things archaeological, with major interests revolving around teaching archaeology, archaeology in North America, the social and political uses of archaeology, and archaeology of the contemporary world.

PREFACE TO THE THIRD EDITION

The principal objective of this book is to introduce students to the nature and scope of archaeology, especially as it is practiced in North America during the twenty-first century.

The substance and style of this book has been guided by the understanding that the content should be substantive enough that students intending on majoring in archaeology and perhaps making a career of it will leave the course for which the book is the text having learned enough to serve them well in future archaeology courses, and keep their interest in archaeology alive. It is also recognized the many, perhaps most, of the students taking the course for which this book is the text, are taking the course as an elective and will take few, if any, other archaeology courses. The choice of content and style is for these students as well. The objective for these students is to create material that is interesting and important, so that they have a lifelong appreciation of what it is that archaeologists do, how they do it, and why they do it.

The first two editions of this book were authored solely by Robert Muckle. The most important change for this edition is the addition of Dr. Stacey Camp as co-author. She brings more balance to this edition, bringing different experiences, perspectives, and areas of expertise.

The changes for this third edition are substantive and many. Regarding the art program, most of the images in this edition are now in color, approximately one-third of the images from the second edition have been replaced, and there are now several ink drawings created for this book. The book has fewer tables than the second edition but more boxes. Each of the eleven chapters now has two boxes. New boxes include those on feminist archaeology; space archaeology; taphonomy after Hurricane Katrina; making archaeology an equitable profession; orphaned and neglected collections; using ceramics to reconstruct ancient foodways; archaeology of children's graffiti; the domestication of dogs; and archaeology and our changing climate.

New sections in this edition include discussions of decolonization in archaeology, digital archaeology, public archaeology, and interpreting the past in the future, which speculates on how archaeologists and others will understand life in the early twenty-first century. Sections on activist archaeology and archaeology of contemporary times have been expanded. Significant revisions have been made to the section on the current state of archaeology, and the Glossary has been expanded. Minor revisions and updates have been made throughout each chapter, which are reflected in the substantial changes in the bibliography which now has a much higher proportion of references by women and Indigenous scholars than previous editions. Further, this third edition addresses some of the more problematic current issues such as sexual harassment and abuse, lack of diversity in the profession, and inclusion.

IT'S MORE THAN VIKING HOARDS, SHIPWRECKS, AND LOVERS ENTANGLED IN DEATH

Being primarily an instrument to provide some backstory to literary works such as novels or plays, a prologue is more than a bit unusual in a textbook. There are, however, things that should be said, and hopefully read, before beginning to read the main chapters and look at the images, and while much of what is said in this prologue could easily have been placed in the "Note to Instructors," "Note to Students," or "Preface," it is understandable that those go largely unread. "Prologue" appears a bit more interesting, at least to some, and especially combined with mentions of Vikings, gold, and lovers in death.

The purpose of this prologue is to let students know that **archaeology** is not what it may seem. For non-archaeologists, perceptions of what archaeology is, who archaeologists are, and how they do their work are based primarily on unrealistic stereotypes perpetuated by media and popular culture.

Stories in mainstream media suggesting that archaeologists have discovered something lost, mysterious, or with enormous monetary value appear almost daily. Media also often confuses archaeology with other subjects, such as **geology** when discussing the discovery of ancient landforms and **paleontology** when discussing dinosaurs.

Most stories about archaeology in media are sensationalized. There are thousands of archaeology projects going on around the world on any given day, and although they may not appear newsworthy, they are important. Choosing which archaeology discoveries make it to the news is very biased, dependent upon the interests of journalists and editors, and what they believe the public will be interested in.

Media tends to sensationalize some archaeology news stories and ignore others. Projects that support **Indigenous** claims to territories and resources, for example, rarely make national or international news, while stories about Viking **hoards**, shipwrecks laden with gold, and lovers entangled in death usually do.

It has become almost routine, for example, to learn of discoveries of hoards of coins and other items buried by ancient Romans or Vikings. These stories often focus on the monetary value of the finds, rather than their value to understanding the human past. They also often tend to overlook when the finds were discovered by amateurs searching for treasure with the use of metal detectors, in no way following the proper methods and ethics of archaeology.

Discoveries of shipwrecks laden with gold and other treasures are becoming increasingly common, as there have been significant advances in technology to find wrecks on the ocean floor and retrieve artifacts from them. What is often left out of the stories, however, is that the discovery and retrieval of the treasure is usually made by actors (often large corporations) with only a commercial interest in the finds, such as selling the treasure. There are real archaeologists who undertake pure research on underwater wrecks, but most of discoveries of shipwrecks are not made by these archaeologists. The discovery and retrieval of items from the *Titanic*, for example, has provided little in the way of a benefit to archaeology, other than perhaps adding to the technology of underwater archaeology, while bringing some measure of closure to the descendants of those who drowned. The exploration of the *Titanic* was far more about a commercial venture, such as charging to see the items and associated documentaries, than about contributing to archaeology.

One of the problems from an archaeological perspective is that there are no laws preventing someone from calling themselves an "archaeologist," unlike, for example, someone calling themselves a lawyer or medical doctor. It isn't unusual for people featured in documentaries to call themselves archaeologists when they have no formal education in archaeology or do not even know the methods, theories, and ethics of professional archaeology.

Stories about archaeology often involve the discovery and analysis of human skeletons and mummies. While these are often interesting and significant, it would be incorrect to believe that most archaeologists are focused on finding and analyzing human biological remains. Most archaeologists, in fact, will stop excavations if they find them. Some governments have put into place strict regulations regarding the protection and study of human remains. Many archaeologists go through their entire careers without coming across a skeleton or mummy, and they are more than fine with that.

Stories about people being buried together, sometimes referred to as lovers entangled in death, are almost always sensationalized. Discoveries of people probably holding on to each other are not common, but they certainly do exist (see, for example, the "Lovers of Modena" or "Lovers of Valdero"). Even though the discoveries of purported lovers entangled in death are often decades old, they are often brought up in current media stories, especially in the weeks leading up to Valentine's Day. In recent years, in keeping with current interests, the stories about people being buried together have often focused on the sexual orientation of the individuals.

Perceptions of archaeology from popular culture and the media could easily and understandably lead one to think that finding artifacts is the endgame for archaeologists; it is clearly not. Finding artifacts is part of the early process of an archaeological research project; it is simply part of the data collection. It is what archaeologists learn from the artifacts and their contexts that is important.

Yet another misconception perpetuated by popular culture and media is that people have only gotten smart recently. This is not true. People have been smart for a very long time. The notion that without intervention by extraterrestrial aliens people could not have built the Egyptian pyramids or Stonehenge, for example, is preposterous. Archaeologists may debate what specific technology was used, but the notion that people were not smart enough is ridiculous.

Other popular misconceptions of archaeology are that it is academic in nature, male-dominated, and comprised primarily of excavation. The reality is that most archaeology is not purely academic, with most professionals making their careers outside of university settings. There are approximately as many females as males working as professionals in archaeology. Most archaeologists spend relatively little time doing fieldwork, and for those that do, much more time is typically spent looking for sites than excavating them.

This following chapters are meant to provide some insight into the world of archaeology – what archaeology really is, how it is really done, what the human past was like, and why archaeology is important. This textbook is a gateway to learning about the human past by examining the things people left behind.

Real archaeology offers a different perspective than the one often portrayed in popular culture in regard to many things, including the story of the human past. It is different from most popular culture versions of how archaeology is done and what it reveals about the human past, but the stories it reveals are no less fantastic.

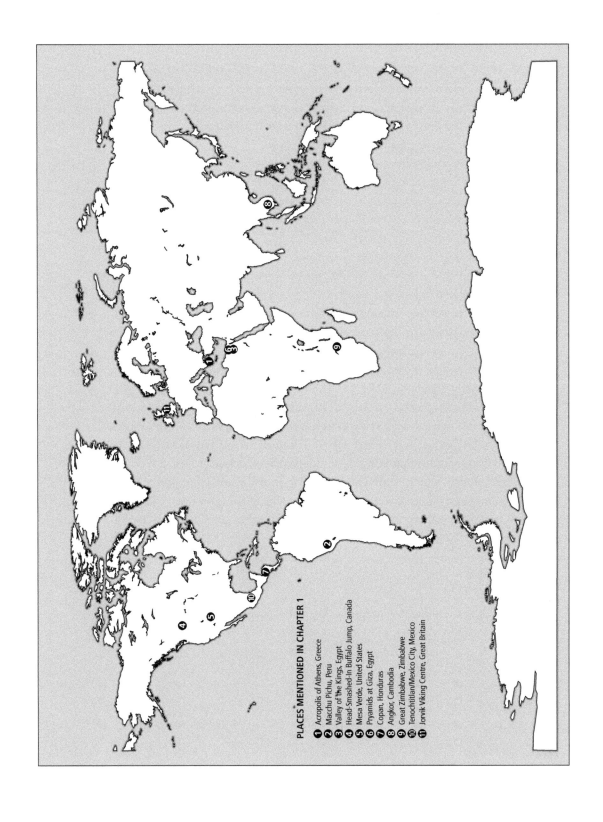

PLACES MENTIONED IN CHAPTER 1

1. Acropolis of Athens, Greece
2. Macchu Pichu, Peru
3. Valley of the Kings, Egypt
4. Head-Smashed-In Buffalo Jump, Canada
5. Mesa Verde, United States
6. Pryamids at Giza, Egypt
7. Copan, Honduras
8. Angkor, Cambodia
9. Great Zimbabwe, Zimbabwe
10. Tenochtitlan/Mexico City, Mexico
11. Jorvik Viking Centre, Great Britain

CHAPTER 1

SITUATING ARCHAEOLOGY

Introduction

Archaeology is everywhere in the early twenty-first century. It is part of the multibillion-dollar **heritage industry**; taught as a scholarly discipline in colleges and universities throughout the world; and firmly embedded in politics, global social movements, and popular culture. It has been defined in dozens of ways and is commonly referred to as a scholarly or intellectual endeavor, a profession, a practice, a craft, and a hobby. It is rationalized in many different ways and relies on several basic concepts.

This chapter introduces archaeology by clarifying these definitions, contexts, rationalizations, and concepts.

The Allure of Archaeology

Many, probably most, people are influenced in their understanding of archaeology by media reports about significant discoveries or through popular culture.

There is no consensus on why so many people are drawn to archaeology, but there is no doubt the allure is widespread. Evidently, people are drawn for multiple reasons.

The general public is often influenced by popular culture, insofar as archaeologists are often presented as heroes, full of adventure, making important discoveries, and preventing evildoers from stealing or destroying important things. There is also the view (problematic as it is) that archaeology is a noble activity and serves the greater good, which may be attractive to some. Although not stated explicitly, archaeologists are often portrayed in media, including popular magazines and documentaries such as those produced by *National Geographic*, as being **white saviors**, with archaeologists from Western countries often presented as saving the tangible heritage of peoples around the world, mostly in developing countries but also including the Indigenous populations of the United States and Canada. (The savior complex is problematic for multiple reasons, including disagreements about who are the rightful stewards of the archaeological record.)

The allure of archaeology may also be fueled by what some have termed **paleofantasy**, including a belief that things were better in the past. This is perhaps best illustrated in the popularity of the **paleodiet**, whose basic assumptions, as discussed in Box 8.1, have been considerably critiqued by archaeologists.

For college and university students, the allure may derive from what they think archaeology is, based on popular culture; or, as may more often be the case, they enroll in an introductory course because it fits their timetable, they know someone else taking it, or it simply sounds interesting.

Those making a career in archaeology may initially be drawn to it through popular culture, but they often get hooked in college or university, especially if they have the opportunity to participate in field research. For some professional archaeologists it is the lifestyle that appeals to them most, letting them spend significant amount of time outdoors or in a college or university classroom. For many it is the interesting mix of the natural sciences, the social sciences, and the humanities that is the draw. Others like the detective work or puzzle-solving nature of archaeology. There are some who are drawn for economic reasons, insofar as one can make a decent living doing archaeology. Others may be drawn primarily for the social contexts, as during fieldwork and laboratory work archaeologists rarely work alone.

The allure for some may lie in the activist aspect of archaeology, such as promoting social justice or the empowerment of marginalized groups. As described elsewhere in this chapter, archaeology is associated with multiple social movements, and for some this may be the driving force for entering the profession. Increasing numbers of Indigenous Peoples, for example, are turning toward archaeology as a career to further empower Indigenous nations. More examples of activist archaeology are provided in Chapter 11.

Many people and institutions place high value on archaeology because they too understand the allure – there are reasons why governments around the world support research and protect **archaeological sites** and artifacts. Besides empowering people and movements, archaeologists can help explain current events, help solve conflicts and assess claims, and assist in solving other problems of living in the twenty-first century, such as dealing with nuclear waste and ever-increasing accumulations of trash.

Archaeology is just one area that focuses on the human past. Many people and disciplines – history, for example – are interested in the past. While historians focus primarily on written records, however, archaeologists focus on landscapes, places, and things. Thus for those who are interested in the past, but also like to work with their hands and deal with physical places and objects that can be seen, touched, measured, illustrated, and studied in other ways, archaeology is a good fit. For many, it is this tangible aspect of archaeology that is the draw.

The allure of archaeology may further be fuelled by what images of ancient sites evoke. In many people's minds, archaeology is correlated with architectural ruins in fabulous settings, such as the Acropolis in Greece and Machu Picchu in Peru.

Comprising the Parthenon and surrounding buildings, the Acropolis is among the most famous archaeological sites in the world, and for many it symbolizes Western civilization and the beginnings of archaeology, which as outlined in Chapter 2 is rooted in the collection of antiquities from ancient Greece and Rome.

Located high in the Andes Mountains of Peru, the **Inka** site of Machu Picchu was abandoned in the early 1500s. Its principal function was likely as a retreat for a ruling Inka family, and it has become a national symbol for Peru.

Besides having architectural ruins in fabulous settings and becoming national symbols, the Acropolis and Machu Picchu, along with many other archaeological sites, accommodate hundreds of thousands of visitors each year making them part of the **archaeotourism** industry, which in itself may be one of the principal gateways to an interest in archaeology.

FIGURE 1.1 The Parthenon on the Acropolis of Athens, Greece. A UNESCO World Heritage Site, for many the Acropolis symbolizes Western civilization, the beginning of archaeology, the political nature of archaeology, Greek identity, and archaeotourism.

PHOTO: Gillian Crowther.

FIGURE 1.2 Machu Picchu, Peru. Located high in the Andes Mountains, Machu Picchu was probably a retreat for a ruling Inka family. It is a UNESCO World Heritage Site, a symbol of Peruvian identity, and one of the most popular archaeotourism destinations in South America.

PHOTO: Barry D. Kass @ ImagesofAnthropology.com.

The Lens of Archaeology

Archaeology may be considered a lens to view the human past. The lens is a framework to guide our interest. Frameworks are important to guide us, helping organize our thoughts and actions. Many frameworks exist for studying and understanding the past. Those interested in ancient landforms follow the framework of geology; those whose primary interest is in dinosaurs study through a lens of paleontology. Of those more focused on the human past, some view the human past through one of thousands of lenses of religion. Others, especially those who like the primacy of the written record, often use the framework of history. Those who prefer explanations involving aliens and supernatural phenomena are often following a framework of **pseudoarchaeology**.

The **lens of archaeology** is defined as viewing humans through a set of archaeological principles, methods, theories, ethics, and research results. These are covered in subsequent chapters in this book. They differ from other frameworks or lenses. There is often overlap with other ways of knowing, but it is the suite of characteristics (methods, theories, etc.) that distinguish the lens of archaeology.

Having a framework for understanding the human narrative is important. Archaeology is a way of knowing. It isn't the only way, but it is a way.

So, on one level, the lens of archaeology is a broad framework for studying the human past. But there are other levels as well. Chapter 2 introduces several more narrow lenses operating within archaeology (e.g., see Figure 2.4), and when it comes to explaining major events of the past (such as the domestication of plants and animals or the collapse of civilizations) there are many different lenses (sometimes referred to as conceptual frameworks) available (e.g., see Chapter 10).

Defining Archaeology

A rough translation of the term *archaeology* from ancient Greek via Latin is "the study of ancient things or stories." The term does not appear in English-language dictionaries until the 1600s, however, and since that time it has been defined and described in many ways.

One of the first and most important things a student of archaeology should learn is that there is no consensus definition of archaeology. Indeed, there are almost as many definitions of archaeology as there are books, dictionaries, encyclopedias, and websites that focus on the subject. Some definitions restrict archaeology to the study of the human past, while others include the present as well as the past as the periods of interest. Some definitions focus on the objects of interest, such as the study of **artifacts** or the study of ancient **civilizations**, yet most do not restrict archaeology to any particular subset of the **material remains** of human physical activity. Many definitions include the phrase "the scientific study of ..." Yet others have rejected the scientific approach in archaeology, promoting more humanistic methods. Some definitions focus on the objectives of archaeology, such as describing the human past or explaining past events, while others make no mention whatsoever of the research goals.

While differences in definitions may lead to some initial confusion for those unfamiliar with archaeology, these differences do provide some indication of the breadth of the discipline. Also, even a cursory examination of the plethora of definitions shows that there are two constants in almost all of them. First, archaeology is focused on humans. Second, the essential database of archaeology is the remains of their physical activities, often referred to as material remains.

Considering these two constants, a good all-purpose definition of the discipline is this: *archaeology is the study of humans through their material remains*. This includes the identification, collection, analysis, interpretation, and management of those remains. This definition does not restrict archaeology to a specific time period, a particular subset of material remains, or the use of the scientific method. It should be understood, however, that most archaeology as it is practiced in the early twenty-first century focuses on the human past and adheres to the fundamental principles and methods of **science**.

To more completely understand the definition, it is necessary to know in greater detail what archaeologists mean by the words *human* and *material remains*. There is no universal agreement about what it means to be human. Almost all archaeologists allow that at a minimum, human is taken to mean all members of the genus *Homo*. As outlined more fully in Chapter 7, the genus appears to have arisen about 2.5 million years ago and coincides with the undeniable evidence of human technology, primarily through the manufacture of stone tools. Many archaeologists are less restrictive and equate human with the biological family **Homininae**. This family includes multiple genera, including *Homo*, and appears to have arisen between about 7 and 5 million years ago. No undisputed evidence of material remains have been found for any genus other than *Homo*, so for many archaeologists, whether one equates human with *Homo* or Homininae is not all that important.

Material remains comprise all kinds of physical evidence of human activities, including, but certainly not restricted to, tools, houses, things buried deliberately or lost, **refuse**, and modifications to the landscape. The variety of material remains is discussed in greater detail in Chapter 4.

A Scholarly Endeavor, a Profession, and a Craft

Archaeology is at once a scholarly endeavor and a profession. There is no question of the scholarly nature of archaeology. It is embedded in colleges and universities throughout the world; it is funded by major research agencies; it makes extensive use of theory at all stages of research; and it produces scholarly, peer-reviewed publications.

There is also no question that archaeology is a profession. Many archaeologists, especially those serving clients in the heritage industry, are more likely to consider their work a business rather than a scholarly pursuit. Professions are generally considered to require specialized knowledge, provide a service to the community, and have a high degree of autonomy, a system of licensing or a registry of qualified members, and self-organized associations. While there are no formal national systems of licensing for archaeologists in North America, registries exist at local, regional, and international levels. These registries typically have codes of ethics and minimum standards of qualification, including postgraduate university degrees and considerable experience in field archaeology. One such registry to which many archaeologists in North America belong is the **Register of Professional Archaeologists (RPA)**.

Although in a clear minority, some archaeologists consider archaeology to be more a craft than either a scholarly endeavor or a profession. For example, some proponents of this view compare archaeology to the craft of **pottery**, suggesting that, like making a pot, archaeology involves both abstract thought and physical labor; thereby they avoid a distinct separation of reasoning and execution, and unify theory and practice. Unlike other academic disciplines that are associated with well-defined subject matter, the essential craft of archaeology is in manufacturing knowledge and interpreting the past.

Archaeology versus Archeology

The variety of spellings of the word *archaeology* confuses many people. There are two common spellings in the English language: archaeology and archeology. Most archaeologists use the longer spelling, with the second *a* after the *h*, while much of the popular press, some professional organizations, and some governments prefer the shorter version. One is more inclined to see the shorter spelling in the United States than elsewhere in the world, but both spellings are considered valid.

FIGURE 1.3 Situating Archaeology in the Early Twenty-First Century. Archaeology in the early twenty-first century is multifaceted, with interests and applications ranging from pure research in academic contexts to involvement with industry, politics, social movements, popular culture, tourism, and more.

IMAGE: Katherine Cook.

Contextualizing Archaeology

How archaeology is perceived and practiced often depends on the framework in which it operates. Archaeology can be considered in many contexts, falling into the principal categories of academia, business, politics, global social movements, and popular culture.

These categories should not be considered mutually exclusive, and any single project can be considered in multiple contexts. It is not uncommon for ongoing projects to be both scholarly and political; and research from purely academic projects is often used to further global social movements long after the fieldwork and analysis has been completed.

ARCHAEOLOGY IN THE CONTEXT OF ACADEMIA

On a broad level, archaeology fits comfortably within the academic world of colleges, universities, and research institutes. Archaeology is an academic discipline that falls within the Western intellectual tradition, with courses taught and research undertaken in academic settings.

Within these academic settings, however, the place of archaeology varies. Archaeology is situated in three basic models, both intellectually and administratively in colleges and universities. Archaeology as a branch of **anthropology** is one model; another is that of archaeology as a stand-alone department; and in the third model, archaeology is recognized as neither a department nor a branch, but rather as specialized courses situated within any of several departments.

Archaeology as a branch of anthropology is the most prevalent model in North America. With the other branches, archaeology shares evolutionary, **holistic**, and comparative perspectives of humankind, and depends on fieldwork for the acquisition of data. An overview of each of the major branches is summarized in Table 1.1.

Anthropology may be a distinct department in colleges or universities, or it may be associated with geography, history, sociology, classics, cultural studies, Near Eastern studies, or other disciplines to form combined departments. In some institutions, this is done for ease of administration, but some people view archaeology as intellectually embedded in these disciplines as well. In some colleges and universities, archaeology courses can be found in multiple departments.

A small percentage of colleges and universities in North America, and many colleges and universities elsewhere in the world, have stand-alone departments of archaeology. These departments sometimes also include courses in biological anthropology.

TABLE 1.1 Branches of Anthropology

BRANCH OF ANTHROPOLOGY	DESCRIPTION
Archaeology	Focuses on past human culture through the analysis of material remains
Cultural anthropology	Focuses on all aspects of contemporary human cultures, including language, economic systems, social systems, art, and ideology; data are usually collected through long-term observation of people; also known as social anthropology or socio-cultural anthropology
Biological anthropology	Focuses on human biology, past and present, including human biological evolution and contemporary biological diversity; also known as physical anthropology
Linguistic anthropology	Focuses on human languages, past and present, including the cultural context in which language is used and the ways in which language, social life, and culture are intertwined

Archaeology is usually considered to be part of a liberal arts education, and is most often associated with the social sciences. However, in some institutions that have archaeological laboratories, use sophisticated technology, and explicitly consider the scientific method, archaeology is considered part of a science education. Other institutions situate archaeology and anthropology within the humanities. This particularly suits those archaeologists who view their role as being one primarily of storytelling, often drawing parallels with literature, visual arts, theater, and other kinds of performance.

As in most academic disciplines, students of archaeology may sequentially work toward a bachelor's degree, a master's degree, and a Ph.D. To meet increased demand for field and laboratory workers since the late 1900s, some colleges in the United States and Canada have developed two-year archaeology programs intended for entry-level employment in the heritage industry.

Most pure scholarly research in archaeology is undertaken by those affiliated with universities, including professors who have usually received money from a funding agency, such as the National Endowment for the Humanities (NEH) or the National Science Foundation (NSF) in the United States, or the Social Sciences and Humanities Research Council (SSHRC) in Canada.

TABLE 1.2 Principal Functions of the Heritage Industry

THE HERITAGE INDUSTRY IS DESIGNED TO

1. Make people aware of the value of heritage
2. Enact legislation to protect heritage
3. Document heritage sites and objects
4. Assess the significance of heritage sites and objects
5. Conserve or preserve heritage sites and objects
6. Interpret heritage
7. Present heritage

ARCHAEOLOGY IN THE CONTEXT OF INDUSTRY

Most archaeologists make their careers in the heritage industry, often working alongside or in cooperation with historians, lawyers, lawmakers, Indigenous groups, tourism operators, and educators.

As outlined in Table 1.2, the heritage industry has several functions. Archaeology is most prominent in the areas of documenting and assessing heritage sites, and archaeologists who perform these functions are generally considered to be working in the field of **commercial archaeology** or **cultural resource management (CRM)**, which is described more fully in Chapter 3.

Although archaeologists have been active in the other areas of the heritage industry, historically they have tended to be secondary to Indigenous advocacy groups, lawmakers, educators, and tourism professionals. In the early twenty-first century, however, archaeologists have been increasing their role in these other areas. They often lobby politicians to protect heritage sites and objects through legislation and other protective measures, and they have become increasingly active in the presentation of heritage to the public.

Heritage tourism or archaeotourism, which has become a multibillion-dollar business, is one aspect of heritage presentation that has created considerable opportunities for archaeologists. For example, the Valley of the Kings in Egypt receives close to 2 million visitors annually; several Maya sites in Central America are major tourist destinations; and despite its remote location and very high altitude, several hundred thousand people visit Machu Picchu each year. Heritage sites throughout North America, Europe, and elsewhere present many opportunities for archaeological research and interpretation. Many sites in North America, including those with

FIGURE 1.4 Angkor, Cambodia. Part of a complex of more than 100 temples built from the ninth through the twelfth centuries AD. After centuries of neglect, Angkor has been designated a World Heritage Site, become embedded in popular culture through movies and video games with an archaeological theme, and become a popular archaeotourism destination in Asia.

PHOTO: Alexa Love.

UN World Heritage status, have created great opportunities for archaeology. These sites include Head-Smashed-In Buffalo Jump and Mesa Verde, which are discussed more fully in Chapter 3. Governments that control heritage sites that are tourist destinations often support archaeological research to enhance the experience for visitors.

Archaeologists often get involved in the authentic presentation of heritage, another aspect of heritage tourism. Many are active in creating and maintaining authenticity at the hundreds, and perhaps thousands, of **living museums** that now dot the globe. Examples include the reconstruction of eighteenth-century Colonial Williamsburg in the United States, which reportedly has about 1 million visitors each year, and the very popular Jorvik Viking Centre in Great Britain, where smells have been recreated to increase authenticity.

Archaeologists are also interested in the lack of authenticity in many living museums. Among other things, they often level criticism against sanitized versions of the past, including inadequate representations of poverty, racism, prostitution, alcoholism, and drug use.

FIGURE 1.5
Reconstructed Neolithic Houses. These Neolithic-style houses are located close to Stonehenge in the UK. They are based on archaeological excavations at a village site close to Stonehenge when it was built and used near the end of the Neolithic period (c. 5,000 years ago). Archaeologists are often involved in constructing and critiquing reconstructions of the physical past such as this and other living museums and **archaeological theme parks** to ensure authenticity.

PHOTO: Bob Muckle.

ARCHAEOLOGY IN THE CONTEXT OF POLITICS

There are three primary political contexts for archaeology: in the creation of a sense of national identity; the protection and investigation of archaeological sites; and the destruction of heritage sites and objects for political purposes.

First, the link between archaeological sites and national identity is not difficult to observe. Archaeological sites often symbolize their countries. As already mentioned, the Parthenon and surrounding buildings of the Acropolis are firmly tied to Greek identity, and Machu Picchu has come to represent Peru. Mayan sites often symbolize Mexico; Stonehenge represents Great Britain; and the pyramids are an emblem of ancient Egypt.

In many countries of the world, national identity is strongly tied to heritage sites even though research doesn't always link contemporary peoples of the region with the builders of the sites. Sites of the ancient Maya, for example, are often tied with national identity in Mexico, even though Mayans constitute a minor percentage of the contemporary population; and a recent Honduran presidential inauguration took place at the Mayan site of Copan. Other examples of well-known heritage sites that are used to create a sense of national identity include the sites of Angkor and Great Zimbabwe.

Angkor, located in Cambodia, was the capital of the ancient Khmer Empire, which controlled much of what is now Cambodia, Thailand, and Vietnam. Angkor is best known for its complex of more than one hundred temples, built between the ninth and twelfth centuries AD. Some scholars believe the complex to be among the greatest architectural achievements of humankind. Following centuries of neglect and looting, Cambodia began to rebuild Angkor in the 1990s, after a civil war. Angkor has now become one of the world's premier tourist attractions, and one of its temples, Angkor Wat, is the centerpiece on the Cambodian national flag.

The country of Zimbabwe takes its name from the site of Great Zimbabwe. When Europeans first started inhabiting the African country once known as Rhodesia, they dismissed the notion that the stone ruins they found there were the remains of a large settlement constructed by the ancestors of the contemporary Indigenous people. During the 1900s, however, archaeologists became convinced otherwise, and one of the largest sites was given the name Great Zimbabwe, which is a word taken from the language of one of the local Indigenous groups. The site had such significance in building a sense of identity among the peoples of the region that when Rhodesia gained independence in 1980, the country was renamed Zimbabwe. It is now believed that the site was built between the fifth and fifteenth century AD, and estimates of the prehistoric population range as high as 30,000.

On occasion, using archaeology to create a sense of national identity can have devastating effects, such as when territorial expansion is justified on the basis of archaeological evidence. In the years leading up to World War II, for example, Nazis used archaeological research by German archaeologists in neighboring areas, including Poland, to make claims that those lands rightfully belonged to Germany, since artifacts recovered there appeared to have had a Germanic origin. In some cases, evidence of swastika-like designs was taken to signify German origin, disregarding the fact that the symbol itself probably originated in India. The rationale behind the Iraqi invasion of Kuwait in the late twentieth century provides another example. Linking modern-day Iraq with the ancient Babylonian Empire that dominated the region thousands of years ago, Iraq's leader at the time, Saddam Hussein, claimed that Kuwait rightfully belonged to Iraq.

A sense of national identity can also be created and maintained by the way archaeological research is portrayed. Some popular American magazines, for example, have been criticized for the way they use archaeology to foster American values and ideology. A comprehensive examination of articles focusing on archaeology in *National Geographic*, for example, shows that the selective slant of the reporting and the choice of images used to accompany the articles validates the American value of rugged individualism and legitimizes American expansionism.

Second, the protection and investigation of archaeological sites is often considered political, in part because heritage legislation and research may be seen as a response to pressure from specific interest groups. In many areas of the world, for example, legislation protecting archaeological sites has been put into place or strengthened following an increase in popular support for Indigenous claims to rights and territories. Archaeological research, undertaken by both Indigenous groups and governments, to investigate legal claims to Aboriginal rights and territories can be viewed as being political, since such claims often pit one nation against another (e.g., an Indigenous nation versus a national government). This view is particularly common in Canada, where dozens of First Nations (as Indigenous groups are called) are negotiating treaties for the first time, and where court cases brought by First Nations against governments are common, with archaeology being used to support both sides.

Protection of archaeological sites can also be considered political at the international level. As we will see in more detail in Chapter 3, many international treaties, conventions, and laws under the umbrella of the United Nations cover the protection of heritage sites. It is not mandatory that individual countries agree to abide by the agreements, but pressure to abide from other member countries gives them the appearance of being political.

Finally, archaeologists are concerned about the political destruction of heritage sites and objects. Despite international laws and agreements (see Chapter 3), many significant heritage objects and sites are destroyed from the direct actions of political regimes and during conflicts between groups or nations. The destruction generally falls within the categories of targeted destruction, **collateral damage**, and **subsistence looting**.

Since heritage sites are often used as symbols of identity, they have frequently been targeted for destruction by political regimes new to an area, in a sort of cleansing of previous regimes and ideologies. Examples include multiple attempts at damaging the Acropolis in Greece over the past few millennia, the leveling of the ancient Aztec capital of Tenochtitlan (under present-day Mexico City) by the invading Spaniards in the sixteenth century, and the deliberate destruction of thousands of important artifacts and at least one United Nations–designated **World Heritage Site** by the Taliban regime in Afghanistan during its reign in the late twentieth and early twenty-first century.

Although not generally thought to be one of the primary areas in which the political context of archaeology is considered, the use of archaeologists in espionage is well known. For example, the American Sylvanus Morley reportedly used his cover as an archaeologist to search for evidence of German submarines along the coast of Central America during World War I. Harvard archaeologist Samuel Lothrop maintained his cover to spy and coordinate intelligence activity for the United States during World War I and II.

ARCHAEOLOGY IN THE CONTEXT OF GLOBAL SOCIAL MOVEMENTS

Archaeology and global social movements are often linked, and their association is commonly viewed as mutually beneficial. Archaeologists seeking to increase the social relevance of the discipline often become involved in social movements, bringing with them the data, methods, and theory of archaeology. Conversely, the impact of social movements often challenges mainstream thinking in archaeology and leads to alternative interpretations of the past. Three social movements that have strong links to archaeology are feminism, Indigenous empowerment, and the environmental movement.

The relationship between archaeology and feminism took serious hold in the 1980s and continues to be an integral force in the evolution of both fields. Feminist thought has challenged the basic assumptions about gender roles in the past, such as the perception that men were the dominant tool makers, artists, food providers, and leaders. Feminism has also been integral in significantly increasing the proportion of women in all levels of the profession, from part-time field-worker to university professor. Archaeology has benefited the feminist movement when archaeologists have debunked unsubstantiated claims of male superiority in past societies and focused increasing amounts of research on topics which hitherto received no or little attention, such as child rearing, plant gathering, and other tasks often associated with women.

Indigenous empowerment and archaeology also have a very close relationship. As Indigenous groups around the world seek to empower themselves and lessen domination by colonial governments, they often include evidence from archaeological research to support their claims to territory and rights. This has created much employment for archaeologists, to the degree that many are considered to be part of the **Indian industry**.

Although less prominent than either feminism or Indigenous empowerment, the relationship between the environmental movement and archaeology is also strong, focusing on environmental sustainability and conservation. Significant contributions made by archaeologists include providing data on previous human use of the environment. Archaeologists are able to provide examples of the negative impacts of some subsistence and economic activities, which may ultimately lead to the abandonment of regions and collapse of civilizations. For example, the **archaeological record** shows that irrigation may lead to increasingly saline soils, rendering them useless for farming.

ARCHAEOLOGY IN THE CONTEXT OF POPULAR CULTURE

Archaeology is very visible in popular culture. This includes many forms of media and entertainment, involving both the results of archaeological research and depictions of archaeologists at work. Examples of archaeology in popular culture can be found in novels, movies, television, advertising, games, and toys.

Although popular culture presents some authentic depictions of archaeologists and their work, archaeologists commonly observe that these constitute a very small minority and that the portrayal is usually inaccurate, inappropriately sensationalized, and generally presents archaeology as a frivolous activity. Examples include the tendency to emphasize archaeology as a treasure hunt in print and visual media, a common European or North American bias in nonfiction books about archaeology (such as overemphasizing heritage sites that are likely to be of most interest to European and North American readers), a common male bias (focusing on male archaeologists and the male activities they discover), and an almost total neglect of the reasons behind archaeology.

Archaeologists have become increasingly concerned about the depiction of their discipline in popular culture for two principal reasons. First, if the popular perception is that archaeology is a frivolous activity, then government funding may be reduced. Ultimately, governments pay directly for most of the pure research done by archaeologists and pay most of the costs associated with the teaching of archaeology at colleges and universities. The feeling is that as demands for government funds increase, archaeology may be subject to cuts because of its perceived lack of importance.

The second reason archaeologists are concerned about the depiction of archaeology in popular culture is the fact that the media increasingly determines the kinds of pure

FIGURE 1.6 Skellig Michael. Located on an island belonging to Ireland, Skellig Michael is a World Heritage Site known mostly for its evidence of early Christian monasteries during the Medieval period, beginning about 1,000 years ago. In more recent times this site has served as a set for movies and other programs, including three episodes in the Star Wars series: *The Force Awakens* (2015), *The Last Jedi* (2017), and *The Rise of Skywalker* (2019).

PHOTO: Alamy / Christopher Hill Photographic.

scholarly research being undertaken. The media has a long history of funding archaeological projects, the results of which then appear in those media magazines or television documentaries (e.g., *National Geographic*). Print and television media are becoming increasingly involved in archaeological projects. Archaeologists are concerned about this primarily because the type of research conducted may be based on what readers and viewers might find interesting, rather than on what might contribute significantly to our understanding of human behavior, past and present.

Archaeologists are also concerned about the use of archaeological sites in advertising, especially the lack of sensitivity to people's identification with the sites and the potential for damage. Coca-Cola, for example, produced an ad that replaced the columns of the Parthenon with Coca-Cola bottles, causing outrage among many Greeks, some of whom felt that they were being humiliated on an international scale. At Machu Picchu, the filming of a beer commercial caused damage to some architectural ruins. A crane used in filming damaged a massive carved stone block known as the Intihuatana, which is presumed to have importance in Inka mythology. As

---

BOX 1.1 ARCHAEOLOGY AND POPULAR CULTURE

Archaeology is embedded in popular culture in many ways, including but certainly not limited to movies, television, news media, advertising, fiction, nonfiction, documentary film, music, comic books, games, and toys. Popular culture both promotes and uses stereotypes of archaeology and the prehistoric past. The way ancient times are portrayed is almost always ridiculous. Similarly, archaeologists in popular culture are almost always portrayed as treasure hunters, which they are not.

It has been said that archaeology is the most popular second choice for a career. If we take them at their word, this is true for celebrities as well as regular folk. Many celebrities associated with the entertainment world have indicated in published interviews that if the acting thing didn't work out, they would have liked to be archaeologists.

It may be that archaeology is so firmly embedded in popular culture because of the stereotypical image of archaeologists – adventurous, smart, good-looking, and fit. The guru of research into archaeology as popular culture is Cornelius Holtorf. In *Archaeology Is a Brand! The Meaning of Archaeology in Contemporary Popular Culture* (2007), he identifies key themes in the portrayal of archaeologists in popular culture: as an adventurer, a detective, making profound revelations, and taking care of ancient sites and finds. In *From Stonehenge to Las Vegas: Archaeology in Popular Culture* (2005, 44), he writes: "Featuring the archaeologist as popular stereotype, the archaeological romance of eerie adventures involving exotic locations, treasure hunting, and fighting for a good cause has become a widely used theme in popular culture."

One of the dangers of the depictions of archaeology in popular culture is that as the real objectives and methods of archaeology are rarely portrayed, there is an increasing tendency for others to see archaeology as a frivolous activity. This may be more important for archaeology than other disciplines. In surveys asking how people learn about archaeology, the overwhelming majority of responses are invariably linked with popular culture sources, especially television. Also, as traditional sources for funding archaeological research become reduced and increasingly competitive, television and other media are increasingly picking up the slack, which leads to decisions about what gets funded lying in the hands of those in media and entertainment rather than science.

Peruvian archaeologist Federico Kauffmann Doig commented, "Machu Picchu is the heart of our archaeological heritage, and the Intihuatana is the heart of Machu Picchu. They've struck at our most sacred inheritance" (BBC News Online 2000).

Rationalizing Archaeology

Historically, archaeology has been justified on the basis that it is intrinsically interesting; it provides information about the past so we can learn from our mistakes; and all knowledge is good. While these are valid rationalizations and worked well for much of the late nineteenth and twentieth century, for most people in the early twenty-first century, they are not good enough reasons to justify the billions of dollars spent each year on archaeological work, including maintaining the discipline in colleges and universities.

To supply context for current global events, archaeology provides a database of more than 2 million years of human events, including instances of warfare, overpopulation, famine, and responses to environmental disasters. In addition, archaeology provides methods of classification and comparison to make this data meaningful, and it has a variety of **conceptual frameworks** that can be used to explain events. For example, although there is no consensus among archaeologists, many believe the archaeological record shows that warfare occurs primarily in times of resource shortages.

The framework archaeology has developed for collecting and interpreting data is most obviously applied in the area of documenting heritage. Archaeological techniques have found other applications as well, such as forensics. Archaeologists are often employed in forensic work, including recovering data from fires in buildings, plane crash sites, and crime scenes. Archaeologists were involved, for example, in the recovery of human remains following the destruction of New York's World Trade Center in 2001. Techniques developed in archaeology have further transferred well into studies of modern **material culture** and have proved beneficial in understanding the effectiveness of recycling and trash disposal programs. Some of these are described in Chapters 3 and 11.

Archaeologists are called upon frequently to evaluate data and ideas. On a very practical level, this includes examining claims of Indigenous groups to their alleged **traditional territory**. Archaeologists evaluate these claims based on many variables, including the evidence itself and how it was collected. At a higher, more theoretical level, archaeologists get involved in evaluating ideas put forward by a wide range of groups and individuals, including academics, about the human past. Archaeologists are often able to show that popular ideas have little basis in fact (see Chapter 10).

Assessing the significance of heritage sites is a common task of many archaeologists working in the heritage industry. These assessments are fundamentally important to help determine whether a site will be destroyed without proper excavation, excavated before destruction, or preserved. Usually only sites determined to be highly significant are protected. Significance is usually assessed in relation to the site's importance to archaeology, other academic disciplines, particular ethnic groups, and the public.

Archaeology has considerable economic value. Much of it is directly associated with the heritage industry, including archaeological research, education, and presentation. With more than 10,000 people making careers in the North American heritage industry alone, its economic impact is real. In countries such as Mexico, Peru, and Egypt, where visits to archaeological sites are very popular, archaeology has become a vital part of the tourism economy.

Some value is given to the role archaeology often plays in support of other disciplines, in both the social and natural sciences. Archaeologists provide material evidence

---

BOX 1.2 ARCHAEOLOGY AND NUCLEAR WASTE

Perhaps one of the most important kinds of work archaeologists can do in addressing some of the problems of living in the twenty-first century is to provide insight into how to help decide on where to store nuclear waste and how to mark it so that people living thousands of years in the future will know the hazards.

The US government has been consulting with archaeologists since the 1980s on how to best mark proposed storage locations for nuclear waste. After all, who better to ask what kind of system is likely to work for 10,000 or more years than archaeologists? Based on their knowledge of the past, archaeologists have been able to make several important suggestions. An important article that has laid the foundation for many subsequent discussions about archaeology and nuclear waste is by Kaplan and Adams (1986), who outline several recommendations, as follows:

- Marking symbols should include symbols, pictures, and languages. Each alone is unlikely to be able to be interpreted properly thousands of years from now, but a combination of the three systems may.
- Structures should be constructed of natural materials such as earth or stone with little or no perceived value. Metal or other materials with perceived value will likely be looted.
- The primary marking system should be detectable at eye level.
- A primary feature should be a series of monoliths ringing the site, each with symbols, pictures, and language conveying information. The monoliths should be granite or basalt, and be at least twice human height.
- Subsurface markers should be included at three different levels. These markers should be ceramic, shaped in a disc or lenticular form with a 12 centimeter diameter, and colored.

One of the biggest problems remaining includes how to mark the site so that people of the future will be able to understand the warnings. While archaeologists can be reasonably certain that monoliths and ceramic markers will withstand thousands of years of weathering and probably not be looted, establishing how to convey the information about the contents of the site and warnings is difficult. Language and symbols used today may be interpretable in a thousand years, but likely not in 10,000 years.

to our basic understanding of human behavior, which is important to anthropologists, sociologists, historians, economists, human geographers, and psychologists. For example, archaeology is often used to validate claims of people with no history of written records. Another example is that archaeology adds to our understanding of the more recent past by supplementing what can be learned through written records and oral history alone.

Through field and laboratory studies, archaeologists study sediments as well as plant and animal remains, which are of interest to physical geographers, geologists, paleontologists, botanists, and palynologists. In this realm, archaeologists contribute to an understanding of the natural world, including the formation and alteration of landscapes, and studies of biological evolution and diversity.

As a final rationale, archaeologists bring awareness and offer solutions to some important problems associated with living in the twenty-first century. For example, archaeologists have made recommendations to the US government for marking deposits of nuclear waste, based on their knowledge of (i) the kind of materials likely to survive the impacts of nature or looters, (ii) the changes that are likely to occur in the landscape over time, and (iii) the problems that arise when the meanings of symbols change or are lost over time, which is common. Other examples include contributions that archaeologists make in debunking popular assumptions about contemporary refuse-discard and recycling programs, and in pointing out the potential problems associated with the ever-increasing amount of space junk in orbit around the earth.

Basic Concepts in Archaeology

Contemporary archaeology rests upon many concepts. The most fundamental of these are **culture**, holism, **deep time**, evolution, reasoning by **analogy**, and using multiple frameworks.

Culture is a concept common to many disciplines in the social sciences. There are many ways to define culture, but one that works well for archaeology is that culture is the learned and shared things that people have, do, and think. There is no minimum number of things that must be shared or number of people sharing to constitute a culture. The things that people have include material objects that are part of the society. In the contemporary world, these include but are certainly not limited to such things as roads, houses, hospitals, churches, colleges, tools, and jewelry. The things that people do include those practices commonly called customs, and involve how people interact with each other, how many hours a day they work, marriage and child-rearing practices, and manners. The things that people think include those commonly linked under ideology, such as beliefs, religion, values, and morals. Sometimes the terms *culture* and *society* are used interchangeably. One way they can be distinguished is to think of the society as the people themselves and culture as those things that are learned and shared by the members of the society.

The reason why culture is a fundamental concept in archaeology is that for most archaeologists their objectives include reconstructing past culture.

The principal spheres of culture are commonly recognized as ecological, social, and ideological. The ecological sphere includes such things as settlement patterns, subsistence strategies, and diet (see Chapter 8), as well as technology (see Chapter 6). The social and ideological spheres include matters of inequality, identity, organization, art, ritual, and religion (see Chapter 9).

In archaeology, holism refers to the notion that all components of culture are linked: an understanding of past culture depends on an investigation of multiple components of that culture, and a change in one component inevitably leads to changes in other components. Archaeologists recognize, for example, that understanding the origins of art, ritual, and **agriculture** depends on an investigation of the earlier technologies, economies, social and political strategies, and belief systems of the people in the region. In many ways, it isn't the individual components of a culture that are under investigation as much as it is the linkages between the components.

In the physical or natural sciences, the phrase *deep time* is generally used to convey the vast billions of years of history of the earth and the universe. Also known as **deep antiquity** in archaeology, deep time is used to convey the long history of humans. The outline of deep time, beginning with the origins of the universe but focusing on the time since humans have been leaving evidence of culture, is included in Chapter 7.

The concept of evolution, both biological and cultural, is central to archaeology. Archaeologists understand that the material evidence left behind by humans extends back in time beyond the existence of *Homo sapiens*. Archaeologists also understand that plants and animals used by humans in the past have evolved, and evidence of this can not only be seen in archaeological sites, but it can also be used to make interpretations about such things as whether the plant or animal was wild or domestic. Archaeologists further understand that cultures are continually changing. The rate of change is not constant, and all components of a culture do not change simultaneously, but change in all aspects of the ecological, social, and ideological spheres is continuous.

Reasoning by analogy is one of the ways in which archaeological interpretations are made. Essentially, analogy is a form of reasoning based on the notion that if two things are the same in some respects, they may be the same in other respects as well. Because archaeologists usually deal with the distant past for which no written records or live witnesses exist, they sometimes rely on analogy to interpret their finds. For example, if an archaeologist finds some clay shaped into a bowl that has been determined to be 7,000 years old, they can reason by analogy that it was used to contain something. The analogy is based on the similarity of the clay-shaped bowl with modern bowls made from clay (the things they have in common). Since modern bowls are used to contain things, then the 7,000-year-old bowl was probably used to contain something as well.

Archaeologists recognize some problems with analogy. They are especially aware that the older the things are that they are trying to interpret, the less confidence they can have in their analogies. The two major kinds of analogies archaeologists use are based on ethnographic research and experiments. **Ethnographic analogy** occurs when archaeologists use similarities with contemporary people, or with people whose culture has been documented in an **ethnography**, to make their interpretations. When archaeologists make observations on contemporary people themselves to provide a source for comparison, it is known as **ethnoarchaeology**. Many archaeologists do experiments to provide a source of comparison (e.g., creating things that can be described as similar to archaeological finds), which is known as **experimental archaeology**.

There are many frameworks for discovery and interpretation in archaeology. There is no single right way to do archaeology. No matter what context archaeology is being practiced within, or what the goals of a particular research project may be, there are always alternative strategies to consider. These include such fundamental things as choosing methods for fieldwork and analysis (see Chapters 5 and 6) and conceptual frameworks for understanding why and how cultures change (see Chapter 10).

Because there are many valid methods, there are also many disagreements among archaeologists. Given the restrictions of specific project goals, time, and budget, some strategies may be better than others, but there is rarely a single best way. When it comes to the broad questions archaeologists investigate, such as why people started to farm and why civilizations collapse, differences in explanations are often based on some basic assumptions on the part of individual archaeologists about how cultures work. These are covered in more detail in Chapter 10.

KEY RESOURCES AND SUGGESTED READING

Schiffer (2017) provides an excellent overview of the contributions of archaeology in contemporary times. Suggested readings on the topic of archaeology and nuclear waste are Kaplan and Adams (1986) and Joyce (2020). Foundational books on archaeology and popular culture include those by Holtorf (2005, 2007). Archaeogaming is covered well by Reinhard (2018).

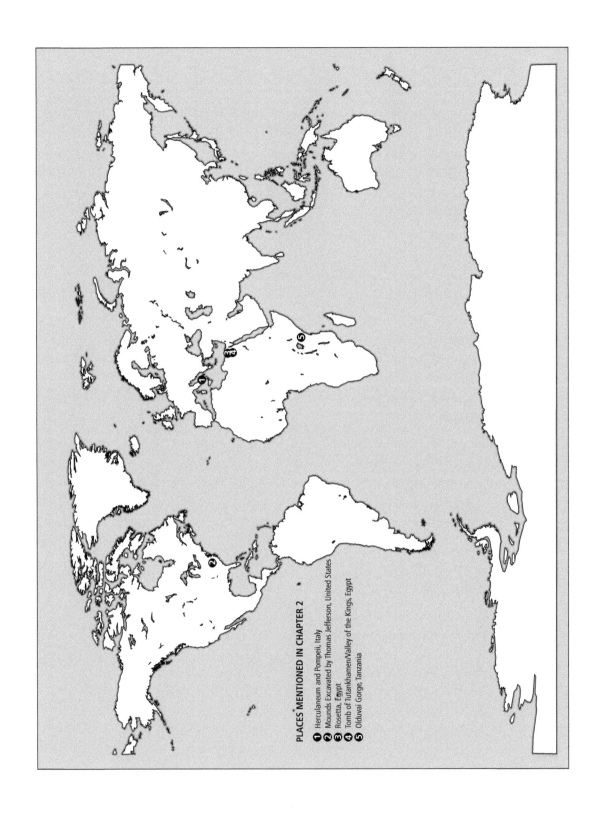

PLACES MENTIONED IN CHAPTER 2

1 Herculaneum and Pompeii, Italy
2 Mounds Excavated by Thomas Jefferson, United States
3 Rosetta, Egypt
4 Tomb of Tutankhamen/Valley of the Kings, Egypt
5 Olduvai Gorge, Tanzania

CHAPTER 2

LOOKING AT ARCHAEOLOGY'S PAST

Introduction

As a widely recognized scholarly endeavor, archaeology has a fairly brief history, extending little more than about 150 years into the past. It has been recognized as a profession for only a few decades. These time frames are somewhat arbitrary, however, and even a cursory examination of the history of archaeology shows that many of the ideas and discoveries upon which the discipline is based come from the distant past, from various fields of study, and from around the globe (even though archaeology has traditionally been considered to be a product of European intellectual history and thought).

This chapter provides an overview of some of the most significant historical events in the emergence and ongoing development of archaeology.

From the Ancient Philosophers to the End of the Eighteenth Century

Some historians of archaeology choose to see the first antecedents of the discipline in philosophical speculations about the human past, which can be traced back to the first millennium BC. Surviving manuscripts indicate that in the ancient societies of Greece, Rome, and China, people were speculating on previous "ages" and cultural evolution. Writings from ancient Greece speculate on previous technologies based on stone; a philosopher from ancient Rome suggested something akin to our modern conception of the Stone, Bronze, and Iron Ages; and it is reported that China had its own version of the **three-age system** more than 2,000 years ago.

Rather than focusing on these speculations, other historians choose to see the origins of archaeology in the first examples of concentrated interest in the material remains of past human activities. Like the philosophical speculations, these go back at least a few thousand years. People who lived in the latter days of the ancient Egyptian civilization spent time restoring some material remains from earlier times, such as the Sphinx, although it may be stretching the imagination to link this with the development of archaeology. Ancient China and Persia provide stronger ties. It is reported that material remains were used in support of historical records in ancient China. And Nabonidus, a king of the Babylonian Empire, is often cited as the first archaeologist because of his deliberate quest, well over 2,000 years ago, for the material remains of the people who preceded the Babylonians.

According to the records retained in **cuneiform**, Nabonidus, who ruled from 556 to 539 BC, attempted to connect himself with the ancient past by excavating artifacts of his predecessors. Because he was excavating with an explicit design to make links with the past, many people call his actions archaeology, although to most this is a very long stretch.

Public museums date to the fifth century BC in Greece and the first century AD in Rome. The oldest museum still in existence, which has been in operation since the eighth century AD, is in Japan. Despite the close relationship between archaeology and museums, the first public museum did not open in Europe until the late seventeenth century.

The Middle Ages – the period from the collapse of the Roman Empire in the fifth century until the beginning of the Renaissance in Europe at about 1400 – was a stagnant period for the growth of archaeology in Europe. Philosophical speculations and interest in the material remains of past cultures gave way to religious doctrine, and the Christian Bible was commonly viewed as the ultimate source of knowledge. Undoubtedly, from the perspective of most people in Europe during that time, speculation about the past was unnecessary. There was little apparent interest in material remains of the past, and little interest or discussion about previous ages.

During the periods widely known as the Renaissance (c. 1400–1600) and the Enlightenment (c. 1600–1800), changes in Europe had important implications for archaeology, beginning with the rise of science as an explanatory framework. As European explorers, traders, and missionaries returned home with tales of foreign places and peoples, Europeans must have found biblical explanations – such as attributing the origin of these cultures to the 10 lost tribes of Israel – increasingly difficult to accept. Parallel developments in the rise of science provided alternative explanations for the natural world. Although the Bible continued to have a prominent explanatory role, it was no longer the ultimate source of knowledge for many.

While the rise of science as a general explanatory framework was perhaps one of the most significant developments in the origins of archaeology, advancements in the more specific areas of geology and biology were equally important. Conventional thinking of the time placed the origin of the earth at somewhere between 6000 and 3700 BC. Various people attempted to determine the origin using religious texts. The most well-known is the calculation based on the Christian Bible by Archbishop James Ussher, who determined in 1650 that the earth was created in 4004 BC. Subsequent calculations were even more precise, pinpointing the origin as October 23, 4004, at 9 a.m. Advances in geology challenged this notion of such a brief history for the earth and led many people to consider a much longer antiquity. Some of the basic principles of geology were formulated during this period, such as the **law of superposition** (stating that each undeformed sedimentary layer is older than the one above it), which ultimately served as a primary technique for assigning relative ages to archaeological sites.

In addition to suggesting a relatively recent origin for the earth, religious doctrine of the period provided for no such concept as biological evolution. All species were generally considered to have been created in their present form. Discoveries of bones we now recognize as those of extinct animals, and stones we now know were shaped by humans, were commonly explained as freaks of nature. Beginning in the 1700s, some people started believing that biological changes in organisms did occur. By the end of the 1700s, many people accepted evidence of biological change.

Although wide support for the concept of biological evolution did not happen until the late 1800s, the recognition and investigation of the phenomena in the 1700s had profound influence on the development of archaeology. The acceptance of biological evolution opened the door to thinking about cultural evolution. After 1,000 years of relatively little philosophical or intellectual interest in previous ages, Europeans once again became open to new concepts dealing with the cultural past.

Other significant developments during this period in Europe include renewed interest in the philosophical speculations and material cultures of the classical civilizations of Greece and Rome. Translations of ancient philosophers who speculated about people progressing through various stages ultimately led to more modern frameworks of the three-age system. By the late 1500s, Europeans were again discussing the possibility of previous ages, and by the late 1700s, many people accepted the notion that European societies had developed in stages now known widely as the Stone, Bronze, and Iron Ages.

In the sixteenth and seventeenth centuries, interest in the material culture of ancient Greece and Rome emerged. Collecting art and antiquities from those classical eras became a hobby of the rich throughout Europe, and the collectors became known as **antiquarians**. Eventually the interest spread to antiquities of ancient Egypt as well.

While antiquarians were focused on ancient civilizations, other people began to document the heritage of their own countries. One of the best known is William

Camden, who produced a compendium of archaeological sites in Britain in the late sixteenth century. Edward Lhwyd and John Aubrey also investigated and wrote about archaeological sites in Britain in the seventeenth century.

European societies were introduced to an immense diversity of cultures from around the world during this time. As European explorers, traders, and missionaries returned from their travels to previously unknown parts of Asia, Africa, and the Americas, they brought with them descriptions of vastly different peoples and cultures, generally portrayed as being greatly inferior to European societies. Religious explanations attempted to account for the existence of these so-called morally and technologically inferior peoples: they were among the lost tribes of Israel mentioned in the Bible, and as they wandered from the Holy Land, they degenerated. Eventually, many would observe some similarities in the material culture of some of the peoples from foreign lands and the finds from earlier times in Europe, suggesting that the non-Europeans were simply not progressing as fast as Europeans (but these views wouldn't be fully worked out until the late 1800s).

The first systematic archaeological excavations are generally considered to have occurred in the eighteenth century. Excavations at three sites are significant for their impact on the development of archaeology. The Roman cities of Herculaneum and Pompeii in Italy were quickly buried by ash from the eruption of Mount Vesuvius in AD 79. Systematic excavations began at both these sites in the eighteenth century, providing a rich database for understanding everyday life in the Roman Empire.

Another significant excavation took place in the United States. During the eighteenth century, considerable thought was given to the thousands of large earthen mounds that dotted the landscape. Although Europeans had observed Indigenous Peoples living on some of the mounds and conducting activities on others, and despite the fact that Indigenous Peoples themselves claimed that they were directly descended from those who built the mounds, many people doubted their origin. Popular explanations included the notion that more advanced civilizations had existed in the mound areas before the Indigenous Peoples.

Some non-Indigenous Americans who were curious about the mounds, including Thomas Jefferson (who would later become the third president of the United States) set out to investigate by excavation. Jefferson's methods, including the recording of mound **stratigraphy**, were remarkable for the time. In many ways, his attention to problem solving (e.g., determining who created the mounds) and his detailed recordings were following scientific method, and he is often credited as the first to undertake scientific excavations. Jefferson determined that the mounds were indeed created by the Indigenous Peoples in previous times, a conclusion that has withstood the test of time.

FIGURE 2.1 Rosetta Stone. Discovered in 1799 in the town of Rosetta, Egypt following the invasion of French troops, the stone repeats the same message in three scripts, providing the key for deciphering hieroglyphics.

Jefferson isn't the only well-known figure from history to have influenced the development of archaeology. When Napoleon Bonaparte, the emperor of France, invaded Egypt in 1798, many people we would describe today as scholars accompanied him. He was interested in Egypt's ancient past, and some of his followers were directed to report on items of potential significance. In 1799, one of Napoleon's officers working in the Egyptian town of Rosetta discovered what was to become one of the world's best-known artifacts. The Rosetta Stone is a large black slab of basalt with an inscription in three languages: an ancient form of Greek, an ancient form of Egyptian script, and **hieroglyphics**. It is 114 centimeters (44 inches) high, 72 centimeters (29 inches) wide, and 28 centimeters (11½ inches) thick.

The Rosetta Stone was immediately recognized for its potential to help decipher hieroglyphics, and although it would take some years, it ultimately did provide the key. Essentially, once it was determined that the ancient Greek and Egyptian scripts said the same thing, the hieroglyphics were assumed to as well, and it was only a matter of time before they were decoded. Despite efforts by the government of Egypt to have the Rosetta Stone returned, it rests today in the British Museum in London.

Archaeology in the Nineteenth Century

The early part of the nineteenth century witnessed further support for the ideas that had begun to form in the preceding centuries. Science was increasingly acknowledged as an appropriate framework for understanding how the world works, and notions of great antiquity for the earth were becoming widely accepted. Although those interested in earth science had developed some basic principles that convinced them that the earth had to be older than several thousand years, as claimed by theologians, the idea of great antiquity, in the order of 100,000 years or more, only became popular after the research and writings of James Hutton in the late 1700s and the publication of Charles Lyell's three-volume series *Principles of Geology* in the early 1830s. These writings were particularly important for establishing the concept of deep time for archaeology. Hutton, often considered the creator of modern geology, developed the principle of **uniformitarianism** (simply, "the present is the key to the past") and wrote *Theory of the Earth*, but by most accounts, his ideas were not easily understood or accepted. It wasn't until the writings of Lyell that theories of geology and geologic time became widely accepted.

In addition, museums played a very important role in the rise of archaeology in the early nineteenth century. Museums became active in their pursuit of collections. While museums were once generally considered to be passive receivers of finds, the desire to fill them in the nineteenth century became one of the principal reasons for the excavation of sites, both in Europe and the rest of world. The nineteenth century is often seen as the golden age of museums. Some of the collecting was done in a professional manner, but in other cases, it amounted to little more than looting. One of the best-known collectors of the early part of the century was Giovanni Belzoni, a purported one-time circus strongman who made a career of looting Egyptian antiquities, some of which made their way to museums. Reports of Belzoni's raids commonly refer to his destruction of tombs and mummies in his quest for specific items, such as **papyri**. Belzoni, who sometimes worked on behalf of the British government, is also well known for his feats of engineering to move huge statues, many of which ended up in Great Britain.

Besides seeking to add to their collections, museums in the early nineteenth century played a role in solidifying thought on cultural evolution and popularizing the notion of the three-age system. Although ideas of cultural evolution can be traced to philosophers more than 2,000 years ago and were rediscovered in the Renaissance, the person usually credited with popularizing the three-age system is Christian Thomsen, who in 1816 was the first museum professional to use it to organize collections. As curator of the Danish National Museum, Thomsen classified objects for public display according to whether they were made from stone, bronze, or iron, and recognized the chronology. The system was quickly adopted by other museums.

Jacob Jens Worsaae was subsequently hired by Thomsen to expand the museum collection. In addition to excavating sites for the collection of objects, Worsaae's work had an intellectual angle: he sought to confirm the chronological sequence of the Stone, Bronze, and Iron Ages. Worsaae also worked for the Danish government, continuing his archaeological research in recording, excavating, and in some cases, preserving archaeological sites. For many, Worsaae is considered the first truly professional archaeologist. He is given this designation because he was paid to be an excavator, had established scholarly research objectives focused on **culture history**, and also was among the first to have a university appointment, beginning his teaching career at the University of Copenhagen in 1855.

Few would dispute that by the mid-1800s, archaeology had not only become a profession involved in the collection of objects of the past, but it had also come to be considered a serious academic discipline. Positions similar to Worsaae's appointment at Copenhagen were being established at other European universities as well.

The mid-1800s were also an influential time for thought about evolution. Many in Europe came to accept the notion of evolution, principally through the publication of Charles Darwin's *On the Origin of Species* in 1859, in which he explained how biological evolution occurs. The widespread acceptance of biological evolution may not have been directly responsible for theories about cultural evolution, since notions

TABLE 2.1 The Unilinear Theory of Cultural Evolution (developed by L.H. Morgan in 1877)

STAGE	DESCRIPTION
1. Lower Status of Savagery	From the infancy of humankind to the acquisition of a subsistence strategy that includes fishing and controlling fire
	No living examples of this stage existed when Morgan developed the theory
2. Middle Status of Savagery	Begins with subsistence that includes fishing and controlling fire, and ends with the use of the bow and arrow
3. Upper Status of Savagery	Begins with the use of the bow and arrow, and ends with the manufacture and use of pottery
4. Lower Status of Barbarism	Begins with pottery and ends with subsistence based on domestic plants and/or animals
5. Middle Status of Barbarism	Begins in the eastern hemisphere with the domestication of animals
	Begins in the western hemisphere with the cultivation of maize and other plants
	Ends with the process of smelting iron
6. Upper Status of Barbarism	Begins with iron smelting and ends with the invention of a phonetic alphabet and writing
7. Civilization	Begins with the invention of a phonetic alphabet and writing

of cultural evolution were already in existence, but it likely made it easier to accept that cultures, like organisms, change over time.

If the three-age system is considered the first major archaeological theory, then the second is the **unilinear theory of cultural evolution** developed by Edward Tylor and Lewis Henry Morgan. In 1871, British anthropologist Edward Tylor developed the idea that based on their culture, peoples and societies of both modern and past times could be classified as either savages, barbarians, or civilized.

The American Lewis Henry Morgan further developed this idea with the publication of *Ancient Societies* in 1877. Morgan's system included three stages of savagery and three stages of barbarism before the stage of civilization. Categorization of any group of people was based primarily on its technology and subsistence strategy (Table 2.1). Since this is what is typically best represented in the material remains of people, Morgan's theory became attractive to many archaeologists. An integral part of the theory was that cultural evolution is directional, with all of humankind beginning at the lowest status of savagery. According to the theory, groups moved through the stages, albeit at different rates.

While many people chose to accept Morgan's model of cultural evolution, not everyone did. Franz Boas, a pioneer of North American anthropology, was one of the principal people arguing against the model. Boas developed the idea of **historical particularism**, which implies that each group's history is unique and does not follow any general pattern of cultural evolution, contrary to the unilinear theory.

The highlight of the last decades of the nineteenth century was the development of systematic and detailed methods of archaeological excavation and recording, which remain in place today. Much of this development is attributed to General Augustus Henry Lane-Fox Pitt Rivers, who took the military precision and rigor he practiced as a general in the British army and applied it to archaeological excavation in his retirement. This included paying close attention to, and making detailed recordings of, stratigraphy; recording the precise **provenience** of all finds; keeping detailed notes; working with trained excavators; and publishing the results of his work. Pitt Rivers is generally credited with providing the foundations for contemporary archaeological fieldwork.

While archaeology in Europe and most other parts of the world continued to develop as a distinct discipline, it was largely subsumed within anthropology in the late 1800s in North America. This is likely due to the fact that in North America, unlike in Europe, direct cultural continuity existed between the original inhabitants of sites and the Indigenous Peoples of the late 1800s. Archaeology was not the only discipline included in anthropology at this time. Many anthropologists in North America during the late 1800s, including Boas, can be described as generalists, practicing all of archaeology, biological anthropology, **cultural anthropology**, and linguistics.

Archaeology in the Twentieth Century

Many important developments took place in archaeology during the twentieth century. These include, but are certainly not limited to, the discovery of new sites; changes in methodological and theoretical orientations; the emergence of archaeology as a profession in addition to an academic discipline; and new interests.

FOCUSING ON DESCRIPTION (c. 1900–1965)

The first several decades of the twentieth century are often depicted as falling within what some call the culture-historical period (focusing on culture history), which means they emphasized describing the chronological development of cultures. Archaeology was primarily focused on finding and describing archaeological sites and the artifacts discovered within them, and then putting the objects and sites of a region into some sort of chronological sequence. Archaeological reports from this time tend to be thick with description and thin on interpretation. The items of interest were generally objects of stone or clay, obviously made by humans.

Archaeology was practiced for a variety of reasons in the early decades of the century. The tradition of antiquarianism continued, and some wealthy benefactors funded excavations led by professional archaeologists. University professors seeking to add to our knowledge base of past societies led many of the projects, and museums continued to expand their collections. Government funding of archaeology for nationalist purposes was also common.

Although dominated by archaeological description, the early decades were not totally devoid of theory. As the century progressed, the reaction against the unilinear theory of evolution became stronger. **Diffusion** was typically used as an explanation for cultural phenomena, and although it wasn't commonplace, archaeologists did theorize about such things as the origins of agriculture.

By mid-century, many archaeologists came to the conclusion that cultures essentially developed as a way of adapting to the environment, and it became widely accepted that there were multiple effective ways of adapting. The notion of a unilinear model of cultural evolution had been dying during the early decades of the century, and was dead by mid-century.

The early decades of the twentieth century were an exciting time for those involved in archaeology. Many important sites associated with ancient civilizations were discovered, perhaps none more inspiring than that of the tomb of Tutankhamen, popularly known as King Tut, in Egypt. Archaeologist Howard Carter had worked in Egypt for many years before coming across the undisturbed tomb of Tutankhamen in 1922. The discovery is significant to archaeology in two major ways. First, it provides the only glimpse we have of an undisturbed royal tomb. All other tombs of royalty that have been discovered were looted long before archaeologists became involved. As such, the tomb of Tutankhamen provides the most comprehensive site of a royal Egyptian burial, and all that we can learn about Egyptian life from that.

Second, the tomb is significant because it marks the beginning of a worldwide fascination with archaeology. Newspapers from around the globe sent reporters to Egypt for the opening of the tomb, bringing the discovery to the attention of readers thousands of miles away. Some of the reporters began taking liberties with the facts, and the idea of the Curse of King Tut, among other things, developed. As the story goes, some newspapers altered the meaning of some of the tomb's inscriptions, leading the public to believe there was a curse. When Lord Carnarvon of Britain, the sponsor of the excavations, died within a year of the opening of the tomb, it was taken as evidence of the curse.

FIGURE 2.2 Howard Carter Examining the Third, Innermost Coffin of King Tut. The discovery of King Tut was among the most significant events for the development of archaeology in the early twentieth century.

Throughout the middle decades of the century, the fascination with archaeology continued. Archaeology was happening around the world, including in Africa by the well-known husband-and-wife team of paleoanthropologists Louis and Mary Leakey. They began searching in East Africa's Olduvai Gorge for evidence of early humans. The Leakeys' archaeological projects resulted in dozens of significant discoveries of both skeletal and cultural remains. Louis Leakey was a great popularizer of research into early humans and was widely revered in his home country of Kenya. Many would say he created an archaeological dynasty. After Louis's death in 1972, Mary Leakey continued to make important discoveries into the 1980s. It was Mary who excavated the oldest known hominin footprints (c. 3.4 million years). Their son Richard replaced Louis as the director of National Museums of Kenya and directed many significant archaeological projects in Kenya throughout the 1970s and 1980s, before turning his attention to conservation and political issues. The Leakey legacy has continued with Richard's wife, Meave, and daughter Louise (Louis's granddaughter) each making new and significant hominin discoveries in the early twenty-first century.

By the middle decades of the century, the basic pattern of cultural chronology for most regions of the world had been established, albeit in a simplified way compared to our current understanding. Ongoing research, of course, has added greatly to our

FIGURE 2.3 Louis Leakey: From Archaeologist to Artifact. This statue of Louis Leakey sits outside the National Museum in Kenya. Leakey was a great popularizer of archaeology, and he and his family have made many significant archaeological discoveries in Africa.

PHOTO: Barry D. Kass @ ImagesofAnthropology.com.

understanding of culture history through the discovery of hundreds of thousands of more sites and many millions of artifacts. A brief overview of world **prehistory** as we understand it in the early twenty-first century is provided in Chapter 7.

The application of **radiocarbon dating** at mid-century was one of the most significant developments in archaeology. Radiocarbon dating began to be applied to material remains in 1950, and since that time it has remained one of the most reliable techniques for determining the antiquity of sites and objects. Prior to 1950, few reliable dating techniques existed for prehistoric sites. By providing specific dates, radiocarbon dating significantly increased the accuracy of dating sites and events of the past. The technique is described more fully in Chapter 7.

BOX 2.1 KING TUT

The discovery of the tomb of the pharaoh Tutankhamun, more popularly known as King Tut, is one of the most significant discoveries in the history of archaeology, not so much for leading to a more complete understanding of ancient Egypt (which is important in itself), but more for catapulting archaeology into the realm of popular culture, especially in regard to mummies and curses.

King Tut was discovered by archaeologist Howard Carter in Egypt in 1922, and since that time has rarely faded from interest. A relatively minor ruler in the overall history of ancient Egypt, in his death, King Tut has likely become one of the most popular people who has ever lived. He is firmly embedded in popular culture – in movies, television, songs, cartoons, comic books, novels, bobble-head dolls, and traveling museum exhibits. In one recent year there were at least three traveling museum exhibits of King Tut in the United States alone; and one of the exhibits reportedly brought in more than $100 million in admissions.

Many are aware of the Curse of the King Tut, which is attributed to the opening of the tomb. The sponsor of the archaeological work on the tomb was Lord Carnarvon, who died less than a year after the tomb's opening (probably due to an infection from a mosquito bite, rather than a curse). The death of Carnarvon and subsequently many others associated with the tomb's contents in more recent years have often been used in support of the curse. In reality, however, support for the curse is nonexistent. Some have suggested that perhaps there were some kind of bacteria or other microorganisms sealed in the tomb that were deleterious to those who breathed them upon opening the tomb. Such explanations are not necessary. Of the 25 people associated most closely with the tomb and mummy, it is reported that the average age at death was 70. Howard Carter himself lived for another 17 years after discovering the tomb, dying at the age of 67.

There appears to be an endless stream of news reports on King Tut, of both the scientific and pseudoscientific kinds. There is no consensus on many aspects of his being, but some recent reports suggest that while alive, he was probably sickly, and may have walked with a limp, had a club foot, cleft palate, and an overbite. Some suggest he may have had a hormonal disorder, scoliosis, and malaria. Various studies in recent years have attributed his death to murder by either poison or a blow to the head, sickle cell anemia, or a combination of an infection, broken leg, and malaria. One recent research project indicates he was the product of an incestuous relationship. Another suggests he may have spontaneously combusted in his coffin. Considerable attention has been paid to the fact that his penis is apparently missing. Some suggest he may have had a genetic disorder leading to underdeveloped genitals while others claim it fell off accidentally or was deliberately removed in recent times.

Archaeology as it was practiced in the early twentieth century was not without its critics from within the profession. It wasn't until the 1960s, however, that significant changes in goals and methods occurred.

A NEW ARCHAEOLOGY EMERGES: THE 1960S

In the early 1960s, archaeology began to change dramatically. Critics argued that instead of simply describing the past, archaeologists should explain the past, focusing on such things as how and why cultures change. Further, the critics argued that archaeologists should use an explicitly scientific approach, which includes testing hypotheses and using quantitative methods. Many archaeologists of the time quickly accepted this new direction, and it became known as the **new archaeology**. Eventually it became more widely known as **processual archaeology**, reflecting the primary focus on understanding **culture process** (i.e., how the various components of culture influence each other, how cultures change, and why cultures change).

Whereas the principal goal of traditional archaeology was to simply describe culture history, the new archaeology added two new goals. One was to reconstruct past ways of life, which essentially means to recreate previous cultures in their entirety. This is also known as **culture reconstruction**, which includes more attention to the social and ideological spheres than had typically been considered. Another goal was to explain the nature of culture, with the hope of generating some scientific laws that govern culture change. The essence of the new archaeology was that it could do much more and become more meaningful than traditional archaeology. Documenting culture history was still important, but by doing more, archaeology would become more socially relevant.

The American Lewis Binford and the British David Clarke are the two archaeologists most often associated with leading these changes in archaeology. Lewis Binford continued to make many important contributions to archaeological method and theory over subsequent decades, especially his contributions to **middle-level research**. Tragically, David Clarke died in a traffic accident in the late 1960s.

Culture history certainly wasn't abandoned, but it started to play a secondary role in many archaeological studies, particularly in the United States. The transition to processual archaeology did not occur in a vacuum. Published criticisms of archaeology had begun in the 1940s, but they were virtually ignored until the 1960s.

Archaeology was not the only field that was changing its nature, and some consideration should be given to the influence of changes in other disciplines. It has been suggested, for example, that David Clarke was influenced by changes occurring in the study of geography in Great Britain. Some historians of archaeology have also speculated that new archaeology caught on so quickly in the United States because of the political climate of the time. The argument is basically that the American government and other major funding agencies started to favor projects that were explicitly scientific and socially relevant.

ARCHAEOLOGY BECOMES DIVERSIFIED: THE 1970S
The 1970s mark the decade when archaeology became significantly diverse. Throughout the earlier history of archaeology, there was always some degree of specialization, such as focusing on a particular geographic region or time period. The increased diversification that occurred in the 1970s is considered important in two major ways. One is that a split began to develop between archaeology undertaken with

scholarly goals (e.g., reconstructing culture history) and archaeology practiced because sites were in danger of being destroyed.

As progressively larger-scale development projects were taking place around the world, people were increasingly concerned that important archaeological sites were being destroyed. During the 1960s and into the 1970s, university- and museum-based archaeologists were called out more frequently to assess potential impacts to sites and sometimes to undertake excavations in advance of their destruction by development. During this time, governments around the world began to strengthen heritage legislation, often making it mandatory that archaeological work be done in advance of development. Eventually, because of increasing development and stronger legislation, a new career track was opened up in archaeology. No longer were employment opportunities restricted to those based in universities or museums. Archaeologists could now work full time in industry: finding sites, assessing their significance, and in some cases, excavating them.

Archaeology also diversified in the 1970s by topical interests. Along with the latest goals and methods of the new archaeology came new topics to be explored. A new type of research known as **middle-range research**, or middle-range theory, began. Middle-range research was designed to bridge the gap between the **low-level research** of documenting culture history and the **high-level research** of theorizing about how cultures work. Examples of middle-range research include experimental archaeology and ethnoarchaeology. Analytical specialties also gained in prominence. Most of the major subfields recognized today (detailed in Chapter 3) arose during the 1970s and early 1980s.

A NEWER, MORE CRITICAL ARCHAEOLOGY EMERGES: THE 1980S

By the early 1980s, it was clear to many that there were problems with processual archaeology. The criticisms included a failure to adequately consider (i) the inherent bias in archaeological research, including gender bias, (ii) nonscientific frameworks for investigating the past, (iii) the multiple stakeholders in archaeological interpretation, (iv) that general laws governing human behavior may not exist, and (v) ideology, ethnicity, and gender in the archaeological record.

Like the development of processual archaeology, this newer, more critical archaeology did not emerge in a vacuum. It is generally considered to have been influenced by what has become known as **postmodernism** in the humanities. Other important and influential developments of the time include assertions of Indigenous Peoples and the continued rise of feminism. During the 1980s, most of the criticisms of processual archaeology were coming from archaeologists working in Britain, most notably Ian Hodder.

This newer, more critical archaeology was originally called **post-processual archaeology**. It has always been understood that post-processual archaeology is not so much a new way of doing archaeology as it is an umbrella phrase for all those who not only criticize processual archaeology, but do archaeology in scholarly, nontraditional methods. Post-processual archaeology includes, but is certainly not limited to, such things as the widespread belief that all archaeology is political; the use of metaphor in interpretations; the explicit recognition of bias in interpretations; and the practice of archaeology in nonscientific ways; and it includes the identification and significance of gender, ethnicity, and ideology as principal objectives of research.

It is difficult to know for sure whether the criticisms of Hodder and other British archaeologists were persuasive enough to alter the kinds of research being done throughout the world, or whether that had more to do with other occurrences, such as the rise of feminism and Indigenous empowerment, or perhaps a change in the way archaeological research is funded.

It is clear that many who profess to be doing processual archaeology early in the twenty-first century have been influenced by the criticisms. Explicit recognition of bias is now common, and topics such as gender, ethnicity, and ideology are now mainstream. Whether the changes are related to world events, intellectual persuasion, funding, or other means remains to be seen. It has been pointed out, however, that after a few decades of National Science Foundation funding for archaeological researchers from the United States, subsequent decreases in funding allocations in the 1980s caused researchers to shift their grant proposals to the National Endowment for the Humanities, in which research on issues of gender and ethnicity are much more likely to be funded.

BOX 2.2 FEMINIST ARCHAEOLOGY

Though gender and sexuality have been explored by other academic disciplines since the 1950s and 1960s, archaeologists did not begin investigating these topics until the early 1980s. It was at this time that female archaeologists who saw themselves as feminists started questioning why archaeologists were so hesitant and late to study gender issues. **Feminist archaeology** pioneers like Dr. Joan Gero, formerly of American University, and Dr. Margaret Conkey, professor of archaeology at the University of California, Berkeley, wrote seminal publications exploring two central problems in archaeology: (i)

the representation of females and gender dynamics in the past, and (ii) gender bias and discrimination in the discipline of archaeology.

Through this work, which is known as first-wave feminist archaeology, archaeologists identified how women in the past were often depicted as passive, inactive people who were solely responsible for birthing and raising children (Conkey and Spector 1984). Men, in contrast, were depicted as active, productive members of society who constructed homes, foraged and hunted for food, and made stone tools. Feminist archaeologists challenged these androcentric representations of the past, arguing that scholars, most of whom were male, had failed to support their claims about how and if labor was divided and organized by gender (Conkey and Gero 1991). Feminist archaeologists discovered that these gender biases made it challenging for women to work in the profession of archaeology. Gero found that female archaeologists were expected to labor in the laboratory, while men were encouraged to pursue outdoor fieldwork. Gero (1985) attributes this to what she calls the "woman-at-home ideology," a pervasive myth in the Western world that circumscribes women's roles in society. This bias permeated granting agencies, including the National Science Foundation (NSF) in the United States; Gero (1985, 347) found that women applying to the NSF were less likely to be funded for field-based research than men.

Second-wave feminist archaeology sought to complicate first-wave feminist archaeology's interpretations of gender relations in the past. It did so by focusing on how identities were constructed in specific time periods, places, and cultures to show that ideas of gender are fluid, not fixed. Dr. Roberta Gilchrist, a professor of archaeology at the University of Reading, for instance, looks at how medieval nunneries constructed specific concepts of religious femininity. Medieval nuns were expected to rid themselves of all vestiges of worldly femininity and individuality in preparation for becoming brides of Christ; this included cutting off one's hair, remaining celibate, and wearing habits (Gilchrist 2000, 91).

Second-wave feminists maintained the work done by first-wave feminists on how female archaeologists are treated in the discipline. In this vein, scholars expressed concern that gender studies was essentially a female pursuit, a field not taken seriously or cited by men in the discipline (Wright 1996, 53). Feminist archaeologists also observed that women pursuing graduate degrees were encouraged to undertake projects exploring themes historically attributed to women, such as gender or household studies (Conkey 2007, 291), themes that were often seen as not as serious as the topics assigned to male Ph.D. students, such as hunting and gathering, the rise of agriculture, and the growth of cities and urbanization.

The third and final wave of feminist archaeology has worked to untangle commonly held beliefs about biological sex, reproduction, sexuality, and gender identity. Biological sex refers to the genitalia and hormones with which one is born; biological sexes include male, female, and intersex. Gender is different from biological sex, as it refers to a variety of identities, such as feminine, masculine, nongendered, and transgender. Sexuality is likewise separate from both gender and biological sex, encompassing sexual practices and behaviors that are not necessarily tied to one's gender identity. Due to the influence of Christianity in Western society, sexual practices have historically been associated with and assumed to be innate to specific genders. For example, in some Western cultures it is assumed that heterosexual (sexuality), masculine (gender) biological (sex) men are innately programmed to desire heterosexual (sexuality), feminine (gender) biological (sex) females for reproductive purposes.

Third wave feminist archaeologists have focused on the intersection of gender-based inequality, in the profession and in archeological analyses of past cultures, with other vectors of identity, including race, class, and sexual orientation. Dr. Barbara Voss, an associate professor of anthropology at Stanford University and co-editor of the now canonical book *Archaeologies of Sexuality*, used archaeological and archival data to argue that relationships formed in Spanish-colonial California involved sexual coercion and violence (Voss 2008a, 2008b). Catherine Jalbert's thesis (2019) has looked at the working conditions and problems of Canadian archaeology, also noting the continual racial disparities in the profession; in her survey of Canadian archaeologists, she discovered that 90 per cent of the 280 respondents were white (Jalbert 2019, 208). Dr. Whitney Battle-Baptiste, an associate professor of anthropology at the University of Massachusetts, Amherst, is one of the few African American archaeologists in an academic institution. Her seminal book *Black Feminist Archaeology* (2011) documents how racism in the field of archaeology has shaped her career trajectory but also how it structures and affects interpretations of African American communities in the past.

(continued)

BOX 2.2 Continued

Recent research has provided sobering statistics that illustrate why many women and people of color may be leaving or no longer considering a career in archaeology. Male respondents to Jalbert's dissertation survey noted continual gender biases and the existence of a "good ole boys club" in the field, with one describing the "treatment of some female coworkers by older male supervisors ... abhorrent" (Jalbert 2019, 209). Clancy et al. (2014) surveyed 666 scientists working in field-based sciences, including archaeologists, to similarly capture the pervasive, widespread nature of sexual harassment and discrimination within the field that pushes many talented scholars out of the field. Muckle (2014), who read Clancy et al.'s findings, notes that archaeologists must take the findings seriously by having clear policies in place before any archaeological field project begins and by reviewing those policies with students before fieldwork begins.

Women who remain in academic archaeology against all odds continue to encounter barriers. Goldstein et al. (2018) observe that while more than half of the Ph.D.s granted in anthropology are produced by women, women remain underrepresented in the academy. Female archaeologists are less likely to both apply for competitive national grants and to find employment at Ph.D.-granting universities. According to Tushingham, Fulkerson, and Hill (2017), female archaeologists are also more likely to publish in lower-tier, non–peer reviewed publications than men, and are substantially underrepresented in top-tier peer-reviewed journals in the Western United States. While the discipline has come a long way from its early days of completely excluding women and minorities from archaeology, these recent studies show that the field still needs to actively work toward equity so that all who are intrigued by the past can find a home in the profession.

Recent History of Archaeology

Important discoveries made during the early twenty-first century include many thousands of previously unknown sites and many millions of artifacts. Many of these discoveries are pushing our understanding of things such as the origins of tool use, the beginning of art, and the movement of people into previously unoccupied territories further into the past (see Chapter 7). Many important new technologies have also been important for finding sites, such as remote sensing techniques including LIDAR and the use of satellite imagery (discussed in Chapter 5), and in the laboratory (Chapter 6).

The early decades of the twenty-first century have seen archaeological interests expand far beyond the interests of culture history, processual, and post-processual archaeology. The diversification of archaeology and emergence of specialties that began in the 1970s has continued, as has the growth of commercial (or CRM) archaeology.

Lenses to guide approaches to the past that have become increasingly common in the early decades of the twenty-first century include **inclusive/queer archaeology, punk archaeology, post-colonial archaeology, digital archaeology,** and **public archaeology** (see Figure 2.4). The first decades of the twenty-first century have also

Colonial

Processual

Post-processual

Feminist

Post-colonial

Queer/Inclusive

Digital

Punk

FIGURE 2.4 The Many Interpretive Lenses of Archaeological Theory. This drawing represents the many theoretical frameworks or lenses through which archaeologists analyze and make sense of their data. These lenses are organized temporally, with the colonial framework representing the discipline of archaeology's formative years as a profession. The most recent theoretical frameworks include post-colonial/Indigenous archaeology; digital archaeology; queer/inclusive archaeology; and punk archaeology.

IMAGE: Katherine Cook.

witnessed a significant interest in archaeology of very recent and contemporary times, including such things as homelessness, undocumented migration, forensics, contemporary disasters, and incarceration. Several of these areas of interest are covered more fully in Chapter 11.

Ethics have also gained a prominent place in the thinking of archaeologists in recent years (see Chapter 3), including recognition of privilege, and having safe workplaces free from harassment, abuse, and bullying.

One of the most prominent archaeology movements within North America during the early twenty-first century is **decolonization**, covered in depth in the following section.

DECOLONIZING ARCHAEOLOGY

Archaeology, as a social science that came of age due to European imperialism, has played a significant role in causing what some see as irreparable harm to Indigenous people (Watkins 2001, 2003, 2005). The American Indian Movement of the late 1960s, the publication of Indigenous scholar Vine Deloria Jr.'s book *Custer Died for Your Sins: An Indian Manifesto* in 1969, and the Civil Rights Movement of the 1950s and 1960s brought global attention to the ethnic genocide of Indigenous groups around the world, the resultant struggles of contemporary Indigenous groups, and the part anthropology and archaeology played in the desecration, devaluation, and destruction of Indigenous human remains, grave goods, artifacts, cultural practices, and sacred landscapes.

Since the 1960s, Indigenous groups across the world have continued to challenge archaeologists' control over Indigenous groups' stories, material culture, and landscapes. This work has taken many forms, resulting in professional archaeological societies recognizing the need for change in their ethical statements and policies as well as the creation of legislation, such as the 1990 Native American Graves Protection and Repatriation Act (NAGPRA) in the United States, to force archaeologists to return and repatriate Indigenous artifacts and human remains. Some federally recognized tribes in the United States and First Nations in Canada have started to take things into their own hands by training members of their tribe or nation in archaeological field and laboratory methodologies, as well as by building archaeological repositories to store and curate their tribe's archaeological collections. Indigenous archaeologists are still significantly underrepresented in the field of archaeology, however. This is due, in part, to the continued discrimination historically marginalized groups in archaeology face in having a seat at the profession's table.

Dr. Sonya Atalay, a professor of archaeology at the University of Massachusetts, Amherst, has outlined what she sees as a way forward for archaeologists committed to rectifying the wrongs committed against Indigenous groups by archaeologists in the past. In her 2006 article "Indigenous Archaeology as Decolonizing Practice," as well as in her 2012 book, *Community-Based Archaeology: Research with, by, and for Indigenous and Local Communities*, she writes that archaeology, as a predominantly Western invention, has mistakenly filtered interpretations of the Indigenous past through a Western lens. In order to "decolonize" archaeology or remove the Western filter from interpretations of Indigenous archaeological sites, Atalay argues that archaeologists must do the following:

1. Conduct archaeological research that Indigenous groups fully support.
2. Research topics that align with Indigenous groups' interests and questions about their ancestors and heritage.

FIGURE 2.5
Indigenous Women Doing Archaeology. Indigenous people in North America have increasingly become involved in archaeology, including controlling archaeological investigations in their territories, working on behalf of their own nations, working collaboratively with non-Indigenous archaeologists, and advocating for decolonizing archaeology. Pictured here are Amanda Vick (Gitxsan name: Siimadam) of the Gitxsan Nation and Tiana Lewis of the Squamish Nation.
PHOTO: Bob Muckle.

3. Seek to understand Indigenous histories through Indigenous ways of perceiving the world, including adopting Indigenous Peoples' conceptualizations of "the past, history, and time."

Atalay states that a decolonized archaeology need not be practiced solely by Indigenous Peoples if archaeologists are willing and able to adopt and adhere to the above principles.

One example of a decolonized archaeology in practice is Dr. Sara Gonzalez's (2018) work with the Confederated Tribes of Grand Ronde in Oregon. Gonzalez is an associate professor of anthropology at the University of Washington who runs a collaborative, community-based participatory research project, Field Methods in Indigenous Archaeology (FMIA). This project is community-driven and community-defined, meaning that the Confederated Tribes of Grand Ronde actively define research questions of interest to their community and have control over the ways archaeologists and field school students engage with and study their land and people. Within this research framework, knowledge is co-created rather than handed down from archaeologist to community (Gonzalez, Kretzler, and Edwards 2018, 94). Researchers have been asked to follow the tribe's protocols for handling sensitive cultural materials that are seen as sacred; these rules include maintaining sobriety while on the project and planning excavation and research after important events such as the Powwow and Salmon Ceremony (95).

While decolonized archaeology is focused on developing ethical practices for working with Indigenous groups, these methods are transferable to a broad range of communities with whom archaeologists work. These best practices provide a set of methodologies that archaeologists can use to help regain the trust of or establish relationships with communities that have been colonized and/or disenfranchised by both anthropologists and/or imperial forces.

KEY RESOURCES AND SUGGESTED READING

Suggested general histories of archaeology include those by Bahn (2014), Fagan (2018), and Trigger (1989). Those focused on the United States include Kehoe (1998) and O'Brien, Lyman, and Schiffer (2005); and the history of archaeology in Canada is covered by Kelley and Williamson (1996). Punk archaeology is covered by Caraher, Kourelis, and Reinhard (2014) and Richardson (2017). Suggested readings on decolonization include those by Atalay (2006, 2014) and Gonzalez, Kretzler, and Edwards (2018). An excellent website focusing on the history of important women in archaeology is https://trowelblazers.com.

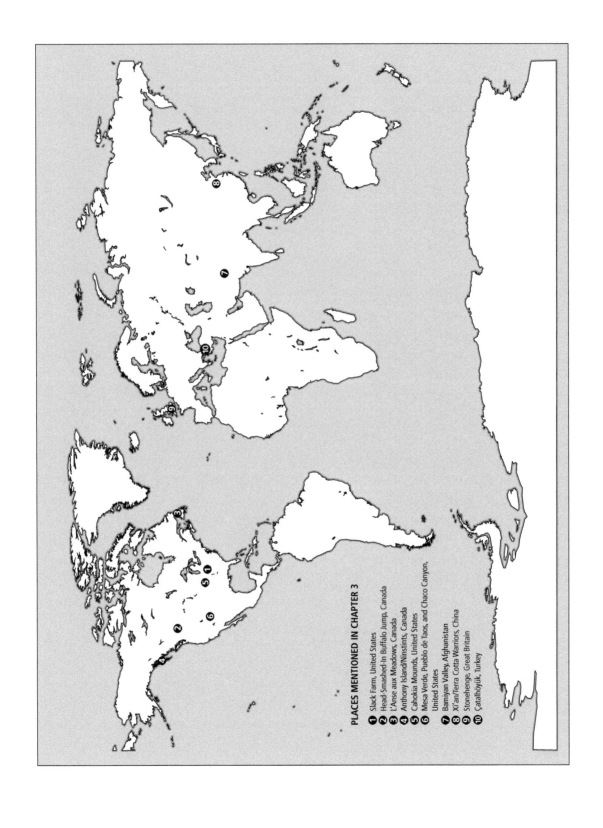

PLACES MENTIONED IN CHAPTER 3

1. Slack Farm, United States
2. Head-Smashed-In Buffalo Jump, Canada
3. L'Anse aux Meadows, Canada
4. Anthony Island/Ninstints, Canada
5. Cahokia Mounds, United States
6. Mesa Verde, Pueblo de Taos, and Chaco Canyon, United States
7. Bamiyan Valley, Afghanistan
8. Xi'an/Terra Cotta Warriors, China
9. Stonehenge, Great Britain
10. Çatalhöyük, Turkey

CHAPTER 3

MANAGING ARCHAEOLOGY IN THE EARLY TWENTY-FIRST CENTURY

Introduction

This chapter provides an overview of the diversity of archaeological work and how it is regulated. It begins with descriptions of the four major domains of archaeology, along with the widely recognized subfields and specialties of archaeological research. This is followed by outlines of laws and other instruments that govern archaeology; the codes of ethics to which archaeologists adhere; and the ways in which archaeologists share information.

The Four Major Types of Archaeology

The four main types of archaeology being undertaken today are **academic archaeology**, archaeology in the context of industry (commonly known as CRM), **Indigenous archaeology**, and amateur (or avocational) archaeology. These categories are not necessarily mutually exclusive, and it is possible for a project to have elements of more than one kind of archaeology.

ACADEMIC ARCHAEOLOGY

Academic archaeology is undertaken for intellectual or scholarly reasons and is based primarily in colleges, universities, and research museums or institutes. There are two basic components of academic archaeology: education and research.

The education component of academic archaeology focuses on teaching students archaeology at the B.A. (bachelor's degree), M.A. (master's degree), and Ph.D. (doctor of philosophy) levels. Academic archaeology often also includes a component of public education, but this is usually secondary.

The research component usually involves the collection of data from the field, including the identification and recording of sites, as well as the excavation and analysis of recovered remains.

Some projects have elements of both education and research. For example, colleges and universities often operate archaeology field schools. These field schools invariably have explicit research goals and the clear objective of training students in archaeological methods. Similarly, students working on their master's degree or Ph.D. do a great deal of research, and it is often said that they learn archaeology by doing it.

Academic research projects are usually directed by an archaeology professor or a student working on a master's degree or Ph.D. Funding for major research projects often comes from large funding agencies, which are often directly or indirectly tied to government (e.g., the National Science Foundation and the National Endowment for the Humanities in the United States, and the Social Sciences and Humanities Research Council of Canada). To ensure that research proposals to large funding agencies will make a worthwhile contribution to society and have a sound research design, they are usually subjected to peer review. In addition to the project director, there are typically field crews consisting of archaeology students.

Of all the major kinds of archaeology, it is academic archaeology that is most dominant in media. The results of research conducted within the domain of academic archaeology form the basis of published information about the discipline. Results of research are often reported in one of many dozens of scholarly journals that include archaeology such as *American Antiquity*, *Historical Archaeology*, and *World Archaeology*. Most articles about archaeology in newspapers and popular newsmagazines, such as *Time* or *Discover*, are written by journalists, but are reporting on academic research. Archaeology stories produced for television, whether news items or documentaries, are also almost always based on academic archaeology.

Academic research often involves multiyear projects, with the amount of time spent doing fieldwork dwarfed by the amount of time involved in analysis and interpretation. The results of academic research projects directed by students are written as master's theses or Ph.D. dissertations, which are held in libraries and are often rewritten as one or more articles in scholarly journals, or as a book. The results of research projects directed by professors are often written as one or more journal articles, a chapter in an edited book, or an entire book.

ARCHAEOLOGY IN INDUSTRY

Most professional archaeologists make their careers in industry, primarily in the documentation and assessment of heritage sites. In North America, this kind of archaeology is usually described as commercial archaeology or as cultural resource management

(CRM). Other descriptors include consulting archaeology, client-based archaeology, and compliance archaeology.

This kind of archaeology is usually done because it is required by legislation, and it involves several stages. Throughout the world, governments have enacted legislation that requires archaeologists to assess the impact of potential land-altering projects on heritage resources, often leading to the documentation and excavation of archaeological sites. The process generally begins when a proposal for land-altering development of some kind, ranging from the widening of a road to building a dam that may potentially flood thousands of square miles, is given to government for approval. The proposal makes the rounds of many different government departments, including the department responsible for heritage. A bureaucrat reads the proposal and determines whether the developer must hire archaeologists to search and document heritage sites in the area. If heritage sites are discovered, archaeologists then assess their significance and make recommendations about protecting or excavating the sites.

One example of a project done in this context is the archaeological investigation associated with the construction of a gas pipeline in Peru. Thirty-three kilometers (21 miles) of pipeline were added to prevent damage to some sites, but many others were excavated. Close to 1,000 archaeological sites were discovered near the route of the 730-kilometer (454-mile) pipeline. It was reported that over 100,000 pieces of textile, jewelry, weapons, and tools were recovered, as well as dozens of mummies.

Compared to those in academic archaeology, archaeologists working in industry generally spend a much higher proportion of their time doing fieldwork (i.e., looking for and excavating sites), and less time in analysis and interpretation. Archaeologists working in industry often attempt to incorporate into their fieldwork a research strategy that will contribute to the broader field of archaeology, but this is usually secondary to fulfilling the needs of their contracts, which usually simply focus on the documentation and assessment of sites.

Whereas field crews and laboratory personnel working on academic archaeology projects are usually affiliated with colleges and universities (as either students or employees), field crews associated with archaeology in industry usually have completed at least a bachelor's degree. Because projects in industry are frequently short-term, many field-workers go from job to job with various employers. These workers are sometimes referred to as **shovelbums**.

Reports of the archaeological projects are always prepared for the clients in industry or government, but they rarely become widely available. Instead, they tend to remain in the client's or government's offices and enter what has come to be known as the **gray literature**.

INDIGENOUS ARCHAEOLOGY

Archaeologists have recently begun to work closely with Indigenous Peoples at all levels of research. This has led to the emergence of Indigenous archaeology, which is archaeology that is done either by, with, or for Indigenous Peoples. It is based primarily out of Indigenous organizations, and the objectives of the projects and the research designs are determined in whole or in part by those organizations. Typical objectives of

---

BOX 3.1 ARCHAEOLOGY AND INDIGENOUS PEOPLES OF NORTH AMERICA

The Indigenous Peoples of North America (commonly referred to as Native Americans in the United States and First Nations in Canada) and archaeologists have had an interesting relationship since the practice of archaeology first began in the late 1800s. Although in recent decades the relationship may generally be viewed as good, it hasn't always been so.

In many cases archaeologists could reasonably be considered agents of colonialism, furthering the colonialist agenda, serving the interests of governments and the settler community (i.e., those of European descent). Although many archaeologists had good working relationships with Indigenous Peoples, until the latter decades of the twentieth century the power balance was clearly in favor of archaeologists. It was common practice for archaeologists to excavate sites, send artifacts to museums, write reports for governments and other archaeologists, and offer nothing to the Indigenous Peoples. The number of skeletons removed by archaeologists numbers in the hundreds of thousands and the number of artifacts, many of them sacred, is in the millions.

Power relationships began to change when Indigenous empowerment in North America took hold in the 1960s. Along with others, archaeologists were entangled in a negative perception of anthropology by Indigenous Peoples. This was led, in part, by Indigenous scholar Vine Deloria Jr., who in 1969 wrote *Custer Died for Your Sins: An Indian Manifesto*. From that book comes a well-known excerpt: "Into each life it is said, some rain must fall. Some people have bad horoscopes; others take tips on the stock market.... But Indians have been cursed above all other peoples in history. Indians have anthropologists" (Deloria 1969, 78). It was Deloria's contention that instead

of preying upon Native Americans, anthropologists should help them.

Political and social events of the 1960s and 70s effectively changed the power imbalance to a much more equal one, and in many cases it is clear that it is Indigenous Peoples who now hold the majority of the power. In many localities, for example, archaeologists are not permitted to work, or will not work, without permission of the local Indigenous groups.

Many archaeologists work collaboratively with Indigenous Peoples, and projects are often initiated by Indigenous groups. Many of the more than 1,100 Indigenous groups in Canada and the United States have their own archaeology programs, and many Indigenous people have become archaeologists themselves, sometimes bringing their own Indigenous perspectives to the field.

In some ways the current relationships between Indigenous Peoples and archaeologists have been supported by the Native American Graves Protection and Repatriation Act (NAGPRA) that took effect in 1990. Basically, the Act says that Indigenous groups in the United States must be consulted prior to archaeological work on tribal or federal lands, and the hundreds of thousands of human skeletons and more than a million artifacts taken from burial sites and kept in museums and universities must be returned to the descendant Indigenous community.

Today there are about 6.5 million people in North America who claim Indigenous ancestry. There are probably about 15,000 people making a career as archaeologists. To some, these 15,000 still hold an unfair power balance, essentially controlling Indigenous Peoples' pasts by using scientific frameworks and vocabulary that is largely accepted by governments, media, and the public.

Indigenous archaeology projects include (i) providing support for claims of Indigenous rights and territory, (ii) archaeotourism, (iii) education for their own and other (non-Indigenous) communities, and (iv) nation building.

AMATEUR ARCHAEOLOGY

Amateur archaeology, also known as avocational archaeology, is an umbrella phrase for the work being done by people without educational credentials in the field, and who do not receive direct income for their work on archaeological projects (although they may receive income from books they write or artifacts they sell). The primary kinds of amateurs are those who volunteer or pay a stipend to work on academic archaeology projects, usually under the guidance of an academic archaeologist, and looters, sometimes known as **pothunters**, who essentially dig up sites to find and sell objects of value. Amateur archaeology also includes people with little or no training in archaeological method and theory who nevertheless theorize and sometimes write popular books explaining the origins of famous heritage sites. Many of the people who fall into this category either have little knowledge or choose to ignore the fundamental principles, methods, and research findings of academic archaeology. Their work is often termed pseudoarchaeology.

Subfields of Archaeology

There are dozens of widely recognized subfields and specialties in contemporary archaeology. Table 3.1 lists several of them, but it certainly is not exhaustive. Many of the subfields and specialties, such as **classical archaeology**, **geoarchaeology**, **historic archaeology**, **lithic** studies, **ceramic** studies, **archaeometry**, **archaeobotany**, **forensic archaeology**, and **zooarchaeology**, are commonly offered as third and fourth year courses in university.

Prehistoric archaeology, which is defined as focusing on a time period before written records existed for a given area, has many subspecialties. These include **paleo-anthropology** (the study of early human biology and culture, usually at least several hundred thousand years ago), or study of one of the widely known temporal periods such as **Paleolithic**, **Mesolithic**, and **Neolithic**.

Historic archaeology, defined as focusing on a time period for which written records do exist, is also known as text-aided archaeology, and similarly has many subspecialties. These include **biblical archaeology** (places and events mentioned in the Bible), classical archaeology (sites and objects of the Greek and Roman empires), **Egyptology** (sites and objects of the ancient Egyptian civilization), **Pre-Columbian archaeology** (civilizations of the Americas before the arrival of Christopher Columbus), **colonial**

TABLE 3.1 Archaeological Subfields and Specialties

NAME	FOCUS
Archaeobiology	Plants and animals in archaeology
Archaeobotany	Plants in archaeology
Archaeometry	Application of physical sciences
Biblical archaeology	Places, people, and events of the Bible
Bioarchaeology	Human remains
Ceramic studies	Baked clay
Classical archaeology	Ancient Greece and Rome
Ecological archaeology	Adaption to natural environment
Egyptology	Ancient Egypt
Ethnoarchaeology	Contemporary people
Experimental archaeology	Creating data for comparison
Forensic archaeology	Crime investigations
Garbology	Contemporary refuse
Geoarchaeology	Sediments
Historic archaeology	Period since writing began
Indigenous archaeology	Indigenous groups
Industrial archaeology	Heavy industry
Lithic studies	Stone
Maritime archaeology	Sites near or under water
New World archaeology	North, South, and Central America
Old World archaeology	Asia, Africa, and Europe
Prehistoric archaeology	Period before writing
Space archaeology	Material remains in outer space
Underwater archaeology	Sites under water
Zooarchaeology	Animals in archaeology

archaeology (study of the time and place of European rule of non-European lands claimed by Europeans), post-colonial archaeology (focusing on the time and place since European colonial governments ceased to rule foreign lands), and **industrial archaeology** (machinery and structures of industrial activity, such as mining, power generation, and road building).

Archaeologists involved in **Old World** archaeology usually specialize in either a continent (Africa, Asia, or Europe), or a specific region within one of the continents. Archaeologists involved in **New World** archaeology often specialize in North, South, or Central America, or a specific region within one of those continents.

Two of the most common types of materials recovered from archaeological sites are fragments of stone and pottery, which have led to the development of the specialties of lithic studies and ceramic studies. The study of sediments from archaeological sites is termed geoarchaeology, and the study of human skeletons is called **bioarchaeology** or **osteology**.

Archaeobotany (also known as paleoethnobotany) is the study of plant remains from archaeological sites, and zooarchaeology is the study of animal remains from archaeological sites. Together, archaeobotany and zooarchaeology are known as **archaeobiology**.

Forensic archaeology is the application of archaeological methods to criminal investigations, as well as the collection of evidence in cases of mass disasters. **Underwater archaeology** focuses on objects and sites underwater, including but not restricted to shipwrecks. Archaeology that depends on the methods of physics, chemistry, mathematics, and computer science is often referred to as archaeometry.

Ecological archaeology focuses on the relationships between people and the environment. Ethnoarchaeology refers to when archaeologists apply their observations of the behavior and material culture of contemporary people to interpretations of the patterning they see in archaeological sites.

There are many other subfields and specialties, which although they rarely warrant a college- or university-level course are common in popular and scholarly writing. These include **dirt archaeology**, which generally is taken to mean working in the field, looking for sites, and possibly excavating them. **Armchair archaeology** is a phrase used to describe both professionals and amateurs who rarely, if ever, do fieldwork, but rather focus their attention on explaining what has been observed by others, without leaving the comfort of their home or office. Experimental archaeology involves replicating possible past events to aid interpretation of archaeological sites and objects.

Some archaeologists focus on contemporary refuse, a subfield popularly known as **garbology**. Although often considered trivial, this is one area that garners much popular attention and has great value to American industry and government agencies.

The best-known archaeologist in the field of garbology is William L. Rathje, who founded the Garbage Project, also known as Le Projet du Garbage, at the University of Arizona in the early 1970s. Since that time, members of the Garbage Project have studied fresh household garbage in several cities throughout the United States, as well as in Mexico and Australia. They have also conducted excavations in more than a dozen landfills in Canada and the United States. Their research has been funded by a wide variety of corporations that are interested in patterns of food consumption and waste, including Heinz,

FIGURE 3.1 Astronaut on the Moon. Space archaeology is a subfield of archaeology, which includes viewing objects left on the moon and other celestial bodies, orbital debris, the International Space Station, and places on Earth associated with the exploration of outer space through the lens of archaeology.

PHOTO: NASA.

BOX 3.2 "TO INFINITY AND BEYOND!": THE ADVENT OF SPACE ARCHAEOLOGY

When we think about archaeology, many of us envision archaeologists toiling away in extreme heat, carefully peeling soil layer upon soil layer back to expose formerly hidden artifacts or architecture. The last thing that likely comes to mind is an archaeologist documenting and counting the trash left behind by astronauts in space. It is only in recent years that the field of "space archaeology" (Capelotti 2010) has emerged. This field was started by the pioneer of contemporary archaeology and garbage studies, Dr. William Rathje (O'Leary 2015; Muckle 2016), who noted that space debris, such as defunct satellites, poses a threat to future space missions.

What do today's space archaeologists do?

Space archaeologists highlight the material stories of the "space race." The space race began after World War II, when the USSR and USA started to develop space and weapons technologies. It has left a lasting material legacy on our planet and beyond. Evidence of this space race includes human-made objects in space, which totaled over 10,000 in 2009. These artifacts include flags, rovers, landers, and abandoned and currently-in-use satellites. Astronauts have left behind bootprints on the moon and robotic explorers have left their marks on asteroids, Titan, the moon, Venus, and Mars.

The space race hasn't stopped, though in recent times some nations have not been able to afford as expensive space exploration as in past years. The space race has expanded to include citizens and private corporations competing for their place in the history of space exploration. Space archaeologists want to understand how cultural values shape our desire to explore beyond our planet (Walsh 2012). They remind us that our care for the past and for the heritage of former space explorations must not be forgotten in our quest to voyage beyond Earth and be the first person, company, or nation to reach formerly unreachable places.

Space archaeologists study how humans interact with their environments and habitats in space. Dr. Justin St. P. Walsh and Dr. Alice Gorman have recently received funding to study the culture and materiality of the International Space Station (ISS),

which has been occupied by astronauts since 2000 (www.issarchaeology.org). The ISS is a unique collaboration that involves a global team of astronauts representing 25 countries, numerous space agencies, and several private corporations.

As archaeologists who are naturally curious about what happens to trash, Walsh and Gorman have examined how trash and supplies move from Earth to the ISS. From what they have learned thus far, cargo and trash is transported between the ISS and Earth by SpaceX, a company owned by Elon Musk, the founder of the electric car company Tesla. SpaceX's Dragon capsule is a spacecraft that brings astronaut trash, scientific specimens, and even the astronauts' dirty laundry (which coincidentally acts as padding to protect the aforementioned specimens!) back to Earth to be picked up by the proper space agency. By studying these materials as well as footage from the ISS, Gorman and Walsh hope to learn how life on a space station is different from that on Earth.

Gorman has not only studied the ISS with Walsh, but has also worked independently to identify the materiality of the space race in space and to investigate how the push to innovate has permanently altered Earth and affected human relationships. Launch and testing sites for shuttles and missiles, and buildings and infrastructure for laborers, have left lasting traces on Earth's surfaces. She argues that the placement of space infrastructure has relied on the exploitation of formerly colonized landscapes and places.

For instance, the UK built the Woomera rocket range in Australia after working with the Australian government. This rocket range featured "nine launch areas, workshops, instrumentation buildings, hangars, tracking and meteorological stations, and roads where none had existed before" (Gorman 2009, 137). Woomera, while described by the British government as a remote desert landscape void of people, was historically and contemporaneously occupied by Aboriginal Peoples. Aboriginals worked as domestic staff at Woomera rocket range and were warned of missile launches in the event they landed near their campsites or housing.

Thousands of historic and prehistoric Aboriginal artifacts canvas Woomera's landscape despite its

(continued)

BOX 3.2 Continued

being reappropriated by the UK and Australia for space exploration purposes. As Gorman describes, this was a place where "the children or grand-children of those who knapped the tools camped nearby" (2009, 138). Gorman's award-winning research has revealed how the space industry, while promising innovative ways of exploring the world beyond Earth, is part of a long trajectory of destroying Indigenous Peoples' lands in the name of "progress."

Frito-Lay, NutraSweet, and Pillsbury, as well as agencies such as the National Livestock and Meat Board in the United States. Regional governments fund work to measure the effectiveness of recycling programs and the amount of hazardous waste in cities.

The members of the Garbage Project have come up with many interesting and sometimes surprising research results. These include the fact that paper remains a dominant class of material in landfill sites and that fast food packaging, Styrofoam, and disposable diapers make up less than 3 per cent of landfill material. They have also found that the average household wastes about 15 per cent of the food it buys and that recycling programs are not always effective (e.g., instead of using up hazardous materials, people will discard them by recycling). They also have found that the average amount of garbage thrown away by individuals continues to increase substantially and that when people receive larger trash containers (as often occurs when a city moves toward a mechanized system of dumping individual containers into trucks), they throw away more stuff.

Among the most recent subfields to emerge, **space archaeology** (also known as **exoarchaeology**) is the study of the off-Earth material remains of space exploration. This includes the study of the tens of thousands of pieces of space junk currently orbiting Earth, as well as the remains of space exploration left on the moon and Mars. Archaeologists are particularly interested in the dozens of sites containing material remains on the moon. One site of particular focus is Tranquility Base, the site of the first landing, where archaeologists funded by NASA have documented over 100 artifacts.

National and International Heritage Management

Governments throughout the world recognize the value of **tangible heritage** and have enacted legislation and other instruments to protect it (Table 3.2). In some countries, the penalty for the unauthorized destruction of heritage resources can be execution. In North America, death is not an option given to the courts, but fines and imprisonment are.

TABLE 3.2 National and International Heritage Regulations

United States

Antiquities Act (1906)

Historic Sites Act (1935)

National Historic Preservation Act (NHPA) (1966)

National Environmental Policy Act (NEPA) (1969)

Archaeological and Historic Preservation Act (AHPA) (1974)

Archaeological Resources Protection Act (ARPA) (1979)

Abandoned Shipwreck Act (ASA) (1987)

Native American Graves Protection and Repatriation Act (NAGPRA) (1990)

Canada

Indian Act (1985)

Historic Sites and Monuments Act (1985)

National Parks Act (2000)

Canadian Environmental Assessment Act (1992)

ICOMOS (International Council on Monuments and Sites)

Charter for the Protection and Management of the Archaeological Heritage (1990)

Charter for the Protection and Management of Underwater Cultural Heritage (1996)

International Cultural Tourism Charter (1999)

UNESCO (United Nations Educational, Scientific and Cultural Organization)

Hague Convention for the Protection of Cultural Property in the Event of Armed Conflict (1954)

Recommendations on International Principles Applicable to Archaeological Excavations (1956)

Recommendations on the Means of Prohibiting and Preventing the Illicit Export, Import, and Transfer of Ownership of Cultural Property (1964)

Convention on the Means of Prohibiting and Preventing the Illicit Import, Export, and Transfer of Ownership of Cultural Property (1970)

Convention Concerning the Protection of the World Cultural and Natural Heritage (1972)

(continued)

TABLE 3.2 National and International Heritage Regulations (Continued)

Second Protocol to the Hague Convention of 1954 for the Protection of Cultural Property in the Event of Armed Conflict (1999)

Convention on the Protection of the Underwater Cultural Heritage (2001)

Declaration Concerning the Intentional Destruction of Cultural Heritage (2003)

UNIDROIT (International Institute for the Unification of Private Law)

Convention on Stolen and Illegally Exported Cultural Objects (1995)

UN (United Nations)

Outer Space Treaty (1967)

Law of the Sea (1982)

WAC (World Archaeology Congress)

Vermillion Accord on Human Remains (1989)

There are several government acts controlling archaeological research in the United States, beginning with the Antiquities Act of 1906, which established the protection of archaeological sites on federal lands and a permit system for archaeological work. This was followed by the Historic Sites Act of 1935, in which it became a national policy to preserve historic sites, buildings, and objects. The majority of archaeological research in the United States today is performed under the National Historic Preservation Act (NHPA) of 1966, which stipulates that archaeological investigations should occur in advance of potential disturbances on federal lands or on lands that may be disturbed by any federally funded project.

The National Environmental Policy Act (NEPA) of 1969 requires federal agencies to consider environmental, historical, and cultural values (including archaeological resources) whenever land owned by the federal government is altered or when private land is altered with federal money. The Archaeological and Historic Preservation Act (AHPA) of 1974 made federal agencies responsible for any damage they caused to archaeological sites. The Archaeological Resources Protection Act (ARPA) of 1979 further strengthened heritage legislation by establishing penalties and fees of up to $100,000 and five years' imprisonment for illegally excavating on federal lands. The Abandoned Shipwreck Act (ASA) of 1987 established that the US government owns abandoned shipwrecks in the country's rivers and lakes, and in the ocean up to three miles off the coastlines.

The Native American Graves Protection and Repatriation Act (NAGPRA) of 1990 requires agencies and museums receiving federal funds to work toward returning native skeletal remains and associated burial objects to the affiliated native groups and also provides native burial sites greater protection in that it requires Native Americans to be consulted when archaeological investigations are anticipated or when cultural items are unexpectedly recovered in their traditional territory.

While the United States has several acts that protect archaeological resources on federal lands, it is virtually the only country that gives ownership of archaeological resources to the owner of private land. In other countries, ownership tends to lie with the government. In some jurisdictions, ownership of recovered prehistoric remains lies with Indigenous Peoples, although the artifacts may be held by the government "in trust."

There is little doubt that the heritage laws in the United States have led to a decrease in the amount of looting on federal lands. But because looting on private land is unregulated, many archaeological resources continue to be unprotected. There are reported cases of people buying "looting rights" to archaeological sites. A well-known example is the Slack Farm in Kentucky, where looters reportedly paid the owner $10,000 for the rights to raid an Indigenous cemetery on the property. Landowners of an Anasazi site in Utah charge "guests" more than $2,000 per day if they want to keep artifacts they discover on the site.

In Canada, heritage legislation falls primarily under provincial and territorial power. All jurisdictions impose penalties for the unauthorized removal or destruction of archaeological resources. The Heritage Conservation Act of British Columbia, for example, stipulates that a corporation that violates the act is subject to a penalty of up to $1 million CAD, while individuals who violate the act are subject to fines of up to $50,000 and a maximum of two years' imprisonment. The removal of heritage objects on First Nation reserves is governed by the Indian Act (1985), and archaeological sites and artifacts on other federal lands are protected primarily through the National Parks Act (2000), the Historic Sites and Monuments Act (1985), and the Canadian Environmental Assessment Act (1992).

Although successful prosecutions for looting or otherwise destroying archaeological sites in North America are rare, they do occur. For example, a recent investigation in the United States resulted in the convictions of seven people and a corporation for looting. Upon conviction, individuals had to pay restitution ranging from less than $10,000 to more than $100,000 and were given prison sentences of up to 37 months.

At the international level, there are many accords, charters, declarations, recommendations, agreements, conventions, protocols, and laws relating to archaeological sites and objects.

The United Nations Educational, Scientific and Cultural Organization (UNESCO) has developed several instruments protecting heritage, beginning with the Convention for the Protection of Cultural Property in the Event of Armed Conflict, also known as the Hague Convention, adopted in 1954. This convention was developed in response to the massive destruction of heritage sites during World War II and stipulates that states are bound to safeguard cultural heritage during times of armed conflict. The convention was adopted with a protocol that prohibits the export of cultural property from occupied territory. In response to the continued destruction of heritage sites during armed conflict throughout the latter decades of the twentieth century, particularly that occurring in the former Yugoslavia and the former Soviet Union, a second protocol was adopted in 1999, which essentially improved the safeguarding measures by defining them, creating a new category for enhanced protection, and providing specific sanctions for violations.

The UNESCO Recommendations on International Principles Applicable to Archaeological Excavations, adopted in 1956, lays out guidelines for member states to legislate the protection of archaeological sites. These include requiring archaeological work to be subject to authorization, declaring archaeological discoveries to proper authorities, providing penalties for violations, defining the legal status of archaeological finds, preserving archaeological deposits for future archaeology, maintaining repositories, and educating the public.

The UNESCO Convention on the Means of Prohibiting and Preventing the Illicit Import, Export, and Transfer of Ownership of Cultural Property, adopted in 1970, stipulates that countries are bound to return cultural property, including the products of both legal and illegal excavations, to the country of origin. UNESCO asked the International Institute for the Unification of Private Law (UNIDROIT) to create a supplement to the convention. The result is the UNIDROIT Convention on Stolen and Illegally Exported Cultural Objects, adopted in 1995, which makes it clear that anyone who has an illegally obtained artifact in their possession must return it.

The well-known World Heritage List was initiated through the UNESCO Convention Concerning the Protection of the World Cultural and Natural Heritage, adopted in 1972. This convention established the framework for having sites added to the list and accessing funds and other forms of assistance to aid in the protection, conservation, rehabilitation, and presentation of heritage. To be included on the list, sites must meet several criteria, including having outstanding universal value. Worldwide, there are approximately 1,000 designated World Heritage Sites, mostly in the "cultural" category. Some of the well-known archaeological sites with World Heritage status are listed in Table 3.3.

TABLE 3.3 Selected UNESCO World Heritage Sites

North America

United States

Mesa Verde

Cahokia Mounds State Historic Site

Independence Hall

Statue of Liberty

Chaco Canyon National Historic Park

Monticello and University of Virginia in Charlottesville

Pueblo de Taos

Canada

L'Anse aux Meadows National Historic Site

Head-Smashed-In Buffalo Jump

Historic District of Quebec

Old Town Lunenburg

Anthony Island

Central America (including Mexico)

Tikal National Park, Guatemala

Maya Site of Copan, Honduras

Historic Center of Mexico City and Xochimilco

Historic Center of Oaxaca and Archaeological Site of Monte Albán, Mexico

Pre-Hispanic City of Chichen-Itza, Mexico

Pre-Hispanic City and National Park of Palenque, Mexico

Pre-Hispanic City of Teotihuacan, Mexico

Pre-Hispanic Town of Uxmal, Mexico

South America

Tiwanaku: Spiritual and Political Centre of the Tiwanaku Culture, Bolivia

Rapa Nui National Park (Easter Island), Chile

(continued)

TABLE 3.3 Selected UNESCO World Heritage Sites (Continued)

Historic Sanctuary of Machu Picchu, Peru

Lines and Geoglyphs of Nazca and Pampas de Jumana, Peru

Europe

Acropolis of Athens, Greece

Archaeological Site of Delphi, Greece

Archaeological Areas of Pompeii, Herculaneum, and Torre Annunziata, Italy

Archaeological Site of Atapuerca, Spain

Altamira Cave, Spain

Archaeological Site of Troy, Turkey

Stonehenge, Avebury, and Associated Sites, United Kingdom

Asia

Cultural Landscape and Archaeological Remains of the Bamiyan Valley, Afghanistan

Angkor, Cambodia

Mausoleum of the First Qin Emperor (Terra Cotta Warriors), China

Peking Man Site at Zhoukoudian, China

Archaeological Ruins at Moenjodaro, Pakistan

Africa

Ancient Thebes and Its Necropolis, Egypt

Memphis and Its Necropolis – the Pyramid Fields from Giza to Dahshur, Egypt

Fossil Hominid Sites of Sterkfontein, Swartkrans, Kromdraai, and Environs, South Africa

Great Zimbabwe National Monument, Zimbabwe

Australia

Kakadu National Park

FIGURE 3.2 **Mesa Verde, Colorado.** This World Heritage Site comprises cliff dwellings and other cultural remains of Pueblo peoples.

PHOTO: Barry D. Kass @ ImagesofAnthropology.com.

Several locations of past cultural activity in Canada and the United States have been accorded World Heritage status. Head-Smashed-In Buffalo Jump in southern Alberta is an excellent example of the Aboriginal practice of driving large animals over a cliff to their death. The site itself consists of a complex of drive lanes that directed buffalo (bison) to a cliff, an accumulation of buffalo bones at the base of the cliff, a butchery location, and camping areas. The site was used for over 5,000 years and is a good example of archaeological tourism in Canada today, with an on-site museum and interpretive programs run by the local Blood and Piikani (Peigan) First Nations, the descendants of the people who operated the jump.

L'Anse aux Meadows is the earliest undisputed evidence of Europeans in North America. Located on the northern tip of Newfoundland, the site consists of the remains of an eleventh-century Viking settlement. Excavated remains include wood-framed, peat-turf buildings like those found in Norse Greenland and Iceland.

Anthony Island, also known as SGaang Gwaay, along the north Pacific coast of British Columbia includes the Haida Peoples' village of Ninstints (Nans Dins) and the remains of their houses, as well as carved mortuary and memorial poles, offering visual keys to their oral traditions.

Cahokia Mounds is an excellent example of the mound-building peoples of the continent. Located near St. Louis, Cahokia Mounds is the largest prehistoric settlement north of Mexico. It was occupied from the ninth to fifteenth centuries, covered nearly 1,600 hectares (3,952 acres) including more than 100 earthen mounds, and at its peak may have had a population close to 20,000. The largest mound, known as Monks Mound, covered more than 5 hectares (12 acres) and stood 30 meters (98 feet) high.

Mesa Verde in Colorado, as well as Pueblo de Taos and Chaco Canyon in New Mexico, includes remnants of the Pueblo Peoples who occupied the southwestern states beginning in the sixth century. Mesa Verde, the best known, consists of both dwellings built into the cliffs and villages on top of the mesa. More than 4,000 sites have been recorded in the area, and some dwellings are comprised of more than 100 rooms. Pueblo de Taos, representing the Pueblo Indians of New Mexico and Arizona, is an adobe settlement consisting of dwellings and ceremonial buildings, and Chaco Canyon was a major center of Pueblo culture in the Four Corners area, known primarily for its distinctive architecture and ceremonial buildings.

The International Council on Monuments and Sites (ICOMOS) adopted the Charter for the Protection and Management of the Archaeological Heritage in 1990. The charter establishes basic principles relating to archaeological heritage management. These include frameworks for legislation, fieldwork, conservation, qualifications, and accessibility to information.

Both the United Nations and ICOMOS have instruments that are meant to specifically protect heritage objects underwater. The United Nations Law of the Sea states that countries have an obligation to protect underwater heritage, and the UNESCO Convention on the Protection of the Underwater Cultural Heritage, adopted in 2001, sets high standards for archaeological investigations in international waters and obligates people to report discoveries or illicit activities. The ICOMOS Charter for the Protection and Management of Underwater Cultural Heritage, ratified in 1996, outlines the appropriate methods for archaeological research underwater, and the qualifications and responsibilities of those undertaking the work.

Recognizing the increase in heritage tourism during the late twentieth century, and the potential challenges that come with it, the ICOMOS International Cultural Tourism Charter was adopted in 1999. The charter includes clauses that recognize differing cultural values and significance of sites, the importance of retaining authenticity, and the value of including Indigenous Peoples in the identification, management, and interpretation of heritage resources.

UNESCO adopted the Declaration Concerning the Intentional Destruction of Cultural Heritage in 2003. This declaration was in response to what appears to have been an increasing number of intentional acts of deliberate destruction of cultural heritage, including two monumental Buddha statues within the World Heritage

FIGURE 3.3 Terra Cotta Warriors, Xi'an. Located near Xi'an, China, excavations at this World Heritage Site revealed about 8,000 life-size warriors constructed from terra cotta placed in battle formation near the tomb of the first emperor of China.

PHOTO: Shutterstock / Jarno Gonzalez Zarra-onandia.

designated landscape of the Bamiyan Valley in Afghanistan. In part, the declaration makes it clear that all states should take appropriate measures to prevent intentional acts of destruction, wherever they are located, during peace and in times of war.

The World Archaeology Congress adopted the Vermillion Accord on Human Remains in 1989. While recognizing the legitimate concern that science should have the ability to study human remains, the accord also establishes that the wishes of the dead, the relatives or guardians of the dead, and the local community be respected.

As archaeologists are becoming increasingly interested in the material remains of space exploration, the United Nations Outer Space Treaty (1967) has important implications. Essentially, the treaty states that land in space cannot be owned by any country, but the material remains of space exploration and other forms of space junk are the property of the country that sent the items into space.

TABLE 3.4 Major Archaeological Associations and Issues Addressed by Their Codes of Ethics

ORGANIZATION	ETHICS ADDRESSED
Archaeological Institute of America	Responsibilities to the archaeological record, the public, and colleagues
Canadian Archaeological Association	Stewardship; Aboriginal relationships; professional responsibilities; public education
Register of Professional Archaeologists	Responsibilities to the public, descendant communities, colleagues, employees, students, employers, and clients; commercialization; standards of research; sharing research
Society for American Archaeology	Stewardship; accountability; commercialization; public education and outreach; intellectual property; public reporting and publication; records and preservation; training and resources
Society for Historical Archaeology	Stewardship; sharing research results; documentation; commercialization; public education
World Archaeology Congress	Responsibilities to Indigenous Peoples

Ethics and Archaeology

Most associations of archaeologists have codes of ethics that stipulate how archaeologists should conduct their work. Although the issues addressed for each organization vary (Table 3.4), some generalizations can be made about the protection of the archaeological record, commercialization, and responsibilities to various groups. In recent years many associations have strengthened their codes of conduct to specifically address sexual harassment and abuse.

PROTECTION OF THE ARCHAEOLOGICAL RECORD

Most professional organizations recognize an obligation to protect the archaeological record. In practical terms, this means that archaeologists should not allow the wanton destruction of archaeological sites or the looting of heritage objects. Some organizations stipulate that archaeologists hold the primary responsibility of protecting and interpreting the human past. Others believe that the responsibility for protecting and interpreting the human past should be shared with or be secondary to **descendant communities**. This brings up the dilemma often expressed in the question, "Who owns the past?" For some,

FIGURE 3.4
Stonehenge, UK. Built in stages between 5,000 and 4,500 years ago, Stonehenge is one of many sites in the UK and elsewhere in Europe involving large stones placed in lines or circles. Stonehenge is a World Heritage Site, linked with British identity, and is a popular archaeotourism destination.

PHOTO: Barry D. Kass @ ImagesofAnthropology.com.

the human past, even if it is the past of one particular group, belongs to everyone. For others, the past of particular groups belongs to the descendants.

The conflicts around the issue of who owns the past can be observed in the example of the prehistoric site of Stonehenge in Britain. Stonehenge, which was constructed between about 4,900 and 4,000 years ago, is comprised primarily of a circular setting of large standing stones, known as **megaliths**. The first discernible feature in the area is a circular ditch, about 100 meters (328 feet) in diameter, dug about 4,900 years ago. About 4,500 years ago, an arrangement of dozens of stones, weighing up to 4,000 kilograms (8,800 pounds) each, were transported about 200 kilometers (124 miles) from Wales to the site and placed within the circular ditch. About a century later, 30 or so larger stones, known as the sarsen stones and weighing up 25,000 kilograms (55,000 pounds) each, were shaped and transported from an area about 30 kilometers (19 miles) away to the site and placed in a circle within the circular ditch. Following this, other stones, known as the lintels and weighing about 5,500 kilograms (12,100 pounds) each, were shaped and placed on top of the sarsen stones to form a complete ring. Most archaeologists believe Stonehenge was primarily a ritual location, although the alignment of some stones with the rising sun on the summer solstice provides some support for the idea that it was, perhaps in part, an astronomical observatory.

Many groups claim rights to visit Stonehenge. In addition to tourists, tens of thousands of people wish to use Stonehenge as a place of ritual, particularly during the time of the summer solstice. These include several different kinds of groups based on ancient religious practices, most notably druids, but also Wiccans and people who practice ancient Viking and Anglo-Saxon beliefs. Many of these people see a connection between Stonehenge and their own beliefs and rituals, and think it is their right to consider it sacred and practice their own rituals at the site. This presents a dilemma for the archaeologist who is concerned about the harm done to the site during the annual summer solstice festivals, which, in addition to damaging the stones, has also included digging into archaeological deposits to make pits for latrines.

COMMERCIALIZATION

Archaeologists are generally dissuaded from participating in the commercialization of artifacts. Archaeologists are faced with the dilemma of placing value on objects, which then may create a market for looting. Working with looted material is another problem. Some archaeology journals (e.g., *American Antiquity* and the *American Journal of Archaeology*) have adopted policies preventing the publication of articles that rely on looted artifacts, although not all archaeologists are in agreement that this is a good thing. Similarly, while most archaeologists acknowledge the severe impact of looting, many sympathize with relatively poor people who do the looting to feed their families, a practice that has become known as subsistence looting.

RESPONSIBILITIES TO VARIOUS GROUPS

Most codes of ethics recognize that archaeologists have responsibilities to other archaeologists and scholars, descendant communities, funding agencies, and the public. However, there is no consensus on how these responsibilities should be prioritized or implemented. Minimally, it is considered proper practice that archaeologists share the results of their research with each of these groups. Many organizations also include responsibilities to the workers involved, especially in matters pertaining to health and safety.

Beyond consulting about research objectives and strategies, and sharing the results of research with various groups, ethical issues about intellectual property rights have also emerged in archaeology, particularly among those who work with Indigenous populations. As archaeology becomes increasingly commercialized, questions of who owns intellectual property arise. Is it the archaeologist, the funding agency, or the descendant community?

There are often conflicts regarding legislation and ethical considerations, especially when it comes to development projects. One recent case in point is the international media firestorm and protests that erupted concerning the 2016 to 2017 construction of the United States' Dakota Access Pipeline (DAPL), which cut through Indigenous and federal lands to transport a maximum of 570,000 barrels of oil a day (Colwell 2016). A company known as Energy Transfer planned to build a pipeline on parts of the Standing Rock Sioux Reservation. Organizations such as Greenpeace and Earthjustice drew attention to the pipeline's construction, which brought thousands of protesters to the area.

Federal legislation, such as the National Historic Preservation Act (NHPA) in the United States, has been put in place to protect precious archaeological resources. Energy Transfer claimed it went through all the proper procedures required by the NHPA, including hiring cultural anthropologists and archaeologists to consult on the project. Some archaeologists, including one of the Standing Rock Sioux Reservation's former Tribal Historic Preservation Officers, tribe members, and anthropologists, made opposing claims, arguing that Energy Transfer knowingly sought to bypass existing knowledge about the impacted sites by hiring consultants who knew little about archaeology and tribal customs in the region to obtain approval for the pipeline's installation (Braun 2020; Colwell 2016).

So if the NHPA is supposed to prevent significant archaeological sites and culturally important landscapes from destruction, what went wrong?

According to both Dr. Chip Colwell, Senior Curator of Anthropology at the Denver Museum of Nature & Science, and Dr. Sebastian Felix Braun, Director of American Indian Studies at Iowa State University, federal legislation fails to take into consideration Indigenous cultural values. Federal legislation is built upon a Western, capitalistic worldview that values the tangible – such as an artifact – over the intangible – such as a natural landscape. This Western framework conflicts with Indigenous groups' definition of heritage, which gives equal weight to a projectile point and a "mountain where spirits dwell" or a place where Indigenous groups have hunted animals and gathered food (Cowell 2016). Additionally, Braun (2020, 10) notes that cultural resource management (CRM) in the United States is built upon a profit-based economic model rather than a model that values consultation and stewardship. For these reasons, some tribes have simply decided not to participate in the consultation process because they know their position on heritage will not be respected. In the case of the DAPL, this silence was "interpreted by the company as a sign that there were no sacred sites" (Braun 2020, 19). However, this silence was a response to the federal government and corporations' continual and repeated neglect of Indigenous ways of defining heritage. As Braun therefore concludes, "when people get silent, it is time to pay attention" (19).

What was the outcome of DAPL?

Energy Transfer, which has a great deal of money and power, has sued Earthjustice and Greenpeace for defamation. These organizations claimed that Energy Transfer had intentionally sought out archaeologists and ethnographers who were unfamiliar with the history and archaeology of the region, thus leading to the discovery of few archaeological and/or culturally significant sites. Energy Transfer argued that whatever sites may have existed on the landscape had likely been destroyed by the construction of the Northern Border pipeline that had been built prior to DAPL. This case study in archaeological ethics shows that there remain many loopholes and problems with federal legislation. For this reason, archaeologists must work to advocate for and understand Indigenous perceptions of what is significant and sacred, which do not always fit neatly within the scope of what is protected by federal legislation.

Career Tracks in Archaeology

Tens of thousands of professional archaeologists are working in the world today. Most have a minimum of a bachelor's degree in archaeology or a related field. With rare exceptions, those in supervisory positions and those in academic positions have a master's degree or a Ph.D.

Most professional archaeologists find employment in industry: working for large companies that do enough land-alteration development to employ archaeologists; working for large environmental consulting companies that offer archaeological services; or working for companies that specialize in archaeology. A master's degree is usually considered the minimum qualification to obtain a supervisory position in archaeology within the heritage industry. Non-supervisory field and laboratory workers usually have a minimum of a four-year bachelor's degree or a two-year diploma in archaeology technology.

Employment as a college or university professor generally requires a graduate degree. Most universities require a Ph.D., although some universities and colleges only require a master's degree.

Many governments employ archaeologists to make sure heritage regulations are being followed, and in some cases to undertake research. As with working in industry or academia, a graduate degree is usually required for these positions.

Some archaeologists find employment in museums. In large museums, a graduate degree is usually required for supervisory positions.

Sharing Information

Archaeologists share the results of their research in many ways, principally through print media, conferences, and the Internet.

Publication in scholarly journals is one way in which the results of academic research projects are shared.

Information is also commonly shared through conference presentations. Many local, national, and international associations of archaeologists have annual conferences, which provide opportunities for sharing research results. One of the most prominent is the annual conference of the Society for American Archaeology (SAA), during which thousands of presentations are given. Another prominent conference is that of the World Archaeology Congress, which has one large conference every four years and many smaller special interest conferences during the intervals.

The impact of the Internet on archaeology has been significant, like it has been with almost all aspects of life in the early twenty-first century. Many journal articles are available online, there are many useful archaeology-related websites, and social media has become a major way of facilitating communication between archaeologists and for outreach. Some government agencies are now making their gray literature more accessible by putting it online.

Some archaeologists have created websites for specific projects, for example the website created for the multiyear excavations led by Ian Hodder at Çatalhöyük, a Neolithic site in Turkey (www.catalhoyuk.com). Among other things, the website contains an extensive archive of analytical reports.

The sharing of information is sometimes referred to as **knowledge mobilization**, which is often an important requirement for obtaining funding for archaeological research. Traditionally, most sharing of research knowledge remained within academia, but in recent times it has become expected that research be shared with non-academic audiences and groups so that they may use it for their benefit.

KEY RESOURCES AND SUGGESTED READING

For more on ethics in archaeology, particularly related to field archaeology, Muckle (2018) is recommended. The codes of ethics of most associations of professional archaeologists can usually be found on their web sites. National, state, and provincial legislation can usually be found on government web sites. International heritage regulations can be found on the websites of UNESCO, ICOMOS, and UNIDROIT. Information on World Heritage Sites, and criteria for inclusion on the list, can also be found on the UNESCO web site.

For those interested in space archaeology, Capelotti (2010) and Gorman (2019) are recommended.

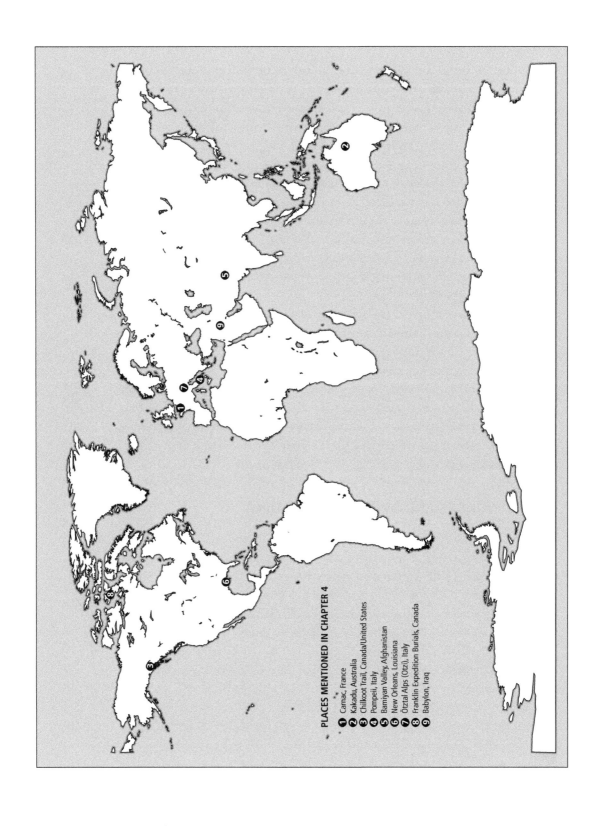

PLACES MENTIONED IN CHAPTER 4

1 Carnac, France
2 Kakadu, Australia
3 Chilkoot Trail, Canada/United States
4 Pompeii, Italy
5 Bamiyan Valley, Afghanistan
6 New Orleans, Louisiana
7 Ortzal Alps (Otzi), Italy
8 Franklin Expedition Burials, Canada
9 Babylon, Iraq

CHAPTER 4

COMPREHENDING THE ARCHAEOLOGICAL RECORD

Introduction

This chapter defines the components of the archaeological record. It also outlines the processes that lead to the creation of archaeological sites, the factors that influence what is preserved, and the range of activities that disturb the original patterning in material remains.

Defining the Archaeological Record and Its Components

There is no consensus definition of the archaeological record. At a minimum, it is taken to comprise all the material remains documented by archaeologists. Many expand this definition to include all material remains left by humans, including those remains yet to be documented. Some consider the archaeological record to include the basic facts about the past, based on material remains. For others, all the documentation pertaining to archaeological investigations, including field notes, maps, photographs, and written reports, constitutes the archaeological record.

However the archaeological record is defined, it is understood that the basic components of the material remains are sites, artifacts, **features**, **ecofacts**, and **cultural landscapes**.

ARCHAEOLOGICAL SITES

Broadly defined, an archaeological site is any location in which physical evidence of human activity exists. In practice, however, archaeological sites are usually defined more narrowly, based on such things as artifact density and time period. Most archaeologists do not routinely record isolated finds of a broken piece of pottery or stone tool as a site, nor do they commonly record deposits less than 100 years old, but they

TABLE 4.1 Major Types of Archaeological Sites

PREHISTORIC SITES	SUBTYPES
Habitation	Open-air; rock shelter; cave; camp; village; city; tell; midden
Earthwork	Embankment; trench; mound
Human remains	Isolated; cemetery
Rock art	Pictograph; petroglyph
Petroform	Megalith; cairn
Resource utilization	Hunting; fishing; gathering; culturally modified trees; quarry; processing; storage
HISTORIC SITES	**SUBTYPES**
Habitation	Single dwelling; multiple dwelling
Industrial	Mining; logging; other
Commercial	Shop; hotel; bar/saloon; other
Human remains	Isolated; cemetery
Military	n/a
Religious	n/a
Medical	n/a

may. Whether material remains are defined as a site is often dependent on the research objectives. Two archaeologists independently looking for sites in an area may see exactly the same material remains, but one may not document any sites, while the other, using different criteria, may document several sites.

There are several common types of archaeological sites. At a very broad level, most archaeologists make a distinction between prehistoric sites and historic sites, each with several discrete categories. The major kinds of sites are listed in Table 4.1.

Classifying a prehistoric site as a habitation indicates that people once lived at the site, but there are no restrictions on the number of people or length of time. Describing a site as a camp suggests a small and temporary occupation, while calling it a village implies at least a **semi-sedentary** pattern of residency. Archaeologists generally refrain from describing a site as a city unless the population is assumed to have been at least 5,000. **Tell** is a term commonly used to describe mounds that have been created by successive settlements in western Asia and northern Africa. Habitation sites usually have large accumulations of refuse, which archaeologists describe as **middens**. When the refuse includes a substantial amount of shell, it is often called a **shell midden**.

The term *petroform* refers to alignments of stones. Alignments of very large stones are known as megaliths. Other common types of petroforms include cairns, hunting

FIGURE 4.1 Carnac, France. Carnac is an example of the many prehistoric sites in Europe involving the alignments of large stone known as megaliths. The functions of the rows of stones at Carnac remain unknown.

PHOTO: Gillian Crowther.

blinds, stone fences, and alignments in rivers and intertidal zones of beaches to direct and capture fish.

The term *earthwork* is used to describe large, deliberately created embankments or mounds. Earthworks are commonly created for defensive purposes, but some have been shaped into animal forms and others have had habitation structures on top.

Burial was not the only way to treat the dead in the past, but certainly it is the most archaeologically visible method. Distinctions are usually made between isolated graves and cemeteries.

Many different kinds of sites fall within the category of resource utilization. Quarries were used to extract clay for making pottery and stone for making tools. People often did some initial manufacture of stone tools at or near the quarry site, creating a **lithic scatter**. Similarly, people often undertook some preparation and preserving of food where they procured their food resources, leaving evidence such as animal parts from butchering, cooking pits, drying racks, and **cache pits**.

The two main categories of rock-art sites are **pictographs** and **petroglyphs**. Using the term *pictograph* indicates that art has been painted onto a large immovable boulder or bedrock, or onto the wall of a cave, cliff, or rock shelter. The term *petroglyph* means the design was carved or pecked into the stone.

FIGURE 4.2
Pictographs at Kakadu, Australia.
With an estimated 15,000 sites and spanning up to 20,000 years in age, Kakadu National Park is a World Heritage Site and has one of the greatest concentrations of rock art in the world.

PHOTO: Gillian Crowther.

Several other classifications of prehistoric sites include cave sites, rock shelter sites, underwater sites, **sacred sites**, and open-air sites. Sometimes a site can be designated on the basis of a single artifact, and these sites are often described as isolated finds. *Culturally modified trees* is a category used to describe the evidence of removing the bark, planks, or small sections of living trees, or cutting the tree down, usually by Indigenous Peoples before the use of tools from the historic period.

Historic habitation sites are usually described as either a single dwelling, such as a cabin, or multiple dwellings, such as a town site. Industrial sites include those associated with logging, mining, manufacturing, and power generation. Commercial sites include those that show evidence of shops, hotels, and saloons. Other common classifications of historic sites are military, medical, religious, social, transportation, and communication sites.

ARTIFACTS

Any object that shows evidence of having been manufactured, modified, or used by people is an artifact. Many archaeologists assert that the object must also be portable. As they do when defining an archaeological site, archaeologists often use narrower criteria to decide whether to classify objects as artifacts. Some archaeologists working at prehistoric sites, for example, may choose to classify individual **potsherds** and **lithic debitage** as artifacts, while others do not. Similarly, others may choose to label every nail and broken piece of glass as an artifact, but most do not. The usual classification of artifacts is outlined in Chapter 6.

FEATURES

The term *feature* is used in a variety of ways. It is commonly used to describe objects that have all the characteristics of an artifact, except that they are non-portable. Feature is also used to describe material that has been patterned in such a way that the arrangement itself is significant, such as when a group of artifacts or food remains are recovered together in a burial. Patternings of natural sediments are often described as features if the arrangement has been caused by human activity. A pattern of soil discoloration, for example, often reflects that wooden posts were deliberately put into the ground, discoloring the soil as they decayed over centuries or millennia. Cobbles and boulders in a circular pattern often represent the outline of a shelter in which hides were weighted down with stones. Similarly, the term *activity area* describes an area in which evidence of certain types of activities are discerned, such as making stone tools. An activity area is often described as a feature. When the activity involves the manufacture of stone tools, the remains of the waste flakes are usually known as a lithic scatter. Some archaeologists make a distinction between constructed features, which include deliberately built structures such as buildings, fire hearths, and burials, and cumulative features, such as the buildup of trash forming a midden.

ECOFACTS

Collectively, **faunal remains**, botanical remains, and sediments from archaeological sites are known as ecofacts. They are collected because, at a minimum, they can provide evidence of the past environmental conditions to which the site's occupants had to adapt. They are also often useful for making interpretations about past lifeways, including settlement patterns, subsistence strategies, diet, and social inequalities, as detailed in subsequent chapters.

Many faunal remains recovered from archaeological sites are bones, but the category includes all parts of animals, including teeth, shell, hide, hair, fur, nails, claws, and soft tissue. Botanical remains similarly include a variety of forms. One of the most commonly recovered botanical remains is wood, usually charred or in the form of wood ash, but also including bark, seeds, nuts, pollen, and **phytoliths**. If faunal and botanical remains have been modified (by food preparation, for example), they could technically be classified as artifacts. In practice, however, unless animal or botanical remains have been made into a tool or piece of jewelry, such classifications are rare.

When discussing sediments, archaeologists usually are referring to non-cultural elements in the archaeological site. This excludes, for example, all artifacts and features.

Sediments are often referred to as the **matrix**, and are typically described as clay, silt, sand, loam, gravel, pebbles, and cobbles.

CULTURAL LANDSCAPES

Although geographers have been using the term "cultural landscape" for over 100 years, archaeologists have only recently begun to use it commonly. Its use has been part of a recent trend to reduce the focus of archaeology on individual artifacts and sites, instead conceptualizing areas as they were likely envisioned by those who used them in the past. UNESCO first recognized cultural landscapes as a World Heritage category in 1992. The operational guidelines for implementing the World Heritage Convention describe cultural landscapes as "illustrative of the evolution of human society and settlement over time, under the influence of the physical constraints and/or opportunities presented by their natural environment and of successive social, economic, and cultural forces, both external and internal."

One example of a cultural landscape with a UNESCO World Heritage designation is the Bamiyan Valley in Afghanistan. The valley contains many material remains associated with Buddhism from the first to thirteenth century in Central Asia and was an important pilgrimage destination. Material remains include monumental Buddha statues as well as other forms of art and architecture in the Buddhist tradition. The Bamiyan Valley received international attention in 2001 when the Afghan militant group the Taliban deliberately destroyed two monumental Buddhas carved into cliffs. The Bamiyan Valley also appears in the UNESCO List of World Heritage in Danger, primarily due to ongoing military action in the area, dynamite explosions, looting, and the presence of land mines.

Although it does not have UNESCO designation, another good example of a cultural landscape is the Chilkoot Trail, which begins on the coast of Alaska and heads inland to Canada's Yukon Territory. The 73-kilometer (45-mile) trail has a long history as an Indigenous trade route, but it is more widely known as the gateway to the Yukon goldfields along which tens of thousands of gold-seekers trekked during the late 1800s, scattering many thousands of artifacts along the way. For many archaeologists, it makes more sense to envision the trail as a single entity rather than as hundreds of discrete clusters of artifacts, features, and sites.

Creating Archaeological Sites

Principal things to consider about the creation of archaeological sites are the circumstances under which initial material remains enter the archaeological record (e.g., discarded as refuse, intentionally buried, lost, or abandoned), and the different ways that material remains can become buried (e.g., intentional burial, sandstorms, or landslides).

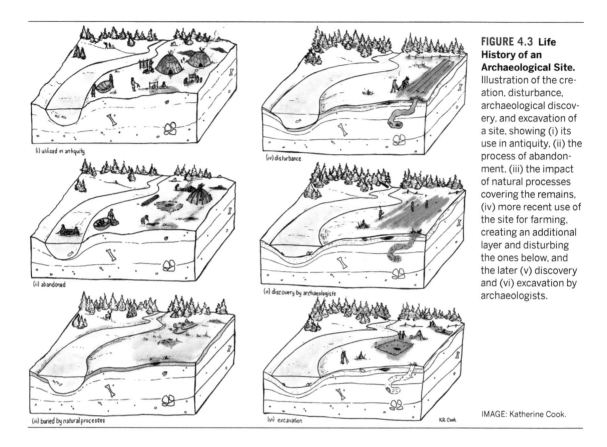

FIGURE 4.3 Life History of an Archaeological Site. Illustration of the creation, disturbance, archaeological discovery, and excavation of a site, showing (i) its use in antiquity, (ii) the process of abandonment, (iii) the impact of natural processes covering the remains, (iv) more recent use of the site for farming, creating an additional layer and disturbing the ones below, and the later (v) discovery and (vi) excavation by archaeologists.

(i) utilized in antiquity

(iv) disturbance

(ii) abandoned

(v) discovery by archaeologists

(iii) buried by natural processes

(vi) excavation

K.R. Cook

HOW SITES ARE INITIALLY CREATED

Many processes lead to the creation of archaeological sites (Table 4.2). Collectively, these are known as **site formation processes**. When the focus is on the initial deposition of material remains, the processes are sometimes called **cultural formation processes** or **behavioral formation processes**. Archaeological sites invariably have sediments in them that are brought in by nature, and the processes responsible for this are generally called **natural** or **non-cultural formation processes**.

Most archaeologists use the term refuse to refer to the collectivity of discarded items. Some, however, prefer to use the term *trash* to describe dry items such as broken artifacts, *garbage* to describe wet or organic items such as food waste, *refuse* to refer to both trash and garbage, and *rubbish* to include all discarded or abandoned items, including house remains.

Archaeologists frequently make a distinction between **primary refuse** and **secondary refuse**. Refuse that was simply abandoned where it was created or used and

TABLE 4.2 Site Formation Processes

CULTURAL FORMATION PROCESSES	NATURAL FORMATION PROCESSES
Deliberate discard	Natural soil formation
Intentional burial	By water
Loss	Through the air
Abandonment	Over land
	By animals

subsequently found in that precise location by archaeologists is called primary refuse. Refuse that was deliberately moved from the area where it was initially created or used and redeposited elsewhere, such as a midden, is called secondary refuse.

To understand the conditions in which items were discarded or abandoned, many archaeologists have done ethnoarchaeology, from which a few generalizations can be made. Research indicates that time and size are the two key variables that determine whether refuse will be left *in situ* or redeposited in a midden. Generally, if people are occupying an area for a very short time, with little expectation of return, they leave refuse in primary context. For example, people who stop to cook a meal while hunting are not likely to create a midden for their refuse. Conversely, few people like to live among their refuse, and if they are going to be staying in an area for at least a day or two, they are likely to create a special area for refuse. Also, people are more likely to leave small items in situ and redeposit larger items as secondary refuse. Potential reuse is another important factor that influences whether people will leave items as primary refuse or secondary refuse.

Many items enter the archaeological record through intentional burial. This includes human burials and associated **grave goods**, as well as **caches** of food in storage pits. Human burials were usually meant to lie undisturbed, but caches of food were buried with the intent of removing the food at some future time. Cache pits for food storage are a common type of feature found in prehistoric habitation sites, sometimes dug into house floors and sometimes outside the houses. It is not uncommon to find cache pits in resource utilization sites, where food preserved by drying or smoking would have been left if it was anticipated that members of the group would return that way in the future.

Some artifacts enter the archaeological record because they were lost. However, this is a relatively rare occurrence. Examples include cargo lost during a shipwreck and coins or jewelry that may have fallen onto, and ultimately under, floors or floor coverings (e.g., wooden floorboards or mats). Isolated finds of arrowheads are likely to be the result of loss, for example by a hunter who missed the target and could not relocate the arrow.

BOX 4.1 DECAY OF HUMAN REMAINS

It is only in rare circumstances that the soft tissue of humans and other animals is preserved for long. This is because the process of decay is not the passive process that many people envision. Rather, it is an active process involving many microorganisms and insects eating the body.

As described by Hyde et al. (2013, para. 1): "Decomposition is a mosaic system with an intimate association between biotic factors (i.e. the individuality of the cadaver, intrinsic and extrinsic bacteria and other microbes, and insects) and abiotic factors (i.e. weather, climate, and humidity)." The process tends to begin with the breakdown of cells, which feeds bacteria in the body. Eventually other organisms, including maggots, flies, and beetles, may feast on the body.

The process is described by Mary Roach (2004) in the book *Stiff: The Curious Lives of Cadavers*, with a focus on the work of bacteria:

> The hallmark of fresh-stage decay is a process called autolysis, or self-digestion. Human cells use enzymes to cleave molecules.... While a person is alive, the cells keep these enzymes in check, preventing them from breaking down the cells' own walls. After death, the enzymes operate unchecked and begin eating through the cell structure, allowing the liquid inside to leak out.... The liquid that is leaking ... [makes] contact with the body's bacteria colonies.... These bacteria were there in the living

body as well.... They've already been enjoying the benefits of a decommissioned human immune system, and now, suddenly, they're awash with this edible goo.... As will happen in times of plenty, the population swells.... Soon bacteria are everywhere. The scene is set for stage two: bloat.

The life of bacterium is built around food.... Like us, they break their food down into more elemental components. The enzymes in our stomachs break meat down into proteins. The bacteria in our gut break those proteins down into amino acids; they take up where we leave off. When we die, they stop feeding on what we've eaten and begin feeding on us.... Bloat is typically short-lived, perhaps a week and it's over. The final stage, putrefaction and decay, lasts longest.

Putrefaction refers to the breaking down and gradual liquefaction of tissue by bacteria.... Dead people, unembalmed ones anyway, basically dissolve.... The digestive organs and lungs disintegrate first, for they are home to the greatest numbers of bacteria; the larger your work crew, the faster the building comes down. The brain is another early-departure organ.... "The brain liquefies very quickly. It just pours out the ears and bubbles out the mouth."

Abandonment is usually considered a site formation process. Most prehistoric sites, including settlements, were abandoned by design, sometimes with the intent of returning and sometimes not. Throughout most of prehistory, people moved, at least seasonally, within their territory, and each time they left for an extended period can be considered abandonment. In other situations, such as abandonment due to environmental, economic, or social reasons, return may not have been anticipated. The implication for archaeology is that when a site was abandoned by design, the inhabitants would have had the opportunity to take what they wanted with them. Sites that have been abandoned, therefore, are usually devoid of artifacts that would have had a relatively high perceived value among the inhabitants.

NATURAL SEDIMENTS IN ARCHAEOLOGICAL SITES

In between periods of occupation and after the final abandonment, many different processes bring natural sediments into a site, which often cause its complete burial. The natural decay of organic matter eventually contributes to soil formation, which in itself can bury a site. Sediments are also brought in by water, such as rivers, tides, and rising lake and sea levels; through mass movement, such as slides or flows; and through the air, such as wind blowing sand over a site. Sediments in archaeological sites may also have been transported and deposited by glaciers.

Burials of sites are usually slow, but occasionally they are sudden and can happen almost instantaneously. Many sites throughout the world are buried by mud slides, avalanches, and volcanic eruptions. The most well-known is the site of Pompeii in Italy.

The city of Pompeii, along with Herculaneum and some smaller settlements, was completely buried by ash from the eruption of Mount Vesuvius in AD 79. Because of the quick burial, Pompeii provides a glimpse into everyday life rarely found in the archaeological record. In most cities, people take their valuables when they leave, and

FIGURE 4.4 Pompeii. Due to a catastrophic eruption of volcanic ash, Pompeii is one of the best-preserved cities in the world, providing an excellent glimpse into the everyday life in a Roman city during the first century AD.

PHOTO: Barry D. Kass @ ImagesofAnthropology.com.

FIGURE 4.5 Collapsed House, Lower Ninth Ward, Louisiana, October 2005. This image represents the impact of Hurricane Katrina on a house in the Lower Ninth Ward, Louisiana. The flood-walls and levees designed to protect New Orleans from flooding in the wake of a massive hurricane collapsed, leading to the destruction of a large portion of New Orleans and surrounding districts, the displacement of more than 1 million people, and the loss of nearly 2,000 human lives.

PHOTO: Shannon Dawdy.

BOX 4.2 PRESERVING THE ARCHAEOLOGICAL RECORD: TAPHONOMY AFTER HURRICANE KATRINA

Archaeologists use the term **taphonomy** to describe how both natural and cultural forces shape the creation of the archaeological record. Natural processes include floods, earthquakes, volcanic eruptions, fires, **bioturbation**, weathering, erosion, tsunamis, hurricanes, and tornadoes. Floods, for instance, can move and displace artifacts from where they were originally deposited by people in the past, meaning that these artifacts are no longer in situ, or in their original location of deposition. Entire buildings and houses can be leveled in a few seconds due to an earthquake. Some cultural processes that can disturb or alter the archaeological record include construction, plowing and tilling fields, leveling houses after natural disasters, and looting archaeological sites. Archaeologists are responsible for reconstructing the many taphonomic events that have disrupted or altered the archaeological sites they excavate.

Archaeologists not only play detective when trying to decipher taphonomic processes in the past; they are also involved in making important decisions about how to preserve and maintain the archaeological record of the present and more recent past when disasters occur. This was the case for Dr. Shannon Dawdy, a professor of anthropology at the University of Chicago and winner of the 2010 MacArthur Genius Award. Dawdy was asked to help formulate a plan for buildings and households destroyed by Hurricane Katrina in New Orleans, Louisiana. These structures were flooded when walls and levees that were supposed to protect the city from torrential hurricanes and flooding collapsed in 2005.

Originally, it was proposed that the buildings affected by the flood "waste in place." This would mean that the city and its residents would rebuild on top of the rubble of former schools, buildings, and homes. This approach would also leave buildings and the

(continued)

BOX 4.2 Continued

goods inside of them in situ, preserving the archaeo-logical record for future researchers. Residents, how-ever, objected to the phrase "waste in place," because it implied that their lives, homes, and possessions that were destroyed were merely "waste." Scientists familiar with New Orleans' geology and soil also re-jected the "waste in place" strategy, arguing that the weight of decaying buildings and abandoned material culture would eventually cause the new buildings to sink into the ground. Finally, government officials raised concerns over the chemicals left behind in the soils from refrigerators, cleaning products, and air conditioners.

Taking these discussions into account, a decision was made to relocate buildings and possessions de-stroyed or significantly altered by Katrina to a neigh-boring landfill. While the provenience of these ruins and objects will not be maintained for future archae-ologists to study, the rubble will still be somewhat close to its original context. Based on the case study of Katrina, Dawdy (2006) concludes that taphonomy is an emotional, political, and cultural process.

environmental conditions lead to the decomposition of organic remains. The people of Pompeii had no time to evacuate, and the quick covering of ash provided excellent preservation. Excavations at Pompeii have uncovered markets, restaurants, shops, an amphitheater, villas, and many other smaller residences. The population is estimated to have been about 20,000.

Besides the obvious processes that bring in sediments over the surfaces of sites, archaeologists also consider that processes operating beneath the surface may also result in site burial. In some regions, for example, sites can be buried by earthworms. Earthworms burrow by swallowing the dirt in front of them, often bringing dirt to the surface where it is redeposited.

Understanding Bias in the Preservation of Material Remains

Archaeologists understand that with the rare exception of a quick and complete burial, as in Pompeii, they usually recover a very biased subset of material culture. This is largely due to the fact that most of the material record was discarded or abandoned deliberately, as described previously. Artifacts of perceived value generally account for a very small percentage of the total items recovered. It is not unreasonable to imagine that for every complete arrowhead or pottery vessel in an archaeological site, there are probably a thousand or more pieces of lithic debitage or potsherds.

Archaeologists also understand that some materials preserve better than others, so that what is recovered is not necessarily an accurate reflection of what originally existed. The major factors that bias the preservation of material remains are the mate-rial itself and the environmental conditions.

MATERIAL BIAS

Items recovered from archaeological sites are often broadly classified as organic or inorganic, and it is widely recognized that inorganic materials will almost always preserve better. However, even within the category of inorganic materials, there are clear differences in preservation qualities.

The three most common types of inorganic materials recovered from archaeological sites are artifacts and features made of stone, clay, and metal. Stone is often characterized as being "hard" or "soft," and the harder varieties such as **obsidian**, basalt, and chert are the most durable, and therefore less susceptible to weathering than softer varieties. Fired clay is as hard as stone in some cases, but tends to be more easily broken and crushed. Metals have varying degrees of durability. Objects made of iron and tin tend to rust and corrode relatively quickly, while objects of gold, silver, bronze, and copper preserve well.

Many types of organic remains are also commonly recovered. Various skeletal elements of animals are recovered, but the parts that preserve the best tend to be bones, teeth, and antlers. Similarly, many types of plant remains are recovered, but the ones that preserve the best tend to be wood (often burned), pollen, and seeds.

To interpret the relative abundance of different types of organic remains in archaeological sites, many archaeologists have become involved in taphonomic studies. Broadly defined, taphonomy is the study of site formation and disturbance processes but is also sometimes more narrowly defined as the study of what happens to organic remains after death. It involves examining the differential rates of decomposition between different organic materials. At a very general level, it is apparent that bone density is a key variable affecting preservation, and since the bone density of large animals tends to be greater than in small animals, the bones of larger animals are more likely to be preserved. Similarly, since mammal bones tend to have greater density than bird or fish bones, mammal bones are more likely to be preserved.

ENVIRONMENTAL CONDITIONS

Many environmental conditions affect the preservation of organic remains, including the rapidity of burial, microbial activity, burning, the chemistry of the matrix, and extreme environments.

Organic remains that are buried quickly often preserve better than those that are left on the surface of the ground. This is particularly true for animal remains, since dead animals left on the ground surface are generally eaten by a variety of other animals, large and small. Rapid burial, whether it occurs deliberately (as in buried garbage) or naturally (as in snowfalls, windstorms, or mudslides) removes the first agents of destruction – scavengers. Rapid burial also generally takes the remains from an aerobic environment to an anaerobic environment, where organisms that eat organic remains are less active. Exposure to air and chemicals at the surface promotes decomposition and weathering. If rapid burial takes place, this exposure is limited, and materials are preserved better.

Although less active in anaerobic environments, many organisms feed on dead matter. These life forms are called saprophytic organisms, and although they include large scavengers such as rodents, the term is more commonly used to describe much smaller forms, such as bacteria, fungi, and insects. These microbial saprophytic organisms need water and air to stay alive, so anaerobic environments inhibit their survival.

Besides an anaerobic environment, several other conditions inhibit the activities of saprophytic organisms. One of these is burning, which removes the nutrients from the remains, making them unattractive to those that feed on dead matter. This is why wood charcoal, for example, is found so frequently in prehistoric archaeological sites.

Very cold environments also inhibit saprophytic activity, which is the usual explanation for the existence of very well preserved bodily remains throughout the world, dating from hundreds to thousands of years ago. The body of a man commonly known as Otzi (named after the Ötztal Alps in Italy, where he died) is an excellent example. He was discovered in a melting glacier in 1991, having died about 5,500 years ago. Current research suggests that after death he probably was covered by a slight layer of snow, dried in the high altitude of the Alps, and was eventually frozen within a glacier. Many of the organic objects he had with him were preserved as well, including clothing and shoes made from animal hides, a grass cloak, and a longbow and arrow shafts. Otzi has become one of the most studied individuals from prehistory, and his excellent preservation has allowed researchers to examine rare soft tissue. Researchers were able to conclude from his intestines that he dined on goat, cereal, and deer shortly before his death. Parasites indicate he was probably suffering from diarrhea, and his fingernails suggest a recent history of illness. X-rays reveal what appears to be an arrowhead in his shoulder, evidently shot from behind and likely the cause of his death.

Another example of human remains preserved in a cold environment comes from northern Canada, where some crew members of an ill-fated nineteenth-century journey through Arctic waters were buried in permafrost. In what is known as the Franklin Expedition, two ships set sail from England in 1845 carrying 129 men to Canada in search of a sailing route through the north of the continent. Despite the apparently well-equipped ships and experienced crew, including Captain John Franklin with his previous Arctic experience, all met their demise in the doomed expedition. It has long been a mystery what led to the relatively quick death of many expedition members shortly after reaching northern Canada, and the seemingly bizarre decision of some to hike out of the Arctic on foot, burdened with luxury items. Owen Beattie sought the answer to these mysteries by investigating both the material remains (including middens) and skeletal remains of expedition members. He concluded that they likely died of lead poisoning due to the poorly manufactured cans in which much of the food provisions were stored for the expedition (evident from the cans found at the sites). Neurological damage is one symptom of lead poisoning, which may explain why some made the bizarre decision to hike out of the Arctic when it would have made much more sense to wait for rescue ships.

Mummy is a term often used by archaeologists to describe human remains that have been preserved by drying. A distinction is often made between deliberate and natural mummification. Deliberate mummification has a several-thousand-year history, and usually involves some sort of intentional drying of the body before burial, as was practiced in ancient Egypt as well as in South America, Southeast Asia, and elsewhere.

Natural mummification has a similarly long history, with remains being preserved through naturally dry environments in North and South America and parts of Asia.

Yet another important condition affecting preservation is matrix chemistry. The precise effects that chemistry has on the variety of organic remains typically found in archaeological sites do not appear to be well understood. In general, however, it is apparent that bone usually preserves best in alkaline soils, and some types of botanical remains survive better in acidic soils.

Organic remains submerged in water or buried in waterlogged sediments tend to preserve well, although not normally for more than a few thousand years. Peat bogs, which are sometimes considered a special class of waterlogged sites, provide excellent conditions for some types of preservation, especially soft tissue. The famous **bog men** of northern Europe are particularly good examples of this. The highly acidic nature of peat bogs generally makes them unsuitable for the long-term preservation of bone, but leads to good preservation of plant remains.

Site Disturbance

In addition to the biasing effects of material and environmental conditions, archaeologists recognize that many other factors potentially alter the original patterning of material culture left by a site's occupants. Collectively, these processes are known as **post-depositional disturbance processes**, sometimes simply called site disturbance processes. They are further subdivided into the categories of natural disturbance and cultural disturbance.

TABLE 4.3 Site Disturbance Processes

NATURAL DISTURBANCE PROCESSES	CULTURAL DISTURBANCE PROCESSES
Bioturbation	Reusing
Cryoturbation	Recycling
Aeroturbation	Trampling
Aquaturbation	Construction
Graviturbation	Looting
	Collateral damage during war

NATURAL DISTURBANCE

Alternatively known as **non-cultural disturbance processes** or **N-transforms**, natural disturbance processes include a wide range of activities that may alter the patterning of the material record.

Bioturbation is a term used to describe disturbance by plants and animals, sometimes more specifically called **floralturbation** and **faunalturbation**, respectively. Disturbance by plants involves such things as the roots of trees and other vegetation growing through archaeological deposits and displacing items of the material record. Tree-throws are a particularly active force in altering the deposits, because when a tree falls over it typically takes a substantial portion of the deposits around the roots and redeposits it on the ground surface. Bioturbation, by aerating the deposits, also allows more oxygen, water, and chemicals into the ground, which can lead to increased rates of physical and chemical weathering of the material remains.

Many types of animals also commonly alter the patterning. This includes the digging and scavenging activities of dogs, rats, and other small animals on or near the surface of a site, as well as the activity of rodents and other burrowing animals, which often creates internal pathways or voids in the matrix where artifacts can fall or be displaced by the animals themselves. Earthworms alone can make significant changes in patterns. One experimental study showed that earthworms buried lithic and ceramic fragments as much as 45 centimeters (18 inches) deep after only five years. In addition to the burial of artifacts, geoarchaeologist Julie Stein observed that earthworms can obliterate stratification and obscure boundaries of sedimentary layers, alter the botanical assemblage within sites, and alter the chemistry of the soils.

The effect of rodents on site disturbance is illustrated in an experimental study reported by Barbara Bocek in 1992. After excavating a 1 × 2 meter (3¼ × 6½ foot) unit, the unit was backfilled with clean (culturally sterile) sediment. After seven years, the unit was re-excavated and found to contain 390 pieces of shell, bone, and **debitage**, as well as 3.4 kilograms (7.48 pounds) of burned and unmodified rock, presumably transported laterally to the unit from the surrounding areas. A simple calculation showed that in the 1,000 years since the site was last occupied, the cultural contents of a single excavation unit could have been totally replaced more than 11 times.

Besides moving artifacts, animals may also mark or break bones in a pattern that could potentially be mistaken for human activity. Archaeologists are aware that the breaks and marks on bones caused by scavenging could be mistaken for deliberate butchery by humans. Similarly, when animals trample over a site, they can easily cause bone breakage.

Archaeologists working in what are now or were once cold environments are usually aware of the potential for cryoturbation to influence the patterning of the material record. Studies have shown that objects can move substantial distances due to frost activity alone. M.R. Hilton (2003), for example, undertook some experiments showing that in a control plot designed to minimize the impacts of wind and other natural processes, freeze-thaw cycles caused artifacts to move an average of almost 8 centimeters (3¼ inches) over a three-year period. Without the constraints to minimize other processes, artifacts in another plot moved an average of almost 32 centimeters (12½ inches) over the same period.

Archaeologists working in windy areas are aware that relatively light items may be displaced or buried by wind, a process known as aeroturbation. Similarly, archaeologists working in areas that are now or once were associated with moving water, whether along a tidal beach, creek, or through simple groundwater percolation, are aware of the potential for water to move material remains, a process known as aquaturbation. And archaeologists working in hilly environments are generally aware that material remains may be displaced as they move downhill, either by slipping down the surface of a slope or when substantial amounts of sediments move, a process sometimes known as graviturbation or mass wasting.

Other natural processes that may influence patterning of material remains are weathering and erosion. Chemical weathering includes the processes that alter the composition of remains when they react with water, oxygen, and other elements. These reactions may weaken the structure of large artifacts and features made of stone, clay, or mud-brick. Physical weathering involves the mechanical breakdown of material into smaller pieces, and erosion means the transport of residual sediments. Extensive wind and water movement potentially removes the matrix surrounding artifacts and features, which makes them more susceptible to displacement by a wide variety of other processes. Wind and water may also erode surfaces of artifacts and features, potentially causing them to break. Physical weathering also describes artifacts that break due to natural fires.

CULTURAL DISTURBANCE

Alternatively known as **behavioral disturbance processes** or **C-transforms**, cultural disturbance processes include a wide range of post-depositional human activities.

A large proportion of sites have been used again after periods of abandonment, a process widely known as reuse. By their very presence, those who occupy a site after a period of abandonment, whether it is measured in years, decades, centuries, or millennia, often disturb it in significant ways. They often modify the site surface and dig in older deposits while involved in such activities as clearing the site of trees; moving shell from a midden to provide increased stability or drainage in another area; using a midden as a burial ground; constructing semi-subterranean houses, cooking pits, and cache pits; or inserting poles for shelters, fences, and enclosures.

Recycling of material remains is commonly recognized as a potential site disturbance process. This includes when people disturb their own middens or those created by previous inhabitants while searching for bone, shell, charcoal, or ceramics to create artifacts such as jewelry, or other items to make dyes, pigments, or pottery temper.

Human trampling is a process widely recognized for its potential to both break and displace material remains. Experimental studies have shown that ceramics and shells are particularly susceptible to breakage by trampling, and that depending on a wide variety of variables, items are also subject to considerable vertical displacement. One study showed that in sandy deposits subjected to human trampling, large artifacts had a tendency to move upwards while smaller artifacts tended to move downwards.

Many contemporary human activities disturb sites in significant ways. It is likely that hundreds and perhaps thousands of archaeological sites are destroyed every day by industrial activities such as mining, logging, and various sorts of construction; albeit, not all of the sites are necessarily significant. Many of these sites are unknowingly destroyed or destroyed with the permission of regulatory authorities because they are of low significance and stand in the way of development projects.

Many sites are mined for the value of the materials in contemporary construction. In various parts of the world, shell middens are mined because the shell is useful for road building. A recent study of Mayan sites in Belize showed that the remains of temples were often used for road fill, and at least one entire Mayan site has been almost completely destroyed by the search and removal of material to build roads.

Deliberate looting of sites for artifacts of a variety of materials and values, often referred to by the generic term **pothunting**, is a major source of site disturbance and results in the total destruction of many thousands of sites, the removal of at least tens of thousands of significant artifacts, and the displacement of artifacts in many thousands more. This practice extends back at least several thousand years to the robbing of ancient tombs for items buried with Egyptian pharaohs and in similar burial sites throughout the world. It continues today around the world, ranging from people collecting arrowheads as a hobby in North America to using metal detectors to search for gold coins in Roman-era sites and deliberate looting to fuel the trade in illicit antiquities.

The impact of warfare on the archaeological record is also significant. Despite the Hague Convention and other instruments to protect archaeological sites during times of conflict, the destruction of many significant sites continues in contemporary times. Bombing of sites, whether intentional or not, is one way they are disturbed. But contemporary warfare affects the archaeological record in many other ways, such as making it logistically difficult to prevent looting and other disruptive effects of conflict in remote locations, and by constructing military bases on or near sites. For example, the ancient city of Babylon has been disturbed by the construction of a military base following the 2003 US conflict with Iraq. The site, which dates back about 2,600 years, was disturbed in a variety of ways: military vehicles damaged much of the brick pavement; trenches were dug into the deposits; deposits were used as fill for sandbags; and large amounts of gravel and other sediments were brought to the site to use as fill in the construction of such things as helipads, parking lots, and accommodations.

KEY RESOURCES AND SUGGESTED READING

The nature of the archaeological record is discussed in the article "Is There an Archaeological Record?" by Patrick (1985). For those interested in cultural landscapes, including the Bamiyan Valley and Chilkoot Trail, the UNESCO web site on World Heritage Sites (https://whc.unesco.org) is recommended. Good overviews of site formation and disturbance processes can be found in Schiffer (1987), and sources on the preservation of material found in archaeological sites can be found in Brothwell and Pollard (2001).

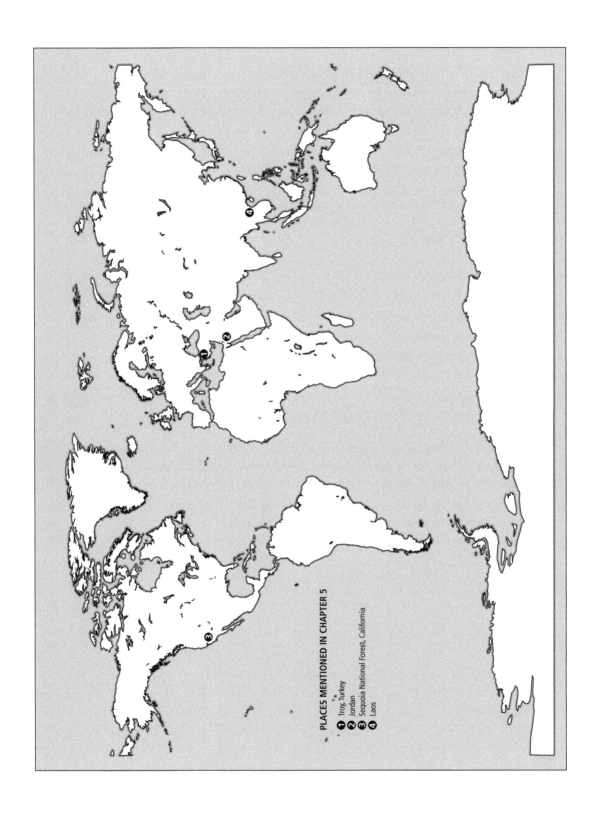

PLACES MENTIONED IN CHAPTER 5

1 Troy, Turkey
2 Jordan
3 Sequoia National Forest, California
4 Laos

CHAPTER 5

WORKING IN THE FIELD

Introduction

This chapter focuses on archaeological fieldwork. It includes sections on archaeological research design, site discovery, excavation, ethnoarchaeology, and the hazards of field archaeology.

Designing Archaeological Field Projects

Archaeological projects are always guided by research design, unless amateurs are undertaking them. Research designs are critical for a variety of reasons. Most importantly, they establish (i) the significance of the project, (ii) the kinds of information being sought, (iii) the preferred methods for obtaining that information, and (iv) the plan for making the research meaningful.

There are always choices to be made in research design. Not only does the design guide the archaeological project director and crew once they begin fieldwork, it also provides a mechanism by which others can evaluate the project.

Archaeological projects that involve the discovery and excavation of sites follow nine basic stages (Table 5.1). Planning the details of each of these stages in advance is what constitutes the research design. Although the basic stages of archaeological research outlined here include excavation, it is important to understand that excavation is not always considered or carried out. Indeed, many purely academic research field projects are based on finding and mapping surface features alone. For cultural resource management (CRM) archaeology, the purpose of most fieldwork is to evaluate the threat development poses to archaeological sites and to work toward avoiding impact on significant sites. In CRM archaeology, excavation is usually undertaken only as a last resort, such as when it is evident that the site will be destroyed.

TABLE 5.1 Basic Stages of Archaeological Research

1. Identifying the need for field research

2. Doing background research

3. Formulating hypotheses or research questions

4. Determining the types of data to collect

5. Determining the field and laboratory methods to use

6. Detailing the logistics of making the project work

7. Collecting data

8. Making the data meaningful

9. Making the research meaningful

IDENTIFYING THE NEED FOR FIELD RESEARCH

In academic archaeology, identifying the need for research generally comes after recognizing the need for more data. Additional data can fill significant gaps of knowledge in a plethora of things that interest archaeologists, whether considered low-level (e.g., culture history), mid-level (e.g., reconstructing past lifeways), or high-level (e.g., explaining culture change). Although individual archaeologists generally identify the need for research, other archaeologists confirm that need before work proceeds, through peer review of research proposals.

For archaeologists working within the context of CRM, the need for fieldwork is usually determined by proposed land-altering activities such as road building, pipeline construction, logging and mining activity, or residential and business development. Major land-altering development proposals are generally sent to governments, where they are subject to review. Typically, a bureaucrat determines whether the person, company, or agency responsible for the proposal is required to fund an archaeological project to assess the impact of the project on archaeological sites and possibly excavate the site as well. Essentially, the need for fieldwork in the context of industry is based on the fact that archaeological sites may or will be destroyed by an impending land-altering development.

BACKGROUND RESEARCH

After the need for fieldwork has been identified, the next stage is background research. This typically involves a literature review, which includes searching for and reading relevant written reports, articles, and books on the geographic area and time period of interest. At a minimum, a literature review takes in all archaeological reports on the area. It often also includes area history, as well as ethnographies of its Indigenous Peoples.

Background research also involves reviewing all the archaeological site records for the study area and consulting a wide variety of people. The site records include completed archaeological site inventory forms as well as reports of site investigations usually held on file with the local, regional, or national government agency responsible for heritage. People consulted are usually those who are potentially very knowledgeable about the location of unrecorded archaeological sites, such as members of local descendant communities and others who spend a good deal of time in the area's outdoors. Historians and anthropologists are often consulted if there is reason to believe that a relatively recent site may be discovered. If an archaeologist is focusing on an area where ancient sites may be discovered, he or she is likely to consult with geologists and paleontologists familiar with the region.

When the project is being undertaken in the context of CRM, background research further includes a detailed review of the development proposal. Most importantly, archaeologists examine the proposal to identify the precise nature and scope of potential impacts to archaeological sites, should they be discovered.

FORMULATING HYPOTHESES AND STATING RESEARCH QUESTIONS

Academic archaeologists usually create one or more hypotheses to guide the research. Essentially, the hypothesis is an explanation of some phenomena that makes some sense to the archaeologist based on background research (e.g., which group of people created a site or why a site was abandoned), but lacks sufficient data to fully support it.

Rather than formulating hypotheses, archaeologists in CRM tend to state research questions in their research design. Typical questions include how many sites are likely to be found in the study area and how the development project will impact the sites.

DETERMINING THE TYPES OF DATA TO COLLECT

It is certainly not practical and not very realistic to think that archaeologists can collect data on matters of interest to all archaeologists while in the field. For example, archaeologists cannot collect and classify every piece of lithic debitage, potsherd, or ecofact recovered during excavations. Thus, while they often take representative samples of the various components of the archaeological record, they focus on the data that can be used most effectively to test their hypotheses or answer their research questions. Basically, archaeologists list in their research designs the kinds of data that they desire to test their hypotheses. Some archaeologists refer to this as **ideal data**.

Different archaeologists will not always collect the same kinds of data. An archaeologist focusing on diet, for example, may recover, classify, and analyze every animal or botanical remain seen during excavations, but take only samples of potsherds and lithic debitage. Conversely, an archaeologist interested primarily in pottery technology is likely to recover, classify, and analyze every potsherd but take only representative samples of ecofacts.

In addition to determining what material to collect, archaeologists must also consider which variables of the material will be most appropriate to address their hypotheses or research questions. An archaeologist interested primarily in stone tool technology, for example, will seek different sorts of data than one interested primarily in stone tool function. The archaeologist interested in technology is likely to consider such variables as the size and shape of the flakes removed to make the tool, while the archaeologist interested in function is likely to consider whether there is residue on the tool, and if so, what kind (e.g., plant, bone, hide, etc.).

DETERMINING THE METHODS TO COLLECT AND ANALYZE DATA

Once the ideal data are determined, the next stage of the research design is to decide the most appropriate methods of obtaining that data, both in the field and in the laboratory. Some archaeologists refer to these as the **ideal methods**. Principal factors that ultimately determine the choice of methods include time and money.

LOGISTICS

Logistics are the details for putting the plan in place. For those working in academia, this usually includes an application for money to undertake the research. Normally, funding agencies subject the proposal to peer review to ensure that the project is important from an intellectual standpoint, and that ideal data and methods are appropriate. For those working in industry, logistics involve submitting a proposal of their work to the government or the developer, and the government agency responsible for archaeology will act as the reviewer to ensure that the methods are appropriate.

Logistics also involve obtaining necessary permissions and permits to conduct fieldwork. This almost always entails obtaining a permit from government and often also means getting approval from landowners and other stakeholders, including Indigenous groups.

Logistics also include hiring the field crew, arranging transportation and accommodation, and buying field supplies.

COLLECTING DATA

The search for sites, their excavation, and laboratory work all produce data. Data collected during the search for archaeological sites typically include basic information on the sites discovered, including their location, number, type, and condition. Data from excavation consist of numbers and types of artifacts, features, and ecofacts.

Data from laboratory analysis may include a wide variety of information, as outlined in Chapter 6.

MAKING THE DATA MEANINGFUL

Raw data are usually made meaningful after they have been manipulated in some way. This usually involves systems of classification, described in Chapter 6. It also often entails statistics. Essentially, data are made meaningful through their application to the stated hypotheses or research questions.

MAKING THE RESEARCH MEANINGFUL

Making the research meaningful brings the project full circle. It is incumbent upon archaeologists to report their research in a timely manner. For those in academic archaeology, this generally means a report to the government and others who have issued the permits or permissions for research, the funding agency, and other archaeologists. Reports to other archaeologists usually take the form of presentations at conferences, journal articles, chapters in edited books, or monographs. Although it does not happen routinely, academic archaeologists are increasingly making their research meaningful to the public, through film productions and articles written for the popular press.

For those in CRM, making the research meaningful generally means reporting the results of the project to the government and others who have issued permits or permissions for research.

BOX 5.1 FROM EXCLUSIVITY TO INCLUSIVITY: MAKING ARCHAEOLOGY AN EQUITABLE PROFESSION

As a discipline that has historically excluded minorities and women, archaeology has been slow to adopt practices that seek to include people of all walks of life. Archaeology has traditionally been defined as field-based science, which poses unique physical, geographical, and logistical obstacles for archaeologists.

Archaeologists are faced with financially and emotionally difficult decisions that include covering the costs of childcare; making the decision to leave their children at home, or bring them to the field if it is permitted on site or if it is safe to do so (Goldstein et al. 2018); dealing with universities or employers who prohibit archaeologists and other field crew members from bringing children to archaeological sites; stereotypes regarding who can be considered an archaeologist (Heath-Stout 2019); and being away from those in their care for long periods of time (Camp 2019). Elder care also presents similar challenges for archaeologists who conduct fieldwork. But child and elder carework are statistically more likely to fall on the shoulders of women around the globe (Covan 1997). In addition, some archaeologists, known as "multigenerational caregivers," find that they are responsible for the care of both children and elders at the same time (Livingston 2018). This is due to two modern factors: (1) women delaying having children until they are done with their education and/or gainfully employed, and (2) people living much longer than previous generations.

(continued)

BOX 5.1 Continued

Archaeologists have also been slow to recognize that archaeology must accommodate people who have disabilities, despite antidiscrimination laws that prevent people with disabilities from being excluded in the workplace and denied access to higher education (Fraser 2007; Phillips and Gilchrist 2012; Enabled Archaeology Foundation n.d.). There is a growing understanding in the discipline that it must become more inclusive, not only to improve and nuance our interpretations of people in the past, but also to ensure our discipline does not actively exclude and create barriers for people with disabilities. The Inclusive Curriculum Project in Britain, for instance, has sought to make archaeological field experiences more inclusive and accessible for students by creating a toolkit called the Archaeological Skills

Self-Evaluation Tool Kit (ASSET) and a handbook for educating archaeology students with disabilities (Phillips et al. 2007). This allows students to identify the abilities that they bring to the field. The toolkit is not only for students who have disabilities, but rather enables all students to assess their strengths and how they could be of benefit to an archaeological project.

Though archaeology has long remained the domain of men with power and privilege, studies acknowledging archaeology's history of exclusion and discrimination against people who don't fit the white male mold are small steps forward for the discipline. Addressing inequality within the field will hopefully open archaeologists' eyes to the problems in their discipline and fuel them to work toward change.

Discovering Archaeological Sites

Archaeological sites can be discovered in many ways. They are generally classified in six major categories: fortuitous discovery, predictive modeling, consultation, aerial-based remote sensing, ground-based remote sensing, and surface survey (Table 5.2).

FORTUITOUS DISCOVERY

Fortuitous discovery happens when sites are found without any deliberate attempt to do so. Common examples include farmers discovering sites as they plow fields; construction workers uncovering sites as they build roads, bridges, and buildings; and people casually detecting artifacts in eroded embankments or lying along the water's edge.

PREDICTIVE MODELING AND CONSULTATION

Predictive modeling involves forecasting where sites are likely to be found by factoring in such things as terrain, weather, and access to resources and transportation routes. **Geographic information systems (GIS)** software is often incorporated in predictive modeling.

Consultation involves seeking information from historical documents and advice from other people. Many sites have been discovered based on historical records.

TABLE 5.2 Methods of Discovering Archaeological Sites

CATEGORY	EXAMPLES
Fortuitous discovery	Plowing fields; during development
Predictive modeling	Using computer programs; maps; knowledge of natural and cultural history
Consultation	With local residents, members of descendant communities, and other academics; written records
Aerial-based remote sensing	Air photos; satellite images; thermography; radar
Ground-based remote sensing	Manual testing with shovels or trowels, augers and corers; geophysical methods such as metal detectors and magnetometers; chemical methods
Survey	Identifying features and artifacts as well as vegetation patterns and anomalies in stratigraphic profiles

Perhaps the most famous occurrence of this was Heinrich Schliemann's search for, and ultimate discovery of, the city of Troy, based on the description written by the ancient Greek author Homer. In North America, many sites have been found based on readings of ethnographies written in the late 1800s and early 1900s, which often detailed the site locations of previous generations.

Consultation also involves talking to people. Members of descendant communities often provide information on site locations, as do non-Indigenous residents familiar with a region's unmodified landscapes. Archaeologists interested in specific time periods often consult geologists and physical geographers to find out where sediments laid down during that period are now exposed. For example, if an archaeologist is interested in finding cultural remains initially deposited between 500,000 and 700,000 years ago, it would make sense to consult with geologists to find out where deposits of that time period are now exposed. Similarly, if an archaeologist is interested in finding evidence of prehistoric coastal or river sites, it may be worthwhile to consult with a geographer to determine the location of past coastlines and river courses. Archaeologists interested in discovering organic remains consult paleontologists and other paleoenvironmentalists to find areas with good organic preservation.

AERIAL-BASED REMOTE SENSING

There are several aerial-based remote sensing techniques, including the simple use of aerial images taken from planes or satellites. Photographs can be used to identify

archaeological features, but more often they are used to locate patterns in the landscape that may have been caused by human use and occupancy. Human impact on the environment often involves changes in natural sediments through such activities as constructing features and discarding food refuse. Human impact can also alter the soil chemistry and soil density so that it is not suitable for supporting certain kinds of plants. Thus, archaeological sites can often be distinguished in aerial photographs by patterns of vegetation. For example, linear patterns of vegetation that differ from surrounding areas may indicate an ancient path or road; an isolated patch of shrubs within a forest of trees may indicate a village or field; and a canopy of vegetation that thrives on soils with a high **pH** may lie over a shell midden.

It was once necessary for archaeologists to either commission their own aerial photos or get permission to use existing photos from those who had them, which was not always easy or inexpensive. In the majority of cases, the Google Earth program has replaced the need or desire to use commercial aerial photos.

Drones, also known as Unpiloted Aerial Vehicles or UAVs, have become a relatively low-cost option for looking for and documenting archaeological sites. The kind of drones used by archaeologists are typically relatively small remote-controlled planes or copters intended for hobbyists rather than military or high-end surveillance. Archaeologists fit the drones with imaging equipment, allowing them to take photos from hundreds or thousands of meters in the air.

LIDAR, an acronym for Light Detection and Ranging, is another recent technology being used by archaeologists to locate and document sites. Essentially, this technique uses laser technology to map ground features, typically from low-flying planes. One of the advantages of LIDAR is that the lasers penetrate forest canopies and other kinds of vegetation that may make it difficult to identify sites with regular photos or satellite images.

Other aerial-based remote sensing techniques are generally more sophisticated and involve methods of detecting subsurface features. These include infrared photography, airborne multispectral scanners, shuttle imaging radar, airborne thermography, and synthetic aperture radar.

GROUND-BASED REMOTE SENSING

Ground-based remote sensing techniques are categorized as manual, geophysical, or geochemical. Manual techniques include simply digging holes with a trowel or shovel to check for subsurface cultural remains. This is the simplest technique and is often employed in combination with surface survey. Twisting augers and corers, which are essentially hollow tubes, into the ground is another manual method commonly used both in the search for sites and in attempts to delineate site boundaries. The hollow tubes retrieve the buried sediments, which are then examined for cultural materials.

Geophysical techniques use a wide range of instruments to measure properties of the subsurface sediments, such as magnetism, density, and soil chemistry. Common examples include metal detectors and magnetometers, which sense metals and other materials with magnetic properties. Other instruments are used to send electric currents, sound waves, and radar into the ground, which can identify dense materials such as walls and roads. Typically, with all of these techniques, archaeologists first determine the measurements that can be expected in non-cultural sediments and then rely on anomalies to identify subsurface features and artifacts.

Geochemical techniques examine the soil chemistry to identify cultural deposits. As with geophysical techniques, archaeologists first determine the chemistry of non-cultural sediments in the area and then use anomalies in the measurements to identify cultural deposits. Most commonly, it is phosphorous that is measured in geochemical sensing. The basic premise is that human settlements tend to have significantly higher measurements of phosphorous in the sediments than occurs naturally. Reasons for this include the substantial amounts of organic matter deposited as waste, refuse, and ash; extensive deposits of manure applied to fields; and the high phosphate content in human skeletons.

SURFACE SURVEY

Also known as ground reconnaissance and field walking, surface survey is undeniably the most usual way in which archaeologists discover sites. It involves physically walking over the ground surface looking for evidence of past human activity.

Despite the vast changes in landscapes as a result of industrial and other activities, it is still common for archaeologists to identify features and artifacts on the ground surface, particularly in areas where there has been little or no deposition of natural sediments.

In places where cultural deposits are likely to have been buried by natural processes, archaeologists sometimes incorporate one or more of the ground-based remote sensing techniques into their survey. Because human occupation alters soil properties, those doing site surveys usually pay very close attention to changes in vegetation patterns.

Surface survey also involves examining natural or culturally created soil profiles for subsurface deposits. These commonly include, for example, eroding river banks and cuts made into the sediments for road building.

An archaeologist doing a survey typically covers several miles per day, often in difficult terrain. Survey work is frequently done in groups, with people evenly spaced

FIGURE 5.2 Looking for Archaeological Sites in a Forest. Archaeological field-work often involves working in groups looking on the ground surface for evidence of past activity. An archaeology crew is depicted here walking through what was once an early twentieth century logging camp.

PHOTO: Mark Galvani.

FIGURE 5.3 Finding Archaeological Sites Using a Magnetometer. Magnetometers are helpful in detecting archaeological sites when very little material culture is visible on the surface. Magnetometers detect magnetic signatures, such as those found in different types of metals, that may be left on a historic site. In this photograph, archaeologist Joanne Sidlovsky Grant is helping locate Kaweah Colony, a late nineteenth-century socialist commune in what is today California's Sequoia National Forest.

PHOTO: Stacy Kozakavich.

and walking roughly in the same direction, often by compass bearing. When sites are found, surveyors complete an archaeological site inventory form, which typically requires details about location and access, as well as descriptions of the site surface and a map. Typical field supplies carried by archaeologists during the survey include topographic maps, a compass, and a Global Positioning System (GPS). Measurement tools such as a 30-meter tape are carried to measure site boundaries and locations of features within a site. Flagging tape is often carried to mark locations where artifacts or features are found. Cameras are also usually taken on the survey.

USING SAMPLES TO SEARCH FOR SITES

When searching for archaeological sites, it is often not practical to cover the entire study area by ground-based remote sensing or surface survey. In most cases, the study area is sampled using either a judgmental sample or a probabilistic sample.

With **judgmental sampling**, also known as **non-probabilistic sampling**, the area chosen for investigation is based on the archaeologist's judgment of where to search. For example, if a study area was 100 square kilometers (39 square miles) and the research design called for a surface survey of 10 per cent of the area, an archaeologist using a judgmental sample would simply choose the best 10 square kilometers (3.9 square miles) to examine based on his or her judgment. The judgment could be based on any number of factors, including past experience working in the area. It may be the case, for example, that 90 per cent of the study area is made up of rugged terrain and 10 per cent is river valley. The project director may reason that since it is unlikely that there were any sites outside of the river valley, the entire 10 per cent sample will be carried out in the valley.

There are both advantages and disadvantages to judgmental sampling. The advantages include the fact that because of the archaeologist's previous background and reasoning skills, more sites are likely to be discovered. Archaeologists can choose to leave out areas with difficult access or low archaeological visibility, so this strategy is also generally easier and less expensive to undertake than **probabilistic sampling**.

Judgmental sampling has two principal disadvantages. For one, the results cannot be used to make predictions with confidence. If, for example, archaeologists found five prehistoric settlements using a 10 per cent sample, they could not then extrapolate the data to infer that there are about 50 settlements in the entire study area. The only inference that can be made with confidence is that there are at least five settlements in the study area. Another disadvantage is that since the archaeologists are looking in areas where they expect to find permanent or semi-permanent habitation sites, then they are not likely to find other sorts of sites, such as quarries or temporary camps.

When the area chosen for investigation is not biased by anyone's judgment, it is called probabilistic sampling, or statistical sampling. There are three basic types of probabilistic sampling: simple random, stratified random, and systematic.

Simple random sampling occurs when each part of the study area has an equal chance of being selected for investigation. For example, a 20 per cent sample of a study area could be determined by dividing the entire area into 100 units of equal size, assigning each unit a number on a piece of paper, putting the pieces in a container, and drawing out 20. Those areas with the corresponding numbers will be investigated.

Stratified random sampling involves subdividing the entire study area, usually based on geographic features such as river valleys and mountains, and sampling a predetermined proportion of each area. For example, if half the study area is river valley and half is mountains, then each area is sampled separately. Stratified sampling is generally used to give greater attention to areas where there is a higher probability of discovering sites (e.g., the valleys), and less attention to those with a lower probability (e.g., the mountains). Thus, 30 per cent of the valley may be chosen for sampling, while only 10 per cent of the mountain areas may be sampled.

When areas are subdivided and sampled at regular intervals, it is called systematic sampling. For a 10 per cent sample of a 100 square kilometer area, the entire area may be divided into 100 distinct units, and every tenth unit is investigated.

Probabilistic sampling has two main advantages. One is that predictions can be made with confidence. Because the areas chosen for investigation are based on chance, extrapolating the data to make predictions about the total number of sites is valid. Archaeologists who find 6 resource utilization sites and 2 settlements using a 10 per cent sample can reasonably infer that approximately 60 resource utilization sites and 20 settlement sites existed in the entire study area.

Another advantage to probabilistic sampling is that archaeologists are more likely to obtain a realistic sense of the variety of sites in the area, because it forces them to look where they might not have based on their own preconceptions.

The principal disadvantage to probabilistic sampling is that it is usually more time-consuming and costly than judgmental sampling. Even if a unit chosen for investigation is on a mountaintop or in a marshy area, the archaeologist is still obligated to search there, which often means more time and money.

Excavation

One of the many things that distinguishes professional excavators from looters, pothunters, and other treasure seekers is that those trained in archaeological method and theory appreciate how necessary it is to carefully choose where to dig and how to recover and record the material remains uncovered during excavation.

DECIDING WHERE AND HOW MUCH TO DIG

By its very nature, archaeological excavation is destructive, and careful attention should be given to both the location and extent of the digging.

Deciding where to dig within a site depends on the research goals. An archaeologist interested primarily in the diet of the site's inhabitants, for example, is likely to excavate in a midden composed of food refuse; an archaeologist interested in pottery technology may focus on areas around kilns; and an archaeologist interested in reconstructing social inequality may choose to excavate burial sites.

Unless a site is likely to be totally destroyed in the near future, it is usually considered unethical to excavate the entire area. In addition to being costly, it violates the principle of preserving portions of sites for other archaeologists who may wish to excavate in the future.

Deciding how much to dig is also dependent on time and money. In CRM work, it isn't unusual for less than 5 per cent of a site to be excavated before being destroyed by development. Several archaeologists have pointed out the problem inherent in such a small sample size. One study of a midden site from southern California demonstrated that despite a systematic sampling pattern and a total number of artifacts exceeding 65,000, **diagnostic artifacts** from the earliest and the most recent occupations were not revealed until almost half the site had been excavated.

As they did when conducting site surveys, directors of excavation projects make an initial choice between using judgmental or probabilistic sampling to decide where to dig. As with site surveys, judgmental sampling is likely to uncover more of what the archaeologist is expecting to find, while probabilistic sampling is generally better for providing statistics to make inferences.

There is no universal way to excavate, but some methods are more suitable than others, depending on research goals and time, among other things. These methods range from small test pits to large-scale excavations.

Excavations sometimes involve creating trenches, and square holes are usually dug. Trenches are often excavated through portions of a site to provide a sense of the overall site stratigraphy. Excavation units are commonly rectangular, measuring one or two meters along each side. Large, continuous areas of excavation are known as block excavations or horizontal excavations.

An excavator's tool kit contains many pieces of equipment. The standard tool is a pointing trowel (a diamond-shaped 5–7 inch metal blade with a wooden handle), typically used to scrape sediments into a dustpan, which in turn is emptied into a bucket. The sediments in the bucket are then usually sieved through a mesh screen. Quarter-inch (6-millimeter) mesh is generally considered the maximum size to use in archaeology. Most sieving involves merely shaking the screen and letting the smaller-sized particles fall through, while artifacts, ecofacts, and other particles larger than the mesh screen are retained. When sediments are difficult to sieve by shaking and water is nearby, water pressure may be used to break apart the smaller particles and push them through the screen.

Several researchers have pointed out the bias in screen size. Muckle (1994) observed radically different recovery rates of various species of bivalve mollusk shells using 4-millimeter and 2-millimeter screens, and James (1997) suggests that 90 per cent of fish remains are likely to fall through quarter-inch (6-millimeter) mesh.

In addition to trowels and screens, the tool kit contains many other items. For particularly delicate items, dental picks and small brushes are often used to clear away particles from an object. In extreme cases of highly compacted sediments, archaeologists have been known to use jackhammers. Archaeologists will often use shovels when there is relatively little time to excavate, or some will use backhoes to dig a trench

FIGURE 5.4
Archaeological Fieldwork. This image captures the slow and sometimes tedious process of excavation. Here, an undergraduate student on the Michigan State University's Campus Archaeology Program 2019 field school, Reid Ellefson-Frank, and his service dog, Llywelyn, scrape away soil to reveal artifacts from an historic homestead on MSU's campus. An excavation unit of this size – 2x2 meters – can take weeks to excavate.

PHOTO: Stacey Camp & the MSU Campus Archaeology Program.

through a site to get a quick idea of the stratigraphy, knowing that objects recovered from the trench will be in secondary context (i.e., not in their original location).

Ideally, artifacts and ecofacts are recorded as they are exposed, and it is only the very small ones that are recovered from the sieves. Generally, once artifacts are uncovered, an inventory form is completed, which minimally includes the artifact's provenience, description, and assigned number. Artifacts are then usually bagged separately. Provenience is established in relation to a site datum. At one extreme, this is accomplished by simply measuring with a tape. At the other extreme, provenience is established with a **total station**, which can record both horizontal and vertical provenience electronically.

Excavators periodically stop and make detailed notes about what they have found, recording such things as the number and types of artifacts and ecofacts, and describing the texture and color of the matrix. These are commonly referred to as level notes. Excavators also typically draw top-view sketches and take photographs of the unit during these intervals.

The timing of these periodic stops for detailed recording is determined by whether the excavation is done by arbitrary levels or by natural levels. Excavating by arbitrary

FIGURE 5.5
Excavation and Sifting. Excavation units are typically 1 or 2 meters square. Dirt and other sediments are usually scraped with a pointing trowel into a dust pan and bucket, which is then emptied into a sifter with wire mesh to look for artifacts or ecofacts that may have been missed by the excavator.

PHOTO: Nadine Ryan.

levels means that the detailed notes will be taken at regular intervals, such as every 10 centimeters, arbitrarily chosen by the project director. Excavating by natural levels means the notes will be taken when the matrix changes, such as when a layer of silt overlies a layer of sand.

Excavating by arbitrary levels has both advantages and disadvantages. The advantages are that it is fast and easy. Essentially, all that is required to follow this system is the ability to read a tape measure. The principal disadvantage to this system is that if the matrix changes partway through the predetermined interval, artifacts and ecofacts from significantly different time periods may be grouped together.

The principal advantage of excavating by natural levels is that material remains from the same matrix, and thus time period, are grouped together. The disadvantage is that it requires very skilled excavators and more time. Differences in the matrix are often very minor and difficult to recognize, such as the difference between sandy silt and silty sand. The ability to recognize such differences in the field generally only comes with considerable experience.

As excavators dig through each level, they often come across ecofacts or other material remains such as potsherds or **microdebitage** that for the purpose of the project may not be classified as artifacts but are nevertheless important. These objects, or at least a representative sample of them, are usually placed in **level bags**.

Field Laboratories

Field laboratories are common on excavation projects. Mostly, they provide a place where initial sorting and cataloging occurs. Typically, for example, items from level bags are sorted in the field lab, separating such things as organic remains from lithics and ceramics. It is also where initial conservation measures can be made on fragile objects. In some cases, especially where it is logistically difficult or illegal to remove material remains from the country, more in-depth analysis occurs in field laboratories, including illustration, photography, detailed description, and microscopic analysis.

Ethnoarchaeology and Experimental Archaeology: Research Design and Field Methods

Ethnoarchaeology projects, which observe contemporary people to promote an understanding of the past, are invariably academic in nature. Some large-scale archaeology projects incorporate ethnoarchaeology as one of several research activities that may also include the discovery and excavation of sites and laboratory analysis. Many projects, however, are entirely ethnoarchaeological in nature.

Ethnoarchaeology can assist our understanding of how archaeological deposits are created and explain the patterning of material remains that archaeologists observe. One of the primary objectives of ethnoarchaeology is to understand the various human behaviors and motivations of contemporary people associated with material remains, to develop models that attempt to explain such processes in the past. In the article "Where the Garbage Goes: Refuse Disposal in the Maya Highlands," Brian Hayden and Aubrey Cannon (1983) report on the disposal of refuse among contemporary Maya, noting that their system is influenced by economy of effort and the potential value or hindrance of the refuse. Once refuse from a household is sorted, it may be dumped in different locations. Hayden and Cannon outline the ways in which their observations assist archaeologists focusing on past communities in that area, by helping them to determine (i) differential sorting and deposition methods, (ii) refuse locations, (iii) biases in the refuse found, (iv) useful quantification techniques, (v) types of behavior the artifacts left in houses or other structures most likely represent, (vi) the significance of refuse found in pits, and (vii) the principles of human behavior that most likely explain major variations in refuse disposal.

Most ethnoarchaeological fieldwork is classified as **participant observation**, a technique borrowed from cultural anthropology in which the researcher becomes immersed in a culture, as both a participant and an observer. In participant observation, the researcher usually relies on one or a few key members of the group being studied, who often serve as interpreters of both the language and the behavior being observed.

The primary differences between participant observation as practiced by archaeologists and cultural anthropologists are those of time and focus. With the exception of some notable multiyear ethnoarchaeology projects, archaeologists usually spend much less time interacting with a group of interest than cultural anthropologists. Archaeologists also tend to be much more focused on material culture than cultural anthropologists, particularly when it comes to observations of site formation processes in general and refuse discard in particular. In some cases, ethnoarchaeologists serve as apprentices to potters and metalworkers to better understand how the material remains become part of the archaeological record.

Conducting interviews and asking questions is another method used by ethnoarchaeologists. For some projects, this may constitute the only fieldwork, while other projects consider it supplemental to participant observation.

As with ethnoarchaeology, experimental archaeology (which attempts to replicate past conditions and events) is primarily academic in nature and may take place in the context of a complete project or be a single component of a large-scale project that might also include the discovery and excavation of sites and laboratory analysis. While some experiments may be done in laboratories, the majority are not. Many experiments are undertaken at archaeological sites, while excavations are ongoing. The most common types of archaeological field experiments involve manufacturing and using stone tools, constructing buildings, and taphonomy. Other field experiments study the effectiveness of early tools in food production, metal working, the creation of pictographs, and the movement of large stones.

BOX 5.2 EATING A SHREW IN THE NAME OF ARCHAEOLOGY

In what has to be one of the most interesting kinds of experimental archaeology and taphonomic research, two archaeologists set out to determine the effects of human digestion on a small animal. The objective was for all archaeologists to be able to better interpret small mammal skeletons in archaeological sites. Basically, one of the archaeologists ate a shrew and then that archaeologist's feces were examined to see the impacts of digestion.

The archaeologists published their work in a paper called "Human Digestive Effects on a Micromammalian Skeleton" in the *Journal of Archaeological Science* (Crandall and Stahl 1995).

As described by the authors, the shrew was skinned, eviscerated, segmented, and boiled for approximately two minutes. It was then swallowed, without mastication, in three parts – limbs, head, and body and tail. The results indicate the effects of human digestion on small mammal skeletal remains is significant. Only 28 of the 131 skeletal elements were recovered. The authors are confident that their analysis was thorough, concluding that the majority of bones succumbed to digestion. Although an unusual experiment, studies like this are important when attempting to interpret animal bones in archaeological sites. The conclusion reads, in part, "The digestive systems of mammalian predators, in this particular case human, appears to severely destroy and weaken bones of small prey items, even when swallowed relatively intact" (Crandall and Stahl 1995, 795–6).

The research received popular attention in 2013 when the archaeologists received an Ig Nobel award, sponsored by the *Annals of Improbable Research* magazine. The awards "honour achievements that first make people laugh, then make them think."

Hazards of Fieldwork

Archaeological fieldwork can be hazardous. Injury, illness, or death may come from several sources. Few areas in the world offer fieldwork without some level of danger. For those doing fieldwork in developing countries, precautions against malaria and other diseases common to the area are routine.

Depending on the geographic location, other common hazards include encounters with bears, poisonous snakes, spiders, and ticks and other insects.

Particularly for those doing historic archaeology, toxic chemicals are a real hazard, and it is not unusual for archaeologists to wear full protection clothing, including hazardous-material suits, when working in areas suspected of containing toxic substances. Archaeologists working in areas with a history of warfare must also be very careful. For example, between 1964 and 1973 about four billion pounds of bombs were dropped in and around the Southeast Asian country of Laos. As many as one-third of them never exploded, and they remain on the land surface today, countless of them in close proximity to areas of archaeological interest.

Archaeologists working with burials from the nineteenth and early twentieth centuries must also be particularly cautious. From the mid-1800s to 1910, arsenic was a prime ingredient in embalming practice, with some embalmers using as much as 12 pounds per body. Because arsenic does not degrade, it has become an extreme health hazard for those who may come in contact with burial grounds of the period. John Konefes and Michael McGee (2001) suggest that if 2,000 people were buried in a single cemetery over a 30-year period, and if only half of those were embalmed with even a very conservative amount of arsenic for the time (about six ounces), then it is reasonable to assume that there is about 380 pounds of arsenic in the cemetery today.

TABLE 5.3 Hazards of Archaeology

HAZARDS	EXAMPLES
Exposure to disease	Exposure to disease-carrying insects, contaminated buried remains, rusty nails, and infected needles
Exposure to toxic wastes of various kinds	Ranging from nuclear waste to the legacies of many sorts of industrial sites
Wildlife encounters	Spiders, snakes, ticks, insects of many kinds, bears, and cougars
Working in difficult terrain and deep units	Falling down cliffs, collapsing walls of excavation units
Field living in general	Extreme weather, unsanitary water, contaminated food, poisonous plants

In the introduction to *Dangerous Places: Health, Safety, and Archaeology*, David Poirier and Kenneth Feder (2001, vii–viii) give the following description of just some of the hazards involved in contemporary archaeological fieldwork:

> Bacterial and viral infections rest quietly hidden in the soil, are concealed in the animals that roam through our sites, reside in the insects that desire our blood, or even lie in wait in the organic remains we discover. Parasites that once resided unharmoniously within the intestinal tracts of past populations may now be lying in wait, ready to blossom once again.... The mortal remains of individuals who died of historical scourges that once afflicted humanity may still host the pathogens that killed them.... Historically disposed of outside the factory and mill door, toxic chemical wastes and manufacturing by-products may continue to permeate.... Infectious diseases, radioactive and chemical contaminants, and volatile explosives are replacing the traditional and somewhat pedestrian archaeological health concerns of poison ivy, sunburn, and mosquito bites.

Despite the fact that shoring the walls of deep excavation units is becoming standard practice in North America and is often required by legislation or government policy, inadequate shoring is another potential problem for fieldworkers. Many archaeologists in even shallow units have experienced collapsing walls, and some have been buried up to their waist or higher in moderately deep units. In 2005, a European archaeologist was buried alive when the walls of the unit he was excavating collapsed and his coworkers could not dig him out quickly.

KEY RESOURCES AND SUGGESTED READING

Good overviews of field archaeology include those by Burke and Smith (2004) and Maschner and Chippendale (2005). For more on the culture of archaeological fieldwork, Edgeworth (2006) is recommended. The use of advanced satellite technology to locate sites is covered by Parcak (2019). The Enabled Archaeology Foundation has a website (https://enabledarchaeologyfoundation.org) that is a good resource for creating inclusive archaeological practices.

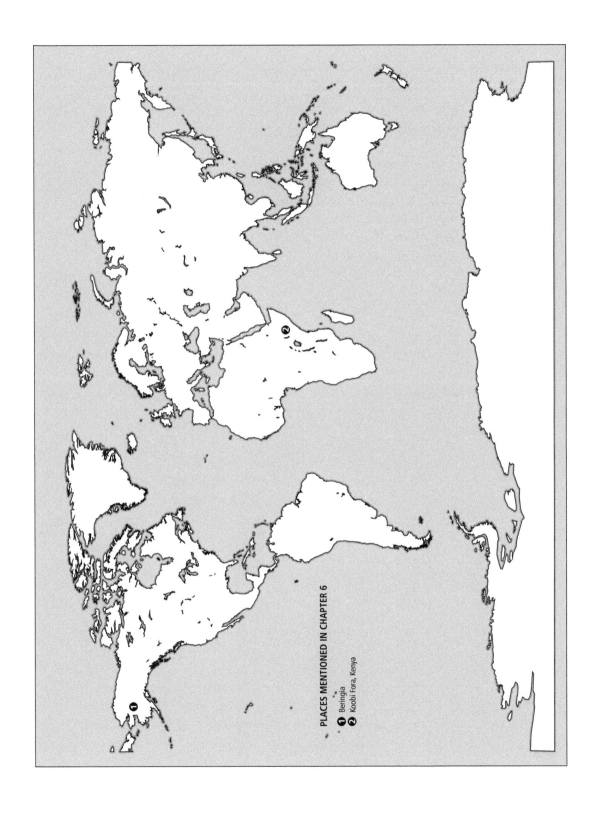

PLACES MENTIONED IN CHAPTER 6

❶ Beringia
❷ Koobi Fora, Kenya

CHAPTER 6

WORKING IN THE LABORATORY

Introduction

The most common popular perception of archaeology is the image of the archaeologist at work in the field. It is primarily in the laboratory, however, that the material remains recovered during excavation are made meaningful.

As described in this and subsequent chapters, laboratory analysis provides the basis for the archaeologist's reconstructions of culture history, technology, paleoenvironments, subsistence strategies, diet, social and political systems, and ideology.

This chapter provides an outline of the common types of laboratory work archaeologists do, beginning with the initial processing of recovered material and then focusing in particular on the analysis of artifacts, ecofacts, and human remains. Methods of determining antiquity are covered in Chapter 7.

Laboratory Processes

Archaeological laboratories may be categorized as either field laboratories or regular laboratories. Field laboratories are most common on large-scale academic research projects, especially where it is logistically difficult or illegal to remove archaeological remains from the area. For example, field laboratories are used for excavations in remote or difficult-to-access locations, such as on islands or in high-altitude regions where archaeologists may want to leave all or a portion of the collected material behind so as not to be burdened by transporting it. In areas where authorities permit excavation but do not wish artifacts to leave the area, field laboratories are used. Field laboratories typically are set up for the duration of the excavation.

Regular laboratories are permanent rooms with specific analytical materials and equipment, and are commonly found in colleges, universities, and commercial

FIGURE 6.1 Working in the Lab. While our image of archaeology usually involves archaeologists sifting through dirt in rugged terrain, the reality of archaeological research is that most of it takes place after excavation has occurred. This drawing represents the complexity and work that goes into post-excavation laboratory research, which can take many, many years after excavation.

IMAGE: Katherine Cook.

archaeology firms. It is not unusual to use a variety of laboratories for analyzing different types of recovered material, such as sediments, faunal remains, botanical remains, human remains, ceramics, and lithics. Besides equipment for various types of measuring, archaeological laboratories generally have comparative collections to aid the identification of various types of material remains.

Laboratory processing generally begins with sorting. This includes sorting items from level bags, typically into the categories of faunal remains, botanical remains, potsherds, and lithic debitage. If the excavations were undertaken at an historic site (from the time for which written records exist), the additional categories of glass and metal pieces are common.

Depending on the research objectives and the skill of the laboratory workers, it is not uncommon to use subcategories in the initial sort, for example, classifying bones as either mammal, bird, or fish, or subdividing the artifacts into lithics, ceramics, glass, metals, or organics. Recognizing that residues on artifacts may provide important clues for current or future studies, artifacts are usually cleaned only to the degree necessary for analysis.

Individual artifacts are entered into a permanent catalog. This process usually begins by looking at the artifact inventory forms completed in the field and adding more detail about the artifacts than could reasonably have been provided when they were first collected. This commonly includes making more precise descriptions of form. The initial processing of artifacts in the laboratory also often includes making line drawings and taking photographs. Perishable or fragile artifacts are often treated with one of a variety of preservatives, and pieces of once-intact objects are often refitted and glued. Artifacts are typically labeled with permanent ink in an inconspicuous place, and if they are not going to be analyzed in the near future, they are packed for storage. The entire process of cataloging, labeling, conserving, and storing artifacts is known as **curation**.

Artifact Analysis

Artifacts are analyzed in many ways. This section provides an overview of the major types of analysis, beginning with classification and including the basic ways in which archaeologists analyze lithic, ceramic, organic, and historic artifacts.

CLASSIFICATION

Artifact analysis often begins with a system of classification known as **typology**, which may be descriptive, functional, or a hybrid of both.

Descriptive typology classifies artifacts according to observable, measurable traits, such as their material, shape, size, and any evidence of their manufacture. Using a descriptive typology, a stone artifact may be classified, for example, as a small, triangular, lithic **biface**. These attributes constitute an artifact **type**. Using a functional typology, on the other hand, this artifact might be classified as an arrowhead. A hybrid classification could categorize the artifact as a small, triangular arrowhead.

There is no consensus on how to best classify artifacts. Some archaeologists believe that typology should be standardized, with everyone using the same criteria to describe artifacts. Others believe that typology should be designed to fit the specific research objectives of the project. Many archaeologists do both, using standard attributes such as material, size, shape, and color to broadly communicate the results of their work, while at the same time using criteria to specifically address the hypothesis or research question of interest.

In general, prehistoric archaeologists are more inclined to use descriptive typology, and historic archaeologists are more likely to use functional typology. This is partly because historic archaeologists work with material from more recent times, so they have more confidence in their inferences of function.

Creating and identifying artifact types allows archaeologists to make sense of the almost infinite number of characteristics prevalent in the recovered remains. Attributes to be recorded are established in the research design on the basis of how important they are to the researcher's objectives. An archaeologist interested in determining how stone tools were made, for example, will likely want to focus on a completely different set of attributes than an archaeologist wanting to focus on how stone tools were used. Attributes such as the position of flake scars on the tools and the size of debitage will be important to the archaeologist interested in lithic technology, while attributes such as linear striations and polish on the tool will be more important to the archaeologist interested in determining the tool's function.

It should be appreciated that there is no one correct way to determine artifact types. It is generally accepted that a minimum of two attributes is required to make a type, but there is no maximum. Provided the same assemblage of 1,000 artifacts, one archaeologist might create 3 types, another might find 100 types, and another might generate 500 types – and they all would be valid.

LITHIC ANALYSIS

In addition to being classified by typology, lithic artifacts are generally analyzed to determine the way they were made and what they were used for, as well as to identify the specific kind of stone.

Archaeologists recognize several ways of making stone tools, including pecking, grinding, drilling, cutting, and chipping. Pecking involves pulverizing one stone with another to rough out a shape, the technique most commonly used to make petroglyphs as well as stone bowls and statues. Grinding uses an abrasive stone to shape another and was often employed alone or in combination with another technique to make smooth and sharp edges, such as with slate arrowheads. Drilling was usually accomplished by using a pointed, hard stone to drill through a softer stone; most stone beads were created this way. Although examples are relatively rare in the archaeological record, cutting was accomplished by scoring a soft stone with the sharp edge of a harder stone. Cutting is sometimes known as incising.

Also known as flaking, chipping is the most common lithic technology observed in the archaeological record, undoubtedly employed in the manufacture of more than 99 per cent of all lithic artifacts and debitage that has been recovered. Chipping involves removing flakes from a core and then using either the core alone or both the flakes and the core for tools.

The principal methods for chipping stone are hard-hammer percussion, soft-hammer percussion, indirect percussion, pressure flaking, and bipolar percussion. Hard-hammer percussion involves holding the core in one hand and striking it with another hard stone held in the other hand. Soft-hammer percussion employs a material softer than the stone to strike blows, typically bone or antler. Indirect percussion involves using a punch of some sort to remove flakes

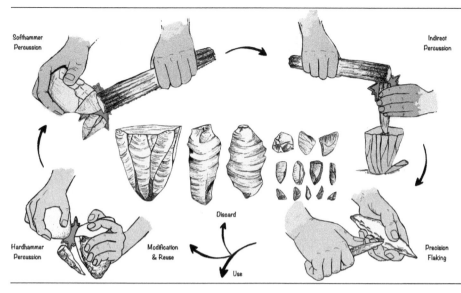

FIGURE 6.2 **Lithic Technology.** This drawing illustrates the principal methods of manufacturing stone tools by chipping or flaking, sometimes known as flintknapping. The drawing also shows the major characteristics of the cores once the flakes are removed and the characteristics of the flakes, which are used by archaeologists to identify the method or methods of manufacture.

IMAGE: Katherine Cook.

by hitting one end of a piece of bone or antler, while placing the other end against the stone to remove the flake. Rather than striking the stone, pressure flaking applies pressure to the stone and forces the flakes off, usually with a piece of bone or antler.

Analysis of stone tool technology usually focuses on determining the method of manufacture, with key variables including the size and shape of waste flakes, including debitage (Table 6.1).

The process of making stone tools by chipping or flaking is known as **flintknapping**, and there are some standard terms used to describe materials produced by this technique. **Core tools** are tools produced by removing flakes from around the original cobble (block of stone). **Flake tools** are tools that have been made from one of the flakes chipped off the original cobble. **Unifaces** are tools that have had flakes removed from only one side, and bifaces are tools in which flakes have been removed from both sides. **Blades** describe flake tools that are at least twice as long as they are wide, and have at least roughly parallel sides. Debitage or **detritus** refers to the waste flakes (i.e., flakes that have been created during flintknapping and are recognized as trash). Very small, usually microscopic pieces are often referred to as microdebitage.

When it is not obvious from the shape, determining the use of a stone tool depends upon magnified views of the tool's edges or chemical analysis of residue on it. It is not unusual to be able to distinguish the type of blood on stone tools. Researchers Thomas

TABLE 6.1 **Attributes of Various Methods of Chipping Stone**

METHOD	TYPICAL ATTRIBUTES
Bipolar percussion	Damage at both ends of flake or core
Hard-hammer percussion	Flakes of various sizes and shapes; most large and thick flakes created this way
Soft-hammer percussion	Flakes of various sizes and shapes, although thick flakes are rare
Indirect percussion	Very small flakes and microdebitage
Pressure flaking	Very small flakes and microdebitage

Loy and E. James Dixon (1998), for example, detected the blood of a variety of large mammal species, including mammoth, on artifacts at least several thousand years old from eastern Beringia – a large mass of land in northwestern North America and northeastern Asia that was freed from ice during the last ice age. Most archaeologists believe the initial migration of people into the Americas was via Beringia.

Based on many experiments over the past few decades, a few generalizations can be made about some physical attributes found near the edges of stone tools. Linear striations running parallel to the sharp edge of a stone artifact, for example, generally indicate that it was used for cutting. A polished or glossy surface along the sharp edge is usually taken to mean that it was used for scraping. When the traits are observed under magnification, they are often termed **microwear**.

Some researchers believe they can use microwear to distinguish tool use for very old artifacts. Lawrence Keeley and Nick Toth (1981) reported that they were able to confidently identify microwear distinctive of meat cutting on some artifacts, and microwear distinctive of cutting soft plant material on others, as well as microwear distinctive of scraping or sawing wood. Artifacts with microwear have been determined to have been used about 1.5 million years ago in the Koobi Fora region of East Africa, which has been studied extensively and where some of the earliest known members of the genus *Homo* and their tools have been uncovered.

Identifying the kind of stone is often dependent on a comparative collection. In general, the coarser the grain of stone, the more difficult it is to control the way it breaks. For very coarse-grained material, such as granite or sandstone, pecking is usually the only effective way of shaping the stone, but it can rarely make a sharp-cutting edge.

One of the most common stones used to make sharp-cutting edges is basalt, which can also be further classified as coarse, medium, or fine-grained. Many projectile points and other fine tools made with sharp-cutting edges are made from a variety of very fine-grained stones. Among the most common are those known as quartzite, chert, flint, chalcedony, and obsidian. Occurrences of these stones are more restrictive, and archaeologists can often trace the original source of the stone through **trace-element analysis**.

Archaeologists often use the same term to describe different things when classifying stone. Although there is no consensus, most American archaeologists and geologists use *chert* as a general term for a wide variety of fine-grained stones, including flint, chalcedony, and jasper. British archaeologists and geologists, on the other hand, usually consider flint to be distinct from chert.

CERAMIC ANALYSIS

Ceramic is a large category of material that is broadly defined as clay baked through the process known as firing. Ceramics include figurines, bricks, tiles, and pipes. The majority of ceramic analysis is undertaken on the class of ceramics known as pottery, defined as ceramic containers. Essentially, if the ceramic artifact was meant to hold something, then it is classified as pottery, even if it is flat like a plate.

In addition to typology, ceramic analysis commonly involves identifying the ceramic body (the composition of the clay) or **fabric**, the method of manufacture, use, and style. The main categories of fabric are **terra cotta**, **earthenware**, **stoneware**, **china**, and **porcelain**. These categories are based on the type of clay and level of porosity, which is dependent on the temperature at which the ceramic was fired. Measured in Celsius, the firing temperature for terra cotta is less than 1,000 degrees (1,832 Fahrenheit); for earthenware, between 900 and 1,200 degrees (1,652 to 2,192 Fahrenheit); for stoneware, 1,200 to 1,350 degrees (2,192 to 2,462 Fahrenheit); for china, 1,100 to 1,200 degrees (2,012 to 2,192 Fahrenheit); and for porcelain, 1,300 to 1,450 degrees (2,371 to 2,642 Fahrenheit). Terra cotta is often considered to be a kind of earthenware.

The primary method of determining ceramic body type involves an examination of color: terra cotta and earthenware usually retain a reddish color; stoneware a light brown or gray; and the categories fired at higher temperatures become white and in some cases translucent. Higher firing temperatures also cause the ceramics to become vitreous.

Most prehistoric pottery is terra cotta or earthenware, likely because it is difficult to create heat in the extreme temperatures required for stoneware, china, and porcelain.

Five primary methods are used in the manufacture of pottery. Pinching and drawing involves manipulating a lump of clay by hand, primarily by using fingers and thumb

to pinch the clay while drawing it upwards to form a bowl shape. When separate pieces of clay are rolled or patted flat and then joined, it is called slab modeling. Molding involves pressing clay firmly into or over a mold. Coiling is the technique of winding worm-like segments of clay upwards in a circular fashion. Throwing refers to pottery manufactured with the use of a pottery wheel. Complete pots and potsherds exhibit several attributes that can be used to distinguish the method of manufacture (Table 6.2).

Archaeologists generally recognize that pottery function falls into four major categories: storage, transport, food preparation, and serving. There are several attributes that distinguish function. Storage containers, for example, usually have restricted openings or closures at the top and, if used to hold liquid, a slip or glaze to reduce permeability. Pots used for transport usually have handles and little or no decoration. Pots used for food preparation generally have wide openings and little or no decoration. Pottery used for serving is relatively flat (e.g., plates) or has unrestricted openings (e.g., bowls), and often has some sort of decorative design. Charring or burning on the base usually indicates the pot was used for cooking, and extensive wear on the interior of the pot is often indicative of food processing.

As with lithics, the study of pottery function occasionally includes residue analysis. By using chemical analysis to identify proteins and lipids, archaeologists are often able

TABLE 6.2 **Attributes of Various Methods of Pottery Manufacture**

METHOD OF MANUFACTURE	ATTRIBUTES OF POTS OR POTSHERDS
Pinching and drawing	Small pots; uneven walls; indentations on walls left by finger and thumb
Coiling	Cracks or breaks along parallel lines; variations in wall thickness; round/smooth edges of potsherds
Slab modeling/building	Rectangular containers; seams; differences in thicknesses of slabs
Molding	Differences in texture between inside and outside of pot or potsherd; parting agents (to prevent clay from sticking to the mold); seams
Throwing	Rilling (a series of small ridges and grooves on the outside of the pot); flat bases; walls may be uneven from top to bottom but not around the circumference

to determine the types of foods and liquids the pots once held. For example, residue analysis of pots is used to determine the antiquity of beer and wine in a region.

ANALYSIS OF ORGANIC ARTIFACTS

The most common types of organic artifacts are those made from bone, wood, shell, and plants. The analysis of organic artifacts usually focuses on taxonomic identification of the material, the technology used in making the artifact, and style.

Identifying the type of material is usually done using a comparative collection. In many cases, it is only possible to distinguish fairly broad categories, such as mammal bone or antler, but identification to the level of genus and species is also common.

As with lithics and pottery, the manufacture of organic artifacts often leaves evidence pointing to the method on the artifact itself. For example, stone and metal tools will leave different sorts of scarring on carved wood artifacts.

Because of the highly perishable nature of **textiles** and woven baskets, they are not commonly discovered and analyzed. When they are, the focus tends to be on the nature of the weave (e.g., coiling, plaiting, or twining). As with pottery, stylistic analysis tends to focus on overall shape and decoration.

ANALYSIS OF METAL AND GLASS

While metal and glass recovered from archaeological sites may be analyzed for its mineralogical components, this is not common. Typically, metal and glass artifacts are subjected to typological studies only.

Metal artifacts are usually sorted into broad categories such as nails, cans, apparel accessories, coins, and household items, and then further classified according to size and manufacturing technology. Nails, for example, are often classified as hand-forged, early machine-cut, and modern machine-cut, in addition to being categorized by size.

The analysis of glass from historic archaeological sites is common. The major categories are flat glass, typically used for windows, and bottle glass. Bottle and bottle-fragment analysis is particularly common. Attributes such as lip form, type of closure, mold marks, and existence and location of seams can often be traced to specific years and places of manufacture.

QUANTIFICATION OF ARTIFACTS

Since most material remains recovered from sites are broken pieces, one laboratory task for archaeologists is to determine how many original artifacts the assemblage of pieces represents. Although there are various ways of quantifying the number, they usually involve refitting as many pieces as possible and then looking at several variables to determine the minimum number of artifacts represented. For example, three potsherds of the same clay fabric and style of decoration conceivably may have come from the same pot and therefore are calculated to represent one pot, whereas three potsherds with different clay fabrics would be calculated to represent three pots. The names and acronyms of some of the methods include the following: estimated vessel equivalent (EVE), estimated tool equivalent (ETE), minimum number of intact tools (MNIT), minimum number of tools (MNT), and minimum number of items (MNI). As described in the next section, the acronym **MNI** is also frequently used in the analysis of animal remains, where it has a different meaning (**minimum number of individuals**).

Ecofact Analysis

The analysis of ecofacts in archaeological laboratories is routine. This section covers the most common types of analysis for animal remains, botanical remains, and sediments recovered from archaeological sites.

ANIMAL REMAINS

Animal remains in archaeological sites include a variety of things such as bone, teeth, claws, shells, hair, and soft tissue. However, it is clearly bone that dominates most assemblages of animal remains and thus receives most attention. The analysis of animal remains routinely involves taxonomic identification and quantification. Taxonomic identification is usually done with the use of a comparative collection. Minimally, a simple list of the species or genera represented is determined in the laboratory. Often, however, there are further, more meaningful quantification calculations to be made.

Although a few standard methods do exist, there is a great deal of diversity in how archaeologists quantify animal remains. In a study of the various methods used to quantify animal remains and the names of those methods R. Lee Lyman (1994) found more than 100 terms.

The two most common ways of quantifying animal remains are **NISP**, which is the acronym for the number of identified specimens, and MNI, the acronym for the minimum number of individuals. Determining the NISP is simply a matter of counting the number of bone pieces, whether complete or fractured. A single, non-fractured rib, for example, would be counted as one piece. If that same rib had been broken into 15 pieces, the count would be 15.

MNI is a method of quantification that indicates how many individuals are represented by all of the remains identified as belonging to one species. The MNI is usually determined by counting the number of bones for which there is only one per individual, such as a pelvis or otherwise distinctive bone (e.g., the front right forelimb of an animal is different than the front left and back forelimbs). For archaeologists, MNI is usually considered the more meaningful statistic. It prevents overrepresentation of animals with more bones or bones that are subject to breakage.

BOTANICAL REMAINS

Many types of botanical remains are recovered from archaeological sites, including pollen, phytoliths, seeds, nuts, bark, and wood. Laboratory analysis usually focuses on taxonomic identification using a comparative collection. Quantification is usually limited to a listing of species or other taxonomic categories present, although some researchers calculate the proportion that individual taxonomic categories such as genus and species represent for each of the types of remains. Proportions are calculated by weight, volume, or number of specimens.

SEDIMENT ANALYSIS

A variety of compositional, **pedological**, and chemical analyses are done on sediments from archaeological sites. The most common, however, determine texture, color, and pH.

Texture is a description of the particle sizes that make up the sample, typically described as a clay, silt, or sand. A combination of sediment sizes is often described as a loam. Determining the texture involves sifting samples of sediments through a series of nested sieves with various mesh sizes, and then classifying the sediments based on the proportion of different-sized particles. As outlined in Chapter 8, soil texture is important for reconstructing paleoenvironments, especially for determining whether the processes of deposition were high energy, like wind storms or fast-flowing rivers, or low energy, like gentle breezes and meandering rivers.

Descriptions of color are usually based on comparisons with standard color charts widely used by archaeologists and other earth scientists throughout the world.

The **Munsell system**, which measures three different dimensions of color known as hue, value, and chroma, is the most common. Color is represented by a series of numbers and letters, such as 10YR 5/4. Such a standard system of color identification is useful for communicating information on color in textual form (with Munsell charts, one can see precisely what 10YR 5/4 looks like).

Soil color reflects the major soil-forming processes and can indicate concentrations of certain elements or compounds. White generally indicates calcium carbonate, and red indicates oxidation. Distinctions in color are also useful for identifying natural and cultural stratigraphic layers within a site, with even minor changes often indicating a distinct process in the formation of archaeological deposits.

Measurements of pH involve determining the acidity of sediments. Since the preservation of organic remains is affected by pH, such measurements are routine. Because pH levels within a site can be altered by human activities, such as the introduction of gardens and middens, pH tests are also sometimes done to help identify areas of human habitation.

A scale from 0 to 14 is used to categorize pH: a level less than 7 is acid; 7 is neutral; and a level higher than 7 is alkaline or basic. All techniques to determine pH involve mixing the sediment with distilled water, which is pH neutral. The simplest and most inaccurate method involves dipping litmus paper into a solution of the sediment mixture, watching the paper change color, and then matching the color against a standard chart. A better method involves mixing a liquid pH indicator with the sediment mixture and comparing the resulting solution color against a standard chart. The most precise tool for measuring pH is an electronic pH meter, which is a glass electrode that is immersed in the sediment mixture and produces a digital value.

Analysis of Human Remains

Although soft tissue is sometimes preserved, most human remains recovered from archaeological sites are bone and teeth. When such remains are excavated, they are commonly in need of preservation and are often in fragmentary condition. Once the remains are stabilized, attempts will be made to identify the particular bones and teeth represented, as well as to infer how old the person was when he or she died and whether the person was male or female. Thus, archaeologists generally are very familiar with human osteology, including not only the characteristics of each bone and tooth of the human skeleton, but also how those characteristics can be used to distinguish the age and sex of the individuals.

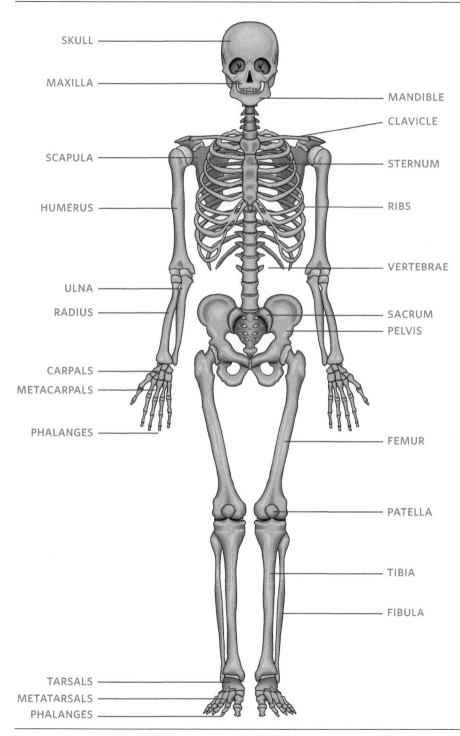

SKULL

MAXILLA

SCAPULA

HUMERUS

ULNA

RADIUS

CARPALS

METACARPALS

PHALANGES

TARSALS

METATARSALS

PHALANGES

MANDIBLE

CLAVICLE

STERNUM

RIBS

VERTEBRAE

SACRUM

PELVIS

FEMUR

PATELLA

TIBIA

FIBULA

FIGURE 6.4 Human Skeleton.
Archaeologists must know how to identify the bones and teeth of the skeleton to distinguish them from other animals in fragmentary form. Most have learned how to use the characteristics of a skeleton to determine how old the individual was when they died and whether they were male or female. Human skeletons are often used in the analysis of diet, disease, status, and ideology.

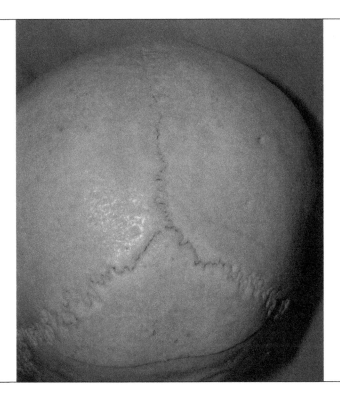

FIGURE 6.5 Cranial Sutures. One way of estimating how old an individual was when he or she died is to look at the degree of closure of the cranial sutures.

PHOTO: Bob Muckle.

DETERMINING AGE AT DEATH

It is difficult to determine precisely how old an individual was when he or she died based solely on skeletal remains. Instead, individuals are usually classified into general age categories. While there is no standard, the basic categories are fetal (before birth), infant (0–3 years), child (3–12), adolescent (12–17), young adult (18–30), middle adult (30–50), and old adult (over 50).

Determining age at death includes examining both bones and dentition. Bone analysis focuses on closure of individual bones and bone parts of both the cranial and post-cranial skeleton. Dental analysis examines both tooth eruption and tooth wear.

The analysis of cranial bones looks at those of the top part of the skull, known as the cranial vault. The main bones of the cranial vault are separate at birth but gradually fuse together during a person's lifetime. The places where the bones come together are known as cranial sutures. By looking at the degree of closure and ultimate fusion at the sutures, archaeologists are able to estimate age. Typically, the bones of adolescents and young adults are interlocked like a jigsaw puzzle, but they can still be pulled slightly apart. For people in the middle adult range, the bones are usually fused, and in old adults the sutures themselves are often difficult to distinguish.

The analysis of the post-cranial skeleton involves examining the degree of fusion of various bones, often known as epiphyseal union. Many post-cranial bones, especially those of the arms, hands, legs, and feet, grow in sections, such as the shaft growing independently from the epiphyses of the long bones. The cartilage separating the pieces turns to bone and fusion is complete by an approximate age. Most unions are completed in adolescence, but some, such as the clavicle (commonly known as the collarbone) and parts of the pelvis, don't fuse until young adulthood.

The most reliable common method of using teeth to determine age of death is identifying deciduous and permanent teeth (alternatively known as baby teeth and adult teeth). The common age ranges at which deciduous teeth erupt and fall out is well established. All the incisors, for example, generally erupt between 6 and 16 months and fall out between 6 and 8 years. Canines and the first molars usually erupt between 16 and 24 months and fall out between 9 and 12 years; and the second molars usually erupt between 23 and 33 months and fall out between 10 and 12 years.

The age of eruption of adult teeth is also well known. Incisors and the first molars generally erupt between the ages of 6 and 9; canines between 8 and 11; premolars between 9 and 12; the second molars between 11 and 13; and the third premolars, commonly known as the wisdom teeth, between 18 and 22. Although some people in the contemporary world never have a third molar eruption and many others find it necessary to have their third molars removed because there is not enough room in their mouth, the third molars remain a part of the human dental formula, and they are commonly found in skeletal remains from archaeological sites.

Since the timing of eruption for all teeth, and shedding in the case of deciduous teeth, is so well known, archaeologists can make inferences about the age of individuals simply based on which teeth are present.

Archaeologists sometimes also use the degree of wear to determine age, but this typically allows only very general inferences and often requires some knowledge of the person's culture. Examining molars is particularly useful, as there is a characteristic pattern of wear on the cusps. Examining the wear on the cusps can give clues to an approximate age. A person whose 6-year molars are worn flat, whose 12-year molars show some wear but with visible cusps, and whose third molars (wisdom teeth) still exhibit prominent cusps probably died as an early adult.

Since it has been the custom of many people in past societies to effectively use their teeth as tools, such as for softening fibers, people from these periods and regions would tend to show considerably more wear than those who did not.

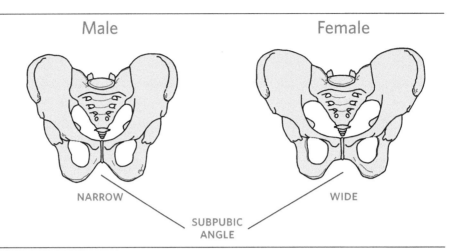

FIGURE 6.6 Male and Female Human Pelvis. Compared to a male, the pelvis of a female is usually wider overall and has a wider subpubic angle.

Male

Female

NARROW

WIDE

SUBPUBIC ANGLE

DETERMINING SEX

There is no single characteristic that indicates with certainty whether an individual was male or female. The pelvis is considered the best indicator, followed by characteristics of the skull and overall robusticity (ruggedness) of the entire skeleton. Most archaeologists would probably agree that with a skull alone, and knowledge of the region from which it came, the sex should be determined accurately about 90 per cent of the time. With the pelvis alone, the sex should be determined accurately about 95 per cent of the time, and with both the skull and pelvis, the sex should be determined accurately 99 per cent of the time.

Of course, what makes the pelvis so good for identifying sex is that the female pelvis typically has many features to facilitate carrying and delivering babies. Two of the most prominent characteristics are that it is wider and more basin-shaped. The subpubic angle is also a key indicator. This is the area of the birth passage and is necessarily wider in females. The angle in females is typically U-shaped, while the angle in males is usually V-shaped.

Compared to many other animals, the degree of sexual dimorphism among humans is generally slight, but it does exist, and it varies on a regional and ethnic basis, at least in prehistory. Differences in skeletal characteristics between males and females among prehistoric Indigenous populations of North America are quite distinct, for example, with the males typically being considerably more robust or rugged than females. Differences in robusticity in Asian populations are very slight by comparison, and differences in those of European ancestry are midway.

OTHER DETERMINATIONS

Human skeletons provide data on many more things of interest to archaeologists. These include determining the stature of an individual by measuring the length of

FIGURE 6.7 A Day in the Life of an Archaeological Laboratory. University of Idaho alumni Emma Scott and Allison Fashing working in the University of Idaho's Alfred W. Bowers Laboratory of Anthropology, counting, weighing, cleaning, identifying, and dating artifacts.

PHOTO: Leah Evans-Janke.

BOX 6.1 **COPROLITES**

Coprolites (the term used in archaeology for preserved human feces) are an important kind of remains from which much can be learned. Following are some facts about coprolites in archaeology.

- Human coprolites are an excellent source of information for studying diets and paleoenvironments.
- The oldest reported human coprolite dates to about 1 million years ago in Africa, but there is some question about whether it is really human.
- There are reports of a 250,000-year-old human coprolite in Asia.
- One of the oldest reliably dated archaeological sites in North America, Paisley Caves in Oregon, which dates to more than 14,000 years ago, has several human coprolites of that age.

- One of the largest accumulations of prehistoric coprolites comes from the Hinds Cave in Texas, with more than 2,000 human feces. They span an 8,000 year period, and are shaped like cow patties. Analysis indicates a diet rich in fiber, although they had a diverse diet. In the hours before defecation, one individual had apparently eaten antelope, rabbit, rat, squirrel, and eight varieties of plants.
- A Viking coprolite discovered in the United Kingdom is probably the largest recorded. It measures 23 cm, provides evidence of a diet of meat and bread, and indicates the person had intestinal worms.
- Routine coprolite analysis often involves reconstituting the dried feces in solution. Sometimes the smell comes back.

long bones; the ethnic affiliation by looking at a complex of characteristics; and stress during an individual's lifetime by looking for periods where the growth of bone and teeth temporarily slowed down. Diet and nutrition are determined by examining carbon and nitrogen isotopes and through trace element analysis (see Chapter 8).

Other determinations include those of disease, **trepanation**, and cannibalism. For example, rickets, caused by a deficiency of vitamin D, is indicated by bowed legs; arthritis is often determined by particular types of bone growth; and bacterial infections often create pitting of bone. Trepanation involves removing a piece of skull bone while the individual is still alive and is widely thought to be an indication of ideology (see Chapter 9). Indicators of cannibalism include butchery marks on bone and evidence of burning.

Where there are abundant skeletal remains, archaeologists sometimes focus on providing an overview of the entire population, known as paleodemography, in addition to examining individuals. This includes determining the relative proportions of males and females, and the age ranges, as well as patterns of fertility, mortality, health, and disease.

Using DNA in Archaeology

Recent advances in the ability to extract and analyze DNA have important implications for archaeology. Archaeologists can now use DNA to determine biological relationships over time in an area. Such was the case on the northwestern coastal region of the North American continent, for example, where researchers have been able to use DNA to link skeletons thousands of years old with living descendants. Archaeologists can also use DNA to link biological relationships throughout a region, to identify diseases, and to make interpretations about population replacement.

Besides human remains, DNA analysis is undertaken on other material remains in archaeological sites, including coprolites, which can provide important information about diet, as well as plant and animal remains.

BOX 6.2 ARTIFACTS IN CRISIS: ORPHANED AND NEGLECTED ARCHAEOLOGICAL COLLECTIONS

One of the most pressing challenges facing archaeologists in the twenty-first century is known as the **curation crisis** (Lipe 1974; Marquardt, Montet-White, and Scholtz 1982; Childs 1995). The curation crisis refers to the constantly growing number of archaeological collections that are neglected, ignored, and/or lack a permanent or safe storage location. The rise of contract archaeology in the United States,

UK, and Canada, along with the growth of archaeology departments at academic institutions, have contributed to this problem (Karrow 2017). Though federal legislation and professional organizations have established guidelines to curtail the growth of **orphaned collections** (in the United States, 36 CFR Part 79, legislation that outlines how archaeological collections are to be handled and curated, is an example of this), such rules have had little impact on neglected collections.

What has caused this immense accumulation of neglected archaeological collections, and why do these assemblages continue to be ignored by archaeologists? For one, archaeologists have traditionally favored archaeological fieldwork over laboratory research. This is partially due to the training requirements for archaeologists. Most professional archaeologists are expected to attend an archaeological field school before graduating with an undergraduate archaeology degree, which involves excavation of archaeological materials. Excavation, in some cases, generates years if not decades of laboratory research. Archaeologists are responsible for funding laboratory research, but often there is little money to spare after excavation is over.

There is also the issue of storing archaeological collections. Professional organizations, federal and state agencies, and legislation have outlined best practices for artifact curation. These curatorial standards include regulating and controlling the temperature of a facility storing collections, ensuring fire suppression systems in the storage facility, maintaining security so collections are protected from looters, and management strategies for avoiding rodent and/or insect infestations of collections. Storage facilities and the management of such repositories cost money and require staff. In some parts of the world, these facilities simply do not exist or cannot be paid for with grants. This means it is the individual archaeologist, federal or state agency, tribe, and/or CRM firm's responsibility to fund and find proper storage for archaeological collections.

How can archaeologists solve the curation crisis? In places where there is simply no physical location to store archaeological collections or on projects where there is no funding to support the long-term storage of collections, archaeologists have practiced what is known as a catch-and-release or no-collections strategy. This means mapping, cataloging, photographing, and analyzing artifacts in the field as an archaeologist excavates and/or encounters them. This is a controversial practice, as the success of this methodology depends on the expertise of the archaeologist. It also does not give other archaeologists the opportunity to replicate the research.

Another practical solution to the problem is encouraging archaeologists to study and analyze orphaned collections that have sat in boxes since they were first excavated. One example of this important, restorative work is Dr. Barbara Voss's Market Street Chinatown Project (https://marketstreet .stanford.edu/) at Stanford University (Voss 2012; Voss and Kane 2012). This project involves cataloging and curating an orphaned archaeological collection consisting of hundreds of boxes of artifacts recovered from San Jose, California's historic Chinese immigrant community. Students and faculty involved in this project have developed presentations, theses, articles, and exhibits on the material culture of this community. This work has been done in consultation and collaboration with the Chinese American community of San Jose, California, and has shed new light on what life was like for Chinese migrants facing discrimination and racism in the mid-nineteenth century western United States.

KEY RESOURCES AND SUGGESTED READING

Good overviews of archaeological laboratory work include Balme and Paterson (2006), Maschner and Chippendale (2005), Banning (2000), and Sutton and Arkush (1996). For archaeobiology, Sobolik (2003) is recommended; for osteology, White and Folkens (2000); for bioarchaeology, Larsen (1997); for lithics, Odell (2004); for pottery, Orton and Hughes (2013) and for DNA in archaeology Matisso-Smith and Horsburgh (2012).

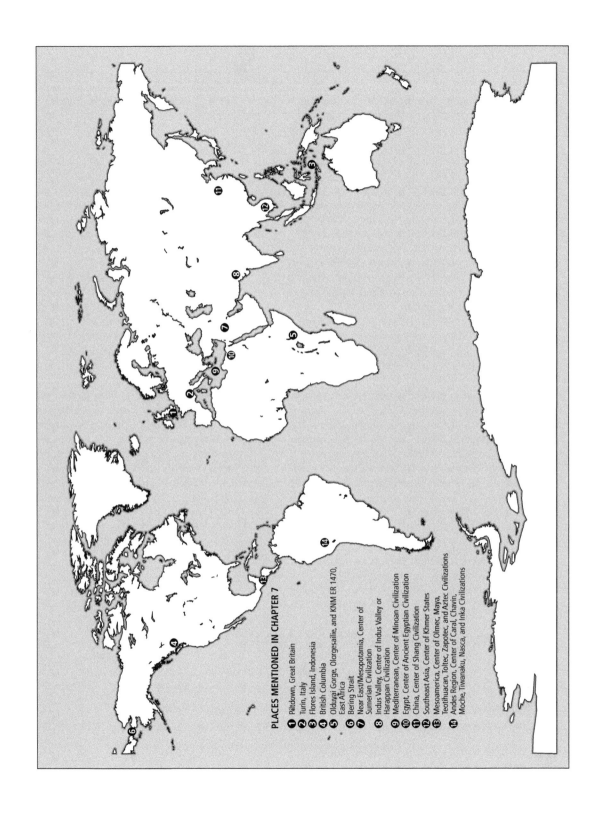

PLACES MENTIONED IN CHAPTER 7

1. Piltdown, Great Britain
2. Turin, Italy
3. Flores Island, Indonesia
4. British Columbia
5. Olduvai Gorge, Olorgesailie, and KNM ER 1470, East Africa
6. Bering Strait
7. Near East/Mesopotamia, Center of Sumerian Civilization
8. Indus Valley, Center of Indus Valley or Harappan Civilization
9. Mediterranean, Center of Minoan Civilization
10. Egypt, Center of Ancient Egyptian Civilization
11. China, Center of Shang Civilization
12. Southeast Asia, Center of Khmer States
13. Mesoamerica, Center of Olmec, Maya, Teotihuacan, Toltec, Zapotec, and Aztec Civilizations
14. Andes Region, Center of Caral, Chavín, Moche, Tiwanaku, Nasca, and Inka Civilizations

CHAPTER 7

RECONSTRUCTING CULTURE HISTORY

Introduction

Archaeologists deal with time in many ways. This chapter begins with an overview of the practical methods of determining how old things are. It follows with a brief description of how archaeologists conceptually organize time and ends with an outline of world prehistory and early civilizations.

Determining Antiquity

Relative dating and **absolute dating** are the two broad categories of dating methods used in archaeology. Relative dating methods have the advantage of being generally cost-free or inexpensive (other than the archaeologist's time), and are applicable to a wide variety of materials. The main disadvantage is that they do not provide precise dates. Conversely, the main advantage of absolute dating methods is that they provide specific dates, but they are often expensive and can only analyze specific kinds of material.

RELATIVE DATING

There are four principal subcategories of relative dating techniques: **chronological sequencing, dating by association, calibrated relative**, and *terminus quem* (Table 7.1).

Chronological Sequencing

Chronological sequencing provides assessments of antiquity in relation to other artifacts and sites, and is thus comparative. Chronological sequencing, for example,

TABLE 7.1 Relative Dating Techniques

CATEGORY	TECHNIQUES
Chronological sequencing	Law of superposition/stratigraphic dating
	Stylistic seriation
	Frequency seriation
	Fluorine, uranium, nitrogen dating
Dating by association	Association with animals of known age
	Association with artifacts of known age
	Association with geological features of known age
Calibrated relative	Obsidian hydration
Terminus quem	*Terminus post quem*
	Terminus ante quem

enables archaeologists to determine that site A is older than site B, or one arrowhead is older than another, but without specific dates attached.

One of the common methods of chronological sequencing is to apply the law of superposition, sometimes known as **stratigraphic dating**. This method is based on the fact that layers of sediments are normally laid on top of each other through time. Accordingly, as archaeologists excavate, they are encountering successively older deposits. In other words, the deeper the deposit, the older it is. Of course, archaeologists recognize that deposits can be mixed after initial deposition and sediments are not always deposited in uniform or horizontal layers, so they are cautious when drawing inferences from this technique alone.

Seriation, or placing objects in chronological order, is another chronological sequencing method with a long history in archaeology. There are two commonly used types: **stylistic seriation** and **frequency seriation**. Stylistic seriation is based on the knowledge that artifact styles change through time, and by knowing what the end or starting styles are, archaeologists can put artifacts in a chronological order. For example, if an archaeologist found 20 clay pots of roughly the same size, shape, and assumed function, she or he should be able to put them in a chronological sequence based on stylistic attributes. As a contemporary analogy, someone provided with a task of putting a collection of 20 automobiles from the past several decades in chronological order could probably do it based on stylistic attributes alone.

Frequency seriation is based on the premise that artifacts of similar function typically go through an initial period of acceptance, then begin to flourish as they become widely used and manufactured (displacing competing styles in the process), and eventually decline as they themselves are replaced by another style or form. For example, large stone projectile points were typically used for spears, medium-sized points were used for darts thrown with a spear-thrower (**atlatl**), and small points were used for arrows. First came spears, then spear-throwers, and then the bow and arrow. Archaeologists can therefore use the relative number of large, medium, and small points to determine the relative age of sites in a region (recognizing of course, that the kind of point may also be reflective of specific kinds of hunting). A modern example is the use of music-recording technology. In the early twentieth century, vinyl was dominant. In the 1960s and 1970s, various forms of tape recordings (e.g., reel-to-reel, eight-track, cassette) rose and flourished, in the 1980s and 1990s, compact discs were all the rage, and in more recent years, digital recordings are in vogue. An archaeologist of the future should be able to determine the decade that a deposit was created by looking at the relative proportions of vinyl, tape, compact discs, and digital devices.

In addition to stratigraphic dating and seriation, there is a third chronological sequencing technique, which is not commonly used anymore but is of historical interest: **fluorine, uranium, nitrogen dating**. It is based on the premise that after the death of an animal, the amount of nitrogen in the bones continually decreases over time through the natural processes of decay. Conversely, the amounts of fluorine and uranium increase over time as they enter the bones from the surrounding matrix, especially through groundwater percolation. This technique is used to assess the relative ages of various bones in a site, reasoning that the bones that have been in the deposit longer will have more fluorine and uranium and less nitrogen than bones deposited more recently.

The fluorine, uranium, nitrogen technique was most famously applied to the **Piltdown Man**, discovered in the early twentieth century in Piltdown, England. The Piltdown Man had characteristics of a human skull but with a very ape-like lower jaw. The skull was widely touted by experts of the day as a "missing link" between modern humans and our apelike ancestors. After decades of controversy over the authenticity of the find, both the lower jaw and the rest of the skull were subjected to fluorine, uranium, nitrogen dating in the mid-twentieth century, reasoning that if the parts belonged to the same individual they would have the same proportions of the three chemical elements. They didn't, and it eventually became clear that the Piltdown

Man was a hoax and that the lower jaw was that of a recently deceased orangutan, while the rest of the skull was from a prehistoric human.

Dating by Association

Many artifacts and sites are dated by their association with objects of known age, such as bones of animals, particular types of artifacts, and geological features. Dating by association is also known as cross-dating.

It is not unusual to find artifacts and bones of an animal that is now extinct in the same stratigraphic layers. Sometimes, paleontologists will have already used absolute dating techniques to establish the time range for the extinct animal, and this then becomes the basis for dating the cultural deposits as well. If, for example, artifacts are found in the same stratigraphic layer as the bones of an extinct form of elephant presumed to have only existed between 600,000 and 200,000 years ago, then the artifacts are presumed to fall within that range as well.

Similarly, archaeologists have used absolute dating techniques to firmly establish the age range for some types of artifacts. The presence of those artifacts in a site, or in a layer within that site, is used to date by association all other material remains.

In many cases, earth scientists assign dates to landforms, including specific dates or ranges of dates to features created during particular ice ages, floods, or other geological events. By their association with these geologic features, cultural remains found by archaeologists are assigned the same dates. For example, a shell midden along a paleocoastline dated by geologists to 8,000 years ago may be assumed to be the same age.

Calibrated Relative Dating

Calibrated relative dating essentially involves techniques that combine those of relative and absolute dating. The most widely applied of these is **obsidian hydration**, which is based on the knowledge that a freshly fractured face of obsidian will adsorb water from the surrounding environment into the core of the stone, creating an observable hydration layer. Because the amount and rate of water adsorption is dependent on the local environment, there is no widely recognized standard against which the thickness of the hydration layer can be measured, and thus obsidian hydration is considered a relative technique. However, at many sites, some of the obsidian pieces with thick hydration layers and some of the pieces with thin layers have been dated by absolute techniques. Researchers are then able to make assumptions about the rate at which hydration layers thicken and can use this to assign dates to other pieces of obsidian.

Terminus Quem Dating

Two types of *terminus quem* dating are commonly used in historic archaeology. **Terminus post quem**, often abbreviated as TPQ, literally means the date after which material remains must have been deposited. Assuming there was no post-depositional disturbance, a Roman coin dating to AD 100 could not possibly enter a deposit before that time, so if a coin of that date is found, this technique indicates that the deposit dates to AD 100 or later.

Terminus ante quem, often abbreviated as TAQ, is applied in two different ways. In one sense, when a specific date is assigned to an artifact found in a particular layer in an archaeological site, archaeologists can use that date in combination with the law of superposition to infer that all materials beneath that layer must be older. In the case of the Roman coin, for example, all deposits below the level in which the coin is found must be older than AD 100. TAQ is also applied to the absence of widely used artifacts to infer that a deposit must have been created before that product became available. For example, an archaeologist working at a site in which all the nails were made by hand may reasonably infer that the buildings were constructed before machine-made nails became common.

ABSOLUTE DATING TECHNIQUES

Also known as chronometric dating, there are several absolute dating techniques widely used in archaeology (Table 7.2). Three of the most important are **dendrochronology**, radiocarbon dating, and **argon dating**.

TABLE 7.2 Absolute Dating Techniques

ABSOLUTE DATING TECHNIQUES
Dendrochronology
Radiocarbon dating
Potassium/argon dating
Argon/argon dating
Thermoluminescence
Archaeomagnetism
Electron spin resonance
Uranium dating
Fission track dating

Dendrochronology

Also known as tree-ring dating, dendrochronology is widely acknowledged to be the most accurate technique for dating prehistoric deposits. However, because wood with identifiable tree rings does not normally preserve well, this technique is also one of the most rarely used. The technique is based on the fact that annual growth rings in trees vary in thickness each year, depending on local environmental conditions. In some regions, such as parts of the American Southwest and northern Europe, tree-ring sequences have been established for the past several thousand years. Starting with trees of modern age where the years corresponding with each growth ring are known, the sequences are created by working backward by matching corresponding growth rings with successively earlier fragments recovered from archaeological or natural sites. Researchers working in areas where a master chronology of tree rings exists simply have to take a wood sample from a site and match it to determine when the tree from which the wood fragment derived lived.

Dendrochronology is used very effectively in the American Southwest, where preservation of organic remains is excellent due to the dry climate and people used wooden beams in house construction. Archaeologists take samples of beams from prehistoric houses to determine when the tree lived. Alternatively, as long as the growth rings are still visible, archaeologists can use remnants of burned wood to determine when a fire associated with a cultural deposit was burning. Of course, archaeologists also must consider that ancient peoples may have recycled beams from older houses, and may have burned wood from long-dead trees.

Radiocarbon Dating

Also known as **carbon-14 dating** or **C-14 dating**, radiocarbon dating is undoubtedly the most commonly applied absolute dating technique in prehistoric archaeology. It is based on the principle that carbon-14 (a radioactive isotope of carbon) decays at a known rate. All living things contain the same relative proportions of carbon-14, and at the instant of death, carbon-14 begins to decay. The rate of decay of radioactive materials such as carbon-14 is often measured in terms of half-lives, which is how long it takes half of the material to decay. For carbon-14, the half-life is 5,730 years, which means that half of the carbon-14 is gone in that time, half of the remaining half goes in the next 5,730 years, half of that half goes in the next 5,730 years, and so on.

Because anything that was alive can be dated by radiocarbon dating, it is widely used. Since charred wood from human-made fires is common in archaeological sites, it is frequently used to date deposits. However, anything organic can be used, including human remains, shells, animal bones, and botanical remains, including materials made of plant fiber.

Radiocarbon dating is applicable for the time period from about 300 to 50,000 years ago. Due to the usual margin of error in calculating radiocarbon dates, which is normally in the order of 200 to 500 years, materials which are presumed to have died within the last few centuries are not usually subjected to this technique. Radiocarbon dates are always expressed with a plus-or-minus figure, such as 15,700 ± 150. At the other end of the scale, current techniques simply are not capable of measuring the very low quantities of carbon-14 remaining in an organism 50,000 years after its death.

For the first few decades of radiocarbon dating in archaeology, beginning in 1950, it was widely assumed that the relative amounts of carbon-14 in organisms had always been exactly the same. We now know that there have been some minor fluctuations in those amounts over time, and archaeologists have sought to correct errors through calibration with tree-ring dates where possible.

Dates produced by radiocarbon dating are always given as "years before present" (meaning 1950), usually expressed as **bp** or **BP**. Using a specific year as a baseline from which all dates are taken is useful to archaeologists because they do not have to know when the lab work was done to calculate the age of the object.

Tens of thousands of dates have been obtained by radiocarbon dating throughout the world. The most famous application of this technique, however, involved dating the Shroud of Turin, a cloth made of plant fibers embedded with the imprint of a man purported to be Jesus Christ, alleged to be the shroud in which he was buried. The authenticity of the shroud has always been in doubt since it was first mentioned in historical records of the Middle Ages. In 1988, several independent radiocarbon dating laboratories throughout the world became involved in tests to determine its age. Samples of various materials from a variety of known ages were submitted to the laboratories without those of the real shroud being identified, so as to not bias the results with expectations. The three laboratories that tested the actual shroud all dated the age of the materials from which it was made to the fourteenth century. Controversy about the authenticity of the shroud still exists, with those that dispute the fourteenth-century date usually focusing on problems of radiocarbon dating or science in general.

Argon Dating

Argon dating involves measuring the amount of argon in volcanic sediments. The most widely known technique is **potassium/argon dating**, commonly known through the abbreviations for the two elements, K/Ar. The basic principle is that radioactive potassium turns into argon gas at a known rate. When volcanic sediments are initially formed, they do not have stable argon gas. Over time, the potassium turns into argon gas. The half-life of radioactive potassium is 1.3 billion years. Accordingly, by measuring how much potassium and argon are in volcanic sediments, the date at which sediments formed can be calculated.

Another argon dating technique is known as argon/argon, or Ar/Ar dating, which is based on the known rate of decay of radioactive argon into stable argon gas.

The primary limitations of argon dating are that it can only be used for dating volcanic sediments, and because the rate of decay is so slow, it is not considered viable for dating materials less than 200,000 years old. Like radiocarbon dating, a margin of error is always given with the dates.

Most applications of argon dating are to determine the ages of early human sites, especially in East Africa, where the stratigraphy of deposits often includes multiple layers of volcanic sediments. Therefore, a discovery of human biological or cultural remains can often be dated by subjecting samples from a volcanic sediment above and a sample from a volcanic sediment below to argon dating.

Other Techniques

Many other absolute dating techniques are commonly used in archaeology but are not generally considered to be as accurate or are not as widely applicable. These include **thermoluminescence**, which measures the amount of energy trapped in material since it was heated to very high temperatures. The date of the original firing can be calculated by measuring the amount of energy released in the form of light when reheated. This technique is sometimes used for dating lithics but is used most frequently for dating the manufacture of pottery.

Archaeomagnetism is a technique that correlates the alignment of magnetic soil particles with known locations of the North Magnetic Pole (which is slowly drifting across the Canadian Arctic) during the past few thousand years. In principle, small magnetic particles in sediments align themselves to the Magnetic North when heated to very high temperatures. By correlating the direction of those particles in specific archaeological features with the historic records of the location of Magnetic North, a fairly accurate dating should be possible. For obvious reasons, archaeomagnetism can only be used on features like pottery kilns or soils on which very hot fires have been built.

Other techniques with even more restricted applications include electron spin resonance, which is based on the premise that some types of electrons accumulate in material only after they are buried, and is used primarily for dating teeth. Uranium dating is based on the radioactive decay of uranium and is used for dating limestone caves. Fission track dating is based on the measurable fission of uranium particles, and is used for dating stone.

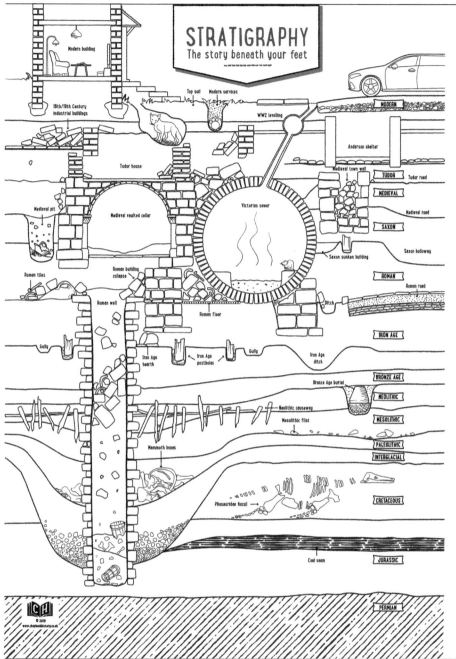

FIGURE 7.1
Stratigraphy: The Story beneath Your Feet. Hypothetical layering of site from millions of years ago to modern times in the UK, including showing how older layers are often disrupted by later occupants of the area, including the building of Roman walls, Medieval activities, construction of sewers, and recent disturbance by animals.

IMAGE: Chapbook History / Ros Lorimer.

Conceptualizing Time

Archaeologists have many ways of conceptualizing time. This section illustrates how the vastness of time can be symbolized by calendars and linear measurement, provides the ranges of dates for geological epochs, and outlines the major descriptive and analytical units in prehistory.

CONCEPTUALIZING DEEP TIME

Relative to the entire time span of the universe as we know it, the period during which humans have existed barely registers a blip. It is often difficult for people to contextualize humankind within the 15-billion-year history of the universe, so it is common to represent the vastness of time symbolically.

One common way of putting humans and their achievements in the perspective of deep time is to imagine the entire 15-billion-year history of the universe as one year, with one day equaling 42 million years, one hour equaling 1.75 million years, and one minute equaling 30,000 years. Assuming that the origins of the universe began on January 1, the first day of that imaginary year, the earliest primates arrived late in the evening on December 30; the first humans arrived about 9:00 p.m. on December 31; the first members of our own species arrived sometime between 11:50 and 11:55 p.m.; and the earliest civilizations arose a mere 10 seconds before the end of the year.

Another way to symbolize deep time is to use linear measurement. Science writer Colin Tudge (1996) suggests translating time into distance, with one millimeter (about the size of a grain of sand) equaling one year, and the entire 15-billion-year history of the universe represented by 15,000 kilometers – the approximate distance from New York to Japan. Using this scale, walking a mere half-meter would take us back 500 years; 5 meters would take us to the earliest civilizations of ancient Mesopotamia and Egypt; and about another 150 meters would take us to the first members of our own species.

GEOLOGICAL EPOCHS

At a minimum, the time period of interest to archaeologists extends 2.5 million years into the past, based on unmistakable evidence of the manufacture and use of stone tools in Africa. To effectively manage archaeological information pertaining to this extensive period in world history, many archaeologists have borrowed frameworks of geological epochs from earth scientists (Table 7.3). Thus, it is not unusual to read about such things as Miocene ancestors, Pliocene humans, Pleistocene sites, and Holocene events in archaeological literature. For perspective, dinosaurs became extinct

TABLE 7.3 Geological Epochs

GEOLOGICAL EPOCH	TIME SPAN
Holocene	10,000 years ago to the present
Pleistocene	1.7 million years ago to 10,000 years ago
Pliocene	5.0–1.7 million years ago
Miocene	24–5.0 million years ago
Oligocene	36–24 million years ago
Eocene	55–36 million years ago
Paleocene	65–55 million years ago

about 65 million years ago, marking the end of the Mesozoic era and beginning of the Cenozoic era, which itself begins with the Paleocene epoch.

In recent years, many have proposed the designation of a new epoch known as the **Anthropocene**, which coincides with the recent time period in which humans have significantly altered environments around the globe. There is no consensus, however, on the validity of using such a term to describe a geological period. Nor is there agreement on when such a period would begin. Some suggest that it should replace the Holocene epoch, for example, while others suggest it began just a few hundred years ago.

MAJOR DESCRIPTIVE AND ANALYTICAL UNITS IN PREHISTORY

Archaeologists and the popular press frequently use a series of time frames to conceptualize prehistory. These typically span several distinct geographic regions and sometimes multiple continents, and range from a few thousand to hundreds of thousands of years in duration (Table 7.4). The temporal boundaries are based primarily on changes in technology, and since not all peoples and cultures make the same technological changes at the same time, the time frames should be viewed as being very general.

The Paleolithic, Mesolithic, Neolithic, Bronze Age, and Iron Age are rarely applied outside of Africa, Asia, and Europe. The term *Paleoindian* is used widely to describe the time period from about 12,000 to 8,000 years ago in North, Central, and South America. The term *Archaic* is used for many, but not all, areas of North and Central America to distinguish the time period from about 8,000 to 5,000 years ago. Because of so many regional differences, there is no comprehensive term to describe time periods throughout North and South America for the past 5,000 years.

TABLE 7.4 **Major Time Frames in Archaeology**

TIME FRAME	DESCRIPTION
Lower Paleolithic	From about 2.5 million years ago to about 250,000 years ago; rarely applied outside of Africa, Asia, and Europe
Middle Paleolithic	From about 250,000 years ago to about 30,000 years ago; rarely applied outside of Africa, Asia, and Europe
Upper Paleolithic	From about 30,000 years ago to about 11,000 years ago; not commonly used outside of Europe
Mesolithic	From about 11,000 years ago to about 9,000 years ago; not commonly used outside of Europe
Neolithic	From about 9,000 years ago to about 5,000 years ago; not commonly used outside of Europe
Bronze Age	From about 5,000 years ago to about 3,000 years ago; not commonly used outside of Europe
Iron Age	From about 3,000 years ago to about 2,000 years ago; not commonly used outside of Europe
Paleoindian	From about 12,000 years ago to 8,000 years ago; application is restricted to the Americas

A rough chronology for **Mesoamerica** for the past 4,500 years identifies the period from about 2,500 BC to AD 300 as Preclassic; the period from AD 300 to AD 900 as Classic; and the period from about AD 900 to AD 1519 as Postclassic.

Reconstructing culture history at a regional level requires more specific descriptive and analytical units, such as **tradition**, **horizon**, and **phase**. Some archaeologists use tradition to describe the temporal persistence of a particular technology in an area, such as a specific pottery tradition or projectile point traditions, with no restrictions (large or small) on geographic area. Most often, however, a tradition reflects a pattern of cultural continuity over a broad area (usually in the order of tens of thousands of square kilometers or miles, or more), spanning at least a few thousand, and often several thousand years. Archaeologist Peter Peregrine (2001b, iv), who has compiled an outline of archaeological traditions around the world, defines the term as

> a group of populations sharing similar subsistence practices, technology, and forms of socio-political organization, which are spatially contiguous over a relatively large area and which endure temporally for a relatively long period. Minimal area coverage for an archaeological tradition can be thought

of as something like 100,000 square kilometers; while minimal temporal duration can be thought of as something like five centuries.

The *Outline of Archaeological Traditions*, compiled by Peregrine, attempts to summarize all the known archaeological traditions. It spans the entire prehistoric period, and covers traditions from all continents. There are currently about 300 archaeological traditions recognized.

Within a tradition, there may be moderate changes in the cultural activities of the people throughout a region, such as in the proportions of different types of foods they eat or the way they make their artifacts. Some archaeologists use the term *horizon* to distinguish these periods. A horizon encompasses the same broad region as the larger tradition, but exists for a shorter period, typically from several hundred to a few thousand years. Within each horizon, archaeologists often distinguish various phases, which are more restrictive in time and area than a horizon, and are based on relatively minor differences in culture. A tradition may be, but is not necessarily, composed of multiple horizons, which in turn may be composed of multiple phases.

The Plateau Pithouse Tradition is one example of using the analytical and descriptive units of tradition and horizon. The tradition, which comprised the last 4,000 years of prehistory in southern British Columbia, is characterized, in part, by a semi-sedentary settlement pattern that included the use of **pithouses** for winter dwellings, a foraging subsistence strategy with a heavy reliance on salmon, storage technology including cache pits, anthropomorphic and zoomorphic carving in stone, and exchange with coastal groups. Within this tradition, three distinct horizons are recognized: the Shuswap Horizon, from about 4,000 to 2,400 years ago; the Plateau Horizon, from about 2,400 to 1,200 years ago; and the Kamloops Horizon, from about 1,200 to 200 years ago. Distinctions between the horizons are based on such things as differences in the size and shape of pithouses, size of cache pits, degree of exchange with coastal groups, projectile-point styles, frequency of stone sculptures, and burial practices.

Reconstructing culture history at an individual site includes identifying diagnostic markers of phase, horizon, and tradition by examining such things as artifact styles. More particularly, this includes comparing the recovered artifacts and ecofacts with the criteria of well-established phases in the region, and if they match, then the assemblage is described as a component of a particular phase, horizon, or tradition.

World Prehistory

The story of world prehistory is based on billions of pieces of evidence, including human skeletal remains, artifacts, features, and ecofacts. The sequence of events described in the following sections should be viewed as only a very basic outline of our understanding of the human past.

HUMAN BIOLOGICAL EVOLUTION

Before examining the details of world prehistory based on the cultural evidence, it is worthwhile to consider human biological evolution. Most anthropologists accept the first humans (defined as the biological family Homininae) probably date to between 7 and 5 million years ago in Africa. They were certainly significantly smaller in height and their brains were probably about one-third that of modern humans. Because they were bipedal primates, they are considered human. We have no evidence of their behavior but reason they were primarily dependent on plant foods and lived in environments that were similar to open woodlands. There were potentially multiple genera of humans living before 4 million years ago, and perhaps as early as 7 million years ago, but we are uncertain which one gave rise to more recent and well-known human genera such as *Australopithecus* and *Homo*.

Beginning a bit more than 4 million years ago and continuing to about 1 million years ago, the genus *Australopithecus*, with several distinct species, emerged and survived in Africa. Some australopithecine species were fairly smooth-featured, while others were more rugged or robust. Some paleoanthropologists believe the remains of the more rugged individuals are sufficient to distinguish a separate genus: *Paranthropus*. Collectively, the remains assigned to *Australopithecus* and *Paranthropus* suggest they ranged in height from about 3.5 to 5 feet, weighed about 50 to 100 pounds, and their brains were approximately the size of a chimpanzee's (about 400 cubic centimeters or 24 cubic inches). As with earlier hominin genera, no remains assigned to the genus *Australopithecus* or *Paranthropus* have been found outside of Africa.

Conventional thinking indicates that one australopithecine population (i.e., one group of one species) evolved into a new genus and species about 2.5 million years ago. Groups of skeletal remains with significantly larger brains (about 700 cubic centimeters or 42 cubic inches) have been found in different areas throughout Africa and have been variously referred to as *Homo habilis* or *Homo rudolphensis*. This species appears to have existed until about 1.5 million years ago, and like the species before, has only been found in Africa.

Sometime around 1.9 million years ago, a new species or group of species evolved, probably from a population of *Homo habilis*. Compared to the earlier forms of *Homo*, these new forms, variously referred to as *Homo erectus* and *Homo ergaster* (some believe the finds all belong to a single species, while others believe they represent two species), had a brain size that overlaps the range of modern variability, with an average size of about 900 cubic centimeters (55 cubic inches), and some individuals were likely more than 6 feet tall.

Homo erectus (and/or *ergaster*) emerges in Africa about 1.9 million years ago and in western Asia, in the country of Georgia, about the same time. (Some refer to the specimens from Georgia as *Homo erectus* while others assign it to a separate species – *Homo georgicus*.) Although the termination date is difficult to determine, it appears likely that they continued to survive there until sometime between 200,000 and 100,000 years ago. It is likely that *Homo erectus*, or other human species, had expanded to East Asia and Europe more than 1 million years ago.

Many skeletal remains from Africa, Asia, and Europe dating between 800,000 and about 30,000 years ago have been found that indicate modern brain size (approximately 1,350 cubic centimeters or 82 cubic inches, but ranging between 1,000 and 2,000), but with the retention of more primitive characteristics like prominent ridges of bone above the eyes. These remains have been variously classified as *Homo antecessor*, *Homo heidelbergensis*, *Homo neanderthalensis*, and archaic *Homo sapiens*. The first remains that appear largely indistinguishable from modern humans appear about 150,000 years ago.

EARLY TOOLS IN AFRICA

The archaeological record of world prehistory begins with stone tools in Africa. A few recent discoveries in suggest people began making stone tools 3 million years ago, and it became increasingly more frequent beginning about 2.5 million years ago. People had learned how to make stone tools by chipping flakes off a cobble, producing tools from both the core of the cobble and the flakes that were taken off. The practice became widespread, and the tools have been recovered from many different areas. The earliest tools have been found in Ethiopia, and some researchers suggest the best candidate responsible for their manufacture is *Australopithecus*. Another area where many early stone tools have been found is Olduvai Gorge in Tanzania, which gave rise to naming these kinds of tools the Oldowan Tool Industry. Despite the possibility that *Australopithecus* was responsible for some of the manufacture, these early tools are generally associated with *Homo*. The fact that they were deliberately manufactured is indisputable, but there is no consensus on what they were used for. Some have suggested they were used for butchering animals, but we do not know for certain the extent to which people were eating meat, if at all. It may have been that the stone tools were used to sharpen sticks to dig roots. Other than the fact that they made and used tools, we know very little of the culture of the earliest members of the genus *Homo*.

NEW LANDS, NEW TOOLS

Homo erectus appears to have spread quickly through Africa and Asia shortly after their emergence 1.9 million years ago. Along with their larger brain, *Homo erectus* developed more sophisticated tool technologies known as the Acheulian Tool Industry, characterized by tear-drop shaped, cobble-sized artifacts with a sharp edge around their entire circumference. The tool is known as a hand ax. Despite the name, we don't really know the function. It was conceivably used to cut, scrape, and pierce, and some have proposed that it was indeed a multifunctional tool. Some researchers believe the "hand axes" are not tools at all, suggesting they are simply cores left behind and it is the removed flakes that were used as tools. Others have proposed that hand axes may have been thrown at large game animals. This throwing hypothesis would explain why there are hundreds of hand axes at single sites, such as at that of Olorgesailie in Kenya. One scenario suggests that the hand axes were thrown at game animals while they were crossing a river that went through the area hundreds of thousands of years ago. All but a few would end up in the river bottom, only to be discovered by archaeologists in the 1900s.

EARLY HUNTING AND FIRE USE

By about 500,000 years ago, it is apparent the *Homo erectus* were hunting and controlling fire, although it isn't clear when precisely this began. Evidence of hunting primarily comes from butchered animal bones, and evidence of fire mainly from charred wood, ash, and burned bone in cultural context.

BOX 7.1 **FIRE!**

The ability to control fire is undoubtedly one of the most significant achievements of humans. There remains uncertainty, however, about the antiquity of controlling fire and the reasons why people initially began to control fire.

Estimates of the antiquity of human-controlled fires range from about 2 million years ago at one extreme to about 30,000 years at the other. Most archaeologists are likely comfortable in placing the origins of human-controlled fires in the range of a few hundred thousand to several hundred thousand years ago. Reasons for debate regarding how long people have been controlling fire include the difficulty of determining whether evidence of fire associated with other human remains was natural or cultural. This is particularly difficult in open-air sites, where natural fires are not uncommon. Even in enclosed sites, such as within caves, the presence of burned organic remains is not enough to rule out burning by natural fires. Burned organic remains could have been blown into caves, or brought into the caves via animals (including, but not restricted to, humans) that frequent caves. Distinct fire hearths where human control of fire is clear only become evident within the last 30,000 years. Most of the evidence prior to this depends on the presence of burned materials such as wood, bone, and stone, but not within a clear and distinct human-controlled fire. The evidence remains circumstantial.

Among those who support a claim for human-controlled fires close to 2 million years ago is anthropologist Richard Wrangham, author of *Catching Fire: How Cooking Made Us Human* (2009). Describing his "cooking hypothesis" to explain human evolution, he writes:

> I believe the transformative moment that gave rise to the genus *Homo*, one of the great transitions in the history of life, stemmed from our control of fire and the advent of cooked meals. Cooking increased the value of our food. It changed our bodies, our brains, our use of time, and our social lives....
>
> Cooked food does many familiar things. It makes our food safer, creates rich and delicious tastes, and reduces spoilage. Heating can allow us to open, cut, or mash tough foods. But none of these advantages is as important as a little appreciated aspect: cooking increases the amount of energy our bodies obtain from our food.
>
> The extra energy gave the first cooks biological advantages. They survived and reproduced better than before. Their genes spread. Their bodies responded by biologically adapting to cooked food, shaped by natural selection to take maximum advantage of the new diet. There were changes in anatomy, physiology, ecology, life history, psychology, and society. Fossil evidence indicates that this dependence arose not just some tens of thousands of years ago, or even a few hundred thousand, but right back at the beginning of our time on Earth, at the start of human evolution, by the habiline that became *Homo erectus*. (2, 14–15)

Unfortunately, as appealing as the cooking hypothesis may be, supporting evidence remains circumstantial and it is far from being considered a most-likely hypothesis by the archaeological community. Widespread acceptance will likely require unequivocal evidence of human-controlled fires close to 2 million years ago; and even if such evidence exists, it will be difficult to identify.

Besides cooking, there are many other advantages of being able to control fire, any one of which may have been the reason why humans initially began to do so. These advantages include providing heat, providing light, and providing protection from predators. Some have suggested a key benefit of fire is that it provides a focus for social interaction, leading to the further development of culture. Fire is also known to have been useful in the manufacture of artifacts, including those made from stone, clay, and wood.

DELIBERATE BURIALS AND SOPHISTICATED ART

The exact date of origin for intentional human burials as a form of ritual activity and symbolic thought is subject to considerable debate among archaeologists. There is some suggestion that humans may have been deliberately discarding human remains down a shaft in a cave in Spain almost 300,000 years ago, but it is unclear if this is or should be taken as an indication of a specific form of ritual or ideology. Many archaeologists believe that by about 50,000 years ago, deliberate human burials were occurring among Neandertals, who according to some were simply a subgroup of *Homo sapiens* occupying portions of Europe and the Middle East from about 250,000 to 30,000 years ago. (Others prefer to classify them as a distinct species, *Homo neanderthalensis*.) However, due to the poor recording of many of the proposed Neandertal burial sites, some archaeologists remain unconvinced of the evidence for intentional burials, instead attributing the origins to modern *Homo sapiens* of the Upper Paleolithic in Europe. Many archaeologists consider the deliberate burial indicative of a belief in an afterlife.

Although the dates of the earliest cave art are debated, it appears that by about 40,000 years ago, sophisticated art was being painted on cave walls. The best-known prehistoric cave art comes from southern Europe in the time period from about 27,000 to 12,000 years ago, and was painted by a particular group of modern *Homo sapiens* known as Cro-Magnon. The meaning of the art is uncertain, but because much of it is in remote parts of the caves and images are painted on top of each other, many believe they reflect ideology-related painting by **shamans** to manipulate supernatural forces, presumably to ensure continued fertility of herd animals and successful hunts. Other beliefs include that it was ritualistic, the work of secret societies, simply art for art's sake, or a method of recording or storing information.

COLONIZING AUSTRALIA AND THE AMERICAS

There is a general consensus that by about 65,000 years ago, humans had expanded their territory to include Australia. Because travel over significant distances of ocean was involved, one of the things archaeologists infer is the ability to make and navigate seaworthy watercraft.

FIGURE 7.2 Spear Thrower in Use. Spear-throwers, also known as atlatls, originated tens of thousands of years ago. They extend the distance, accuracy, and force of a spear thrown by hand and could be used to efficiently kill large animals. Their use declined with the adoption of bows and arrows, which further enhanced distance, accuracy, and force of projectiles.

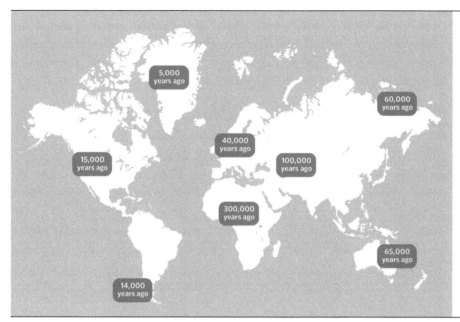

FIGURE 7.3 Human Expansion across the Globe. This map illustrates the origin of *Homo sapiens* (in Africa about 300,000 years ago) and subsequent emergence through migration and expansion of territories in other parts of the world.

There is no consensus on when humans first colonized the Americas. Conventional archaeological thought indicates that the first migrants came from Asia via the area around the present-day Bering Strait, following either an inland route or traveling along the coast during the latter stages of the last ice age, sometime between 20,000 and 15,000 years ago. Some postulate colonization occurred before 20,000 years ago, and others have suggested the first humans arrived via an Atlantic Ocean crossing, but these hypotheses lack enough convincing data to achieve widespread support.

CERAMICS AND POTTERY

The first evidence of ceramic technology comes from Europe, in the form of baked clay figurines dating to about 25,000 years ago. Pottery appears to have been first invented in eastern Asia about 15,000 years ago, but didn't become widespread until several thousand years ago, by which time it is found in **sedentary** communities of Asia, Africa, Europe, and the Americas.

DOMESTICATING PLANTS AND ANIMALS, SETTLING DOWN, RISING POPULATIONS, AND INCREASING SOCIAL COMPLEXITY

There is no consensus on when people first began the process of domesticating plants and animals for food, but many suggest that it was about 15,000 to 12,000 years ago.

One of the problems in identifying the origins of **domestication** is that it is likely that people were managing plants and animals, such as by modifying the environments to increase productivity, on some scale thousands of years earlier, and the difference between managing and domesticating becomes a somewhat arbitrary distinction. Regardless, relying on domestic plants and animals for subsistence in a significant way appears to have begun about 12,000 to 11,000 years ago.

Likely all correlated with the domestication of plants and animals, evidence of increasing sedentism, rising populations, and increasing social inequality appears in the archaeological record about 10,000 years ago. Domestication both requires and allows for increasing sedentism. By necessity, people depending on domestic plants and animals must be around more often to provide care, such as weeding around food-producing plants or moving animals to various grazing lands. By producing more food than it is possible to consume from wild versions, domestic plants and animals also allow people to stay in areas for longer periods without fear of depleting the resources. Rising populations result when food surpluses can support larger

---

BOX 7.2 **BEER!**

Archaeologists tend to have a special relationship with beer. They study its origins, they talk about it, and they drink it.

The Origins of Beer. Although most archaeologists suggest that the domestication of plants occurred to increase plant productivity for its food value, there are some who believe the driving factor may have been to make beer. Besides the obvious good feelings brought on by beer, early beer making would have increased the nutritional value of wheat and barley and perhaps killed pathogens in water. Brewing beer may have begun more than 10,000 years ago and pre-dates wine and other spirits. The oldest potential evidence of making beer in North America comes from Greenland, where evidence suggests Vikings may have been growing barley for beer 1,000 years ago.

Ancient Beers. A biologist reportedly used yeast extracted from 45-million-year-old amber as the starter for a larger batch used to make beer for a brewery in California. Some archaeologists and breweries specialize in recreating beers from ancient

times. Beer residue dated to 9,000 years ago in China was used to develop a recipe for recreating that beer, and written recipes from ancient Sumeria and Egypt have been used to recreate beers from those civilizations. A leading candidate for the oldest bottled beer was discovered in a shipwreck in the early twenty-first century. It was about 200 years old, and was drunk by professional beer tasters, who described it as tasting very old.

Beer as the Beverage of Choice. Beer is the alcoholic beverage of choice among many archaeologists. Possible explanations for this include: beer-lovers self-select archaeology as a profession; beer is simple to take to remote field locations (e.g., no glasses, corkscrews, ice, or mix required); in many locations where archaeologists work it is safer to drink beer than water; and the low cost of beer suits those in the profession. While the association of archaeologists with beer was once prominent and almost celebrated in the late twentieth and early twenty-first century, it is less so now for multiple reasons, including the social problems that are associated with alcohol.

populations. There is considerable debate among archaeologists about the reasons for the origins of social inequality, but it is clear that it was correlated with food surpluses and increasing populations, perhaps as a way of maintaining social control.

There is also archaeological interest in the domestication of animals not normally used for food. Box 10.2 focuses on the domestication of dogs from wolves.

Ancient Civilizations

There is no consensus definition of civilization among archaeologists, but most agree that to be counted as one, a society has to have at least most of the following: **monumental architecture**, at least one city, a system of writing, an agricultural base, and a state-level political organization. Some of the best-known civilizations of the ancient world are those that were centered in the Near East, Egypt, the Indus Valley, China, the Mediterranean, Mesoamerica, and the Andes of Peru.

The Near East includes the region of the Tigris and Euphrates rivers, commonly known as Mesopotamia when referring to ancient times. The earliest civilization in both Mesopotamia and the entire world is generally considered to be that of the Sumerians, who developed the first known system of writing, called cuneiform, about 5,100 years ago. Other major civilizations of the Near East that followed in the succeeding millennia include the Akkadians, Babylonians, Assyrians, and the Persian, Roman, and Islamic empires.

Civilization in Egypt began about 5,000 years ago, with the system of writing known as hieroglyphics. As occurred in the Near East, the region was subsequently dominated first by the Roman Empire and then by the Islamic empires.

The first civilization of the Mediterranean region is that commonly referred to as the Minoans. Rising about 4,000 years ago and centering on the island of Crete, they had many ports in and around the Mediterranean Sea. Civilizations that followed in the region include those of the Hittites, Mycenaeans, and Etruscans, and Classical Greece and the Roman and Byzantine empires.

Civilizations have a long history in Asia. In the area of the Indus Valley in Pakistan, the first civilization emerged about 4,400 years ago. Sometimes known as the Harappans, the people of this civilization built some of the most well-planned cities of the ancient world. In China, the Shang civilization emerged about 3,800 years ago and was subsequently followed by the Zhou and Han. In Southeast Asia, the Khmer states emerged about 1,000 years ago.

The first civilization of Mesoamerica was the Olmec, which began about 3,500 years ago. Later civilizations include those of the Maya, Teotihuacan, Toltec, Zapotec, and Aztec.

FIGURE 7.4 Egyptian Pyramid. The building of pyramids is associated with the earliest states of Egyptian civilization, beginning about 5,000 years ago.

PHOTO: Nadine Ryan.

In the Andes region of South America, the first widely recognized civilization is the Chavin, which rose about 2,500 years ago and was later followed by the Moche, Tiwanaku, Nasca, and Inka. Recent research suggests that a civilization known as Caral may have arisen as early as 4,600 years ago.

KEY RESOURCES AND SUGGESTED READING

The *Handbook of Archaeological Sciences,* edited by Brothwell and Pollard (2001), includes several contributions on dating in archaeology. The two multivolume series *Outline of Archaeological Traditions* (Peregrine 2001b) and *Encyclopedia of Prehistory* (Peregrine and Ember 2001) are both comprehensive. A comprehensive overview of world prehistory is provided in *The Human Past: World Prehistory and the Development of Human Societies* by Chris Scarre (2013).

Archaeological dating methods are covered in Brothwell and Pollard (2001). For overviews of world prehistory Peregrine (2001a, 2001b) and Scarre (2013) are suggested, and for ancient civilizations, Scarre and Fagan (2016). Lesnick (2018) provides an interesting view on the notion of eating insects in the past.

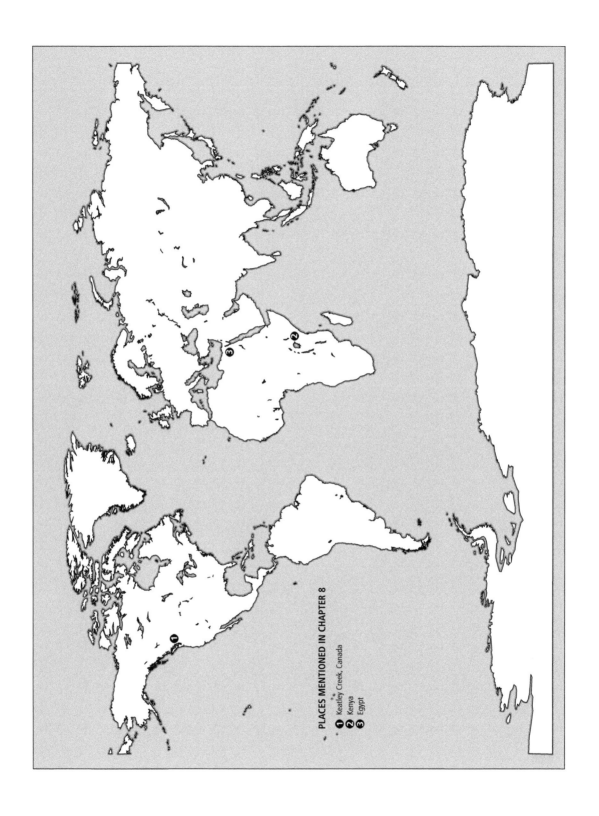

PLACES MENTIONED IN CHAPTER 8

1 Keatley Creek, Canada
2 Kenya
3 Egypt

CHAPTER 8

RECONSTRUCTING ECOLOGICAL ADAPTATIONS

Introduction

Studies of how people adapt to their environments have a long history in archaeology. Several important archaeological studies of an ecological nature were undertaken in the early twentieth century, and many archaeologists in the middle decades of the century were influenced by the development of **cultural ecology** – the study of the relationship between people and the natural environment. Ecological research became a focus of processual archaeology in the 1960s and has continued to be a mainstay of archaeological projects in the twenty-first century.

The study of the interplay between natural environments and humans in the past is widely known as ecological archaeology, with major areas of interest including reconstructing paleoenvironments, settlement patterns, subsistence strategies, and diet. Archaeological investigations into each of these areas are outlined in this chapter.

Reconstructing Paleoenvironments

Archaeologists reconstruct paleoenvironments for three principal reasons: to determine what it was that people were adapting to; to discover where to look for archaeological sites; and to reconstruct site formation and disturbance processes (Table 8.1).

DETERMINING WHAT PEOPLE WERE ADAPTING TO

Cultures are, at least in part, an adaptation to the natural environment. Knowing about past environments provides a base of information archaeologists can use to explain aspects of culture. For example, knowledge of the diversity and relative abundance of plants and animals in an area can be used to infer why people were there, what they might have been eating, and what kinds of organic materials might have

TABLE 8.1 Reasons for Reconstructing Paleoenvironments

REASON	EXAMPLES
1. To know what people were adapting to	Availability of plants and animals, temperature, precipitation, raw materials, hazards, carrying capacity
2. To know where to look for sites	Paleocoastlines, underwater sites, old river and stream courses
3. To reconstruct site formation and disturbance processes	Fluvial or aeolian deposition, erosion, high- or low-energy deposition

been incorporated into culture in the form of tools, clothing, and shelter. Information on plants and animals can also be used to get an idea of what hazards the people might have faced, such as sharing territory with dangerous animals and poisonous plants. Knowing about climate can provide insight into site location, housing, clothing, soils, and vegetation. Using the width of tree rings, archaeologists working in the American Southwest have been able to demonstrate that some areas underwent lengthy periods of drought before settlements were abandoned.

DISCOVERING WHERE TO LOOK FOR SITES

When considering where to look for sites, archaeologists recognize that waterways and landforms change through time. Sea levels, for example, have been fluctuating in many parts of the world for thousands of years, and sites that were close to a beach while they were occupied may be many meters above or below current sea levels. Therefore, an archaeologist searching for coastal sites must rely on paleoenvironmental evidence of ancient coastlines. Similarly, rivers and streams frequently change course, and since settlements are often alongside them, archaeologists searching for sites should be aware of where they once flowed.

RECONSTRUCTING SITE FORMATION AND DISTURBANCE PROCESSES

An archaeologist's interpretation of site formation and disturbance can be accepted with confidence only if he or she has some knowledge of the natural processes active during and after the creation of the site. Understanding the natural environment allows the archaeologist to judge the potential impact of myriad processes upon the archaeological record. For example, the knowledge that a river once flowed by a site may be used to support inferences of fluvial deposition or erosion of sediments.

METHODS OF RECONSTRUCTING PALEOENVIRONMENTS

Archaeologists reconstruct both biotic and abiotic environments using a variety of techniques and frequently rely on research from experts in the biological and earth sciences.

Reconstructing the biotic environment means identifying the species of plants and animals that were living in the area. Most plants and animals can only survive within a limited range of temperatures and levels of precipitation, so diversity also provides information on past climate.

Identifying plants is usually accomplished by examining preserved remains, including seeds, wood, nuts, bark, pollen, and phytoliths. Animals are usually identified by examining bones and teeth, but also hair, fur, antlers, claws, nails, and soft tissue. Reconstructions may also be based on animal coprolites and fossil impressions. Archaeologists alone are often able to identify species of plants and animals that are commonly found in cultural contexts, such as food remains. However, the identification of many other plants and animals usually requires specialists, such as palynologists (scientists who study pollen and spores) and paleontologists.

Reconstructing the abiotic environment means determining the non-living aspects, such as topography, soil characteristics, and location of waterways, as well as the natural processes of deposition, erosion, and disturbance. The study of climate involves looking at temperature, precipitation, humidity, winds, and seasonal changes. Reconstructing the abiotic environment relies on methods developed in the earth sciences. These include geomorphic research to understand where and when features such as ancient coastlines may have existed; pedological research to distinguish soil formation processes; lithological research to determine where the sediments originated; hydrological research to determine the nature of waterways; chemical research to identify areas of significant organic activity; and sedimentological research to understand the processes that bring sediments into sites and may subsequently disturb them.

Geomorphological, pedological, lithological, and hydrological research is often performed by experts in those fields. As outlined in Chapter 6, however, chemical and sedimentological analysis is considered standard procedure in archaeology and most archaeological laboratory technicians are proficient at it.

Sedimentological analysis includes determining particle size distributions and is very useful for reconstructing the conditions under which natural sediments are deposited in archaeological sites. Layers of fine-grained sediments, such as clay and silt, are generally considered indicative of low-energy deposition, such as by a meandering river, a lake flooding, or slight winds. Coarse-grained sediments such as sand, gravel, and pebbles, on the other hand, indicate high-energy deposition, such as fast-flowing rivers, ocean tidal action, and strong winds. The reasoning is that high-energy processes pick up fine-grained sediments and hold them in suspension until the energy in the process decreases. A fast-flowing river, for example, picks up particles of clay and silt as it erodes the river bottom and banks, keeps them in suspension, and deposits them when it slows down. A river or creek bottom with little evidence of clay and silt particles indicates a fast flow.

Sediment sorting (the degree to which sediments are the same size) also indicates the transporting agent. Water, wind, and glacier meltwaters sort sediments according to size (deposits will be uniform in size), whereas glacial ice is a poor sorter (deposits of glacial till are of varying sizes and shapes).

The characteristics of individual particles can also be used to indicate whether the sediments were deposited in the site by air or water. Generally, a dull or matte surface on the particles suggests deposition by air. A polished or glossy surface on the particles suggests deposition by water.

Sediment shape can also be a useful indicator. Angular-shaped sediments have not been transported far from their source (less exposure to erosion). Rounded sediments have been transported further (more exposure to erosion). Glaciers are the exception to this. Sediments can be transported within ice for great distances without the edges being eroded.

Reconstructing Settlement Patterns

Archaeologists study settlement patterns at four different levels: individual houses, single settlements, traditional territories, and regions (Table 8.2). Estimates of population are common in all levels of study and are described separately.

TABLE 8.2 Types of Settlement Pattern Studies in Archaeology

LEVEL OF STUDY	FOCUS
Individual houses	Physical characteristics of house; architecture; construction methods; social uses of house; defining the makeup of the household
Single settlement	Layout of settlement; variability of houses; season of occupation; site catchment area
Traditional territory	Seasonal rounds; diversity of site types; evidence of cultural continuity
Regional analysis	Relationship of sites to the natural environment; relationship of sites to each other

FIGURE 8.1 Turkana Village, Africa. Research has shown that in many areas, particularly in warm climates, people such as the Turkana spend relatively little time in houses, so the houses are small. Knowledge such as this is important when making inferences about settlement patterns.

PHOTO: Bob Muckle.

INDIVIDUAL HOUSES

The study of one or a few houses in a settlement is an emerging focus of archaeological interest and is sometimes known as **household archaeology**. The physical characteristics of houses, such as construction materials and methods, are commonly studied, along with the architecture.

Archaeologists also investigate the social uses of houses, focusing on such things as the kinds of activities that were done in the house. In many societies, particularly those in warm climates, most activities are done outdoors and the houses are reserved primarily for sleeping. Examples of this are the relatively small grass houses of the Turkana (Figure 8.1) and the earth-walled houses of the Maasai (Figure 8.2).

In addition to estimating how many people lived in a house, archaeologists are often interested in how membership in the household was established. Archaeologists often use the number of fire hearths and identifiable internal dividing structures within the house to infer how many nuclear families or other groupings may have lived there. Stylistic similarities in artifacts and features are also examined to see if they point to family relationships. On the northwest coast of America, for example, carvings on the outside of houses, as well as artifacts found inside, often depicted the clan of the people who lived there.

In multifamily houses, differences in the status of the inhabitants are often determined by comparing the artifacts and ecofacts found in the identifiable family divisions within the house. In multifamily dwellings, it is not unusual for the higher quality artifacts and food remains to be unequally distributed between different family areas.

SINGLE SETTLEMENTS

At the settlement level, archaeologists commonly investigate such things as variability among houses within the community, the distribution of houses, and the spatial relationship of all features within a site (e.g., middens, houses, burial grounds, and common areas).

Data on the variability and distribution of houses often supports inferences of social inequality between households (as does similar information about artifacts and ecofacts found in multifamily dwellings). Excavations at Keatley Creek, a large prehistoric village in western Canada, show that smaller houses had significantly lower proportions of foods that were ethnographically described as better quality and had less diversity of food types overall. The smaller houses, for example, revealed substantially smaller amounts of the highly valued sockeye and spring salmon and much more of the low-quality pink salmon than the larger houses.

The patterning of houses observed in settlements is almost always planned. In the Maasai villages in Africa, for example, houses are situated around the perimeter of the village, with the large common area in the center (Figure 8.2).

For archaeologists working with settlements created by non-sedentary peoples, determining the season in which the site was occupied is a common objective, and research on this is often known as **seasonality studies**. Determining the season of occupation is accomplished primarily through examining the animal and plant remains recovered from the site. The shells of some mollusk species exhibit seasonal growth rings that can be identified in cross section, which makes determining the season in which shell midden sites were occupied quite straightforward. When the remains of young animals are recovered and the birthing season is known, the level of skeletal development can sometimes be used to infer when the animal was killed. Based on the knowledge that the pigs found in some prehistoric deposits in southern England were born in springtime, archaeologists were able to use immature pig bones to determine that the sites were probably created in winter. Similarly, for species that shed and regrow antlers at fixed times, the state of antler growth may be used to infer when the animal died. The presence of the remains of animals that routinely migrate through an area is another method of inferring season of occupation.

Plant remains are also often used to infer the season a site was occupied. The inference is usually based on the time of year when most or all of the plant remains found in cultural context were edible. For example, if a site has nuts that typically ripen from

FIGURE 8.2
Maasai Village, Africa.
The Maasai are cattle herders, mostly living and working on the savanna. Their villages are often encircled by fences of thorns to protect them from lions. The houses are situated around the edge with a communal area in the middle. This kind of knowledge is important when making inferences about settlement patterns.

PHOTO: Bob Muckle.

August to October, berries that ripen from September to November, a wild grass that is edible from April to October, and a wild root that is edible from September to November, then it can reasonably be inferred that the site was occupied in the late summer and early autumn.

Another common objective for archaeologists focusing on a single settlement is to locate the source of all the recovered remains. This includes determining the source of raw materials, such as the stone used in artifact manufacture and the clays used for making pottery. Such data are often integral to making inferences about trade, and their study is known as **site catchment analysis**.

TRADITIONAL TERRITORY

In recent decades, many archaeologists have begun to focus their study of settlement patterns on areas habitually used by specific groups. The study area is known as either the traditional territory of the group or the **site exploitation territory**.

The focus on traditional territories is especially prevalent in Indigenous archaeology, where much of the work is undertaken to prove prehistoric use and occupancy of an area. Archaeological research usually includes examining the number and diversity of site types, searching for evidence of cultural continuity within the traditional territory, and establishing the evidence of a **seasonal round**, which explains the diversity of sites.

REGIONAL ANALYSIS

Archaeologists study settlement patterns at the regional level in a multitude of ways. They usually examine the data from studies of individual houses, settlements, and traditional territories, and search for similarities and differences in patterns throughout a geographic region or **culture area**, encompassing multiple traditional territories.

Many archaeological studies of regional settlements adapt methods and theories from geography to examine the different ways in which humans are apt to order their settlements in relation to each other. These methods involve such things as measuring distances between settlements of various sizes and looking for geometrical patterns illustrating standard differences between cities, towns, villages, and camps. Another major method focuses on how settlements are patterned in relation to the natural environment. This includes examining the preferred locations of settlements, such as hilltops versus valley bottoms.

ESTIMATING POPULATION SIZE

Population sizes of houses, sites, territories, and regions can be estimated in many ways, such as by looking at the number of people buried in cemeteries, the numbers of specific types of artifacts, the local or regional carrying capacity, and ethnographic and historical records. Table 8.3 lists the major types of settlement data used in most estimates.

Ecological information, burial data, and artifacts are among the least reliable sources. While ecological information may provide some measure of how many people an area could support, the estimates are usually too broad to be of value, and the carrying capacity would not necessarily have been reached. Burial information is likewise unreliable, especially for the prehistoric period. While it is not unusual to find cemeteries when excavating sedentary communities, archaeologists would have to establish the contemporaneity of the remains and consider that some remains may have completely decomposed and that others may have been buried off-site. Using burials to estimate population size for non-sedentary peoples is a non-starter. Some archaeologists use artifacts, such as the number of cooking pots, to make population estimates. However, this method has its limitations in that archaeologists would need to make many assumptions about the use and discarding of pots in addition to recognizing pots in a deposit (especially difficult considering pots are often recycled).

For recent times, historic and ethnographic records are the most reliable tool for estimating populations. However, as with all ethnographic and historic records, archaeologists must exercise caution when using observations to draw analogies to the past.

The amount of floor space; the number of rooms, dwellings, and hearths; and the volume of deposits are all commonly used as estimates of population. They are all dependent on ethnographic analogy. One study used a wide sample of ethnographies

TABLE 8.3 Methods to Estimate Population

Ecological information
Burials
Artifacts
Ethnographic and historic records
Covered floor space
Number of rooms, dwellings, and hearths
Volume of site deposits

to determine that population size could be estimated by calculating one person for every 10 square meters (12 square yards) of floor space. Considering the variability of environments and cultures throughout the world, however, the indiscriminate use of this calculation would be naïve.

When determining population size in traditional territories and regions, archaeologists must ensure that sites being used in the calculation are contemporaneous. This includes, for example, not counting settlements whose occupants were already accounted for in another seasonal site. It also involves determining normal patterns of behavior. During prehistoric times in some parts of the world, for example, it was common for dozens or hundreds of people to live together during some weeks or months, and spend the rest of the year traveling throughout the territory in much smaller groups.

Because the original number of sites in most regions is unlikely to be known, estimates of regional populations during prehistory are filled with assumptions and speculations. Estimates of the prehistoric population of North America before the arrival of Europeans, for example, range from less than one million to tens of millions.

Reconstructing Subsistence Strategies

Subsistence strategy refers to the way in which people get their food. Archaeologists recognize five basic patterns of subsistence for people living in pre-industrial times (Table 8.4).

GENERALIZED FORAGING

Classifying people as **generalized foragers** means that most of their food comprises a wide variety of wild plants and animals that they collect themselves. They are some-

TABLE 8.4 Major Subsistence Strategies

STRATEGY	DEFINITION
Generalized foraging	Subsistence based on a wide variety of wild plants and animals
Specialized foraging	Subsistence based on a wide variety of wild plants and animals, but specializing in one type
Pastoralism	Subsistence based on the herding of animals
Horticulture	Subsistence based on plant cultivation, using only hand tools
Agriculture	Intensive plant cultivation, often with the aid of animals and irrigation

times described as hunters and gatherers. Prior to about 15,000 years ago, all people were generalized foragers. In addition to being primarily dependent on a wide variety of wild plants and animals, generalized foragers typically live in groups of less than 50 people, are **egalitarian**, and are highly mobile, moving at least several times each year within their territory. There are few remaining generalized foraging groups today, but some can be found in the Australian outback and parts of southern Africa.

Archaeological indicators of generalized foraging include a preponderance of wild foods in cultural context; small, temporary settlements; and equal distribution of resources. Because generalized foragers move frequently, pottery, which is often bulky and relatively heavy, is rare in their settlements.

SPECIALIZED FORAGING

Also known as **complex foraging** or complex hunting and gathering, and probably emerging about 15,000 years ago, **specialized foraging** describes a subsistence based on a wide diversity of plants and animals, but with a primary dependence on a single resource. A good example is the people of the northwest coast region of North America who for several thousands of years had a diverse diet of dozens of different plants and animals, but salmon was overwhelmingly predominant. The size of specialized foraging groups was typically in the range of a few hundred to a few thousand, although they did not all reside together. Specialized foragers are also characterized by semi-sedentism and marked social inequality.

Archaeological indicators of specialized foraging include a great diversity of animal and botanical remains with a preponderance of one kind, semi-permanent villages, and an unequal distribution of resources.

FIGURE 8.3
Pastoralists in Kenya.
A Turkana woman providing water to livestock. Subsistence focusing on domestic herd animals began more than 10,000 years ago. Pastoralists can often be identified in the archaeological record by little variety in animal remains, larger populations, and more permanent structures compared to foragers, and some unequal distribution of resources.

PHOTO: Alamy / John Warburton-Lee Photography.

PASTORALISM

Emerging about 11,000 years ago, **pastoralism** describes subsistence based on the herding of animals such as cattle, sheep, goats, and pigs. Characteristics of pastoralism include groups of up to a few thousand spread among several villages, seasonal mobility, and slight social inequality.

Archaeological indicators of pastoralism are the preponderance of one or two species of animals in a site, with those animals showing evidence of domestication, seasonal movement (to graze the herds), and some social inequality in the distribution of resources.

HORTICULTURE

Like pastoralism, **horticulture** emerged about 11,000 years ago. It describes subsistence based on plant cultivation with hand tools only (i.e., no plows or animals involved in the preparation of fields or harvesting). Horticultural groups generally range in size from the hundreds to several thousand, although they are spread among many different villages. Each village is typically occupied for several years while the nearby land is farmed. When the nutrients from the land are exhausted, the people move to a nearby location, create new garden plots, and build new residential structures.

Archaeological indicators of horticulture include a preponderance of domestic plant remains, evidence of multiyear occupation, garden plots, and slight to moderate inequality in the distribution of resources.

AGRICULTURE

Agriculture involves intensive plant cultivation, often (but not always) with the use of animals to assist in the preparation of fields (e.g., to pull plows) and harvesting (e.g., to transport the crops). Agriculture emerged about 6,000 years ago and was the subsistence strategy of all ancient civilizations and states. Populations supported by agriculture have very high densities (ranging from the thousands to the millions), the presence of cities, and marked social inequality. Agriculturalists often have armies, writing, and monumental architecture. All of the above are evidence of agriculture.

Distinguishing Wild Plants and Animals from Domestic

There is no consensus definition of domestication in archaeology. At a minimum, it is taken to mean that plants or animals are under the control of humans. At most, it means that plants and animals are dependent on humans for their survival. Many archaeologists consider plants and animals to be domestic if humans are somehow involved in the breeding. Identifying domestic versus wild plants and animals in the archaeological record is difficult, especially for those plants and animals in the early stages of domestication (Table 8.5).

PLANT DOMESTICATION

There is no single attribute for distinguishing a plant as wild or domestic, and archaeologists often use a combination of morphological and cultural evidence. The principal variable used to identify domestic plants in the archaeological record is size. The part of the plant that people use is usually larger among domestic varieties than wild. A domestic cob of corn, for example, is larger than a wild cob; and a domestic squash is larger than a wild squash. It is uncertain why this is, but one possibility is that larger plants were selected for breeding, and the genes for the large sizes were passed to subsequent generations. The size increase may also have been due to human intervention in the form of watering and weeding, and in more recent times, fertilizing.

Since size is easily measured and compared, and since it is usually the edible part of the plant that is preserved in archaeological sites, it makes sense that this is the way

TABLE 8.5 Criteria for Distinguishing Domestic versus Wild Plants and Animals (of the same species)

ATTRIBUTES OF DOMESTIC VARIETIES OF PLANTS
The part of the plant that people use is usually larger
The plant may have lost its mechanism for natural dispersal
The part of the plant that people use may have become clustered
There is often a genetic change
There may be a loss of dormancy
The plants tend to ripen simultaneously
There is a tendency for less self-protection, such as thorns and toxins

ATTRIBUTES OF DOMESTIC VARIETIES OF ANIMALS
The animals are smaller (at least in the early stages of domestication)
There is a tendency to find more complete skeletons in the faunal assemblage
There is likely to be a high percentage of young animals in the faunal assemblage
There is likely to be a high percentage of young male animals in the faunal assemblage
There is likely to be a high percentage of old female animals in the faunal assemblage

many inferences about plant domestication are made. Generally, if archaeologists see an increase in the size of the edible parts of the plants through time, it is usually reasonable to infer that the plant was becoming domesticated.

As outlined in Table 8.5, several other attributes of plants can be used to distinguish whether they are of the domestic or wild variety. However, due to the fact that the non-edible parts of plants domesticated for food are rarely preserved, most have limited application in archaeology.

Cultural evidence of plant domestication comes in a variety of forms, including the presence of gardening artifacts such as hoes, features such as irrigation canals, and soil chemistry indicating a previous garden plot.

ANIMAL DOMESTICATION

Ways of distinguishing domestic versus wild animals in archaeological sites include size, the completeness of the skeleton, and age and sex ratios of the slaughtered remains, as well as cultural evidence.

FIGURE 8.4 Butchery in a Village. The completeness of the skeleton is one way to distinguish domestic from wild varieties of animals. As depicted here in this rural Egyptian village, an entire domestic animal is being butchered in the village. If the animal was wild there is a good chance some preliminary butchery would have been undertaken before returning to the village.

PHOTO: Bob Muckle.

At least in the early stages of domestication, domestic animals were usually smaller than their wild counterparts. A domestic goat, for example, was smaller than a wild goat. The reason for the size difference is not completely understood. One popular explanation is that smaller animals were selected for domestication because they were easier to capture and control. Another possibility is that domestic animals generally would have had a worse diet than their wild counterparts, which was reflected in the stunted growth of the skeletons.

The completeness of skeletons is a good way to tell whether animals were domestic. A complete or nearly complete skeleton of a moderate-sized or large animal in a settlement suggests that it was probably domestic, likely because if the animal was hunted, some butchery would have taken place at the site of the kill. Hunters routinely discarded parts of the animal of little value to them to lighten the load to carry back to the settlement. For example, a hunter of a wild goat who kills an animal 25 kilometers (15 miles) from the settlement is unlikely to bring the entire skeleton back.

Assemblages of butchered remains are also examined for age and sex ratios to make inferences about domestication. A high percentage of young adults, particularly males, is probably indicative of domestication. One reason for this is that when hunting wild animals, the young adults are typically the most difficult to kill due to their strength and speed. Also, groups who have domestic animals often preserve most females, but rely on a few males for breeding. Thus, relatively few young female remains are likely to be found in an assemblage of domestic animals.

Fencing is one type of cultural evidence of domestication, usually indicated by post holes. Large accumulations of animal dung in or near a village may also indicate domestication. In some cases, there may be some associated artifacts, such as collars.

Reconstructing Diet

Several kinds of evidence are used to determine the particular foods that people were eating. These are (i) plant and animal remains in cultural context, (ii) human skeletal remains, (iii) **human waste**, (iv) human soft tissue, and (v) residue on artifacts.

BOX 8.1 THE PALEODIET AND OTHER FANTASIES

Much of the world seems to be in a paleo-craze these days, or in some people's view, living in the world of paleofantasies. Much of the focus has been on the paleodiet, known to some as the Caveman diet.

The first edition of *The Paleo Diet: Lose Weight and Get Healthy by Eating the Foods You Were Designed to Eat*, by Loren Cordain, was published in 2002. According to the revised edition published in 2011, the book became one of America's best-selling diet and health books, with more than 200,000 copies sold. Cordain (2011, xi) describes the diet as

> the diet to which our species is genetically adapted. This is the diet of our hunter-gatherer ancestors, the foods consumed by every human being on the planet until a mere 333 human generations ago, or about ten thousand years ago. Our ancestors' diets were uncomplicated by agriculture, animal husbandry, technology, and processed foods. Then, as today, our health is optimized when we eat lean meats, seafood, and fresh fruits and veggies at the expense of grains, dairy, refined sugars, refined oils, and processed foods.

Repeating this basic premise elsewhere, he asserts that indeed, for most of the 2.5 million years (when the genus *Homo* emerges) "every human being on Earth ate this way."

Archaeology and biological anthropology simply do not support this. To archaeologists the notion that there was such thing as a common diet in prehistory is absurd. The idea that we have not continued to evolve, especially in regard to digestion, is also ridiculous. A good example is the evolutionary change occurring several thousand years ago facilitating the ability of many adults to effectively digest dairy products.

The success of the book, as with other diet and health books, may have more to do with the fact it works – but not for the reasons people think. The premises and assumptions of the paleodiet are faulty. The popularity of the diet may also be related to what some refer to as "paleo-nostalgia," which is taking a view of the "good old days" to the extreme.

Another example of a paleofantasy is associated with the exercise regimes based on assumptions about past lifestyles. Popular paleo-workouts emphasize such things as simulating perceived lifestyles in the past, including lots of running, jumping, spear-throwing, and fighting, which once again are based on faulty perceptions. As with diet, there was never a single lifestyle activity, and notions that most people of the past were involved in spear-throwing on a daily basis are equally absurd. In fact, for many people of the past, running, spear-throwing, and fighting were probably rare occurrences. A more realistic paleo-workout would likely involve lots of walking.

For more debunking of the paleodiet and other popular thoughts and actions based on misunderstandings of the past, *Paleofantasy: What Evolution Really Tells Us about Sex, Diet, and How We Live*, by Marlene Zuk (2013), is recommended.

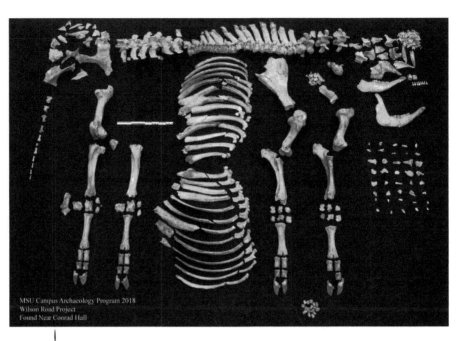

FIGURE 8.5 Cow Skeleton. In 2018, an entire articulated cow skeleton was found as construction workers on Michigan State University's campus were working to build a road. The MSU Campus Archaeology Program was called out to identify the bones and tell a story about them to the campus community. The cow appears to be of old age due to the presence of bone spurs and worn teeth. The cow was either associated with MSU's historic bull barn or a family who operated a farm prior to MSU owning the property.

PHOTO: Autumn Painter and the Michigan State University Campus Archaeology Program.

PLANT AND ANIMAL REMAINS IN CULTURAL CONTEXT

The most obvious indicators of diet are the plant and animal remains found in good cultural context, such as in or around middens, fire hearths, containers, cache pits, and houses. This is the most common and one of the most reliable methods of determining diet. As outlined in Chapter 6, the plant and animal remains are often quantified.

HUMAN SKELETAL REMAINS

Through an analysis of isotopes and trace elements in bone, human skeletal remains provide a good indication of the kinds of foods eaten. The ratio of carbon and nitrogen isotopes is different among various kinds of plants and animals; when foods are eaten as a regular part of people's diet, those ratios are imprinted in their bones.

The ratios of isotopes can be used to make inferences about the relative amounts of protein coming from marine and terrestrial species. On the west coast of Canada, for example, the ratios of carbon-13 and carbon-12 in dozens of excavated skeletal remains have indicated that over the past 5,000 years those living there obtained about 90 per cent of their protein from marine species (e.g., salmon). And those living in the interior along salmon-bearing rivers obtained about 50 per cent of their protein from marine species. Isotope analysis is also used to make inferences about the types of plants eaten. Root crops, nuts, and berries, for example, have different ratios than cereal grains.

The relative proportion of meat in diets can be distinguished using trace element analysis of human bone. A meat-rich diet will typically show higher levels of copper and zinc and lower levels of manganese and strontium than diets with relatively little or no meat.

An analysis of human teeth can also indicate dietary preferences. Wear patterns on teeth can be used to make some broad inferences. A diet with a lot of hard, gritty foods, for example, is likely to be reflected on the surface of the teeth. Cavities are often correlated with a dependence on agricultural products.

HUMAN WASTE

Although rare in archaeological sites, human waste provides one of the best and most reliable methods of reconstructing diet, and comes in a variety of forms. Coprolites may appear in the form of cylinders, pellets, or pads, and are most commonly found in dry caves. The study of coprolites is a specialty in archaeology, and it is reported that when reconstituted, even the smell comes back sometimes. Since coprolites contain the remnants of food products, they are highly valued for reconstructing diet. It is not unusual to be able to identify plant species from partially digested seeds or leaves, as well as small bones of birds and fish. Indicators of diet also include other parts of plants, such as stalks and roots, and other parts of animals, such as hair and feathers that may have adhered to the meat, as well as fish and reptile scales.

Another type of human waste is cess, which is an accumulation of human waste including feces and urine. Cess is often used to describe the entire contents of latrines or sewers. Because it is much less likely to be preserved than coprolites, prehistoric archaeologists do not usually encounter cess.

HUMAN SOFT TISSUE

The absolute best method of determining diet is from food found in the stomachs and intestines of human remains preserved through extreme environmental conditions. As with coprolites, analysis involves identifying food products. A study of the intestines of the well-preserved bog bodies from Iron Age Europe, for example, shows meals consisting of beef, pork, wheat, barley, oats, peas, bread, and blackberries.

RESIDUE ANALYSIS

Diet may also be reconstructed using residue analysis. As outlined in Chapter 6, foods often leave residue on artifacts. A chemical analysis of residue left in a pot, for example, can often determine the type of food stored in the pot; and blood residue on stone tools leads to inferences about the kind of animal killed and butchered, presumably for food.

KEY RESOURCES AND SUGGESTED READING

A good source for environmental archaeology is Reitz and Shackley (2012). Books focusing on subsistence and diet include Outram and Bogaard (2019), Hastorf (2017), and Twiss (2019). Brothwell and Pollard (2001) includes multiple contributions on reconstructing subsistence and diet.

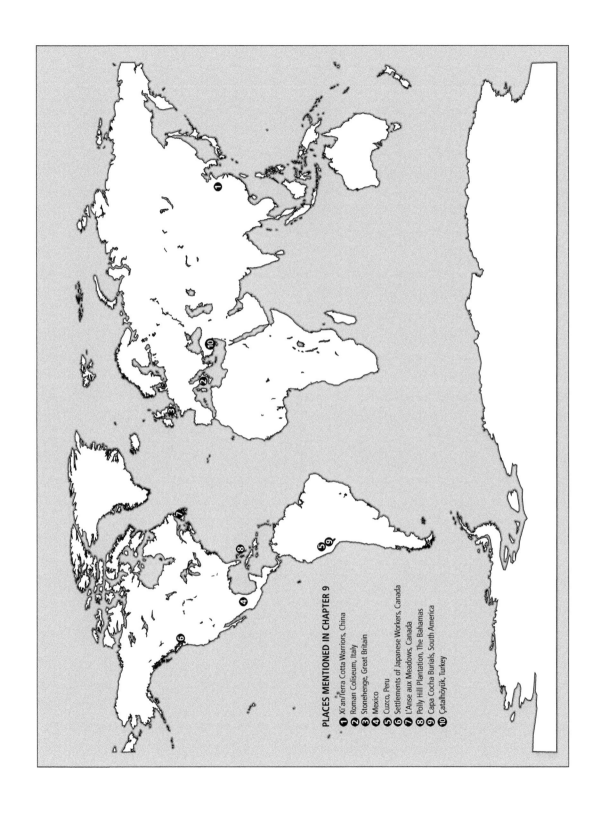

PLACES MENTIONED IN CHAPTER 9

1. Xi'an/Terra Cotta Warriors, China
2. Roman Coliseum, Italy
3. Stonehenge, Great Britain
4. Mexico
5. Cuzco, Peru
6. Settlements of Japanese Workers, Canada
7. L'Anse aux Meadows, Canada
8. Polly Hill Plantation, The Bahamas
9. Capa Cocha Burials, South America
10. Çatalhöyük, Turkey

CHAPTER 9

RECONSTRUCTING THE SOCIAL AND IDEOLOGICAL ASPECTS OF CULTURE

Introduction

Although some archaeological work in the early twentieth century examined the social and ideological aspects of past cultures, these types of studies have only become popular in recent decades. The new or processual archaeology that emerged in the 1960s tended to focus on ecology, but many archaeologists at this time also began to study social systems, attempting to identify social inequality and categorize societies into the classification systems developed by anthropologists. Identity and ideology emerged as a focus in the 1980s, associated with the development of post-processual archaeology.

Reconstructions of the social and ideological aspects of culture tend to be more difficult than those of culture history and ecological adaptations. Because most of what archaeologists excavate, including ecofacts and features, is directly related to ecological adaptations, it is relatively easy to make inferences about paleoenvironments, settlement patterns, subsistence strategies, and diet. For example, inferring diet from plant and animal remains found in pots or a midden can hardly be considered a great intellectual leap.

Using those same remains, usually people's garbage, to make inferences about the social and ideological aspects of culture is clearly more difficult. It can be done; it just isn't as easy. While inferences about subsistence and diet, for example, are made by identifying the remains themselves, the patterning of those remains tends to be more important to archaeologists interested in reconstructing the social and ideological aspects of culture.

In sequence, the remainder of this chapter covers the reconstruction of (i) inequality, (ii) the type of society, (iii) identity of various sorts, and (iv) ideology.

Reconstructing Inequality

Reconstructing inequality involves determining differences of status and access to resources within a group. Groups are usually classified as being egalitarian, ranked, or stratified.

Describing a group as egalitarian means that everyone in the group has roughly equal status and equal access to resources. A ranked group means that everyone has a different status: if there are 500 people in the group, then there are 500 different statuses. **Stratification** refers to a class system, in which there are typically at least three distinct classes, commonly referred to as lower, middle, and upper class. Sometimes groups exhibit ranking within classes.

Groups are not always easily categorized. In recent years, for example, archaeologists have increasingly used the word **transegalitarian** to describe groups that are transitioning between egalitarian and ranked or stratified systems. The principal evidence archaeologists use to determine levels of inequality is variability in burials and in houses.

The very fact that some members of a group were buried while others were not can be an indication of inequality. Low status people, such as slaves, may have been merely thrown out along with trash, while people with higher status were buried. Variability in grave goods also indicates differences in status: people with higher status were generally buried with more and higher quality goods. Levels of inequality may also be gauged by variability in the preparation for burial, including the building of tombs. The pyramids and tombs of the ancient Egyptian rulers and the thousands of terra cotta warriors associated with the Emperor Qin from China (see Figure 3.3) are extreme examples of how grave goods and tombs can reflect high status.

Skeletal remains themselves may also provide indications of status. Some groups along the west coast of North America and others in Mesoamerica, for example, artificially shaped the forehead as an indication of high status. Binding a flat object to the forehead of an infant for lengthy periods produced a distinctive elongated shape.

Houses are another common way of gauging status. Settlements with highly variable houses usually indicate inequality. People with higher status typically have the largest houses, which are more costly to build and maintain. Examples of extreme differences in status as reflected in house size abound in the archaeological record, from several thousand years ago to the present. One example is the Keatley Creek site in the Pacific Northwest region of North America. The over 100 semi-subterranean houses, commonly known as pithouses, found at the site were occupied in prehistoric times, ranging in size from several meters to more than 20 meters in diameter. Excavations indicate that the larger houses were occupied by groups with higher quality artifacts and other prestige items confirming that they were occupied by higher status and wealthier groups.

Examining the range and variability of material remains within houses is a further way to determine social inequality. An unequal distribution of luxury items or **prestige goods** between houses or within multifamily houses likely indicates inequality. Prestige goods include raw materials in short supply, such as high-quality stone for making tools or shell coming from great distances. Manufactured objects can also be classified as prestige goods, often in the form of jewelry that required a tremendous investment of labor.

Reconstructing Types of Societies

A variety of anthropological models categorize types of societies based on their economic, social, and political systems (Table 9.1). As outlined in Chapter 2, the

TABLE 9.1 **Reconstructing Categories of Societies in Archaeology**

THE MAJOR CATEGORIES OF SOCIETIES
Bands
Tribes
Chiefdoms
States
Empires

THE MAJOR KINDS OF EVIDENCE ARCHAEOLOGISTS USE TO RECONSTRUCT TYPES OF SOCIETIES
Size of population
Size of settlements
Sedentariness
Subsistence strategy
Variability among houses
Variability in the distribution of material remains
Monuments
Architecture
Evidence of specialization (e.g., craft areas)
Iconography
Mortuary data

unilinear theory of cultural evolution, with the stages of savagery, barbarism, and civilization, was one of the first attempts to categorize people in this way.

Anthropologists created two popular models in the 1960s, and these were readily adopted by archaeologists. Despite their shortcomings, both models are still widely used in the twenty-first century. One model is primarily political in nature and categorizes societies as egalitarian, ranked, or stratified. Classification of prehistoric societies is based primarily on evidence of inequality.

Another model is based on a variety of criteria, including subsistence strategy, level of inequality, leadership, population, and occupational specialization.

This model remains the most widely used, although not without some modifications over the past several decades. The categories are **bands**, **tribes**, **chiefdoms**, **states**, and **empires**.

BANDS

Bands are characterized by their small group size (usually less than 50 members), high mobility throughout their territory, egalitarianism, and subsistence strategy of generalized foraging. Each band is autonomous, but they form economic, social, and ideological alliances with neighboring bands. Marriage patterns among bands are always **exogamous**, meaning that marriage partners are found from outside one's own band. Everyone in a band has roughly equal status. Leadership is informal: the person who is recognized as being best at a specific task takes on the role of leadership for that task. There is little occupational specialization among band members (other than shamans), with each man doing what all other men do and each woman doing what all other women do. Even the role of shaman is considered a part-time task, and he or she is still expected to do what all the other men or women in the group do. All groups before about 15,000 years ago were bands, and although rare, they continue to exist in the twenty-first century.

Archaeological indicators of bands are also characteristics of generalized foragers and typically include an equal distribution of resources, little variability in house size or form, relatively small settlements, seasonal occupations, temporary structures, and plant and animal remains identified as wild. Territorial boundaries are difficult to define and often overlap with neighboring bands. Because bands are mobile, pottery, which is relatively heavy and bulky, is rarely found in their sites.

TRIBES

Also known as **segmentary societies**, tribes are characterized by populations typically ranging from a few hundred to a few thousand. Subsistence is usually based on pastoralism or horticulture (or both), although there are numerous examples of tribal hunting and gathering societies in resource-rich areas such as the Great Plains in North America. The level of social inequality within tribes can be described as transegalitarian. They generally have multiple villages, each with their own leader, who is often described by anthropologists as a **Big Man** or **Head Man**. These leadership positions hold no authority and are usually based on the personal qualities of a person, who then parlays his role into a higher status. Leadership is typically effective only at the village level. There is no central authority over the entire tribe, but the bonds between villages are maintained through kinship ties and common interest associations.

Archaeological indicators of tribes are similar to those of pastoralists and small-scale horticultural communities. Tribal societies will usually have a preponderance of plant and animal remains identified as domestic. Slight social inequality, based on the presence of a Big Man or Head Man, is likely to be reflected in a minor unequal distribution of resources and perhaps one house that is slightly larger than the others.

Considering that both pastoralists and horticulturalists spend relatively long periods in one area, there may also be some evidence of structures intended for long-term use.

CHIEFDOMS

Chiefdoms are characterized by populations ranging from a few thousand to tens of thousands, a subsistence strategy based on horticulture, and marked social inequality, including formal leadership positions. Members of a chiefdom are spread among multiple communities. Leadership extends beyond the community to the entire chiefdom. The central leader is known as the **chief**, who has authority over all members of the group. Leadership is **ascribed** and is usually based on ancestral ties with the supernatural or mythical world. The populace pays taxes to the chief and his ruling extended family. Taxation may be in the form of goods, such as a percentage of the crops harvested, or labor, such as a given number of weeks in service to the chief in subsistence or construction activities. Chiefdoms exhibit much social inequality and usually a system of ranking. One's status is typically dependent on how closely one is related to the chief. Craft specialization, including artisans, is common. Although not evident in all cases, chiefdoms are also characterized by monuments. These include incised monoliths to mark territory or declare ownership, such as **stelae**, or for ritual activities, such as Stonehenge.

Archaeological indicators of chiefdoms include those associated with large-scale horticulture, such as storage facilities. Other indicators are a preponderance of food remains identified as domestic, a marked unequal distribution of resources, considerable variability in houses and burials, evidence of craft specialization areas, signs of ascribed leadership (e.g., **iconography**), and monuments.

STATES

States are characterized by populations ranging from about 20,000 to several million, a subsistence based on agriculture, the presence of cities, a **bureaucracy**, monumental architecture, and armies. States also usually have a system of writing. One of the essential differences between chiefdoms and states is that in a state, the leader's power is legitimized or at least supported by an army. In states, leadership can be either achieved or ascribed. The surplus created by agriculture is used to support not only artisans, crafts specialists, and armies, but also a bureaucracy, which is primarily responsible for carrying out the wishes of the leadership, including enforcing laws and collecting taxes. States invariably are associated with civilization.

Archaeological indicators of states correlate with those of agriculturalists and civilizations. Evidence of a system of writing is perhaps the easiest way to distinguish a state from a chiefdom, although it is understood that some states, such as the Inka, lacked writing. Monumental architecture, cities, unequal distribution of resources, and domestic foods are other types of evidence that are commonly associated with states, but these characteristics are also common among chiefdoms.

EMPIRES

An empire is a special kind of political system that is territorially expansive, with one state exercising control over other states, chiefdoms, tribes, or bands. Territorial expansion is supported by the actual or potential threat of military power. Archaeological indicators of empires include the commingling of cultural traditions, such as architecture, and the creation of elaborate road systems linking the territories.

The most well-known empires of the past include the Aztec, Inka, and Roman. The dominance of the many distinct societies throughout Mesoamerica by the Aztec peoples of northern Mexico from the fourteenth to the early sixteenth centuries is referred to as the Aztec Empire. The Spaniard Hernán Cortés was able to conquer the empire with relative ease in part because he enlisted many volunteers from cultures under Aztec domination.

During the Inka Empire, millions of people in dozens of different cultures were dominated by one group originally based in Cuzco, Peru, beginning in the early

FIGURE 9.1 Roman Coliseum. Similarities in architecture, such as that of the Roman Coliseum, is one way to identify empires.

PHOTO: Barry D. Kass @ ImagesofAnthropology.com.

fifteenth century and ending with conquest by Spanish forces led by Francisco Pizarro in the early sixteenth century. At its height, the Inka Empire controlled much of the western coastal region of South America, including areas now recognized as Peru, Bolivia, Ecuador, and portions of Argentina, Chile, and Columbia. The Inka legacy includes a reported 12,000 or more miles of roads, used in part to exert military control over those living throughout the empire. As with the conquest of the Aztec, the Spanish forces were able to enlist the aid of subjected peoples in their fight against the Inka.

The Roman Empire, which existed from about the third century BC to the fifth century AD, included domination of much of Europe, northern Africa, and western Asia. The Roman Empire's presence in the archaeological record can be seen throughout the region, including its trademark roads and architecture.

Reconstructing Identity

Archaeologists attempt to reconstruct several kinds of identities, primarily using artifacts, symbols, and mortuary remains (Table 9.2).

TABLE 9.2 Reconstructing Identity in Archaeology

THE MAJOR KINDS OF IDENTITY ARCHAEOLOGISTS ATTEMPT TO RECONSTRUCT
Ethnic identity
Descent group
Gender
Children
Specific individuals

THE MAJOR KINDS OF EVIDENCE ARCHAEOLOGISTS USE TO RECONSTRUCT IDENTITY
Artifacts
Symbols
Mortuary data

ETHNIC IDENTITY

An **ethnic group** is defined as a group of people who share a common language, culture, history, and territory, with members consciously identifying with the group.

Reconstructing ethnicity in archaeology, particularly for the prehistoric period, is notoriously difficult and controversial. There is much debate about the reliability of inferring ethnicity from material remains, especially considering that neighboring groups frequently shared many cultural attributes and that cultures continually change. Many people have attempted to reconstruct ethnicity for political reasons, including those who work in the field of Indigenous archaeology and who aim to support claims of Aboriginal rights and territory.

Reconstructing ethnicity is often based on **ethnic markers**. Examining evidence of African American ethnicity in the archaeological record of the New World, archaeologist Timothy Baumann (2004) describes three forms of ethnic markers: (i) artifacts that were made in or are indigenous to Africa, such as a clay pipe from Ghana found in a New World cemetery; (ii) artifacts made in the New World that exhibit African styles, such as a pipe made in a European form but exhibiting West African decorative motifs; and (iii) non-African materials used in African ways, such as European-made bowls (which were found in greater proportion to plates) that were used for gumbos and stews. Similar types of ethnic markers are commonly used to identify Asian ethnicity in late-nineteenth- and early-twentieth-century sites in western North America. The ethnic markers are most frequently

FIGURE 9.2 Japanese Bottles. Line drawings of bottles recovered from an early twentieth century logging camp in Canada. These bottles are an example of an ethnic marker.

IMAGE: Bob Muckle, Seymour Valley Archaeology Project.

artifacts that have been manufactured in China or Japan, such as rice bowls and bottles (Figure 9.2)

Chapter 3 briefly discussed the site of L'Anse aux Meadows, which achieved UNESCO World Heritage Site status largely based on the fact that it provides the earliest reliably dated evidence of Europeans in the Americas. The ethnic markers used to identify Viking ethnicity included characteristic iron nails and rivets, soapstone spindle whorls, and distinctive boatsheds.

Ethnicity may also be identified through rock art. It has been suggested that, in at least some situations, people new to an area may create distinctive rock art as a means of establishing their presence (Quinlan and Woody 2003).

DESCENT GROUPS

A **descent group** is defined as a group in which all members can trace lineal descent to a single ancestor. The ancestor may be mythical or real. Lineage is one kind of descent group in which all the links to the ancestor are known. Groups of lineages often form clans, in which all members assume common ancestry, but only some of the links are known.

Clans typically number in the hundreds and thousands, with members spread out over expansive territories. Symbols are frequently used to identify clan membership, and it is these symbols that archaeologists often use to reconstruct descent groups. On the northwest coast of North America, for example, carvings and paintings on houses and grave markers can be used to infer clan membership.

SEX AND GENDER

As outlined in Chapter 6, skeletal remains can determine whether an individual was male or female. Gender, however, is a cultural construct and encompasses the way people are perceived and expected to behave, including the traditional female and male roles, as well as other categories for hermaphrodites, androgynous people, homosexuals, and transgender people, depending on the society.

Inferences of gender are usually made using ethnographic analogy. It is not unusual to have some types of artifacts associated with men and others associated with women, with ratios of these taken to indicate gender. Among foragers, for example, projectile points are often considered to be men's artifacts, and digging sticks or baskets are often considered women's artifacts. The presence of either artifact as grave goods would be a good indication of gender.

In historic resource utilization camps in North America, such as those associated with mining and logging during the late nineteenth and early twentieth centuries, men-only and mixed camps both operated. One way archaeologists determine whether women were in the camps is by the ratios of artifacts commonly associated with women, such as jewelry and fancy dishes.

Homosexuality is frequently inferred based on art. Pictographs and portable art (e.g., small carvings) sometimes depict sexual acts, often between two or more members of the same sex.

CHILDREN

The identification of children is an area of interest in archaeology that emerged in the late twentieth century. In addition to human remains, the principal archaeological indicators of children are artifacts and art. These include toys, although distinguishing an artifact as a toy is in itself somewhat problematic. Children are also depicted in art, and in some cases, the art itself is interpreted as having been created by children because of its simple qualities. Experiments have shown that fingerprints found on ceramics and wall surfaces can be used to estimate the age of the maker.

FIGURE 9.3 Children's Graffiti at Polly Hill Plantation. This photograph illustrates what Dr. Jane Baxter is calling children's graffiti, done at Polly Hill Plantation in the Bahamas. This particular image is of ship iconography prevalent at Polly Hill Plantation.

PHOTO: Jane Baxter.

BOX 9.1 FINDING CHILDREN IN THE PAST: CHILDREN'S GRAFFITI AT POLLY HILL PLANTATION

Archaeologists have often failed to consider the material traces left behind by children in the past. Dr. Jane Eva Baxter of DePaul University has attempted to address this issue in her numerous publications and research projects on the subject. One particularly innovative project Baxter has undertaken concerns the archaeology of children at Polly Hill Plantation, which is located on San Salvador in the Bahamas.

San Salvador has a complex history, including occupation by British Loyalists in the late 1700s, who brought native-born African slaves and Creole slaves from the Caribbean and the Southeastern United States. While San Salvador's enslaved population were emancipated in 1834, many of them remained marooned on San Salvador and other islands because they did not have the finances to return

back to their homelands. In the 1950s, the United States military built two bases in the region, marking renewed outsider presence and occupation at San Salvador.

During Baxter's research at Polly Hill Plantation, she discovered two buildings featuring incised graffiti that depict ships. The first building was used to house the enslaved who worked at or near the manor house; this building only had one graffito. The second building was a former office and industrial processing building; this building had over 25 graffiti. Baxter believes that some of this graffiti may have been the work of formerly enslaved children post-emancipation. How did she come to this conclusion? For one, Baxter, who is 5'2" tall, observed that much of the graffiti was not at her eye level, nor could the

(continued)

BOX 9.1 Continued

artwork have been drawn if someone of her height was sitting in a chair or standing. Second, the ship graffiti also appeared to have been created by a wide variety of "artists" with differing skill levels and appeared to lack details that an adult familiar with ships or shipbuilding might include.

Baxter believes this ship iconography goes beyond merely child's play. She suggests that ships may have been important to enslaved children for three reasons. First, ships were not commonplace during the time in which graffiti was incised and symbolized a "lifeline to the world beyond San Salvador." Second, ships may have been important to the enslaved because they are part of their "origin story" as to how they arrived on San Salvador. Lastly, Baxter believes that the ships were etched onto the buildings after the white enslavers left San Salvador. Ship graffiti may be the enslaved's attempt to reinscribe and claim landscapes formerly controlled by the enslavers.

SPECIFIC INDIVIDUALS

Many individuals of the past, including some rulers of the ancient civilizations of Egypt and China, have been identified, primarily by analyzing written records that accompany the burials. In recent years, archaeologists have expanded their interest to include identifying individuals of the prehistoric past. Rather than focusing on the names and positions of leaders, current research concentrates on identifying characteristics of individual commoners, craftspeople, or artisans. This includes, for example, determining physical stress on the body by examining skeletal remains, which could provide an indication of occupation; examining special characteristics of artifacts that may indicate the work of a particular craftsperson (e.g., the way lithic tools or pots were finished); observing the wear on tools to determine if an individual was right- or left-handed; and looking at characteristics of art to determine whether multiple pieces were created by the same or different artists.

BOX 9.2 **IDENTIFYING PIRATES IN THE ARCHAEOLOGICAL RECORD**

Pirates, especially those of the "golden age of piracy" in the Caribbean and the Americas – from about 1650 to 1750 – have been firmly embedded in popular culture. With advances in underwater archaeology in recent decades, these pirates and their material have become an area of interest for historic archaeologists, especially those focusing on doing archaeology underwater.

Some archaeological research concentrates on pirate lairs, but mostly the archaeology of pirates focuses on the identification, documentation, and interpretation of the wrecks of their vessels and the remains found onboard. One of the most obvious things that has resulted from the archaeology of pirates is the knowledge that identifying people, ships, and cargo as being associated with pirates is difficult. Research shows that popular images of pirates are far from reality, and identifying them in the archaeological record is difficult. Some researchers (Babits, Howard, and Brenckle 2006), for example, intimate that it isn't as if we are likely to find a cabin on a ship with arm hooks, wooden legs, eye patches, and a parrot on someone's shoulder, and note that the clothing pirates wore was largely indistinguishable from other sailors, that any pirate modification to a ship is unlikely to have preserved, and that cargo would not necessarily be a good indicator of piracy, but a variety of weaponry might.

Much of the work on pirate archaeology was brought together in the book *X Marks the Spot: The Archaeology of Piracy*, edited by Skowronek and Ewen (2006). A core theme of the book is that the popular image of piracy is not very realistic, and identifying pirates and their ships and cargo usually requires complementary research by historians and archaeologists. The book provides some case studies of archaeological research on pirate lairs and pirate ships.

Reconstructing Ideology

Reconstructing ideology involves making inferences about what people thought, including worldviews, beliefs, intellectual frameworks, and values. Although the material remains of ideology form an obvious part of the archaeological record, there have been relatively few attempts until recent times to establish a body of archaeological method and theory to deal with it. Inferring ideology from material remains has long been considered the most difficult of all archaeological inferences. As a major theme of archaeological research, it emerged in the late twentieth century and is often known as **cognitive archaeology**. The research primarily focuses on evidence of sacred sites and **religious ritual**; mortuary practices; and art. Although not routinely encountered in the archaeological record, cannibalism and trepanation are also often considered in the framework of ideology.

SACRED SITES AND RELIGIOUS RITUAL

Sacred sites are those presumed to have religious significance. For the purpose of archaeology, religion is defined as a shared belief about supernatural powers. Religious rituals are formalized, repetitive acts associated with religious beliefs, and often take place at sacred sites.

In a seminal paper on archaeology and religion, Colin Renfrew (1994) suggests that religious ritual can be identified by material evidence that focuses attention, reflects boundary zones between this world and the next, represents images or symbols of a **deity**, and demonstrates participation and offering (Table 9.3). Site location, features, and artifacts may serve to focus attention. Mountaintops and caves are particularly common ritual sites, which in addition to providing a focus can also represent

TABLE 9.3 Archaeological Indicators of Ritual

Evidence that focuses attention	Special, natural locations, such as a mountaintop or cave
	Special building designed for religious functions, such as a church or temple
	Features and artifacts that focus attention, such as an altar
	The repetition of symbols
Evidence that suggests a boundary zone between this world and the next	Features and artifacts that promote concepts of pollution and the need to purify, such as pools and basins of water
	Architecture that may reflect both public displays and hidden mysteries
Evidence that suggests the presence of a deity	Images of the deity
	Animal symbolism relating to specific powers
	Symbols also seen in other ritual contexts, such as funerary
Evidence of participation and offering	Art and iconography reflecting prayer and worship
	Devices for inducing religious experiences, such as music and drugs
	Animal or human sacrifice
	Offerings of food, drink, and other material objects
	Great investment of wealth in the offerings and the facilities

Source: Based on Renfrew 1994.

the interface between worlds. Features such as altars, artifacts such as figurines, and repeated symbols also function to focus attention.

The boundary zones between this world and the next may also be reflected in the presence of water, such as in basins or pools. Evidence of deities may come in a variety of forms, including carved figurines, painted images, and **frescoes**, all of which may be abstract or realistic.

Evidence of participation and offering may be reflected in many ways, including art and iconography representing prayer or worship. The presence of drugs or musical instruments may represent induced religious experiences. Offerings of various kinds may also be interpreted as evidence of ritual. These include both human and animal sacrifice as well as offerings of food, drink, and artifacts.

One example of ritual that is reflected in material evidence is the practice of **capa cocha**, an Inka ritual involving the sacrifice of children to the gods on mountaintops. Pilgrimages through Inka territory, some of which took months to complete, climaxed with the sacrifice of a child on high altitude sites in the Andes. In addition to the sacrifice, a wealth of goods was offered, including figurines made of gold, silver, and exotic shell.

At least four archaeological indicators of ritual are evident in the capa cocha sites: the mountaintop locations, which represent both a place for focusing attention and a boundary zone between this world and the next; the sacrifice of children; the presence of figurines; and a great investment in time (trekking to the very high altitudes of the Andes).

MORTUARY PRACTICES

The deliberate and ritualistic postmortem treatment and disposition of the body is usually taken to indicate a belief in an afterlife. While some have suggested that disposing of bodies by burial is simply a way to remove rotting corpses, this can easily be countered with arguments that burial is far more time-consuming than other means of disposition, such as simply dragging the corpse to a midden. Although not all archaeologists accept that burial indicates a belief in an afterlife, at a minimum it is taken to represent a reverence for the dead.

The presence of grave goods usually strengthens inferences about a belief in an afterlife. When the grave goods include food, this is almost always taken to affirm a belief in an afterlife. When the grave goods consist of personal artifacts, however, some archaeologists may counter that this simply represents further reverence for the dead and perhaps a belief in bad luck (from using artifacts associated with a deceased individual).

The positioning of a body may provide some indication of belief systems. It is not unusual for archaeologists to find bodies laid out in cardinal directions, such as an east-west alignment correlated with the rising and setting of the sun. The alignment of the bodies may even be used to make inferences about specific religions. For example, in some cemeteries that have been excavated, the individuals were buried on their side and aligned toward Mecca, suggesting the individuals were Muslim. In a study of almost 500 Inuit burials from Siberia, Alaska, and Canada, Barbara Crass (1999) identified distinctive alignments in directional orientations that she suggests can be correlated with Inuit ideology about different realms of the afterlife, with the positioning of the body directing the soul to the proper realm.

It is not uncommon for archaeologists to discover human remains buried in the fetal position, which provides an indication of people's thoughts about the life cycle. It is also not uncommon to discover **ochre** sprinkled around or painted on bodies, which also suggests belief systems strongly tied to the earth. Usually red and powdery, ochre is roughly translated in many languages as "blood of the earth."

FIGURE 9.4 Mortuary Archaeology. Reconstructing the life history stories of people who have long passed on involves using multiple lines of evidence. As this drawing shows, these data sets include historic photographs that can come from family photo albums, museums, or archives; artifacts recovered from the people's homes or neighborhoods; an understanding of the family's religious practices and belief systems; and analysis of material culture using resources like historic catalogs to understand how much a family made and how much they spent on their goods, including headstones.

IMAGE: Katherine Cook.

Whether burials were individual or collective can be used to make inferences about the values of the society. When a collection of individuals buried together are identified as a family, for example, it may be inferred that the sense of family was highly valued.

Similarly, it is not uncommon for individuals to have undergone a primary burial followed by a secondary burial. In this case, individuals who were buried shortly after death would be exhumed after several years so that all the individuals of a group (e.g., a lineage) could then be interred together, providing evidence of the value placed on descent groups.

THE MEANING OF ART

Both visual and performing arts are recognizable in the archaeological record, but the visual arts receive most attention.

Pictographs and petroglyphs are often considered to be the work of shamans attempting to influence supernatural powers. This interpretation primarily comes from the fact that pictographs and petroglyphs are often located in remote and

FIGURE 9.5 Goddess Figurine from Çatalhöyük. This 8,000-year-old "goddess figurine" was found during excavations overseen by the Çatalhöyük Research Project in 2016 at the Neolithic site of Çatalhöyük, Turkey. Some scholars believe this figurine represents reverence for older women or elders who were perceived as bearers of sacred knowledge. Other scholars believe that this figurine represents fertility worship across the globe, as similar figurines have been found in Europe and the Middle East.

PHOTO: Çatalhöyük Research Project, Ian Hodder and Jason Quinlan.

difficult-to-access locations, such as cliff faces and deep recesses of caves. Also, the style of rock art is often distinct from other art associated with the community, suggesting a different purpose. Further, pictograph images are often superimposed over each other, suggesting that it is the process of doing art, rather than the final product, that is most important.

Non-shamanistic explanations of rock art include those tied to economics and social life. Art is often seen as a mechanism of recording and measuring, which is also often seen as a component of ideology. Similarly, art is often perceived to be a reflection of gender, sexuality, and power, which are both social and ideological.

Most studies of art in the context of reconstructing ideology focus on two-dimensional artistic depictions (such as painting) as well as three-dimensional sculptures manufactured from wood, stone, clay, antler, bone, and metal. Sculptures, both large and small, are represented around the world. The **Venus figurines** are one well-known type found in many sites in Europe dating between about 30,000 and 20,000 years ago. The figurines, averaging about 11 centimeters (4.4 inches) in height and made from a variety of materials, generally portray women, often with large buttocks and breasts and explicit genitalia. Features of the face are often simple or nonexistent. There is no consensus on what these figures mean, but they are usually correlated with ideology. The figures have been variously interpreted as symbols of fertility, goddesses, or matriarchies; self-portraits by women artists; educational tools; and prehistoric pornography.

CANNIBALISM AND TREPANATION

Although not common, evidence of cannibalism does exist in the archaeological record. It isn't likely, however, that cannibalism has ever been a regular component of any group's subsistence strategy. The major types of cannibalism and its archaeological indicators are listed in Table 9.4.

TABLE 9.4 **Types and Archaeological Indicators of Cannibalism**

TYPES OF CANNIBALISM	DEFINITION
Exocannibalism	Eating non-group members
Endocannibalism	Eating group members
Ritual cannibalism	Eating people, usually in very small or symbolic portions, as part of a ritual
Vengeance cannibalism	Eating enemies
Aberrant behavior	Deranged individuals eating people
ARCHAEOLOGICAL INDICATORS OF CANNIBALISM	**EXAMPLES**
Modification to human bone	Butchery marks on human bone
	Artificially enlarged foramen magnum
	Charring or burning of human bone
Coprolites	Human coprolites containing human remains
Context	Human bone found mixed with food refuse

Considering the amount of meat returned for the effort and risk, hunting, killing, and butchering humans does not make economic sense. Hunting deer, for example, is less dangerous (a deer isn't typically going to have a weapon to fight back), and provides more meat per individual than most humans.

Where cannibalism does occur, it is often interpreted as being opportunistic, such as when killing enemies, which is a form of both exocannibalism and vengeance cannibalism. This may explain why some archaeological sites exhibit some human remains that have been obviously cannibalized, while some other individuals have been buried.

Based on ethnographic observations, some evidence of cannibalism can be inferred to be ritualistic in nature. Ethnographic observations of cannibalism in recent times suggest that cannibalism usually demonstrates a reverence for the dead. When a prominent person of a particular lineage dies, for example, parts of that individual may be cannibalized by other members of the lineage in a show of respect and perhaps in the belief that they may obtain some of that person's qualities and abilities. These are examples of both endocannibalism and ritual cannibalism.

Archaeological indicators of cannibalism include bones that have been cooked, bones that have been broken in a particular fashion to get marrow, butchery marks on the bone, and disposal with other trash. These indicators are most likely to suggest that food was the primary reason for the cannibalism. Another indicator of cannibalism, particularly ritualistic cannibalism, is an artificially enlarged **foramen magnum**. A common method of extracting the brain was to extract it through the foramen magnum, which was enlarged by removing some of the bone around the edges of the hole. Ethnographic observations suggest that with ritualistic cannibalism, the brain was a favored part of the body, perhaps because it was perceived to be the most likely location of a person's essence.

Trepanation, also known as trephination, is the removal of a piece of bone from the skull. Trepanation is known to have occurred in prehistoric times in Europe, Africa, Asia, and the Americas, with more than 1,000 known cases in total. Bone was typically removed by incising or drilling.

Trepanation is often considered in the context of ideology because a common explanation for the phenomenon is that the procedure was done on people who may have been thought to be possessed by evil spirits, with the removal of bone providing a route for them to escape. It has been thought to be ritualistic and a medical procedure to relieve perceived pressure on the skull and perhaps some conditions like epilepsy.

Because many trepanned skulls show no signs of healing around the edges of the incised or drilled hole, it is assumed that death was a not unlikely consequence of the procedure, presumably by infection setting into the brain. Evidence of healing around the edges of the hole on many others, however, indicates that the procedure wasn't

FIGURE 9.6
Trepanated Skull.
Trepanation is known to have occurred in many places around the world during pre-historic times. The reasons are not always clear. Trepanation may have occurred for ideological reasons, such as to release evil spirits, or for medical reasons, such as releasing pressure on the brain.

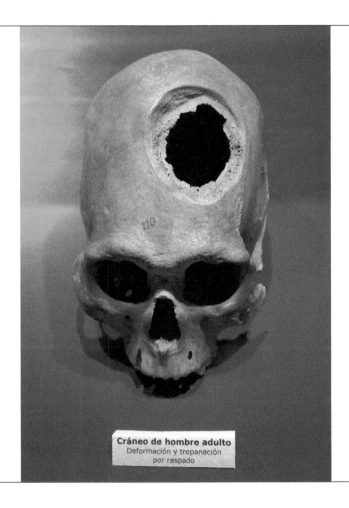

Cráneo de hombre adulto
Deformación y trepanación por raspado

PHOTO: Barry D. Kass @ ImagesofAnthropology.com.

always fatal. Some individuals evidently went through the procedure up to several different times during their lifetimes.

KEY RESOURCES AND SUGGESTED READING

Children in archaeology is covered well by Baxter (2005, 2007, 2008, 2019), and the archaeology of pirates by Skowronek and Ewen (2006). Ideology is thoroughly covered by Insoll (2011).

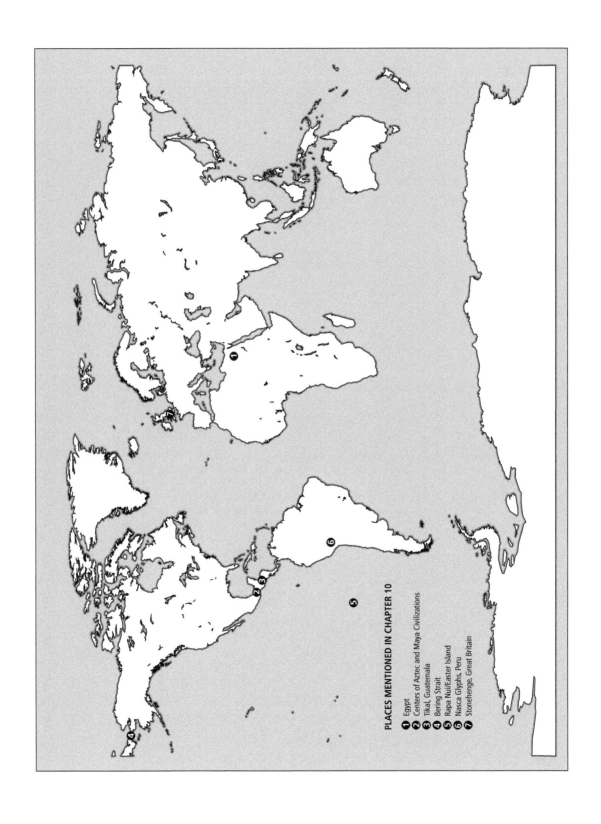

PLACES MENTIONED IN CHAPTER 10

1. Egypt
2. Centers of Aztec and Maya Civilizations
3. Tikal, Guatemala
4. Bering Strait
5. Rapa Nui/Easter Island
6. Nasca Glyphs, Peru
7. Stonehenge, Great Britain

CHAPTER 10

EXPLAINING THINGS OF ARCHAEOLOGICAL INTEREST

Introduction

This chapter focuses on explaining how and why things change. To situate the kinds of things that archaeologists need to explain, it begins with an overview of three levels of archaeological research. It then focuses on culture change, covering its mechanisms and conceptual frameworks, and explanations for the rise of food production and the collapse of civilizations. The final sections examine bias in archaeological explanations and how archaeologists evaluate competing hypotheses.

Three Levels of Archaeological Research

Archaeological work usually falls within one of three levels (Table 10.1). Low-level research, also known as low-range research, constitutes most types of field and laboratory work. It involves such things as finding, recording, and excavating sites as well as basic laboratory analysis. Although ultimately governed by some theoretical considerations in the research design, low-level research is the least explicitly theoretical aspect of archaeology. Reconstruction of culture history may also be thought of as low-level research. Matthew Johnson (2019, 4–7, emphasis in original) describes the theoretical aspect of low-level research as follows:

> In practice, every day of our working lives as archaeologists, *we decide on which order to put our facts in*, what degree of importance to place on different pieces of evidence. When we do this, we use theoretical criteria to decide which facts are important and which are not worth bothering with.... What makes us archaeologists as opposed to mindless collectors of old junk is *the set of rules we use to translate those facts into meaningful accounts of the*

TABLE 10.1 Three Levels of Archaeological Research

Low-level research	The least explicitly theoretical aspect of archaeology includes most kinds of field and laboratory work, and the reconstruction of culture history includes such things as recording sites and describing artifacts
Middle-level research	Attempts to understand the patterning of material remains, primarily through ethnoarchaeology, experimental archaeology, and taphonomy
High-level research	Focuses on explaining significant events in the human past, how various parts of cultures influence each other, and why cultures change

past, accounts that "make sense" to us as archaeologists and (it is hoped) to those that read or engage with our work. And those rules, whether they are implicit or explicit, are theoretical in nature. Facts are important, but without theory they remain utterly silent.

Middle-level research, also known as middle-range research or middle-range theory, is most often identified with ethnoarchaeology, experimental archaeology, and taphonomy. The study of site formation and disturbance processes clearly falls within the realm of middle-range research. Middle-range research provides the links between the material remains observed by the archaeologist and human behavior. It can then be used to make broader inferences about cultures and culture change.

High-level research, also known as **grand theory** or **general theory**, attempts to explain significant events in the human past and the basic nature of cultures, including how the various parts of cultures influence each other and why cultures change. Research at this level is the most explicitly theoretical, and includes studies of what are commonly referred to as revolutionary developments or big events in the history of humankind (Table 10.2).

The production of food and the collapse of civilizations are perhaps the two types of major events that have both academic and popular appeal. The conditions under which these events occur are discussed in more detail later in this chapter.

Many other types of archaeological work fall under the category of high-level research. Studying the use and production of tools involves determining the antiquity of the establishment of tool making (currently dated to about 3 million years ago) and the conditions under which the spread of new technologies throughout prehistory occurred – including stone tools, fire, spears, atlatls, and bows and arrows. Biological

TABLE 10.2 Major Areas of Grand Theoretical Interest in Archaeology

The rise of social complexity
The collapse of civilizations
The origins of tool use and tool making
The development of home bases and division of labor
The origins of abstract thought
Migrations and expansions of territory in prehistory
The origins of food production

anthropologists and archaeologists are both interested in the development of home bases and the division of labor, and study in this area involves determining the antiquity of these events and the conditions under which they occurred. Archaeological interest in the origins of abstract thought includes examining the development of and evidence for speech, art, and beliefs. Studies of migration and territorial expansion focus on the initial spread of the genus *Homo* out of Africa close to 2 million years ago, the expansion of modern *Homo sapiens* throughout Africa, Asia, and Europe beginning about 100,000 years ago, and migrations to Australia about 65,000 years ago and to the Americas at least 15,000 years ago. Studies of the rise of social complexity focus on understanding the conditions that lead to different forms of inequality and types of societies, including the emergence of states and civilizations.

Mechanisms of Culture Change

There are two basic kinds of culture change: **synchronic change**, meaning change through space, and **diachronic change**, meaning change through time. The major mechanisms of cultural change include in situ evolution, diffusion, trade, and migration.

Studies of synchronic change usually focus on the mechanisms under which ideas and materials spread relatively quickly through broad areas, such as continents or hemispheres. Diffusion, trade, and migration are the usual explanations for synchronic change.

Studies of diachronic change examine expansive geographic areas, but focus as well on explaining change in specific sites. In situ evolution in specific sites or regions can be established by observing the same basic pattern of culture persisting through time, although a few major changes and many minor ones may occur. Sometimes major and relatively sudden changes, in settlement patterns or subsistence strategies for example, are thought to be indicative of population movements, but they are often in situ adaptations to changes in the environment. Changes in house size during prehistoric times in some areas of North America, for example, are strongly correlated with significant alterations in temperature. The incorporation of certain types of fish and shellfish in diets is correlated with the stabilization of rivers and sea levels (which is assumed to have led to increased productivity of these resources).

Invention is the primary mechanism of in situ technological change. Generally defined as the creation of a new artifact type, invention is identified in the archaeological record by the discovery of prototypes. Much like mutations are the ultimate source of change in biological evolution, invention may be seen as the ultimate source of change in technology. Archaeologists also often refer to innovation, which is usually taken to mean the application of an existing technology in a new way. For example, the technology of firing clay to make ceramic figurines (evident about 25,000 years ago) was later applied to the making of pottery (beginning about 15,000 years ago).

Diffusion (the spread of ideas) is undeniably the principal source of cultural change. It is widely agreed that more than 90 per cent of the traits of any one culture, past or present, have spread through diffusion. The notion that good ideas spread quickly is not new, and applies to the simplest stone tools dating to more than 2 million years ago and electronic technology in contemporary times. It is not necessary to find evidence of the physical movement of material technology, whether through trade or changing populations, to explain why new technologies appear suddenly in a culture. But because diffusion deals with the spread of ideas rather than material objects, it is somewhat difficult to identify with certainty in the archaeological record. Inferences about diffusion are often based on the relatively sudden incorporation of a technology, with no apparent prototypes in the area. Examples include the spread of atlatls and bows and arrows around the world during prehistory.

Trace-element analysis of raw material often indicates an artifact was acquired through trade. Many types of stone, such as obsidian, exhibit trace elements that are unique to the original source. Trade routes and spheres of interaction are often established by linking sites with specific raw materials to their original source. Chemical fingerprinting of obsidian, for example, indicates that it has been traded over the past 10,000 years through various linguistic and ethnic areas of the Pacific Northwest.

Specific kinds of seashells are also often used to infer trade. Shell studies have demonstrated that shells were a part of extensive trade networks extending thousands of miles in both North and South America. Conch shells from the Gulf of Mexico, for example, have been found in archaeological sites in Ohio and Manitoba.

Migration, which infers the replacement of one ethnic population with another, is commonly used to explain cultural change. Archaeological indicators of migration include the relatively sudden occurrence of multiple cultural traits, including new settlement patterns, subsistence strategies, diet, artifact types, art, and burial practices. This includes the use of local raw materials in new ways, such as obsidian suddenly being used for making jewelry instead of for arrowheads. Inferences about migration are more credible if they are supported by significant and sudden differences in skeletal remains and if the homeland of the migrant population can be identified, based on the similarities of cultural traits.

Conceptual Frameworks

Archaeologists seeking to explain cultural change usually identify with a particular conceptual framework, also commonly known as a **paradigm**, research strategy, grand theory, or **heuristic theory**. These frameworks provide starting points and guides for archaeologists in their research.

Describing the nature of such frameworks, Philip Salzman (2004, 30–32) defines and describes heuristic theories as

> [those] that guide our inquiries. Heuristic theories are very general in the sense that they are very abstract and purport to cover myriad facts from many times and places.... Heuristic theories guide anthropological thought by offering a vision of social and cultural reality and directing attention to what it deems important. Each heuristic theory proposes a way of looking at the world, a way of carrying out research, and a way of understanding research findings.... Heuristic theories cannot really be tested to see whether they are true or false but instead are generally judged to be useful or not useful, fruitful or not fruitful in generating interesting results.

Table 10.3 lists a sample of conceptual frameworks used in archaeology. Unilinear cultural evolution is of historical use only, and many others (e.g., Annales School, catastrophe and chaos theories, environmental determinism, Darwinian archaeology, and sociobiology) are not commonly used. The dominant frameworks used in archaeology in the twenty-first century fall into the broader categories of ecological, social, and ideological.

ECOLOGICAL FRAMEWORKS
Ecological frameworks assume that the driving force of cultural change lies within the sphere of ecology, including changes in the environment, economy, technology, or demography. Cultural ecology and cultural materialism fall within the realm of ecological frameworks, and they have been the dominant conceptual frameworks in

TABLE 10.3 **Conceptual Frameworks in Archaeology**

Agency theory	Focuses on intentional actions of individuals in creating change
Annales School	Stresses the interrelationship of short- and long-term events
Catastrophe theory	Views culture change as a buildup of minor factors that suddenly overload a cultural system, causing major changes
Chaos theory	Views culture change as being caused by small-scale and apparently random phenomena
Cognitive idealism	Views ideology as the driving force of culture change
Conflict theory	Focuses on social conflict within and between cultures
Critical theory	Focuses on the inner, hidden workings of societies (also known as the Frankfurt School)
Cultural ecology	Focuses on the interrelationship between humans and the natural environment
Cultural materialism	Focuses on the environment, economy, technology, and demography as the driving force of culture change
Darwinian archaeology	Modeled after Charles Darwin's theory of biological evolution, but with "cultural" rather than biological traits being subject to selection processes
Diffusionism	Focuses on the spread of ideas
Environmental determinism	Views culture as primarily an adaptation to natural environments
Feminist archaeology	Addresses inaccurate depiction of gender roles in the past and systemic gender inequality
Functionalism	Focuses on the interrelationship of the various components of a culture
Historical particularism	Views the evolution of each culture as being unique
Marxist archaeology	Focuses on the economy and conflict between classes
Sociobiology	Views cultural behavior as driven by biology
Structuralism	Focuses on social systems and institutions
Unilinear cultural evolution	Views cultural evolution as following a singular, predetermined course; of historical interest only; no longer considered valid

archaeology for the past several decades. The basic idea is that all, or almost all, cultural change is triggered by something that initially occurred within the ecological sphere. Archaeologists using ecological frameworks tend to consider the ecological sphere of culture as the most important, and view aspects of culture change in the social and ideological spheres as primarily reflections of or repercussions from occurrences in the ecological sphere. Religion, values, patterns of social inequality, and type of society can be all explained by an initial change in environment, technology, economy, or demography.

SOCIAL FRAMEWORKS

Social frameworks begin by assuming that cultural change may be initiated in the social sphere of culture. Archaeologists using social frameworks look first to social phenomena as a cause of change in all aspects of culture, including the ecological and ideological spheres. Common social frameworks in archaeology are conflict theory, feminist archaeology, and Marxist archaeology.

IDEOLOGICAL FRAMEWORKS

Ideological frameworks start with the basic assumption that the ideological sphere of culture initiates culture change, with repercussions in the social and ecological spheres. Agency theory and cognitive idealism (also known as cognitivism) are considered ideological frameworks.

The conceptual framework an archaeologist uses usually reflects the way she or he thinks cultures work. Most people have some ideas about what the most important parts of culture are, although outside of academia, labels such as "conceptual frameworks" and "paradigms" are rarely used.

Consider, for example, aid agencies seeking assistance for an impoverished people. Change may be initiated in different ways for the overall betterment of the people. Some groups may wish to introduce new varieties of high-producing crops to the area to initiate change, reasoning that once food shortages are taken care of, everything else will fall into place. These groups are working within an ecological framework. Other groups, also claiming to be working for the betterment of all in the region, may wish to initiate change by replacing a particular leader or overthrowing the government – clearly working within a social framework. Others may wish to initiate change in the ideological sphere, reasoning that if you can change people's beliefs and values, then everything else will fall into place.

Another example can also serve to illustrate the different frameworks. Imagine three different experts attempting to explain the rise of youth violence. One expert, using a materialist framework, suggests that it has been caused by lack of permanent, well-paying jobs for youth. Another expert, using a social framework, may believe the root cause of youth violence lies in the breakdown of the nuclear family. The final expert, using an ideological framework, may attribute the cause to the decreasing participation of youth in church activities and subsequent loss of moral guidance.

Although both examples above (i.e., aid for impoverished people and youth violence) provide ecological, social, and ideological views, no one view is necessarily better than the other. Each view is based on the sphere of a culture the people involved believe is most important to initiating or explaining change.

The fact that conceptual frameworks are neither right nor wrong, true nor false, means that there will always be disagreements among archaeologists about why cultures change. Choosing a conceptual framework to guide research is an archaeologist's personal choice, based on a plethora of factors, including but certainly not limited to his or her own evaluations, experience, and belief systems.

The need for choosing a conceptual framework to guide research is perplexing for many newcomers to archaeology. Those who are familiar with archaeology, however, usually understand the necessity. Archaeologists recognize that facts do not speak for themselves, and there is no objective truth. At a very elementary level, conceptual frameworks narrow down the types of facts that are collected. The types of data that can be collected to explain any phenomena are almost infinite. Conceptual frameworks serve to organize thoughts and define the methods of research.

Because there is no agreement on a universal research strategy, and there never will be, debates will always be a part of archaeology. It is unlikely, for example, that consensus on the conditions underlying the origins of food production and the collapse of civilizations will ever exist.

Explaining the Transition to Food Production

Food production is the term used to describe the advent of plant and animal domestication, which led to pastoralism, horticulture, and agriculture. Early theorists postulated that a solitary genius had come up with the idea for food production or that plants were accidentally discovered growing in middens. They then invoked diffusion to explain the relatively widespread adoption of food production around the world. Food production has long been considered a milestone in human development, and before the 1960s most assumed that it made life better overall for those who made the transition, by creating more leisure time and better health.

In the mid-twentieth century, as ethnographers and ethnoarchaeologists began research on various groups of food producers (pastoralists, horticulturalists, and

FIGURE 10.1
Agriculture in Egypt.
A primary area of interest in archaeological research is to understand the conditions leading to the transition to reliance on domestic foods. This photo illustrates a water buffalo rigged to a wheel mechanism designed to enable the irrigation of fields.

PHOTO: Bob Muckle.

agriculturalists), and non-food producers (generalized foragers) in the contemporary world, and as bioarchaeologists studied the activity of those groups in the past, it became clear that life for the earliest food producers was probably more difficult than for foragers. In particular, ethnographic research showed that food producers work longer in subsistence activities than non-food producers. Thus, foragers have more leisure time than food producers. Research from bioarchaeology showed that early food producers suffered worse nutrition and health than foragers.

Once archaeologists realized that food production did not immediately lead to a better life overall, they discounted all the early hypotheses that saw only the benefits and none of the ill effects of relying on domestic foods. In recent decades, archaeologists have been examining other potential benefits that may have been viewed as a worthy trade-off to increased work and worse health.

One of the most oft-cited benefits of food production is that it supports larger populations and allows increased sedentism. The debate, however, is whether these are really advantages. There is no doubt that domestication, because of the increased productivity of plants and animals, supports higher populations, but many people would argue that higher populations, with all that they bring in the form of conflict and transmission of disease, may be at least as much a disadvantage. While domestication also clearly allows for increased sedentism, not all view that as an advantage either.

Many foragers, for example, place a high value on mobility and resist efforts to become sedentary. However, sedentism allows for the accumulation of material things, and some perceive this to be an acceptable trade-off for more work and worse health. In Western industrialized nations, it is not uncommon for people to work very long hours, often leading to deteriorating health, so that they can drive nice cars, live in nice houses, and have an array of electronic devices.

Many archaeologists focus on the fact that increased productivity of plants and animals can provide a surplus of food to be used in times of stress on the natural resources. Others argue, however, that since food production tends to focus on considerably fewer plants and animals than a foraging way of life, it is actually riskier. They reason that if a particular disease decimates one or two wild plant or animal species in a region, foragers can still rely on the dozens of others they normally use. But if a disease were to hit one or two of the crops or animal species upon which food producers rely, the results would be catastrophic for the people.

Few archaeologists would dispute that people were aware of their ability to increase the productivity of plants and animals. People likely did some occasional weeding and watering of plants and perhaps ensured supplies of food and water for animals long before these activities emerged in the forms we recognize as pastoralism and horticulture. Research by archaeologists, ethnobotanists, geographers, and others shows that before the arrival of Europeans, the Indigenous Peoples of the northwest coast of North America managed their landscapes, plants, and animals in a variety of ways to increase productivity, without reaching the stage known as domestication. These management techniques included weeding, burning, transplanting, removing rocks from clam beds, and introducing some types of fish into waterways in which little or no productivity of those species previously existed.

Contemporary archaeological explanations of the transition to food production can be considered in the context of ecological, social, and ideological frameworks.

Ecological explanations often invoke **population pressure** as the trigger for food production, reasoning that there was no longer enough food to support the extant population numbers. In other words, the carrying capacity of the region was no longer large enough to support the population. This may have been caused by environmental changes. For example, the wild plants and animals in a local area may have supported a population of about 1,000 for many thousands of years. Then, due to any of several environmental changes, the wild resources were only sufficient to support about nine hundred. This reduction in food availability led to population pressure, and the people eventually had to spend more time in food production, initiate strategies to get food from others, or reduce their population size. They chose food production.

Explanations within social frameworks suggest that the trigger for the transition lay in the social sphere of cultures. Some adherents of this view suggest that it was the acquisition of increased social status that led to food production. For example, leaders who wished to raise their status may have put pressure on their kin groups to create food surpluses for feasting or trade, further elevating their status and wealth. Another social explanation is that domestication originated as a way to use the marginal members of societies, such as children and the elderly.

Ideological frameworks provide various explanations for food production, and most consider the domestication of plants and animals for subsistence to be a by-product of ideology. One such explanation is that domestication is a by-product of shamanism, reasoning that the first domesticates may have been pharmaceuticals. James Pearson (2002) suggests that shamanism might have been an underlying factor in the origin of agriculture because the experience with pharmaceutical plants may have been transferred to food plants. Others reason that food production was a by-product of producing plants for alcohol, leading humorist Dan Murphy to write, "There are academics who now think that we gave up our nomadic ways and started tilling the soil mostly so we could get the hops and rye and grapes with which to concoct drinks. If they're right, it means that the cocktail is the basis of civilization. And we settled in towns and cities primarily so our waiters could find us."

It is worth considering that people making the transition to food production did not necessarily know the disadvantages. However, once started, it is near impossible to revert to a foraging way of life without significant reductions in population. Both archaeology and history have demonstrated that as carrying capacity increases, human populations invariably also increase to catch up.

Explaining the Collapse of Civilizations

All civilizations collapse, eventually. The collapse of individual civilizations and of civilizations in general is a topic of much interest and debate in archaeology. Table 10.4 lists some of the explanations for collapse, within ecological, social, and ideological frameworks.

The most common materialist explanations for the collapse of civilizations, both in particular and in general, tend to focus on the degradation of soils used for growing crops and ever-increasing populations. One common explanation is that with growing populations and the correlated need for larger amounts of food, fields were not left fallow long enough to replenish the nutrients for productive crops. Consequently, the amount of food that was produced began a continual decline until the population could no longer be supported. Other ecological explanations suggest the following reasons: population growth increased faster than crop yields could keep up, salts left by irrigation water rendered the soils unsuitable, climate change caused droughts, and epidemic diseases damaged crops.

TABLE 10.4 Explanations for the Collapse of Civilizations

Ecological	Ecological catastrophe (e.g., earthquakes, volcanic eruptions)
	Climatic change (e.g., drought)
	Epidemic diseases to crops
	Depletion of soil nutrients through overuse
	Rendering the land useless through irrigation, leading to increased salinity of soil
	Overpopulation
Social	Collapse of trading networks
	Warfare with other groups
	Peasant revolts and other forms of internal conflict
Ideological	Too much effort spent on religious activities, drawing people away from the agricultural labor force
	Fatalism, stemming from religious prophecy forecasting doom

Social explanations for the collapse of civilizations include internal conflict, warfare, and failure to maintain trading alliances. Explanations involving internal conflict usually suggest a class revolt of some kind or ethnic rebellions within empires, which require that resources normally allocated to agriculture be redirected to the conflict, leading to the collapse of the economic system.

Ideological explanations often suggest that excessive resources were expended in religious activities. For example, the construction of religious monuments may have drawn people away from the agricultural labor pool, and that may have started a chain reaction of events. In the first year of construction, the reasoning goes, crop production may have been reduced, and this reduction was then interpreted as evidence that the gods were unsatisfied. Therefore, people may have further increased their religious activity in the next year, making that year's crop even worse, and so on.

Another ideological explanation suggests that collapses resulted from a degree of fatalism, reasoning that religious prophecies predicted doom and people simply accepted it. It has been suggested, for example, that when the Spanish became a threat to the Aztecs about 500 years ago, the Aztec emperor was a fatalist who believed in omens of disaster. To the emperor, overthrow by foreigners was inevitable, and the Aztec strategies for dealing with the Spanish were formulated with this assumption in mind.

FIGURE 10.2 Tikal, Guatemala. A major Mayan site, with population estimates ranging up to 200,000, Tikal (like many other Mayan sites) was abandoned relatively suddenly about 1,000 years ago. Understanding the conditions leading to the collapse of civilizations is a primary area of interest in archaeology.

PHOTO: Alamy / Yaacov Dagan.

Understanding Bias in Archaeological Explanations

Table 10.5 lists some of the types of bias in archaeological explanation. Some kinds of bias are obvious and others are not. One of the most obvious is the inherent bias of the archaeological record. As outlined in Chapter 4, this includes the bias the original inhabitants showed when they chose what to abandon or discard and what to recycle or keep. It also includes preservation bias, such as the fact that stone and clay are more likely to be preserved than are metal and organic remains.

The bias of conceptual frameworks should be at least equally obvious. As outlined earlier in this chapter, the conceptual framework an archaeologist chooses usually reflects what he or she perceives to be the most important sphere of culture and the driving force of cultural change. This kind of conceptual bias can usually be seen in the introductory sections of research articles. The bias is rarely explicitly stated, but after reading the first few paragraphs of an article, the basic assumptions of the author usually become obvious. Ecological frameworks are the ones most commonly used by archaeologists over the past several decades. The bias toward ecological frameworks may stem from the fact that archaeologists deal mostly with remains that are directly related to the ecological sphere of culture (e.g., physical remains of environments, settlement patterns, subsistence, and diet), leading to a tendency to overemphasize their importance.

TABLE 10.5 Major Kinds of Bias in Archaeological Explanations

Inherent bias of the archaeological record
Bias of conceptual frameworks
Bias of age
Bias of sex
Bias of nationality
Bias of ethnicity
Bias of training and education
Bias of time and place

Biases of age, sex, nationality, and ethnicity may also be obvious. Our perspectives are colored by who we are. People of different ages, sexes, nationalities, and ethnic groups have different experiences and agendas. Like many academic disciplines, the history of archaeology has been shadowed with heavy male bias, although this has begun to change significantly in recent decades. One example of this bias is the focus in the archaeological record on what are generally perceived to be male activities, such as hunting and warfare. Similarly, throughout most of its history, archaeological research could fairly be called **Eurocentric**. A study of atlases of "world prehistory" by Chris Scarre (1990) showed an extreme bias toward European prehistory. In a sample of archaeological atlases produced by European publishers, Scarre found that despite purporting to be about world prehistory, they devoted about 30 per cent of their space to Europe and more than 20 per cent to the Near East. The UNESCO list of World Heritage Sites is similarly biased in that Europe is overrepresented. Post-processual archaeologists often make biases of age, sex, nationality, and ethnicity explicit. Most others do not.

The bias of training and education may not be so obvious, but is nevertheless important to understand. Students are usually heavily influenced by their professors. One of the reasons it is usually considered preferable for professional archaeologists to receive their degrees (B.A., M.A., and Ph.D.) at different universities is that it exposes them to a variety of frameworks, ideas, and experiences.

The biases of time and place are among the least obvious, but perhaps most important, to understand. It has become increasingly apparent in recent years that whether consciously or not, archaeologists are strongly influenced by current events. Examples include explanations of European cave art and the collapse of the Mayan civilization.

Paul Bahn (2000) shows how explanations of European cave art reflect obsessions and prejudices of the times. In the late nineteenth and early twentieth centuries, simplistic notions about "primitive" people correlated with the idea that the cave art must have been mindless graffiti, play activity, or associated with magic. The sexual revolution of the 1960s is correlated with a plethora of studies examining the sexuality depicted in the cave art; the general interest in space exploration is correlated with interpretations of cave art as astronomical in nature; the burgeoning use of computers led to descriptions of the art as "a series of giant floppy disks or CD-ROMs"; and the legacy of drug culture and its associated hallucinogens and altered states of consciousness is correlated with explanations that the art reflects trance imagery.

In the article "The Ancient Maya and the Political Present," Richard Wilk (1985) examined explanations for the collapse of the Mayan civilization 1,000 years ago in the context of American history, suggesting that archaeological explanations by Americans are influenced by informal and often hidden philosophical and political debates. Explanations pointing to warfare as the cause of the Mayan collapse, most prominent in the 1960s, are strongly correlated with American military involvement in Vietnam. Ecological explanations, gaining prominence in the 1970s, are strongly correlated with environmental movements of the time; and ideological explanations parallel the rise of religious fundamentalism, also in the 1970s. This trend has continued, with researchers observing that the rise of economic explanations in the 1990s occurred in tandem with economic globalization during that time, and the recent shift back to explanations of warfare and ecological disaster becoming increasingly common in the twenty-first century correlate with contemporary American concerns with terrorism, war, and climate change. The implication is that the current events surrounding archaeologists on a daily basis through popular media are likely to affect the way they think about the past.

Evaluating Competing Explanations

Table 10.6 outlines criteria for evaluating explanations in archaeology. These criteria are a guide, part of the package called critical thinking skills.

The idea that explanations are testable is fundamental to all scientific inquiry. Quite simply, if the hypothesis cannot be tested empirically, then it should be considered no further. Gods and extraterrestrial aliens may exist, but there is no empirical evidence of their presence. Therefore, explanations relying on god(s), aliens, or other supernatural phenomena are simply not acceptable in archaeology. When faced with a hypothesis, archaeologists should first ask if there is a way of testing it with material remains.

TABLE 10.6 Criteria for Evaluating Archaeological Explanations

Is the hypothesis testable?	If not, consider it no further
Is the hypothesis compatible with our general understanding of the archaeological record?	If not, be cautious
Can the hypothesis be used to explain more phenomena than competing explanations?	In general, the more phenomena a hypothesis can explain, the better
Occam's razor	The simplest explanation is usually the best
Have all competing explanations been considered equally?	Do not accept one hypothesis by merely rejecting the others

In general, hypotheses that are compatible with our general understanding of the archaeological record are more likely to be accepted than those that are not compatible. Despite recent claims that the first migrants to the Americas may have come via the North Atlantic Ocean or the South Pacific, the hypothesis that they came from northeast Asia via the area around the Bering Strait remains the most plausible explanation for most archaeologists. The Bering Strait route is most compatible with our understanding of world prehistory, which places people in northeast Asia before the Americas, and provides evidence of similarities in culture.

Hypotheses that can explain several phenomena are usually considered to be better than others. This is often referred to as the explanatory power of the hypothesis. A hypothesis that explains the collapse of all or many civilizations, for example, is usually considered better than one that explains the collapse of a single civilization.

Occam's razor, also known as Occam's rule, is based on the notion that the simplest explanation is usually the best, and the simplest explanation is the one requiring the fewest assumptions. It is named after William of Occam, the thirteenth-century philosopher who developed it.

It is good practice to consider all explanations equally. A common mistake is to begin with a series of possible explanations and then systematically eliminate them one by one until there is only one remaining, and then declare that hypothesis the best.

Almost all explanations invoking gods or aliens use this approach, ruling out all sorts of explanations that can be empirically tested and then concluding the phenomena must be attributable to a god, extraterrestrials, or some other supernatural phenomena.

Figure 10.3 illustrates the image of a hummingbird in the Nazca desert of Peru. It is one of the dozens of animal figures that, along with hundreds of miles of straight

BOX 10.1 PSEUDOARCHAEOLOGY

Pseudoarchaeology involves explanations of places, people, and things from the past using unusual, far-fetched, often bizarre, and extremely unlikely scenarios. Although proponents of outlandish theories often purport to be following scientific methods and contextualize their explanations within archaeology, they are clearly not following the principles or methods of science in general and archaeology in particular, and usually demonstrate a poor understanding of the prehistoric and historic past.

Pseudoarchaeology is big business. One well-known pseudoarchaeologist, Erich von Daniken, has sold tens of millions of books, opened a theme park, and produced multiple documentaries, all purporting that many of the major features of the prehistoric past have been either created or facilitated by visits to Earth by extraterrestrial aliens. Pseudoarchaeology persists in mainstream media, in print, online, in movies, on video, and on a multitude of television programs, including documentaries and reality programming.

Pseudoarchaeologists often make fantastic claims, including, but certainly not limited to, that the lines on the Nazca desert in Peru are in fact landing strips for alien spacecraft; that the Egyptian pyramids were built with knowledge obtained from extraterrestrials; that the statues of Rapa Nui were created to relieve boredom by stranded extraterrestrials awaiting rescue; and that Mayan art depicts ancient astronauts.

One of the most common ploys of pseudoarchaeologists, especially those claiming to be following the scientific method, is to frame possible explanations as a series of several hypotheses. They then proceed to rule out all the hypotheses but the last one, which invariably is the most fantastic, bizarre, and outlandish of all, often invoking extraterrestrials and occasionally conspiracies by mainstream archaeologists to keep things quiet. This is far from acceptable science. A basic rule of science is that one should never accept a hypothesis by merely ruling out the others. And this is what pseudoarchaeologists do, almost every time.

---

lines, concentric circles, and geometric shapes, are known collectively as the Nazca glyphs. They were evidently created by sweeping the top layers of pebbles on the desert to expose the lighter soil underneath, and research indicates that they were created about 1,000 years ago.

Many people have proposed explanations for the glyphs. One common archaeological explanation suggests they served as sacred pathways and symbols. Competing explanations by non-archaeologists often invoke the influence of extraterrestrial aliens. The leading proponent of extraterrestrial influence is Erich von Daniken, author of several books promoting supposed evidence of extraterrestrial aliens on Earth. According to von Daniken, the straight lines may have been landing strips for alien spacecraft, and the images may have been created by earthlings based on instructions from the aliens.

When we go through the criteria for evaluating competing explanations for the glyphs, we need look no further than testability. The hypothesis that they were landing strips for alien spaceships or were created under instructions by aliens is simply not testable. But it is certainly easy enough to empirically test the hypothesis that they are sacred pathways. In fact, data has been collected depicting similar images

FIGURE 10.3 Hummingbird Glyph on the Nazca Desert, Peru. Dozens of animal forms and several hundred miles of straight lines are found in the Nazca desert. Archaeologists have no problem correlating them with the Nazca peoples living in the area 1,000 years ago, although some other people prefer to believe they are associated with extraterrestrial aliens.

PHOTO: Shutterstock / Dmitry Gritsenko.

on the pottery of the Nasca people of the time, and ethnographic and historic research shows numerous examples of people walking straight lines as part of religious rituals.

The sacred pathway and symbol hypothesis also wins as the most compatible with our current understanding of the archaeological record. The lines and images are both compatible with Nasca culture. The alien hypothesis is not compatible at all. The application of Occam's razor suggests a clear preference for the archaeological hypothesis of sacred pathways as well. The only assumption that has to be accepted for the sacred pathway and symbol hypothesis is that the Nasca people had the capability to create the lines (which experiments have demonstrated to be quite simple). Supporting the alien hypothesis, on the other hand, requires assumptions that extraterrestrials exist, have come to Earth and landed their craft, and have had successful communication with earthlings who have then followed instructions in creating the animal images.

The Nazca glyphs are among hundreds of sites and features throughout the world for which popular, nonscientific explanations invoking lost civilizations, extraterrestrials, and supernatural forces abound. Other well-known examples include Stonehenge, the statues of Rapa Nui (Easter Island), and purported evidence of Atlantis. As with the Nazca glyphs, it is difficult to accept the nonscientific explanations when pitted

FIGURE 10.4 Statues of Rapa Nui. There are approximately 1,000 of these large stone statues, also known as moai, on Rapa Nui, which is also known as Easter Island. For some, these moai are mysterious and best explained as being associated with extraterrestrial aliens. To archaeologists there is little mystery. They are associated with the art and other cultural aspects of the Indigenous Peoples of Rapa Nui. They were carved in quarries on the island and transported to their current positions several hundred years ago.

PHOTO: Nadine Ryan.

against archaeological explanations and evaluated against the stated criteria. Proponents of the non-archaeological explanations often prey upon the fallacy that people without a European heritage were not smart enough or did not have the intrinsic cultural imperatives to construct monumental architecture and other large-scale features. Research in archaeology and anthropology suggests the opposite is quite true – people throughout the world in prehistoric and recent times had both the ability and the imperative.

BOX 10.2 FROM WOLF TO FIDO: THE DOMESTICATION OF DOGS

Have you ever wondered how wolves went from growling predators to tail-wagging, eager-to-please pets?

Dogs occupy a very special place in, believe it or not, *human* history. Some archaeologists believe that dogs not only managed to make the transition from aggressive wolves to faithful fidos, but that they also helped humankind develop more complex thinking and cognition in the process. According to Dr. Donna J. Haraway, Distinguished Professor Emerita of the

(continued)

BOX 10.2 Continued

History of Consciousness program at the University of California, Santa Cruz, dogs are "companion species" to humans, with both species engaging in a mutually beneficial, co-evolved relationship throughout time (Haraway 2003).

So how did dogs become humankind's best friend and vice versa?

Dogs broke away from their ancestral wolf tendencies through a process known as domestication. Domestication is defined as the process through which humans exert control over an animal or plant. The domestication of dogs likely happened at several places across the globe and at different moments in time, though it is believed that dogs were first domesticated in either Asia or Europe (Thalmann et al. 2013). Recent evidence suggests dog domestication started in Asia approximately 20,000 to 40,000 years ago (Handwerk 2018).

There are multiple theories as to why and how domestication occurred. Some scholars postulate that wolves started trailing hunter-gatherers, who left behind tasty refuse piles and bones for wolves to consume. Soon, wolves got braver and began approaching hunter-gatherer settlements, with hunter-gatherers feeding wolves in exchange for protection from predators. Aggressive wolves who bit or attacked humans were culled from the herd, while wolves who exhibited positive, friendly traits were bred by humans. This process of humans selecting desirable traits from plants or animals is known as **artificial selection** or **selective breeding**.

Domestication has come at a cost for dogs. In watching and listening carefully to their human companions, dogs have lost skills that are necessary to survive in the wild. For instance, dogs have lost their ability to work well as a pack due to their reliance on their human counterparts (Handwerk 2018).

What are some examples of artificial selection we can see in dogs today? Scientists have compared the facial muscles and eye movements of domesticated dogs to wolves and have found that dogs are able to produce "puppy eyes" that may release oxytocin in humans (Kaminski et al. 2019). New human mothers release oxytocin so that they can bond with and care for demanding newborn infants and, in this case, with their canine companions. Tail-wagging and eye contact with humans (Hare et al. 2002) are two additional evolutionary adaptations that helped build the bond between human and dog. Dogs continue to serve important roles in today's society: they aid humans in hunting parties, warn humans of threats by barking, protect the public as police dogs, and work as service dogs to people who are blind, who have epilepsy, and who use wheelchairs.

KEY RESOURCES AND SUGGESTED READING

For more on conceptual frameworks, Trigger (1989), Johnson (2019), and Dark (1995) are recommended; for the collapse of civilizations, Yoffee and Cowgill (2001). For more on the areas of grand theoretical interest, Kintigh et al. (2014) is suggested. A good source on pseudoarchaeology is Feder (2020).

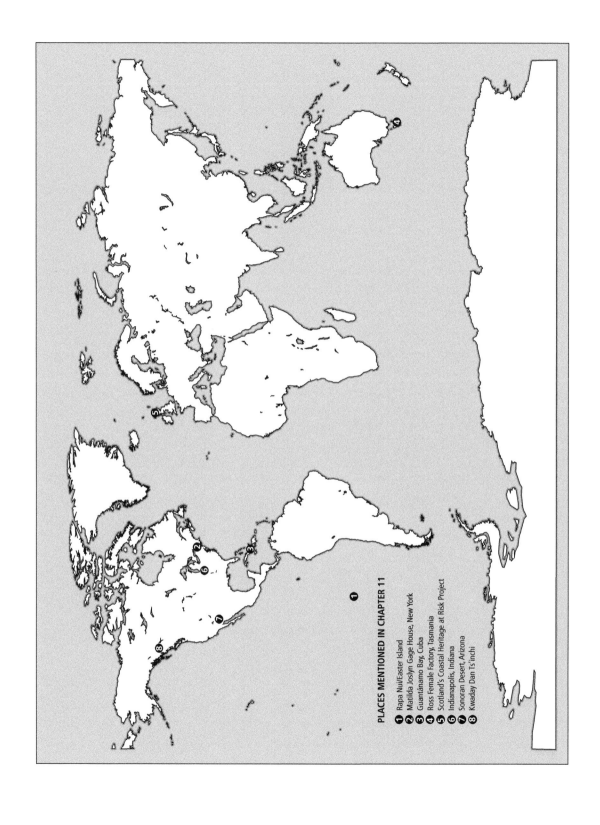

PLACES MENTIONED IN CHAPTER 11

1 Rapa Nui/Easter Island
2 Matilda Joslyn Gage House, New York
3 Guantánamo Bay, Cuba
4 Ross Female Factory, Tasmania
5 Scotland's Coastal Heritage at Risk Project
6 Indianapolis, Indiana
7 Sonoran Desert, Arizona
8 Kwaday Dan Ts'inchi

CHAPTER 11

THE ARCHAEOLOGY OF YESTERDAY, TODAY, AND TOMORROW

The Current State of Archaeology

The current state of archaeology can be described in multiple ways. On some fronts, little has changed since 2003, when archaeologist Geoffrey Clark (2003, 61) stated:

> In sum, American archaeology at the beginning of the twenty-first century is many things. At a minimum, it is a science-like endeavor, an industry (the "heritage industry"), a platform for promoting various political agendas, a medium for educating the public, and an exercise in public relations.

It is tough to make a decent living in most parts of North America without at least a Master's degree. One of the reasons for this is that in addition to a specific amount of fieldwork experience, governments often require permit holders and field supervisors to have a graduate degree. A recent survey of archaeologists in North America showed that average salaries for those with a Master's degree or Ph.D. were between $50,000 and $100,000. Not surprisingly, university professors and owners of commercial archaeology firms, or those in senior positions with government, are usually the highest paid. A 2019 report by the US Bureau of Labor Statistics states the median income for an archaeologist in 2018 was $62,000 per year, or $30.00 per hour. The hourly median income for Canada, by contrast, was $36.00 per hour.

The proportion of males and females active in archaeology remains roughly equal, yet recent studies show that males tend to receive more research money and there is a recent trend toward more women receiving Ph.D.s than men (see Goldstein et al. 2018; http://saa-gender.anthropology.msu.edu).

Archaeology tends to remain highly valued in academia, politics, and global social movements. Governments around the world, for example, still protect archaeology through legislation, support the teaching of archaeology in colleges and university, and offer financial support for research.

Archaeology is not without its problems, however, and there are many issues of major concern. One is precarious employment, with little or no guarantees of work. Many working in CRM, for example, are hired only for the duration of specific projects, and many of those teaching archaeology in colleges and universities are on short-term contracts, often for far less pay than regular instructors or professors. Archaeologists working in colleges and universities are not alone in precarious employment. The American Association of University Professors has noted a distinct rise in part-time positions, and for the year 2016, 73 per cent of university instructors were non-tenure track, or contingent laborers.

Other important issues that are at least in the initial stages of being addressed include the lack of diversity and safety in the workplace, including addressing sexual abuse, harassment, and bullying.

Archaeology has a broader scope than ever before, in regards to both time and place. The time period for studying material culture has now been pushed back to around 3 million years, and there is significant interest in the very recent past and the contemporary world. And archaeologists aren't restricted to Earth anymore, as is evidenced by considerable research documenting and studying orbital debris and material culture left on planets and asteroids.

Archaeology has changed considerably over the past few years. While in the past archaeologists in training would almost always be involved in finding and excavating sites and analyzing artifacts, it is now common for people making careers in archaeology to have little or no involvement in fieldwork or laboratory work, instead finding careers focusing on recently emergent areas of interest such as digital archaeology and public archaeology.

"Archaeologies of the Heart," or heart-centered archaeology, is yet another kind of archaeology to emerge in very recent times. As described by Lyons, Supernant, and Welch (2019, 6), it is part of a shift away "from the disconnected ethos that pervades (much of) archaeology as objective science and towards the unification of our intellectual and emotional selves to produce a more holistic and integrated practice," which invokes notions of love and is characterized by care, emotion, relationality, and rigor.

Many archaeologists are currently reflecting on and in some cases changing their vocabulary, especially when considering the archaeology of Indigenous Peoples of North America. One of the critiques of archaeology is that by using traditional academic and scientific terms, and centering Europeans in understanding the human past, archaeologists are complicit in the disassociation of Indigenous Peoples from people, places, and resources important to them.

Consequently, some archaeologists try to avoid using the term "prehistory" to describe the period before the arrival of Europeans, since it both centers Europeans and carries a negative connotation – insofar as using the prefix "pre" suggests a more primitive time, which it was not. Some archaeologists are replacing terms such as "site" and "midden" with more functional terms such as "village," replacing "skeletons" and "human remains" with "ancestors," and replacing "artifacts" with "belongings."

Archaeology is currently blurring the boundaries of disciplines within areas commonly described as the humanities, especially in regard to storytelling, art, and music. It is not uncommon, for example, to have sessions at archaeology conferences that focus on the intersections of archaeology and art, including music and other soundscapes; and archaeologists are increasingly using photo essays and stories illustrated by graphic artists to convey information to both academic and non-academic audiences.

Archaeologies of the Contemporary

An emerging trend in archaeology has been to focus on the material culture of the very recent past (e.g., the last few decades) and contemporary times. Some examples have already been included in this text, such as the study of contemporary landfills and efforts at marking nuclear waste. Some of the many other kinds of archaeology that focus on bringing archaeological method and theory to the material culture of modern times include (i) a wide variety of studies variously referred to as activist, action, applied, public, and collaborative archaeology; (ii) studies that focus on the disenfranchised and voiceless; (iii) forensic and disaster archaeology; and (iv) studies of contemporary waste.

ACTIVIST, ACTION, AND SIMILAR ARCHAEOLOGIES

Activist archaeology is described by M. Jay Stottman (2010, 8–9), one of the most ardent supporters of the field, as

> more about intentionality and advocacy, which should be focus for projects, not an aside ... To use archaeology to affect change in and advocate for contemporary communities, not as the archaeologist sees it but as the community itself sees it, defines activist archaeology.... It is about understanding a community and integrating its needs and wants into our work and using the process of archaeology and the knowledge it produces to help satisfy community needs.

FIGURE 11.1 Activist Archaeology. Over the past 10 years, archaeologists sought both to demand change from those within the discipline and to study how activists in the past went about their work to change their society for the better.

IMAGE: Katherine Cook.

The focus of activist archaeology is on contemporary people and issues, such as those relating to gender, ethnicity, class, and education. *Archaeologists as Activists*, a book edited by Stottman (2010), for example, includes contributions by several archaeologists practicing such archaeology, including using archaeology to address issues such as gender and feminism, race in a variety of contexts, and education and the educational system, as well as to help redefine community identity and create economic vitality in stigmatized and economically depressed communities. This type of work is continuing to grow in archaeology, and Christopher Barton has a forthcoming edited volume on this topic entitled *Trowels in the Trenches: Archaeology as Social Activism*.

Rather than calling these and similar kinds of archaeological projects addressing contemporary problems in the world "activist archaeology," others prefer the descriptor "action archaeology." In *Archaeology Matters: Action Archaeology in the Modern World*, Jeremy Sabloff (2008, 17) defines it as "*involvement or engagement with the problems facing the modern world through archaeology*" and "archaeologists working *for* living communities, not just *in* or near them" (emphases in original). One example is the identification of a particular kind of agricultural practice from ancient times in parts of South America known as **raised field agriculture**, which was more productive than the kinds of farming used in more recent times. Archaeologists were able to work with local farmers in the region, teaching them the techniques of previous systems based on their research and resulting in improved crop yields for contemporary farmers.

Other examples described by Sabloff (2008) include archaeologists working on an American slave plantation with descendants of the slaves who are now living in nearby communities; archaeologists working with Native American communities; and archaeologists working with students in Rapa Nui (Easter Island) to teach them multiple skills.

Distinctions between activist, action, applied, public, collaborative, and community archaeology are not always clear, and there is no consensus about precise definitions. In common usage, activist archaeology and action archaeology are roughly synonymous, although using the descriptor activist archaeology brings the focus of an activist agenda front and center. Any application of archaeology beyond pure research may be considered applied archaeology, but in practical terms, applied archaeology has usually been reserved for archaeology done under the umbrella of commercial archaeology or cultural resource management. Public archaeology can be used to describe archaeologists working with the public in almost any capacity, including K–12 and public education and outreach. Collaborative archaeology is often used to describe projects in which archaeologists work in partnership with various groups, including Native Americans. Community archaeology is sometimes used to refer to archaeology being done in association with descendant communities and sometimes working with local government or special interest groups such as neighborhoods or community groups.

Not every archaeologist can identify as activists; some are legally prohibited from identifying themselves as social activists. In the United States, federal and state employees are not permitted to perform any activist or partisan party work during their hours of employment. The legacy of the New Archaeology and the processualist movement in archaeology has also made archaeologists hesitant to adopt an explicitly social activist framework for archaeological practice, since processualism argued for a more scientific, objective, apolitical, and value-natural archaeological practice.

As mentioned, activist archaeology takes many forms. Some scholars study the archaeology of social activists in the past and how they worked to change the social conventions of their time. Activists studied by archaeologists include Gerrit Smith, Harriet Tubman, Elizabeth Cady Stanton, and Thomas and Mary Ann McClintock (Christensen 2010, 22). One example of this kind of work is Dr. Kim Christensen's research on Matilda Joslyn Gage, a prominent female social activist and abolitionist who lived in nineteenth-century New York. Gage helped found the National Woman

Suffrage Association out of her home, which became an epicenter for activist work. Based on her research on Gage, Dr. Kim Christensen argues that activism comes in many forms beyond the stereotypical ones we often see in media, such as protests and marches. Activism requires invisible work behind the scenes, such as mobilizing and organizing people and writing petitions, newspaper and magazine articles, and books.

One particularly interesting find from Christensen's excavation of Gage's household is the discovery of delicate ceramic teawares. Archaeologists studying this time period have historically interpreted ceramic teawares recovered from domestic (household) contexts as reflecting women's adherence to nineteenth-century ideas of middle-class femininity and domesticity. Some archaeologists have asserted that the consumption, use, and display of matching ceramic teawares was participation in what is known by historians as "the cult of domesticity." This ideology was prevalent in the nineteenth century, and posited that women are biologically designed to take care of their children, their husbands, and the private sphere of the home. Christensen's work turns this idea upside down, as Gage was serving tea while actively trying to overthrow social norms and conventions such as the cult of domesticity.

Another strand of activist archaeology actively seeks to change laws, ideas, and behaviors of the present using archaeological data. This work overlaps with many of the goals of public archaeology, in that it prioritizes how archaeology can be used to address problems of the present and right wrongs done in the past (including the wrongs of past archaeologists) (Stottman 2010; Atalay et al. 2014; Atalay 2014; Barton forthcoming). Some archaeologists, like Christensen, identify with multiple strands of activist archaeology. Christensen was involved with the (Matilda) Gage Foundation as an undergraduate. It was through her work there and a course of women's suffrage that she came to see herself as a feminist. She started the Matilda Joslyn Gage House Archaeological Project wearing multiple hats – archaeologist, activist, and stakeholder – and used archaeological data to help further her cause of championing women's rights in the past and in the present.

Not all activist archaeology, however, is equal. Some activist archaeology frames heritage as an asset belonging to the world without critically examining the political consequences of such rhetoric. An example of this is UNESCO's list of World Heritage Sites that are to be protected during conflict. As Dr. Maria Theresia Starzmann (2008) observes, powerful first world nations may invoke this notion of protecting heritage of "universal" importance to justify war and the loss of human lives. For this reason, Starzmann argues that archaeologists must be reflexive about their role and position in defending the profession and, consequently, be cognizant of how they may be playing a part in an imperialist project.

THE ARCHAEOLOGY OF INCARCERATION AND FORCED REMOVAL

As you have learned from this book, archaeology isn't simply digging in the dirt looking for the remnants of ancient civilizations. Rather, archaeology is a way of viewing the world through a unique kind of disciplinary lens: one that seeks to address how change occurs over time and investigate what social factors influenced those changes. These questions are critical to understanding human impulses and behaviors over time, whether in the archaeology of thousands of years ago or of ten seconds ago. Archaeologists look for changes in landscapes, food and dietary patterns, ceramic styles, and architecture, to name just a few. Archaeologists are also becoming increasingly interested in answering questions about our contemporary world using archaeological methodologies.

One example of this kind of work and unique methods of pursuing it is Dr. Adrian Myers's Camp Delta Project, which uses geographic information system (GIS) data via Google Earth's free open source platform to investigate the development of US Naval Station Guantánamo Bay, the US government's secretive and highly politicized prison. This prison's existence has been highly criticized by both American-based media and international news outlets since its founding in 2002. Camp Delta is one of several facilities at Guantánamo Bay and, as of Myers's 2010 publication, it incarcerated 215 men and boys accused of terrorism. Reporters and investigative journalists have claimed that Camp Delta's prisoners have been subjected to inhumane treatment, including being housed in cages and torture. They also claim that many prisoners have never formally been convicted of crimes.

Camp Delta's design and layout mirror that of "US supermaximum security prisons, where inmates are subjected to twenty-three hours per day of solitary confinement" (Myers 2010, 489). A number of scholars have argued that Guantánamo Bay's geographical location outside the margins of mainland America have made it an ideal liminal space where the United States government can act outside the US and international laws that govern how prisoners should be treated.

Myers uses GIS to investigate a covert government operation outside the American public's eye and in a space made physically inaccessible to scholars, lawyers, and human rights organizations. By looking at Google Earth satellite imagery from 2003 to 2008, Myers discovered that Camp Delta had expanded a great deal; floor space increased by 43.5 per cent, the fence surrounding Camp Delta increased by 35.5 per cent, and an additional 42 buildings were added to the landscape (Myers 2010, 461). According to Myers, this demonstrated that the US government anticipated incarcerating more individuals as it initiated a "Global War on Terror" in a post-9/11 world.

Former President Barack Obama ordered the Central Intelligence Agency to close Guantánamo Bay and to return some of its prisoners to their home countries in 2009.

Despite Obama's executive order, the prison remained open, though it incarcerated a smaller number of prisoners than in the years preceding his presidency. More recently, President Donald Trump ordered in 2018 that Guantánamo Bay be kept open indefinitely. Google Earth photos from 2019 show that the facility has grown substantially since Myers' article was published in 2010 (see Figure 11.2), which suggests that the prison will continue to be used by the US government for covert operations in the coming years.

Myers is not the only archaeologist to use archaeological methodologies to investigate incarceration. Over the last 15 years, archaeologists have drawn attention to the history of incarceration in the United States and beyond. They have studied a wide range of sites of imprisonment, including government-run boarding schools for Indigenous children in the United States; World War II internment camps for Japanese Americans and Japanese Canadians; World War II POW prisons for Germans and Italians in the United States; World War II concentration camps; and historic prisons and detention facilities around the globe.

Indigenous children around the globe have a shared history of being forcibly removed from their homes and placed in residential or boarding schools by the colonizing nation. In Finland, native Sámi children were forced to leave their families when the Public Education Act of 1947 was passed, requiring that all children in

FIGURE 11.2 Guantánamo Bay Detention Camp (GITMO). This image is taken from Google Maps footage of GITMO in 2020. Though the US government claims it has reduced the number of people GITMO incarcerates and its capacity for detaining people, the detention center has grown in size over the years.

IMAGE: Google Maps.

Finland attend public schools (Huuki 2016, 7). For the Sámi, this meant that children frequently had to relocate far away from their Indigenous lands, leaving their families and communities behind. We find the same pattern of violence and forced removal of Indigenous and Aboriginal children in Canada, Australia, and the United States during the nineteenth and early twentieth centuries (Trafzer, Keller, and Sisquoc 2006).

Archaeologists have recently begun to study these institutions to understand not only the impact this practice had on the children who were ripped from their families and held against their will by foreign governments, but also how it impacted and traumatized generations to come. In the United States, several Native American boarding schools have been excavated, including the Old Leupp Boarding School in Arizona (Two Bears 2019), Mount Pleasant Indian Industrial Boarding School in Michigan (Surface-Evans 2016), the Fort Spokane Indian Boarding School in Washington (Brunson 2012), the Steward Indian School in Nevada (Cowie, Teeman, and LeBlanc 2019), and the Phoenix Indian School in Arizona (Lindauer 2009). In Canada, the Victoria Jubilee Home sought to assimilate the Piikani Nation children (Dielissen 2012).

The goal of these institutions was to force Indigenous children to abandon their cultural and religious beliefs and to convert to a Western way of thinking and living. Upon entry into a boarding school, children were forced to cut their hair and part with clothing that was associated with their tribes. Part of this assimilation process involved gender-segregated instruction, inspired by Christian ideologies of the time. Boys and girls were housed in separate buildings and taught different skills, with the ultimate goal of funneling Indigenous children into low-paying jobs. Boys were taught carpentry, blacksmithing, baking, and how to farm and work in the agricultural industry. Girls, in contrast, received instruction in sewing, housekeeping, table-setting, meal preparation, nursing, and laundressing in preparation for work as domestic servants. Some girls and boys were even released to do this kind of work in towns neighboring their boarding schools.

The consequences of defying assimilation were severe. Discipline involved physical and emotional abuse, denying children food and/or water, public humiliation, and isolation from other children and people in prison or solitary confinement cells. Some children died at the hands of their supposed teachers. These conditions, along with homesickness and despair, compelled some children to run away. Other students confronted the institution head on. At the Mount Pleasant Indian Boarding School, a female student set the girls' dormitory and laundry building on fire as a last resort (Surface-Evans 2016, 585). Some children smoked tobacco and drank alcohol in sadness as well as in defiance.

What archaeological evidence exists documenting children's resistance to boarding schools' attempts at the cultural genocide and eradication of Indigenous Peoples? At the Fort Spokane Boarding School, it appears that boys resisted the clothing given to them by removing military-issue buttons on their uniforms, as demonstrated by the numerous military buttons recovered during excavations (Brunson 2012, 115). At the Phoenix Indian School, flaked pieces of glass, projectile points, and a clay bird effigy – objects considered contraband, since they were associated with Indigenous lifeways – found during excavations also document children's resistance to the United States government's federal assimilation policy (Lindauer 2009).

Another example of the use of incarceration to punish marginalized groups in society is Dr. Eleanor Casella's (2000, 2001, 2007) archaeological and documentary work on British female prisoners transported to Australia. Britain used female prisoners to create a labor force and build their empire in Tasmania, Australia. Tasmanian prisoners were convicted of petty theft and were sentenced to between 7 and 14 years of imprisonment and laboring for the British government. They were then transported to Tasmania by the British government to prisons, where they would labor to help build Britain's colony in Tasmania. Casella has excavated several of these female convict prisons, including the Ross Female Factory, which was reserved for women who committed additional offenses when they arrived in Australia. Offenses that would result in imprisonment at the Ross Female Factory include "illegitimate pregnancy, public drunkenness, insubordinate behavior, homosexuality, inciting riot, or trafficking in goods forbidden to convicts – particularly alcohol, tobacco, and money" (Casella 2001, 60). Female prisoners were not allowed to have currency or other worldly possessions. Punishment for violating the Ross Female Factory's rules was dehumanizing and violent, involving "solitary confinement, decreased food rations, distinctions in prison uniform, and public humiliation, including headshaving and periods of bondage in an iron collar" (Casella 2001, 49).

Despite severe consequences for insubordination, female prisoners engaged in illicit trade of forbidden goods, as revealed by Casella's archaeological research. The presence and density of buttons – particularly ferrous and bone buttons only recovered from sites associated with Aboriginals, former convict laborers, and prisoners – in solitary cells and across the prison landscape suggest that buttons may have been used as a form of currency within the prison and/or as gaming pieces (Casella 2000, 214). Fragments of alcohol bottles and kaolin smoking pipes likewise document an underground economy in the prison. There is also archaeological evidence of a fire – perhaps due to arson – in the solitary cells of the prison reserved for the "worst" offenders. Archival data also shows that female prisoners resisted the incarceral environment by rioting, by setting other prisons in Tasmania on fire, and through vandalism.

One of the lessons we can take from Casella's research on boarding schools is that heavy-handed disciplinary techniques of incarceration were ineffective in the past. Nonetheless, we continue to use similar forms of punishment tactics in the hope that this will "reform" prisoners. In the United States, some strategies still used in prisons include solitary confinement, using prisoners as a labor force for the government, and transporting prisoners out of their home state to another state. Archaeology shows that some lessons have yet to be learned when it comes to incarceration.

ARCHAEOLOGY OF THE DISENFRANCHISED, THE VOICELESS, AND THE INVISIBLE

Similar to activist archaeology is an emerging kind of archaeology that focuses on the disenfranchised, the voiceless, and those who many would prefer remain invisible in contemporary societies. Unlike archaeologists who claim to be doing activist archaeology, those who research the material culture of these groups may be more focused on research than on explicitly operating within an activist agenda, although they may indeed be attempting to shed light on social and political issues and to change social and political policies. These archaeologists do this by working with and studying concerns shared by the public.

Public archaeology is a field dedicated to the development, study, and assessment of attempts to educate the public about archaeology. Some, such as Dr. Gabe Moshenska, have defined public archaeology more broadly (see Figure 11.3) to include popular archaeology featured in the media; archaeology that is open and freely available online (websites, 3D models of artifacts, etc.) or offline (brochures, maps, etc.); archaeology done by amateur archaeologists, independent scholars, metal detectorists, and local archaeological societies; academic investigations into the relationship between politics and archaeology; and archaeology conducted within the context of the public sector, often with the aid of taxpayers' funds.

Archaeology has many publics, including stakeholders who live near to and/or have an interest in a particular archaeological project or site, the public at large, and descendant groups whose family once inhabited the landscapes and archaeological sites that archaeologists study. Public archaeologists are interested in studying how these groups respond to various forms of outreach, such as traditional, permanent or semi-permanent, and pop-up, temporary museum exhibits, curriculum, and open house events at archaeology laboratories and excavation sites. Archaeologists use this information to improve upon the messages they communicate about archaeology to the public.

Some examples of this work include studies on homelessness, climate change, and studies on undocumented migrants making crossings into the United States.

FIGURE 11.3 The Many Faces of Public Archaeology. This illustration by Gabe Moshenska shows the numerous ways archaeologists and the discipline of archaeology interact with the public.

ARCHAEOLOGISTS WORKING **WITH** THE PUBLIC

COMMUNITY ARCHAEOLOGY AND HERITAGE PROJECTS RUN BY MUSEUMS, UNIVERSITIES OR COMMERCIAL UNITS. ①

ARCHAEOLOGY **BY** THE PUBLIC

LOCAL ARCHAEOLOGICAL SOCIETIES, METAL DETECTOR CLUBS, AMATEUR INTEREST GROUPS, INDEPENDENT SCHOLARS. ②

PUBLIC SECTOR ARCHAEOLOGY

HERITAGE RESOURCE MANAGEMENT WORK CARRIED OUT ON BEHALF OF NATIONAL, REGIONAL OR LOCAL GOVERNMENT. ③

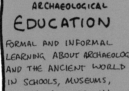

ARCHAEOLOGICAL **EDUCATION**

FORMAL AND INFORMAL LEARNING ABOUT ARCHAEOLOGY AND THE ANCIENT WORLD IN SCHOOLS, MUSEUMS, ONLINE, AND OUT IN THE WORLD. ④

SOME COMMON TYPES OF **PUBLIC ARCHAEOLOGY** BY GABE MOSHENSKA

OPEN ARCHAEOLOGY

ARCHAEOLOGICAL WORK THAT IS MADE PUBLICLY ACCESSIBLE THROUGH VIEWING PLATFORMS, WEBCAMS, GUIDES OR INTERPRETATION MATERIALS. ⑤

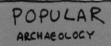

POPULAR ARCHAEOLOGY

TELEVISION SHOWS, MUSEUM EXHIBITIONS, BOOKS, MAGAZINES AND WEBSITES ABOUT ARCHAEOLOGY AND THE ANCIENT WORLD. ⑥

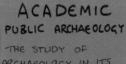

ACADEMIC PUBLIC ARCHAEOLOGY

THE STUDY OF ARCHAEOLOGY IN ITS ECONOMIC, POLITICAL, SOCIAL, CULTURAL, LEGAL AND ETHICAL CONTEXTS. ⑦

OTHER TYPES

THIS ISN'T SUPPOSED TO BE AN EXHAUSTIVE LIST, SO LET ME KNOW IF I'VE MISSED ANYTHING! g.moshenska@ucl.ac.uk @gabemoshenska © GABE MOSHENSKA 2015

IMAGE: Gabe Moshenska.

One of the best-known archaeologists studying the contemporary problem of homelessness is Larry Zimmerman, who has been focusing his research on American cities, particularly St. Paul, Minnesota, and Indianapolis, Indiana. He and others who study homelessness are often explicit in making their research relevant to policy makers and seek to work collaboratively with local communities. Ultimately, these archaeologists wish to help the homeless while at the same time contributing to scholarship. In part, they are able to do this by offering some assessment of the effectiveness of social services agencies and volunteer organizations.

One particularly well-received example of public archaeology is Scotland's Coastal Heritage at Risk Project (SCHARP). SCHARP is a project that relies upon the

goodwill and interest of Scotland's citizens to document and protect fragile archaeological sites found along Scotland's coast. Interested community members are encouraged to take SCHARP trainings that teach the public how to use SCHARP's free app, available to download on a phone, to document coastal archaeological sites at risk of being destroyed due to climate change. SCHARP researchers have studied the effectiveness and outcomes of their trainings in order to improve upon them in the future. SCHARP's award-winning work is discussed in a film (https://vimeo.com/channels/scharpevaluation), in reports, and in academic publications.

Many professional organizations and granting agencies explicitly state that archaeologists must disseminate their research and work to the public, as SCHARP has done. For this reason, the onus will continue to be on archaeologists to continue to develop new and innovative ways of communicating with the various communities we serve.

The Undocumented Migration Project, led by Jason De León, is a long-term ethnographic and archaeological project examining the processes and realities of undocumented border crossings from northern Mexico into the desert areas of southern Arizona. The archaeological component of the project focuses on learning from such artifacts such as water bottles and clothing left behind by the migrants in the desert.

FIGURE 11.5
Archaeology of Undocumented Migration. By studying artifacts left by migrants crossing from Mexico into the southern United States, archaeologists learn much about the processes and impacts of undocumented crossings.

PHOTO: Jason De Leon.

BOX 11.1 **ARCHAEOLOGY OF UNDOCUMENTED MIGRATION**

The Undocumented Migration Project is a long-term ethnographic and archaeological study of undocumented crossings in contemporary times, by foot, from northern Mexico into the United States via the Sonoran desert. The project is led by Jason De León at UCLA.

The archaeological component of the project focuses on documenting the material remains left behind during the desert crossings. The artifacts provide a plethora of insight into the process of border crossing. De León (2012, 478) uses discarded water bottles, shoes, and clothes, for

example, to "illustrate that the use of these items is determined by a complex and culturally shaped set of processes influenced by many factors including economic constraints, folk logic, enforcement practices, migrant perceptions of Border patrol and the human smuggling industry." He writes that "those who characterize the artifacts left behind by migrants as mere trash ... fail to recognize the historical, political, and global economic forces that have shaped border crossing into a well-structured social process." One example is the recent production of black plastic water bottles to capitalize on migrant folk logic that holds black bottles help prevent detection.

The project has documented dozens of "migrant stations" in the desert where the migrants typically eat, rest, change clothes, and leave things behind – sometimes intentionally, such as empty water bottles, worn shoes, and bloodied clothes, and sometime unintentionally, such as personal photos and letters. Thousands of artifacts have been recorded, but hundreds of thousands, perhaps millions, of empty water bottles and other artifacts remain uncataloged.

Interestingly, De León uses the concept of use-wear in his artifact analyses. Use-wear studies are well-known in prehistoric archaeology, where archaeologists determine the function of lithic tools and pottery by looking at wear patterns on the artifacts. De León (2013) brings the concept to the study of contemporary material culture in general, and border crossings in particular, focusing on wear patterns on empty bottles, shoes, clothing, and backpacks. He recognizes three major categories of use-wear, including wear patterns on shoes, clothes, and other artifacts; biological traces on artifacts (e.g., sweat, urine, menstrual blood, skin); and modifications to artifacts, including writing on packs, repair, and repurposing. He uses wear patterns on water bottles, for example, to infer that migrants refill their bottles from bacteria-laden stagnant pools and water tanks for livestock. Difficulties of the journey are also shown by such things as bloodied clothing and gauze, and urine-soaked clothing caused by dehydration ultimately leading to loss of bladder control.

The dangerous nature of border crossings through the desert should not be underestimated. Many do not survive. De León shows how archaeology can effectively be used to understand contemporary human activities, including not only the actual process of border crossing, but also the larger contexts of economic, social, political, and legal aspects surrounding it.

In short, results indicate that rather than deterring undocumented crossings, government policies and practices simply reshape the crossings into a dangerous social process, involving elements of the human smuggling industry and businesses quick to accommodate the needs of those planning on crossing the desert, such as by producing black plastic containers for water.

FORENSIC AND DISASTER ARCHAEOLOGIES

Forensic archaeology and disaster archaeology both emerged relatively recently, and although they are often linked, there are subtle differences.

Forensic archaeology is usually considered to involve the identification, recovery, and interpretation of buried human biological and cultural remains in legal contexts. Such work may range from assisting local police in locating and identifying a missing person to working with the United Nations to document genocide. Forensic archaeology is sometimes used synonymously with forensic anthropology, although in practice forensic anthropology tends to be used to describe studies that focus on human biological remains, while forensic archaeology tends to be used to describe studies that focus on cultural and biological remains.

TABLE 11.1 Defining Attributes of Disaster Archaeology

1. Problem solving: Disaster archaeology is intended to solve problems, such as determining the identification of victims and collecting evidence relevant to the disaster.

2. Assigned task: Disaster archaeology does not follow an archaeological research agenda; instead, it responds to requests of authorities at the scene.

3. Medicolegal requirement: Disaster archaeology requires very high standards of collection, recording, and interpretation, so as to possibly withstand court challenges.

4. Empirical minimalism: Disaster archaeology requires conclusions to be based on the simplest and fewest assumptions.

5. Archaeology leads: Disaster archaeology depends on archaeologists maintaining very high standards in their initial identification and documentation, since other specialists will depend on the reports for their own studies.

6. Situational awareness: Those working in disaster archaeology must be knowledgeable about what the various agencies involved are expected to do.

7. Attitude is everything: Those working in disaster archaeology must be aware of the structure of emergency services management, including its hierarchical structure, and archaeologists must be able to work in a cooperative and egalitarian way.

8. Safety is always first: The safety and health (including emotional health) of those involved in disaster archaeology is always the first priority.

9. Confidentiality is critical: It is important that evidence and information is not compromised or contaminated; discretion must be used in discussing information on-site and afterwards, and archaeologists should not be doing interviews at the scene; limits on disclosure may go on for many years and perhaps indefinitely; archaeologists should not necessarily expect to publish their work, including photos, in peer-reviewed journals.

10. Archaeology speaks for the victims: Those working in disaster archaeology are uniquely situated to provide emotional and legal closure.

Source: Based on Gould 2007.

Disaster archaeology is archaeology done in the context of identification, recovery, and interpretation following large-scale disasters, either cultural or natural, that usually lead to mass fatalities. Archaeologists involved in disaster archaeology are also actively involved in the processes of memorialization and bringing closure to relatives who have lost family. Disaster archaeology took hold in North America as part of the recovery efforts following the targeted attacks on the World Trade Center towers in New York City in 2001. Since then, archaeologists in this field have been involved with numerous other disasters, including night club fires and hurricanes.

The most ardent supporter of disaster archaeology is Richard Gould, who outlines the 10 defining attributes of the field in his 2007 book *Disaster Archaeology* (see Table 11.1).

ARCHAEOLOGY AND CONTEMPORARY WASTE

Few would doubt that waste of all sorts is a major problem on several levels, including its sheer volume, the danger posed by chemicals and other toxic substances in it, the pollution it causes, the ill-effects and fatalities in animals feeding on polluted things and plastics, the environmental costs of wasting resources on packaging, the financial costs of satellites and space stations avoiding orbital debris and ships avoiding enormous floating accumulations of trash in the Pacific and Atlantic Oceans, and the financial and labor costs of dealing with waste.

The enormity of the problem is described by Edward Humes (2012) in *Garbology: Our Dirty Love Affair with Trash*, as outlined in Table 11.2.

Although the initial archaeological studies of contemporary waste, described in Chapters 1 and 3, were popular and valued in the late twentieth century, they largely faded from popular perceptions of archaeology. In the early twenty-first

TABLE 11.2 American Trash

SOME BASIC DATA AND COMMENTS ON AMERICAN TRASH

Total pounds of trash created per person, per day:	7.1 pounds
Yearly loads of garbage trucks:	enough to fill a line of trucks that reaches halfway to the moon
Percentage of world's waste created by Americans:	25%
Money spent on waste management:	more than on fire protection, parks and recreation, libraries, and schoolbooks
Number of water bottles discarded each day:	about 60 million
Aluminum discarded each year:	"enough to rebuild the entire commercial air fleet four times over" (Humes 2012)
Plastic wrap discarded each year:	enough to shrink-wrap Texas
Wood deposited in landfills each year:	enough to heat 50 million homes for 20 years

Source: Based on Humes 2012.

FIGURE 11.6
Archaeology Students Sorting Contemporary Trash. Archaeology students sorting trash during an annual waste audit at Capilano University. This provides students with practical experience sorting objects, enables them to use trash to make inferences of behavior, and provides information leading to a significant reduction of waste on campus.

PHOTO: Bob Muckle.

century, the academic study of waste became the purview of other disciplines, especially human and environmental geography, environmental science, and sustainability studies.

Archaeologists, however, are beginning to reestablish themselves in academic studies of waste, bringing their theories and methods to problems of waste and what can be learned from it. An example includes professors and archaeology students on college and university campuses across North America becoming involved in campus waste audits. Waste is sorted and, when the results are determined, this gives campuses a baseline of data from which they can assess and improve upon discard behavior, such as strategically placing more and varied composting and recyclable containers on the grounds. Bob Muckle's archaeology students at Capilano University, for example, have participated in multiple campus waste audits, which have contributed to a significant reduction in waste and to learning about human behavior on a university campus. In this manner, waste archaeology can be referred to as a kind of activist or action archaeology.

Digital Archaeology

An area of considerable growth in recent years is digital archaeology, which refers to the use of technology to gather, interpret, disseminate, and preserve archaeological data. While there are many different approaches to digital archaeology, there are three core principles guiding digital archaeological work.

The first concept is that archaeological data and the technologies used to acquire it must be free. This means using open-access software and digital platforms. One example of non–open access software (also known as proprietary software) is ArcGIS. Many archaeologists use ArcGIS to create maps of the data they collect in the field. A license to use ArcGIS's software, however, is very expensive and is cost-prohibitive to even some cultural resource management firms. Some digital archaeologists have pushed for alternative mapping programs that are free to use. Dr. Benjamin P. Carter (see http://benjaminpcarter.com/digital-data-collection /tools/) has published a blog explaining how archaeologists can use open-source mapping software and digital platforms like QGIS and KoBoToolbox (https:// kobotoolbox.org).

A second core principle of digital archaeology is encouraging archaeologists to play with new technology and to experiment with new methods of interpreting and communicating information about the past. Feminist archaeologists were among the earliest archaeologists to adopt and explore using new modes of communicating and disseminating archaeological data using technology. Dr. Ruth Tringham and Dr. Rosemary Joyce, both professors of archaeology at the University of California, Berkeley, were the first to propose using the Internet to make space for discussions about archaeological interpretation. Tringham created a CD-ROM of photographs, audio, and texts associated with a Neolithic village in Yugoslavia, while Joyce shared primary texts from Tenochtitlan, an Aztec city, that have been interpreted in multiple ways by scholars. In more recent times, archaeologists have used augmented reality to enhance visitor experiences at museums and historic cemeteries; developed free apps for museum and archaeological site tours; reconstructed ancient cities, historic communities, and archaeological sites in virtual worlds like Minecraft and Second Life; and created and printed 3D models of artifacts so that the public can touch artifacts without fear of breaking them.

The third and final concept is that archaeological data, like the technology used to collect and interpret it, must be democratized so that researchers can use them in the future. This means that the digital data generated from archaeological projects, such as field maps, field photographs, artifact databases, site reports, and field notes, are preserved and actively curated by an organization or company. Funding agencies such as the National Science Foundation (NSF) and the National Endowment for the Humanities (NEH) in the United States now require that archaeologists receiving grants have a digital data management plan. Digital data must be taken care of in a manner similar to artifacts placed in storage. In the United States, archaeologists are encouraged to deposit all data generated from archaeological projects in the state in which the site is located. State Historic Preservation Offices are funded by taxpayers to support the preservation of archaeological site records. However, these offices often do not have the technological know-how or cloud or digital storage space to curate vast amounts of digital data generated by archaeological projects.

The Digital Archaeological Record (tDAR; https://core.tdar.org) provides a solution to this problem. It has the digital infrastructure needed to store and archive archaeological data from around the world for the long haul. In 2015, the Society for American Archaeology (SAA) reached an agreement with tDAR to allow presenters at the SAA annual meetings to upload their abstracts and papers for free. Since 2013, the Society for Historical Archaeology (SHA) has also allowed presenters at the SHA annual meetings to upload their paper abstracts and presentations for free.

Despite these advances, archaeologists who do not have funding to upload, organize, and curate their digital archaeological data are unable to guarantee the long-term preservation of their projects' data for future researchers beyond local repositories that may or may not be able to store and curate these digital data. Data sustainability will be an ongoing challenge for archaeologists in the coming years; past file formats and software programs used to generate archaeological reports or data tables have, in some cases, already become obsolete due to what is known in the tech world as "planned obsolescence." This renders valuable data inaccessible unless non-profits like tDAR or Open Context are actively managing such data.

Archaeology, Climate Change, and Sustainability

Archaeologists have much to contribute in regard to understanding human adaptations to climate change, including global warming. The archaeological record is replete with examples of how people adapt to environmental change, including modifying residential structures to better suit the climate, dietary changes to take advantage of changes in species availability, and sometimes abandonment of areas, including large settlements.

Some archaeologists believe that some of the land management practices of the past are more effective than those used in the present, and could be key to maintaining sustainability in times of ongoing climate change. Guttmann-Bond (2010), for example, suggests several approaches that could be tried: raised field agriculture (discussed earlier in this chapter) is quite effective in wetland areas – which may be particularly useful to know, since it is expected that wetland areas will increase with global warming; applying more effective methods of farming in deserts, which are also expected to increase with global warming; planting several species together, as many of the Indigenous groups of the Americas did with maize, beans, and squash, to increase productivity; and increasing yields by replacing pesticides with natural predators.

One interesting aspect of global warming for archaeology is that, as ice and snow melt, new evidence of past lifeways are emerging. This is especially prevalent in high-altitude areas such as the Alps, the Andes, and the Rockies, and in high-latitude areas such as the Arctic region. The discovery of Otzi the Iceman in the Italian Alps, for example, was facilitated by the melting of ice that had kept him preserved for more than 5,000 years. A similar discovery was made in the northwest region of North America, near the intersection of Alaska, British Columbia, and the Yukon, when melting ice exposed an Indigenous person and his or her belongings. The individual was given the name Kwaday Dan Ts'inchi, meaning "Long Ago Person Found" in a local First Nation language. For many, the discovery and recovery of cultural evidence from areas of melting snow and ice is called ice patch archaeology. Besides revealing inorganic remains, these melting ice patches are providing unique glimpses into artifacts made of organic materials that have survived several thousands of years or more. At least hundreds, possibly thousands of organic artifacts have been recovered by a relatively small group of archaeologists working in North America. From melting ice patches in the Yukon, for example, archaeologists have recovered prehistoric atlatl darts, arrows, and moccasins. A 10,000-year-old atlatl dart was recovered from a melting ice patch in the Rocky Mountains, near Yellowstone National Park.

Some archaeologists have commented on how it is somewhat paradoxical that although archaeologists study what kinds and how much waste others have, they are oblivious to their own waste (Wells and Coughlin 2012). This isn't the case with all archaeologists, however, and many are addressing issues of sustainability and addressing the ecological impact of their own work.

It is becoming increasingly common, for example, to save paper by using laptop computers, tablets, and other devices for recording. Some field projects are entirely paperless. Similarly, lab reports are often done digitally only, thus reducing paper. Other suggested ways of reducing waste include using biodegradable flagging tape and recyclable water containers, reducing electricity and other kinds of energy use in labs, and replacing plastic with glassware (Wells and Coughlin 2012).

BOX 11.2 FIRE AND ICE: ARCHAEOLOGY AND OUR CHANGING CLIMATE

Our rapidly changing climate has been a double-edged sword for archaeological sites and resources. Dramatic changes in weather patterns and temperatures have revealed previously unknown archaeological sites and artifacts, but these changes have also placed such resources in grave danger. If archaeologists and governments do not act promptly, sites and artifacts may be destroyed or looted.

Two new fields of archaeological research have emerged due to climate change: ice patch archaeology and fire archaeology. Ice patch archaeology is the study of archaeological sites and artifacts made visible due to melting ice patches found at high altitudes. Ice patch archaeologists are working in the Yukon, the Alps, Norway, and the United States to save artifacts revealed due to increasing temperatures. What is particularly exciting about ice patch archaeology is that it has resulted in the recovery of organic materials rarely found on traditional dirt-based archaeological projects. Organic artifacts, such as objects made out of wood, textiles, plant fibers, and bone, are unusual archaeological discoveries because they degrade quickly in the soil.

Ice patch archaeology has produced some of the oldest organic artifacts in the world (Muckle 2012). Canada's Yukon Ice Patches, located in First Nations territory, have recovered one of the oldest moccasins in Canada, dating to 1,400 years ago (Hare et al. 2012, 125). At Schnidejoch, a ridge of mountains located in the Swiss Alps, the left side of a pair of pants or leggings was found (Schlumbaum et al. 2010). It is considered to be an exceedingly rare and exciting find, considering that it dates to the Neolithic period and is made of leather. Further research was done on the leather to determine what animal was used to make the leggings. Upon further analyses, scientists discovered that the pants were made from a goat and, more importantly, a goat that is not present in contemporary Europe. The goat is only found in Southeast Asia, which provides new information about animal domestication and migratory patterns across the world.

You may be wondering why people would have sought high altitudes and crossed ice patches in the past. Ice patches served a variety of purposes, which differ across time and place. Schnidejoch is the longest continuously used pass, as artifacts dating to the Neolithic period, "the early Bronze Age (4100–3650 cal BP), the Roman period (2150–950 cal BP), and the Medieval period (1250–1050 and 650–450 cal BP)" have been recovered (Reckin 2013, 351). Researchers believe Schnidejoch was desirable because people used it for travel and trade (Reckin 2013, 352). Scholars believe that Canada's Yukon Ice Patches may have served multiple purposes. Woodland caribou have historically migrated to these ice patches to escape insects, cool down, and find a continuous water source during the summers. Indigenous Peoples recognized the caribou's migratory patterns and hunted them on the ice patches. Nearly all of the artifacts recovered from ice patches in the Yukon are associated with hunting, including darts, stone projectile points, and arrows (Hare et al. 2012, 121). This stands in contrast to artifacts recovered from the Alps, which are mostly related to human and not hunting activities. Some scholars have interpreted the discovery of basketry and containers found in the Olympic Mountains of Washington State and in the Yukon (Reckin 2013, 325) as an indicator that people were carrying ice off of the mountains as a water source. Finally, some researchers postulate that people may have used ice patches as an early refrigeration technique to keep meat cool.

Despite the exciting new information these organic artifacts have revealed about the past, ice patch archaeology presents significant challenges. Ice patches are typically difficult and expensive to access. In some cases, they are only accessible via helicopter or plane (Hare et al. 2012, 120). Some ice patches can only be explored during warmer seasons, meaning that archaeologists may only have a month or two of the year during which they can retrieve artifacts. Thawed-out organic artifacts must also be collected within a short period of time, as exposure to the elements, such as wind, UV radiation, and sunlight, means organic artifacts will likely disintegrate within a few years' time. The provenience of ice patch discoveries is also problematic, as artifacts typically drift to the base of the ice patch as the snow melts (Hafner 2012, 193).

Fire archaeology is another emerging subfield related to climate change. Fires have been around since time immemorial, but urbanization and our rapidly changing climate have created higher-temperature, fast-moving fires that have in recent times devastated large swaths of North America and Australia. In the western United States, fire seasons have expanded due to rising temperatures, which have created longer summers. Readers of this textbook are likely familiar with the frightening media images of people's houses burning to the ground and animals killed by rapidly spreading fires. Archaeology, too, is a threatened resource due to fires (Buenger 2003; Ryan 2010).

What happens to artifacts and archaeological sites during a fire?

For one, fire often removes the brush covering archaeological sites and artifacts, making them visible for, in some cases, the first time in thousands of years (Dunn 2018). Exposure means that archaeologists need to conduct post-fire surveys to identify and potentially collect archaeological resources before the sites are looted or post-fire processes, such as rain, wind, and erosion, move artifacts, causing

their provenience to be lost. Fire can completely destroy or dramatically alter historic and prehistoric artifacts, pictographs, and rock art. Similarly, they can make it nearly impossible to collect radiocarbon dates for an archaeological site. Fires can also distort stratigraphic sequences in the soil; some fires can burn as deep as 2 meters down into the ground, which can cause multiple occupational layers to be combined into one (Leslie 2019). Fire-fighting and suppression activities, such as the use of construction equipment to clear brush, can also cause archaeological resources to be damaged or destroyed.

What are archaeologists doing to try to lessen the impact of fire on cultural resources in the future?

Some archaeologists have worked with natural resource and fire experts to identify places most likely to be negatively impacted by fire in forests (United States Department of Agriculture 2012). Archaeologists can use these models to prioritize the survey and excavation of landscapes with a high likelihood of fire activity. This way archaeological resources can be identified and saved before fire sweeps through the area, destroying everything in its wake.

Predicting the Future of Archaeology

The use of sophisticated technologies is likely to increase in field and laboratory work. Despite the potential application of high-tech field and laboratory methods in some research projects, the fact remains that most projects are still relatively low-tech due to budget constraints. Many archaeological projects are quite small in scale and operate with minimal budgets. But continued decreases in costs for many once-prohibitive technologies, such as remote sensing techniques and total stations, will make the application of these technologies routine. It is also likely that the trend toward a less invasive and more sustainable archaeology will continue.

Archaeologists will continue to explore new avenues of research. Recently emergent areas of interest, such as Indigenous archaeology, activist archaeology, the archaeology of the very recent past and contemporary life, and community archaeology, are likely to flourish. Perhaps one of the most enlightening areas will be in the use of DNA research in archaeology.

The prospects of making a career in archaeology remain good. The US Bureau of Labor predicts a 10 per cent growth in the field between 2018 and 2028.

Archaeological issues, research, and practitioners will become increasingly connected on a global scale. This has already started with the widespread use of online archaeology periodicals, open-access journals, websites for projects and institutions, and social media.

Archaeologists will also undoubtedly continue to find and record many thousands of archaeological sites each year, lament the destruction of sites, and work toward the preservation of the archaeological record.

Academic archaeologists are dealing with increasing competition for money from government-funded research organizations, such as the NSF and the NEH in the United States and the Social Sciences and Humanities Research Council (SSHRC) in Canada. In addition to less money for archaeology, in many cases archaeologists are being asked to rationalize why they should be funded at the expense of other kinds of research. In the economic and political climates of the early twenty-first century, traditional rationales that are often framed in social frameworks seem inadequate. If research archaeologists are to increase funding opportunities, they likely will have to rationalize their work within the frameworks of economics and politics, making the economic and political benefits of archaeology explicit.

As funding for pure research becomes increasingly difficult to obtain, the entertainment industry is likely to continue to pick up the slack. The problem with this, of course, is that research will then be driven primarily by what makes good television or other forms of entertainment rather than what makes good archaeology. The entertainment industry clearly likes archaeology with skeletons, mummies, and historic objects that have a high monetary value. Consequently, we can expect the public to gain an even more skewed vision of archaeology as it is really practiced in the twenty-first century.

The future of archaeology may increasingly rely on non-archaeologists for assistance. A recent example is the GlobalXplorer program begun by archaeologist Sarah Parcak, in which non-archaeologists use an app to look at satellite images she provides to identify potential archaeological sites. In its first few years, approximately 100,000 people participated in the program.

The future of commercial archaeology is difficult to predict. Commercial archaeology is strongly linked with the economy; when the economy suffers, development projects slow or cease, and there is thus less work for archaeologists on archaeological sites. As fossil fuels deplete, energy resource companies continue to explore and develop, often resulting in more work for archaeologists; so in those areas of megaprojects involving oil and gas, for example, archaeology will likely continue to flourish.

A wildcard in the future of commercial archaeology is government views on archaeology and environmental protection in general. In some jurisdictions, it is clear that government regulations are reducing the need for archaeological assessments or not requiring them at all. Whether these views will continue, leading to even less protection of archaeological sites, or revert back to a focus on heritage preservation is unknown.

Another thing to consider is that the boundaries of disciplines are blurring. It isn't unusual anymore for people trained in other disciplines, such as data science, to find employment in archaeology. Similarly, people trained in archaeology often find employment in related but distinct disciplines such as criminology or digital humanities.

Interpreting the Present in the Future

Predicting how people living 500 or more years into the future will view the peoples and cultures of early twenty-first century North America is fraught with difficulties. Based primarily on our understanding of the nature of the archaeological record and our understanding of human behavior based on archaeological research, however, we may speculate.

There are many things to consider. For one, the further we go into the future, the archaeological record of contemporary times will become increasingly biased toward inorganic materials. For example, 500 years from now, based on the preservation of plant and animal remains alone discovered in cultural contexts, people will have a good sense of the diversity of our diets. Five thousand and more years from now, the ability to identify most plant and many animal remains will be more difficult, and may lead to a sense of us having more meat in our diets than we really do. This may be mitigated by the application of technology such as the ability to extract plant and animal DNA from soils, but for the most part, macroscopic evidence of our diet will not be as evident.

Five hundred years from now, it is likely that some written records of current times will exist, but it would be a mistake to assume that people will be able to access all the words written with computer technology. Storage devices may still exist, but there is no guarantee, even if the preservation of storage devices is good, that we will have the ability to access them. Floppy discs, anyone? We are likely to have good preservation of some writings on paper because some archives have taken care to preserve them as best they can. It is reasonable to assume that 5,000 years from now, nobody may be able to understand our writing. Once the paper records are gone, there are few inorganic records of language. Unlike some ancient civilizations, whose writing was etched on clay tablets and on stone, we don't see that very much today. Ten thousand years from now, people may think that we had no written language at all.

Settlements and other impacts on the landscapes that are obvious now may be difficult to identify in the future. This is due to multiple reasons, including the long-standing practice of simply building over top of things. Finding evidence of early twenty-first century cities, for example, will likely require excavating through substantial cultural remains built over top, and it is likely to be rubble of the buildings that last, not the buildings themselves.

People in the future will be able to see many things preserved in the sediments. A significant disposal of plastics is already visible in stratigraphy. Advanced technology will likely be able to detect many other toxic things going into our soils. Human-caused global warming will be identified in the stratigraphy by rising sea levels and visible changes in the record of plants and animals. These changes are already being seen – for example, plants and animals normally restricted to warm climates are increasingly present in areas that are warming.

Human biological remains may provide some insight into life in the early twenty-first century. Analyses of human skeletons will show a significant increase in life expectancy compared to earlier times. People will also see a significant rise in height, and the use of artificial body parts. The study of bones and teeth may show that people of this time had considerable opportunity to live extremely healthy lives, including nutritious diets, but also that many are malnourished.

It would be a mistake to think that people of the future will be able make good interpretations of life in the early twenty-first century based on discrete piles of our refuse, such as landfills. Of course most of the organic remains will decompose, but many of the inorganic materials are likely to be gone as well. Landfills are already viewed as storehouses of valuable materials that can be recycled.

It is also possible that people of the future will not be as interested in the past as many people are today. Recall that archaeology is intertwined with politics and social movements, and the rationales for supporting archaeology now may not exist in the future. Speculating on the nature of archaeology in the future also requires speculating on the economic, social, political, and ideological aspects of those peoples and cultures, assuming that a mostly scientific knowledge of the material culture of the past will be important to them. We don't even know that the framework of archaeology will be a valued way of knowing in the future.

Archaeologists often name time periods and peoples based on the material remains left behind, such as the Stone, Bronze, and Iron ages; Beaker people (based on a style of pottery); Clovis people (based on style of spearpoint); and more. Thus, 500 years from now, we may be referred to as living in the Plastic Period; and 5,000 years from now we may be known as part of the Concrete Culture.

Final Comments

Introductory archaeology texts are meant to do many things, including familiarize students with the basic objectives, vocabulary, concepts, history, and methods of the discipline. All this information is a lot to remember. At a minimum, here is what we hope all readers retain for years to come, and perhaps pass on to others.

1. *Archaeology is important and relevant to everyday life.* This includes its role in providing the following: (i) contexts for current events; (ii) methodological and theoretical frameworks for collecting and interpreting data; (iii) expertise to support, refute, or assess claims and ideas about the past from diverse people and groups; (iv) an economic base for many people and nations; and (v) an awareness of and solutions to some important problems of living in the twenty-first century, including but not limited to marking nuclear waste sites, addressing homelessness, and dealing with contemporary waste.

2. *The archaeological record is vast.* It includes the material remains of human activity for at least 2.5 million years and from every continent. There are hundreds of thousands of recorded sites and probably billions of recorded artifacts. Tens of thousands of sites and their associated artifacts are added each year.

3. *Archaeology is firmly grounded in scientific method and theory.* This is not usually obvious from the popular press and media, but archaeologists are not treasure hunters.

4. *Archaeological sites are being destroyed at an alarming rate.* Natural processes are agents of destruction, but the loss of sites from industrial development and looting is of greater concern.

5. *Archaeology is filled with bias.* This includes the bias of the archaeological record itself (e.g., inorganic materials are overrepresented), the bias of conceptual frameworks used to investigate the past, and the bias of individuals. The recognition of bias is not necessarily a bad thing. Research in all disciplines is inevitably biased in some way. It is important to understand that alternative explanations almost always exist. There is little certainty about anything in archaeology.

6. *People have been smart for a very long time.* Tool technologies have been around for more than 2 million years; people have been controlling fire for hundreds of thousands of years; sophisticated art has been in evidence for more than 30,000 years; plants and animals were manipulated to the point of domestication more than 10,000 years ago; and civilizations began rising more than 5,000 years ago.

Over the past few decades, the world of archaeology has changed substantially. It is likely to continue changing in all aspects of the discipline. For anyone involved with archaeology as a career or as a mere observer, interesting times are ahead.

KEY RESOURCES AND SUGGESTED READING

For more on the archaeology of contemporary archaeology, Graves-Brown, Harrison, and Piccini (2013) is suggested.

On the topics of activist and action archaeology, books by Stottman (2010) and Sabloff (2008) are excellent. For archaeological studies of homelessness, see Little and Zimmerman (2010), Zimmerman and Welch (2011), and Zimmerman, Singleton, and Welch (2010); and for more on the archaeological study of undocumented migrants, see De León (2015). Forensic archaeology is covered in the very comprehensive volume edited by Blau and Ubelaker (2009), and disaster archaeology is covered by Gould (2005, 2007). For more on public archaeology, Moshenska (2017) is suggested. For more on archaeologies of the heart, see Lyons, Supernant, and Welch (2019) and Supernant et al. (2020). For those interested in the GlobalXplorer progam, to help find archaeological sites, there is a website – www.globalxplorer.org.

GLOSSARY

absolute dating: Dating that provides specific dates or range of dates, in years. Examples of absolute dating techniques include dendrochronology, radiocarbon, and potassium/argon dating.

academic archaeology: Archaeology undertaken for intellectual or scholarly reasons and based primarily in colleges, universities, and research museums and institutes.

agriculture: A subsistence strategy characterized by the intensive cultivation of food plants, often involving the use of plows, draft animals, and irrigation.

analogy: A form of reasoning based on the premise that if two things are alike in some respects, they may be alike in other respects as well. Many explanations in archaeology, particularly about how sites were created and the function of artifacts, are based on analogy. Analogies in archaeology are commonly drawn from existing ethnographies, ethnoarchaeology, and experimental archaeology.

Anthropocene: A proposed time period to describe the years in which humans have had a significant impact on the environment, observable in the geological record. There is no consensus on the validity of the term to describe geological time periods or when such a period began.

anthropology: The evolutionary, holistic, and comparative study of humans. In North America, archaeology is usually considered to be a branch of anthropology.

antiquarians: Hobby collectors of ancient art and antiquities, particularly from ancient Greece and Rome.

archaeobiology: A subfield of archaeology focusing on animal and botanical remains recovered from archaeological sites. Archaeobiology includes both archaeobotany and zooarchaeology.

archaeobotany: A subfield of archaeology focusing on plant remains recovered from archaeological sites; also known as paleoethnobotany.

archaeological record: Minimally includes all the material remains documented by archaeologists. More comprehensive definitions also include the record of culture history and everything written about the past by archaeologists.

archaeological site: Any location where there is physical evidence of human activity. To be defined as an archaeological site, a location need not meet minimum requirements for age or contents, although some government jurisdictions may dictate minimum criteria for inventory purposes.

archaeological theme park: Extreme versions of heritage tourism, consisting of heritage-related theme parks where entertainment appears to take precedence over archaeological data and interpretations.

archaeology: The study of humans through their material remains. Most archaeology focuses on the human past and is undertaken within the framework of science.

archaeomagnetism: An absolute dating technique based on the knowledge that when heated to high temperatures, magnetic particles in clays and other sediments align themselves toward the North Magnetic Pole. In situ measurements of particle alignments are correlated with historical records of the location of the North Magnetic Pole.

archaeometry: Archaeology associated with the methods of natural sciences, such as math and physics, usually used in the analysis of materials.

archaeotourism: Tourism focusing on promoting visits to archaeological sites as well as heritage interpretation centers and museums.

argon dating: Absolute dating techniques (potassium/argon and argon/argon) based on the rate at which potassium and radioactive argon change into stable argon gas.

armchair archaeology: A phrase used to describe both professionals and amateurs who focus on describing or explaining what others have done, without participating in fieldwork themselves.

artifact: Any object that shows evidence of being manufactured, modified, or used by people. Most archaeologists also restrict the term artifact to items that are portable.

artificial selection: Involves the intentional selection of desirable traits in plants or animals. Also known as selective breeding.

ascribed: Predetermined by birth.

atlatl: A spear-thrower usually about a meter long, upon which the spear was laid to effectively increase the length of the arm to power the spear.

band: A type of society characterized by relatively small groups (usually less than 50) that act autonomously, are egalitarian, and have a subsistence based on generalized foraging.

behavioral disturbance processes: Human processes such as trampling, scavenging, construction, and looting that affect the original patterning of archaeological remains; also known as cultural disturbance processes and C-transforms.

behavioral formation processes: Human processes that lead to the creation of archaeological sites, such as deliberate discard, loss, and abandonment; also known as cultural formation processes.

biblical archaeology: Archaeology that focuses on peoples, places, and events mentioned in the Bible.

biface: Tools, usually stone, that have been modified on both of the major surfaces.

Big Man: One kind of village leader in tribal societies, with no real power or authority. Also called Head Man.

bioarchaeology: The study of human remains from archaeological sites.

bioturbation: Disturbance of archaeological sites by plants and animals. Examples include a rodent burrowing into the ground and tree roots spreading horizontally and vertically through a site.

blade: A stone tool that is at least twice as long as it is wide, and has at least roughly parallel sides.

bog men: Dozens of human bodies preserved in the bogs of northern European countries, especially Denmark. Also known as bog people.

bp or BP: Abbreviation for *before present*, which is taken to mean AD 1950; used to indicate dates in years before present when materials are dated by radiocarbon dating only.

bureaucracy: Full-time government workers, characteristic of state-level societies.

C-14 dating: An absolute dating technique based on the known rate of decay of carbon in organisms, beginning at the instant of death. Also known as carbon-14 dating and radiocarbon dating.

cache: A stored quantity of something, usually food or artifacts.

cache pit: A pit dug into the ground to store something, usually food.

calibrated relative dating: A category of dating techniques that is a hybrid of absolute and relative techniques.

capa cocha: An Inka religious ritual involving child sacrifice at high altitudes.

carbon-14 dating: An absolute dating technique based on the known rate of decay of carbon in organisms, beginning at the instant of death. Also known as C-14 dating and radiocarbon dating.

ceramic: Baked clay.

chief: The leader of a chiefdom, with real power and authority.

chiefdom: A type of society characterized by populations ranging from a few thousand to tens of thousands, marked social inequality, subsistence based on horticulture, and formal positions of leadership.

china: A category of ceramics based on the type of clay and its porosity, and requiring a firing temperature between 1,100 and 1,200 degrees Celsius.

chronological sequencing: A category of relative dating methods that puts sites and objects in sequence. Includes stratigraphic dating, seriation, and *terminus quem*.

civilization: There is no consensus definition of civilization, but most archaeologists agree a society must have most of the following: monumental architecture, at least one city, a system of writing, an agricultural base, and state-level political organization.

classical archaeology: Archaeology focusing on the empires of ancient Greece and Rome.

cognitive archaeology: Archaeology that focuses on ideology; also known as archaeology of the mind.

collateral damage: Unintended damage. Used primarily in archaeology to describe the impact of military actions on archaeological sites.

colonial archaeology: Archaeology focusing on the time periods and places under European colonial rule, especially in Australia, Canada, and the United States.

commercial archaeology: See **cultural resource management**.

complex foraging: A subsistence strategy based on gathering and hunting a wide variety of plants and animals, but with a specialization in one type, leading to increasing social complexity.

conceptual framework: A theoretical framework that guides research; also known as a paradigm, research strategy, research approach, grand theory, and heuristic theory.

coprolite: Human feces and other animal waste, preserved through drying or mineralization.

core tools: Stone tools that are produced by removing flakes from the original cobble, with the remaining core of the cobble becoming the tool.

CRM: An acronym for cultural resource management.

C-transforms: Also known as cultural disturbance processes or behavioral disturbance processes, these are human activities that alter the original patterning of archaeological remains, including trampling and construction activities. The term *C-transforms* was widely used in the 1970s and 1980s but is rarely used in the twenty-first century.

cultural anthropology: The branch of anthropology focusing on contemporary human cultures.

cultural ecology: Focuses on the relationship between people and the natural environment.

cultural formation processes: The human processes that lead to the creation of archaeological sites, such as deliberate discard, abandonment, and loss; also known as behavioral formation processes.

cultural landscape: A distinctive geographic area with cultural significance.

cultural resource management: Archaeology undertaken within the context of the heritage industry, often because archaeological assessments are required by legislation, to be completed in advance of potential disturbance to areas where sites are known or suspected to exist. Often abbreviated as CRM.

culture: The learned and shared things that people have, do, and think.

culture area: Broad geographic area in which there are general similarities in cultures. There are 10 culture areas in North and Central America (Arctic, Subarctic, Northwest Coast, Interior Plateau, Great Basin, Plains, California, Southwest, Eastern Woodlands, and Mesoamerica).

culture history: A description of the archaeological record and the chronological sequence of events in an area.

culture process: How cultures work, including how and why they change.

culture reconstruction: An interpretation of past lifeways, including subsistence and settlement patterns, social and political strategies, and ideology.

cuneiform: An early form of writing found in Mesopotamia.

curation: Refers to the process of properly housing and maintaining an archaeological collection for the duration of its lifespan. Curatorial work usually involves ensuring researchers in the future can easily locate and understand all important information associated with the archaeological collection, including when it was excavated, who excavated it, where all the artifacts were found on the archaeological site, and reports and publications on the site.

curation crisis: A mounting problem in North America where archaeologists have excavated more artifacts than they can store in repositories designed to curate archaeological collections permanently.

dating by association: Dating artifacts and sites by their association with other artifacts, ecofacts, or geological features of known age; a subcategory of relative dating.

debitage: Waste from the manufacture of artifacts, usually stone. Also known as detritus.

decolonization: Refers to attempts to radically transform the discipline of anthropology by privileging the voices and discourses of people historically on the periphery of the field and from cultures that have been written about by anthropologists and colonized in the past. Indigenous archaeology is an example of decolonizing practice. See also post-colonial archaeology.

deep antiquity: A phrase used to convey the long history of humankind, including the 2.5-million-year record of human culture.

deep time: A phrase used to convey the 15-billion-year history of the universe.

deity: A god.

dendrochronology: Tree-ring dating.

descendant community: A group of people who can trace their ancestry to others who lived in an area. In archaeology, descendant community usually refers to the Indigenous Peoples of a region.

descent group: People who trace their common lineal descent from a real or mythological ancestor, including lineages and clans.

detritus: Waste from the manufacture of artifacts, usually stone. Also known as debitage.

diachronic change: Change through time.

diagnostic artifact: An artifact that is characteristic of a particular time, group, or culture.

diffusion: The spread of ideas.

digital archaeology: Digital archaeology involves both the use and critical analysis of technology in archaeology. Many digital archaeologists emphasize the importance of using free, open-source software and of democratizing data; this means that archaeologists share their findings and data sets on public accessible websites, in online databases, and using non-proprietary software. Finally, many digital archaeologists also believe in using technologies that are inclusive so that people of all skill levels and backgrounds can understand and access information about the past.

dirt archaeology: Fieldwork, including looking for and excavating archaeological sites.

domestication: There is no consensus definition of domestication in archaeology, but at a minimum it means that plants and/or animals are under the control of humans.

earthenware: A category of ceramics based on the type of clay and its porosity, and requiring a firing temperature between 900 and 1,200 degrees Celsius.

ecofact: Items from archaeological sites, not recorded as artifacts or features, but that are relevant to archaeological interpretations. Includes animal remains, botanical remains, and sediments.

ecological archaeology: Archaeology focusing on the relationships between people and natural environments.

egalitarian: A level of equality where everyone has roughly equal status and access to resources.

Egyptology: A multidisciplinary field of study focusing on ancient Egyptian civilization. Prominent specialties within Egyptology include archaeology, history, and art.

empire: A special kind of political system that is territorially expansive, with one state exerting control over other states, chiefdoms, tribes, and bands.

ethnic group: People who share, or once shared, a common language, history, and territory, with members who have a self-conscious identification with the group.

ethnic marker: Artifacts, features, or other material remains that are indicative of particular ethnic groups.

ethnoarchaeology: A subfield of archaeology that involves making observations of contemporary people to better understand the archaeological record.

ethnographic analogy: When archaeologists make interpretations of the archaeological record based on similarities observed in ethnographically described cultures.

ethnography: A written description of a culture, based on first-hand observation by a cultural anthropologist.

Eurocentric: Focused on Europe.

exoarchaeology: A subfield of archaeology focusing on the physical remains of human space exploration.

exogamous: Marrying someone from outside one's own group.

experimental archaeology: Conducting experiments to replicate past conditions and events, and using the results to interpret archaeological remains.

fabric: Also known as the ceramic body, fabric refers to the composition of the clay.

faunal remains: Animal remains, including bones, teeth, shells, horns, antlers, fur, hair, nails, claws, talons, and soft tissue.

faunalturbation: Disturbance of archaeological sites by animals.

feature: A non-portable object that shows evidence of being manufactured, modified, or used by people, or an arrangement of material remains in which patterning is significant.

feminist archaeology: A movement within archaeology that arose in the 1980s to address systematic gender inequality in the profession of archaeology as well as inaccurate depictions of gender roles and sexuality.

flake tools: Stone tools that are made from a flake originally removed from a cobble.

flintknapping: Manufacturing stone tools by chipping or flaking.

floralturbation: Disturbance of archaeological sites by plants, including trees.

fluorine, uranium, nitrogen dating: A relative dating technique based on the premise that after the death of an animal, the relative amounts of fluorine and uranium in bone will increase and the amount of nitrogen will decrease.

foramen magnum: The hole at the base of the skull through which the spinal cord passes to connect to the brain.

forensic archaeology: Archaeology done in the context of criminal investigations, including the search for evidence using archaeological methods and the identification of human remains.

frequency seriation: An archaeological dating technique based on the relative frequency of certain artifact types; based on the premise that artifact types go through a period of acceptance, after which they flourish and then decline.

fresco: Decorative painting on a plastered surface.

garbology: The study of fresh household trash and contemporary landfills.

general theory: Focuses on explaining the significant events of the human past and the nature of culture; also known as grand theory and high-level research.

generalized forager: A person who employs a subsistence strategy based on collecting a wide variety of wild food resources, with no primary dependence on one kind.

geoarchaeology: Archaeology focusing on sediments from sites and the reconstruction of abiotic environments, including natural landscapes.

geographic information systems (GIS): Computer software that allows layering of various types of data to produce complex maps; useful for predicting site location and for representing the analysis of collected data within sites and across regions.

geology: The study of the physical components of the earth, including minerals, rocks, and other sediments and deposits on and below the earth's surface.

grand theory: Focuses on explaining the significant events of the human past and the nature of culture; also known as general theory and high-level research.

grave goods: Items, usually artifacts and food, included with a human burial.

gray literature: Archaeological reports with limited distribution.

Head Man: One kind of village leader in tribal societies, with no real power or authority. Also called Big Man.

heritage industry: A growth industry involving the promotion, preservation, documentation, assessment, interpretation, and presentation of heritage. In North America, some view cultural resource management to be equivalent to the heritage industry, while others view it to be only a component of the industry.

heuristic theory: A theoretical framework that guides research; also known as conceptual framework, paradigm, research strategy, research approach, general theory, and grand theory.

hieroglyphics: The pictorial form of writing used by ancient Egyptians.

high-level research: Archaeological studies that focus on explaining significant events in the human past and the nature of culture in general; also known as grand theory and general theory.

historic archaeology: Focuses on a time period in an area for which written records exist. Also known as historical archaeology.

historical particularism: The conceptual framework that suggests the evolutionary course of every culture is unique, disregarding any general laws of cultural evolution.

hoard: In archaeology, the accumulation of valuable items hidden for future retrieval and use.

holistic: The recognition that all components of a culture are interrelated.

Homininae: The biological family to which modern humans belong and which appears to have originated several million years ago. Includes multiple species within the *Homo*, *Australopithecus*, and other early human genera.

Homo: The biological genus to which modern humans belong and which appears to have originated about 2.5 million years ago.

horizon: A descriptive unit reflecting cultural continuity over a broad area, typically from several hundred to a few thousand years.

horticulture: A subsistence strategy based on plant cultivation with hand tools only.

household archaeology: Focuses on individual houses, including physical characteristics, construction methods, and social uses.

human waste: Biological waste of humans, including coprolites and cess.

inclusive/queer archaeology: Archaeology that confronts essentialist, Eurocentric, and heteronormative ideas about sexuality, sex, gender, race, class, and identity in the past.

iconography: Forms of art and writing that are thought to symbolically represent ideology.

ideal data: Data that archaeologists desire to test a hypothesis.

ideal methods: The preferred methods to obtain data, both in the field and the laboratory.

in situ: In its original context, undisturbed; literally meaning "in place."

Indian industry: All the work revolving around the assertions of Aboriginal rights, especially in Canada, and specifically regarding the activities of lawyers, historians, sociologists, anthropologists, and archaeologists involved with First Nations claims.

Indigenous: Usually applies to populations that have been in an area for a very long time. In Canada and the United States it refers to people and groups whose ancestry can be traced in the region prior to the arrival of Europeans, and includes those sometimes known as Aboriginal, Eskimo, First Nations, Indians, Inuit, Métis, and Native Americans.

Indigenous archaeology: Archaeology done by, with, or for Indigenous Peoples; most often associated with the Aborigines of Australia, Native Americans of the United States, and First Nations of Canada. Indigenous archaeology represents an attempt to bring oppressed and neglected theoretical and methodological approaches informed by Indigenous groups to the forefront of anthropological scholarship.

industrial archaeology: A subfield focusing on sites and objects of heavy industry such as mining, logging, and power generation.

Inka: A civilization that was centered in Peru but developed into an empire that dominated many other groups in western South America for about a century until the conquest by the Spanish in the early 1500s. Also known as the Inca.

judgmental sampling: A sampling strategy based on an archaeologist's judgment or opinion of where to look for sites or excavate; also known as non-probabilistic sampling.

knowledge mobilization: An umbrella term used to describe multiple ways of sharing knowledge between researchers and knowledge users, including both academic and non-academic groups.

law of superposition: In undeformed sequences of sedimentary rock, each bed is older than the one above it. It is recognized that deformation can fold or overturn sedimentary layers, placing them out of sequence, and that rock can also form from rising magma, making deep layers younger than those above.

lens of archaeology: A framework for studying the human past, including a set of archaeological principles, methods, theories, ethics, and research results.

level bags: Bags used by excavators to collect material remains (usually excluding artifacts, which are collected separately) while excavating a particular level in an archaeological site.

lithic: In archaeology, usually means stone tool or the waste from stone tool manufacture.

lithic debitage: Waste from the manufacture of stone tools.

lithic scatter: A scattering of lithic waste flakes (debitage or detritus) created during the manufacture of stone tools.

living museums: Museums where people dress in period costume and often reenact the time being portrayed, such as acting as shopkeepers and blacksmiths.

low-level research: This generally refers to archaeological field and laboratory work.

material culture: The physical aspect of culture, such as things that can be touched; distinct from behavior and ideology.

material remains: The physical remains of human activities and ecofacts.

matrix: The sediments surrounding the artifacts, features, and ecofacts.

megalith: A large stone, often in association with others and forming an alignment or monument, such as at Stonehenge and Carnac.

Mesoamerica: Central America, including Mexico.

Mesolithic: The time period from about 11,000 to 9,000 years ago; not commonly used outside of Europe.

microdebitage: Very small, often microscopic pieces of waste created during the manufacture of artifacts, usually stone.

microwear: Wear on tools from use by people, usually only seen under magnification.

midden: A large, discrete accumulation of refuse.

middle-range research: See **middle-level research**.

middle-level research: Refers to research that links field and laboratory work with the grand theories. It focuses on interpreting patterning in archaeological sites, primarily through ethnoarchaeology, experimental archaeology, and studies of taphonomy; also known as middle-range research and middle-range theory.

minimum number of individuals: On a broad level, it means the minimum number of individuals of any category of material remains represented by an assemblage of bone. In practice, however, it usually refers to the minimum number of individuals of a particular species.

MNI: An acronym for minimum number of individuals.

monumental architecture: Large-scale construction of buildings, earthworks, and other large features.

mummy: Well-preserved animal remains (usually human and including soft tissue) that result from drying, including those intentionally dried and those dried through fortuitous circumstances.

Munsell system: The standard system of measuring color in archaeology, based on hue, chroma, and value.

natural formation processes: The natural processes that bring sediments into archaeological sites, such as through water and air. Also known as non-cultural formation processes.

Neolithic: The time period from about 9,000 to 5,000 years ago; not commonly used outside of Europe.

new archaeology: Also known as processual archaeology, it emerged in the 1960s and focused on using explicit scientific method, attempting to explain (rather than merely describe) culture change. Although common in the 1960s and 1970s, the phrase "new archaeology" is rarely used in the early twenty-first century.

New World: The Americas.

NISP: Acronym for number of identified specimens.

non-cultural disturbance processes: Natural processes that affect the original patterning of archaeological remains; also known as natural disturbance processes and N-transforms.

non-cultural formation processes: Processes associated with wind and water that bring natural sediments into archaeological sites; also known as natural formation processes.

non-probabilistic sampling: A sampling strategy based on an archaeologist's judgment or opinion of where to look for or excavate sites. Also known as judgmental sampling.

N-transforms: Natural processes that affect the original patterning of archaeological remains; also known as natural disturbance processes and non-cultural disturbance processes. Although common in the 1970s and 1980s, the term *N-transforms* is used rarely in the early twenty-first century.

obsidian: A fine-grained volcanic stone, classified as a glass. Because of its excellent quality for stone tool manufacture, it was traded widely in prehistory.

obsidian hydration: A calibrated relative dating technique, based on the knowledge that freshly exposed surfaces of obsidian adsorb moisture from the surrounding environments in measurable layers.

ochre: A naturally occurring mineral pigment, usually red and often used in ritual and for color in paints or dyes.

Old World: Africa, Asia, and Europe.

orphaned collections: Refers to an archaeological assemblage that has been severely neglected or ignored for many years, resulting in poor curation and/or destruction to artifacts in the collection. Some orphaned collections lack provenience, meaning that archaeologists are unable to discern where artifacts found.

osteology: The study of the human skeleton.

paleoanthropology: The study of early human biology and culture.

Paleolithic: The time period from about 2.5 million to about 11,000 years ago; commonly referred to as the "Old Stone Age" and subdivided into the Lower, Middle, and Upper Paleolithic.

paleodiet: A popular contemporary diet based on largely incorrect assumptions about human diets in the past and the evolution of human digestive systems.

paleofantasy: The belief that things were better in the past.

paleontology: The study of ancient animals and plants, incorporating aspects of geology and biology. Usually excludes humans, although some studies of early human fossils are described as human paleontology.

papyri: The writing material produced from plants in ancient Egypt.

paradigm: A theoretical framework that guides research; also known as conceptual framework, research strategy, research approach, heuristic theory, general theory, and grand theory.

participant observation: A technique of ethnographic research in which researchers immerse themselves in a culture as both participants and observers.

pastoralism: A subsistence strategy based on the herding of animals.

pedological: Having to do with the study of soils. Pedology is also known as soil science.

petroglyphs: Designs carved or pecked into large boulders, bedrock, or the walls of cliffs, caves, and rock shelters.

pH: A measure of acidity. Archaeologists measure the pH of sediments.

phase: A descriptive unit reflecting cultural continuity in a region or subregion for a relatively short period (i.e., usually less than 2,000 years).

phytoliths: Small particles of silica from the cells of plants.

pictographs: Paintings on large, immovable boulders or bedrock, or the walls of cliffs, caves, and rock shelters.

Piltdown Man: Skeletal remains discovered in Piltdown, England, in the early twentieth century, purported to be a "missing link"; eventually revealed as a hoax through the application of fluorine, uranium, nitrogen dating.

pithouse: Semi-subterranean dwelling, consisting of a large depression in the ground covered with an above-ground roof. The roof is usually supported by a log and pole framework and the roof itself is often composed of bark and other forms of vegetation overlain with a layer of earth. Entrance may be through the side or top via a ladder.

population pressure: The condition where human population is at or exceeds the carrying capacity of the environment.

porcelain: A category of ceramics based on the type of clay and its porosity, and requiring a firing temperature between 1,300 and 1,450 degrees Celsius.

post-colonial archaeology: Post-colonial archaeology refers to attempts to radically transform anthropology and archaeology by privileging the voices from people historically on the periphery of the field and from cultures that have been written about by anthropologists and colonized in the past. See also decolonization and Indigenous archaeology.

post-depositional disturbance process: Any process, cultural or natural, that affects an archaeological deposit after it was initially created.

postmodernism: A conceptual framework, generally considered anti-scientific in nature, focusing on the subjectivity of interpretation.

post-processual archaeology: An umbrella phrase for archaeology done since the 1980s in scholarly but nontraditional ways, often focusing on topics of ideology, gender, and ethnicity, and explicitly recognizing bias in the undertaking and exploitation of archaeological research.

potassium/argon dating: An absolute dating technique based on the known rate at which potassium changes to argon in volcanic sediments. Often abbreviated as K/Ar.

pothunter: A generic term used to describe a person who loots archaeological sites.

pothunting: A generic term used to describe the looting of archaeological sites.

potsherd: A broken piece of pottery.

pottery: Baked clay containers, such as bowls, cups, jars, and vases.

pre-Columbian archaeology: Archaeology focusing on the Americas before the arrival of Christopher Columbus; usually used to describe the archaeology of the large chiefdoms and states of Mesoamerica, such as the Maya and Aztec.

prehistoric archaeology: Archaeology focusing on a time period before which written records exist in a given area.

prehistory: The time before written records were kept in an area. The prehistoric period ends at different times around the world, distinguished by when the inhabitants invented writing or when people with the knowledge of writing entered the area.

prestige goods: Items that are more a function of high status than practical utility; also known as luxury items. Prestige goods may also include raw materials in short supply.

primary refuse: Refuse that was abandoned where it was created or used and left undisturbed until found by archaeologists.

probabilistic sampling: Sampling not biased by any person's judgment or opinion. Also known as statistical sampling and includes simple random sampling, stratified random sampling, and systematic sampling.

processual archaeology: Also known as the new archaeology, it emerged in the 1960s and focused on using explicit scientific method, attempting to explain (rather than merely describe) culture change.

provenience: The precise, three-dimensional location of an artifact.

pseudoarchaeology: The study of the human past based on material remains, but not following the methods of archaeology.

public archaeology: In its broadest definition, public archaeology is the study of how archaeologists engage the public. A central component of public archaeology is collaborating with different stakeholder groups to identify and investigate questions of mutual interest.

punk archaeology: While adhering to methods and ethics of professional archaeology, punk archaeology operates on the fringes or margins of mainstream archaeology, critiques scholarly convention, often takes a do-it-yourself approach, and tends to focus on the very recent past.

radiocarbon dating: An absolute dating technique based on the known rate of decay of carbon-14 in organisms after death. Also known as C-14 and carbon-14 dating.

raised field agriculture: A kind of agriculture involving the raising of garden plots above ground level by digging ditches around the plots and adding the sediments to the raised plots. An effective land-management technique in prehistoric South America that has been reintroduced in recent times to increase crop yields.

refuse: An umbrella term used to refer to discarded items, including trash (dry items) and garbage (wet or organic items such as food waste).

Register of Professional Archaeologists (RPA): An international list of archaeologists who meet minimum standards of qualification and agree to abide by a strict code of ethics.

relative dating: Determining the relative antiquity of sites and objects by putting them in sequential order, but not assigning specific dates.

religious ritual: Formalized, repetitive acts associated with religious beliefs.

sacred site: Site with presumed religious or spiritual significance.

science: A method of inquiry based on the collection of empirical data as well as the formulation, testing, and continual reevaluation of hypotheses.

seasonal round: Where people will be and what they will be doing within their traditional territory at various times of the year, following a schedule.

seasonality studies: Determining the time of year a site was occupied.

secondary refuse: Refuse that was moved from where it was initially created.

sedentary: Settling permanently.

segmentary society: A type of society characterized by slight social inequality, subsistence usually based on pastoralism and/or horticulture, and populations ranging from a few hundred to a few thousand spread among many villages. Also known as a tribe.

selective breeding: Involves the intentional selection of desirable traits in plants or animals. Also known as artificial selection.

semi-sedentary: Semi-permanent settlement pattern.

seriation: Placing objects in chronological order based on their style (stylistic seriation) or relative frequency (frequency seriation).

shaman: An individual with a perceived connection to the supernatural world.

shell midden: An accumulation of refuse with a substantial amount of shell.

shovelbum: A term applied to itinerant archaeological fieldworkers, who often go from project to project working for various employers in the CRM industry.

site catchment analysis: Determining the source location of all material remains found in a site.

site exploitation territory: The area habitually used by a group throughout the year; also known as traditional territory.

site formation processes: The variety of cultural and natural processes leading to the creation of archaeological sites.

space archaeology: The study of how humans' desire to explore the "last frontier" – space – has left material traces on Earth, the moon, and Mars, and in orbit.

specialized foraging: See **complex foraging**.

state: A type of society characterized by all or most of the following: large populations, cities, bureaucracies, monumental architecture, writing, and armies.

stelae: An upright stone, often inscribed; common in both Egypt and Mesoamerica.

stoneware: A category of ceramics based on the type of clay and its porosity, and requiring a firing temperature between 1,200 and 1,350 degrees Celsius.

stratification: A system of social inequality involving classes, such as lower, middle, or upper class.

stratigraphic dating: A relative dating technique based on the knowledge that layers of sediments are normally laid on top of each other through time; based on the geological law of superposition.

stratigraphy: The description or study of the observable layers of sediments.

stylistic seriation: A relative dating technique based on changing artifact styles through time.

subsistence looting: The practice of looting sites, usually by local peoples, to provide the basic necessities of life.

synchronic change: Change over space.

tangible heritage: The material aspect of heritage, such as artifacts and sites; compared to intangible heritage, which includes such things as folklore and traditions.

taphonomy: In a broad sense, both the natural and cultural forces that shape the archaeological record. A narrower and more restrictive definition is that it is the study of what happens to organic remains after death.

tell: A term used to describe mounds that have been created by successive settlements in the Middle East, western Asia, and northern Africa.

terminus ante quem: A relative dating technique in which the presence of an object of known age is used to infer that all other finds must be at least as old as that object. Often abbreviated as TAQ.

terminus post quem: A relative dating technique in which the presence of an object of known age is used to infer that all other finds must be no older than that object. Often abbreviated as TPQ.

terminus quem: Relative dating based on finding an object of known age and then inferring that other objects must be either older or more recent than that object.

terra cotta: A category of ceramics based on specific types of reddish clay and its porosity, and requiring a firing temperature less than 1,000 degrees Celsius.

textiles: Fabrics manufactured by spinning or weaving plant or animal fibers.

thermoluminescence: An absolute dating technique based on the premise that energy becomes trapped in objects when they are heated to very high temperatures. Reheating the objects releases stored energy in the form of light in a way that can determine the length of time since the object was originally heated. Most commonly used for dating ceramics, but stone tools have also been dated with this technique.

three-age system: Conceptualizing the past through the Stone, Bronze, and Iron Ages.

total station: An electronic device that can measure distances, angles, and elevations from a fixed point. It runs on software that allows the data to be downloaded and used to create maps.

trace-element analysis: Subjecting materials to analysis to determine their composition.

tradition: A descriptive unit reflecting a pattern of cultural continuity over a broad area for at least a few thousand years.

traditional territory: The area habitually used by a group throughout the year. Also known as site exploitation territory.

transegalitarian: A term used to describe societies transitioning between egalitarianism and distinct social inequality.

trepanation: Removing a piece of bone from the skull of a living person; also known as trephination.

tribe: An intermediate category of society falling between egalitarian foragers and ranked or fully stratified societies, with the beginnings of formal leadership and subsistence usually based on horticulture and/or pastoralism. Exhibits populations between a few hundred and a few thousand, spread among many villages.

type: A category of artifact based on typology; types may be descriptive and/or functional.

typology: A system of artifact classification based on physical attributes and/or presumed function.

underwater archaeology: Archaeology that focuses on sites and objects underwater, including shipwrecks.

uniface: A stone tool that has been modified on one side only.

uniformitarianism: A geological principle often articulated as "the present is the key to the past," meaning that the geological processes in operation today are the same as those that operated in the past. The implication is that since most geological processes are relatively slow, the earth must be very old.

unilinear theory of cultural evolution: A theory developed in the nineteenth century that proposed cultural evolution was on a singular course and people in various stages of that course could be classified as either savages, barbarians, or civilized.

Venus figurines: Small (about 4½ inches or 11 centimeters on average) figures made from stone, clay, and antler, usually depicting women. Found in Europe and dating to between 20,000 and 30,000 years ago.

white savior: The white savior complex includes the idea that white people impose their belief systems and power over those who have less power or privilege, often with the goal of uplifting the marginalized. Based on the assumption that Westerners have the skills needed to help or save others. Examples in archaeology include archaeologists claiming to save and protect archaeological sites and artifacts for the benefit of others.

World Heritage Site: A site that has received designation from the United Nations Educational, Scientific, and Cultural Organization (UNESCO) in recognition of its high significance.

zooarchaeology: The study of animal remains from archaeological sites.

BIBLIOGRAPHY

This bibliography provides complete information on all the articles and books cited within or at the end of chapters, as well as some other important sources for students interested in expanding their knowledge of archaeology. It also includes some of the principal sources the authors consulted but that are not cited in the text.

Adams, Amanda. 2010. *Ladies of the Field: Early Women Archaeologists and Their Search for Adventure*. Vancouver: Greystone.

Allison, Penelope M., ed. 1999. *The Archaeology of Household Activities*. New York: Routledge.

Ames, Kenneth M., Doria F. Raetz, Stephen Hamilton, and Christine McAfee. 1992. "Household Archaeology of a Southern Northwest Coast Plank House." *Journal of Field Archaeology* 19 (3): 275–90. https://doi.org/10.1179/009346992791548851.

Ashmore, Wendy, Dorothy T. Lippert, and Barbara J. Mills, eds. 2010. *Voices in American Archaeology*. Washington, DC: SAA Press.

Association Research Inc. 2005. *2005 Salary Survey Conducted for the Society for American Archaeology in Cooperation with the Society for Historical Archaeology*. Rockville, MD: Association Research Inc. https://documents.saa.org/container/docs/default-source/doc-careerpractice/salary_survey2005.pdf?sfvrsn=44a76241_8.

Atalay, Sonya. 2006. "Indigenous Archaeology as Decolonizing Practice." *American Indian Quarterly* 30 (3/4): 280–310. https://doi.org/10.1353/aiq.2006.0015.

———. 2012. *Community-Based Archaeology: Research With, By, and For Indigenous and Local Communities*. Oakland: University of California Press.

———. 2014. "Engaging Archaeology: Positivism, Objectivity, and Activist Archaeology." In *Transforming Archaeology: Activist Practices and Prospects*, edited by Sonya Atalay, Lee Rains Clauss, Randall H. McGuire, and John R. Welch, 45–60. Walnut Creek, CA: Left Coast Press.

Atalay, Sonya, Lee Rains Clauss, Randall H. McGuire, and John R. Welch, eds. 2014. *Transforming Archaeology: Activist Practices and Prospects*. Walnut Creek, CA: Left Coast Press.

Aufderheide, Arthur C. 2003. *The Scientific Study of Mummies*. New York: Cambridge University Press.

Babits, Lawrence E., Joshua B. Howard, and Matthew Brenckle. 2006. "Pirate Imagery." In *X Marks the Spot: The Archaeology of Piracy*, edited by Russell K. Skowronek and Charles E. Ewen, 271–81. Gainseville, FL: University of Florida Press.

Bahn, Paul. 2000. *Archaeology: A Very Short Introduction*. Oxford: Oxford University Press.

————, ed. 2014. *The History of Archaeology: An Introduction*. Abingdon, UK: Routledge.

Balme, Jane, and Alistaire Paterson. 2006. *Archaeology in Practice: A Student Guide to Analyses*. Oxford: Blackwell.

Banning, E.B. 2000. *The Archaeologist's Laboratory: The Analysis of Archaeological Data*. New York: Kluwer.

Barton, Christopher, ed. Forthcoming. *Trowels in the Trenches: Archaeology as Social Activism*. Gainesville: University Press of Florida.

Battle-Baptiste, Whitney. 2011. *Black Feminist Archaeology*. Walnut Creek, CA: Left Coast Press.

Baumann, Timothy. 2004. "African American Ethnicity." *SAA Archaeological Record* 4: 16–20.

Baxter, Jane Eva. 2005. *The Archaeology of Childhood*. Walnut Creek, CA: Altamira.

————. 2007. "A Different Way of Seeing: Casting Children as Cultural Actors in Archaeological Interpretations." Paper presented at the American Anthropological Association Annual Meeting, Washington, DC.

————. 2008. "Archaeology of Childhood." *Annual Review of Anthropology* 37: 159–75.

————. 2019. *The Archaeology of American Childhood and Adolesence*. Gainesville: University Press of Florida.

BBC News Online. 2000. "Fury at Sacred Site Damage." *BBC News*, September 13, 2000. http://news.bbc.co.uk/2/hi/americas/923415.stm.

Bell, Martin. 2004. "Archaeology and Green Issues." In *A Companion to Archaeology*, edited by John Bintliff, 509–31. Oxford: Blackwell.

Bintliff, John, ed. 2004. *A Companion to Archaeology*. Oxford: Blackwell.

Black, Stephen L., and Kevin Jolly. 2003. *Archaeology by Design*. Walnut Creek, CA: Altamira.

Blau, Soren, and Douglas H. Ubelaker, eds. 2009. *Handbook of Forensic Anthropology and Archaeology*. Walnut Creek, CA: Left Coast Press.

Bocek, Barbara. 1992. "The Jasper Ridge Reexcavation Experiment: Rates of Artifact Mixing by Rodents." *American Antiquity* 57 (2): 261–69. http://dx.doi.org/10.2307/280731.

Bradley, Bruce, and Dennis Stanford. 2004. "The North Atlantic Ice-Edge Corridor: A Possible Palaeolithic Route to the New World." *World Archaeology* 36 (4): 459–78. http://dx.doi.org/10.1080/0043824042000303656.

Braun, Sebastian Felix. 2020. "Culture, Resource, Management, and Anthropology: Pipelines and the *wakan* at the Standing Rock Sioux Reservation." *Plains Anthropologist* 65 (253): 7–24. https://doi.org/10.1080/00320447.2018.1554550.

Brodie, Neil, Jennifer Doole, and Colin Renfrew, eds. 2001. *Trade in Illicit Antiquities: The Destruction of the World's Archaeological Heritage*. Cambridge: McDonald Institute for Archaeological Research.

Brodie, Neil, and Colin Renfrew. 2005. "Looting and the World's Heritage: The Inadequate Response." *Annual Review of Anthropology* 34: 343–61. http://dx.doi.org/10.1146/annurev.anthro.34.081804.120551.

Brodie, Neil, and Kathryn Walker Tubb. 2002. *Illicit Antiquities: The Theft of Culture and the Extinction of Archaeology*. New York: Routledge. http://dx.doi.org/10.4324/9780203165461.

Brothwell, D.R., and A.M. Pollard, eds. 2001. *Handbook of Archaeological Sciences*. New York: Wiley.

Brown, Marley. 2019. "Proof Positive." *Archaeology*, November/December. https://www.archaeology.org/issues/359-1911/trenches/8100-trenches-egypt-ancient-yeast.

Brunson, Tiffany. 2012. "What Boys and Girls are Made of: Personal Adornment and Social Identity and Gender at the Fort Spokane Indian Boarding School." M.A. thesis, University of Idaho.

Buenger, Brent A. 2003. "The Impact of Wildland and Prescribed Fire on Archaeological Resources." Ph.D. diss., University of Kansas.

Burke, Heather, and Claire Smith. 2004. *The Archaeologist's Field Handbook*. Crows Nest, Australia: Allen & Unwin.

Camp, Stacey L. 2019. "Fieldwork and Parenting in Archaeology." In *Mothering in the Field: The Impact of Motherhood on Site-Based Research*, edited by Bahiyyah M. Muhammad and Mélanie-Angela Neuilly, 27–42. New Brunswick, NJ: Rutgers University Press.

Canti, M.G. 2003. "Earthworm Activity and Archaeological Stratigraphy: A Review of Products and Processes." *Journal of Archaeological Science* 30 (2): 135–48. http://dx.doi.org/10.1006/jasc.2001.0770.

Capelotti, P.J. 2010. *The Human Archaeology of Space: Lunar, Planetary, and Interstellar Relics of Exploration*. Jefferson, NC: McFarland & Co.

Caraher, William, Kostis Kourelis, and Andres Reinhard, eds. 2014. *Punk Archaeology*. Grand Forks: Digital Press of North Dakota.

Carman, John. 2002. *Archaeology and Heritage: An Introduction*. New York: Continuum.

———, ed. 1997. *Material Harm: Archaeological Studies of War and Violence*. Glasgow: Cruithne Press.

Casella, Eleanor Conlin. 2000. "'Doing Trade:' A Sexual Economy of Nineteenth-Century Australian Female Convict Prisons." *World Archaeology* 32 (2): 209–21. https://doi.org/10.1080/00438240050131199.

———. 2001. "To Watch or Restrain: Female Convict Prisons in 19th-Century Tasmania." *International Journal of Historical Archaeology* 5 (1): 45–72. https://doi.org/10.1023/a:1009545209653.

———. 2007. "Prisoner of His Majesty: Postcoloniality and the Archaeology of British Penal Transportation." *World Archaeology* 3 7(3): 453–67. https://doi.org/10.1080/00438240500168533.

Chamberlain, Andrew T., and Michael Parker Pearson. 2001. *Earthly Remains: The History and Science of Preserved Human Bodies*. New York: Oxford University Press.

Chapman, John. 1994. "Destruction of a Common Heritage: The Archaeology of War in Croatia, Bosnia, and Hercegovina." *Antiquity* 68: 120–26. https://doi.org/10.1017/S0003598X00046251.

Childs, Terry S. 1995. "The Curation Crisis." *Common Ground: Archaeology and Ethnography in the Public Interest* 7 (4). https://www.nps.gov/archeology/cg/fd_vol7_num4/crisis.htm.

Chisholm, Brian S., D. Erle Nelson, and Henry P. Schwarcz. 1983. "Marine and Terrestrial Protein in Prehistoric Diets on the British Columbia Coast." *Current Anthropology* 24 (3): 396–98. http://dx.doi.org/10.1086/203018.

Christensen, Kim. 2010. "Archaeology and Activism of the Past and Present." In *Archaeologists as Activists: Can Archaeologists Change the World*, edited by M. Jay Stottman, 19–35. Tuscaloosa: University of Alabama Press.

Clack, Timothy, and Marcus Brittain, eds. 2007. *Archaeology and the Media*. Walnut Creek, CA: Left Coast Press.

Clancy, Kathryn B.H., Robin G. Nelson, Julienne N. Rutherford, and Katie Hinde. 2014. "Survey of Academic Field Experiences (SAFE): Trainees Report Harassment and Assault." *PLoS One* 9 (7): e102172. https://doi.org/10.1371/journal.pone.0102172.

Clark, Geoffrey A. 2003. "American Archaeology's Uncertain Future." In *Archeology Is Anthropology: Archeological Papers of the American Anthropological Association*, vol. 13, no. 1, edited by Susan D. Gillespie and Deborah L. Nichols, 51–67. Arlington, VA: American Anthropological Association.

Cleere, Henry, ed. 1989. *Archaeological Heritage Management in the Modern World*. London: Unwin Hyman.

Cole, Teju. 2012. "The White-Savior Industrial Complex." *The Atlantic*, March 21, 2012. https://www.theatlantic.com/international/archive/2012/03/the-white-savior-industrial -complex/254843/.

Colwell, Chip. 2016. "How the Archaeological Review Behind the Dakota Access Pipeline Went Wrong." *The Conversation*, November 20. http://theconversation.com/how-the -archaeological-review-behind-the-dakota-access-pipeline-went-wrong-67815.

Conkey, Margaret W. 2007. "Questioning Theory: Is There a Gender of Theory in Archaeology?" *Journal of Archaeological Method and Theory* 14 (3): 285–310. https://doi.org/10.1007 /s10816-007-9039-z.

Conkey, Margaret W., and Joan M. Gero, eds. 1991. *Engendering Archaeology: Women and Prehistory*. Oxford: Blackwell Publishers.

Conkey, Margaret W., and Janet D. Spector. 1984. "Archaeology and the Study of Gender." *Advances in Archaeological Method and Theory* 7: 1–38. https://doi.org/10.1016/B978-0 -12-003107-8.50006-2.

Cooper, Malcolm A., Antony Firth, John Carman, and David Wheatley, eds. 1995. *Managing Archaeology*. New York: Routledge.

Corbey, Raymond, Robert Layton, and Jeremy Tanner. 2004. "Archaeology and Art." In *A Companion to Archaeology*, edited by John Bintliff, 357–79. Oxford: Blackwell.

Cordain, Loren. 2011. *The Paleo Diet: Lose Weight and Get Healthy by Eating the Foods You Were Designed to Eat*. Revised edition. Hoboken, NJ: John Wiley.

Covan, Eleanor Krassen. 1997. "Cultural Priorities and Elder Care: The Impact on Women." *Health Care for Women International* 18 (4): 329–42. https://doi.org/10.1080 /07399339709516288.

Cowie, Sarah E., Diane L. Teeman, and Christopher C. LeBlanc, eds. 2019. *Collaborative Archaeology at Steward Indian School*. Reno: University of Nevada Press.

Crandall, Brian D., and Peter W. Stahl. 1995. "Human Digestive Effects on a Micromammalian Skeleton." *Journal of Archaeological Science* 22 (6): 789–97. http://dx.doi.org/10.1016/0305-4403(95)90008-X.

Crass, Barbara A. 1999. "Gender in Inuit Burial Practices." In *Reading the Body: Representations and Remains in the Archaeological Record*, edited by Alison E. Rautman, 68–76. Philadelphia: University of Pennsylvania Press.

Cunliffe, Barry, Wendy Davies, and Colin Renfrew, eds. 2002. *Archaeology: The Widening Debate*. New York: Oxford University Press.

Daniel, Glyn. 1981. *A Short History of Archaeology*. London: Thames and Hudson.

Dark, K.R. 1995. *Theoretical Archaeology*. Ithaca, NY: Cornell University Press.

Darrin, Ann Garrison, and Beth Laura O'Leary, eds. 2009. *Handbook of Space Engineering, Archaeology, and Heritage*. New York: CRC Press. http://dx.doi.org/10.1201/9781420084320.

David, Nicholas, and Carol Kramer. 2001. *Ethnoarchaeology in Action*. New York: Cambridge University Press.

Dawdy, Shannon Lee. 2006. "The Taphonomy of Disaster and the (Re)Formation of New Orleans." *American Anthropologist* 108 (4): 719–30. https://doi.org/10.1525/aa.2006.108.4.719.

De León, Jason. 2012. "'Better to Be Hot than Caught': Excavating the Conflicting Roles of Migrant Material Culture." *American Anthropologist* 114 (3): 477–95. http://dx.doi.org/10.1111/j.1548-1433.2012.01447.x.

———. 2013. "Undocumented Migration, Use Wear, and the Materiality of Habitual Suffering in the Sonoran Desert." *Journal of Material Culture* 18 (4): 321–45. http://dx.doi.org/10.1177/1359183513496489.

———. 2015. *The Land of Open Graves: Living and Dying on the Migrant Trail*. Oakland: University of California Press.

Delgado, James P., ed. 1997. *Encyclopedia of Underwater and Maritime Archaeology*. London: British Museum Press.

Deloria, Vine Jr. 1988 [1969]. *Custer Died for Your Sins: An Indian Manifesto*. Norman: University of Oklahoma Press.

Derry, Linda, and Maureen Malloy, eds. 2003. *Archaeologists and Local Communities: Partners in Exploring the Past*. Washington, DC: Society for American Archaeology.

Diamond, Jared. 1987. "The Worst Mistake in the History of the Human Race." *Discover* 8 (5): 64–66.

———. 2005. *Collapse: How Societies Choose to Fail or Succeed*. New York: Viking.

Dielissen, Sandra. 2012. "Teaching a School to Talk: Archaeology of the Queen Victoria Jubilee House for Indian Children." M.A. thesis, Simon Fraser University.

Dunn, Carolyn. 2018. "Archaeologists Find Treasure in Aftermath of Giant Forest Fire." *CBC*, June 29, 2018. https://www.cbc.ca/news/canada/calgary/kenow-fire-blackfoot-archeology-sites-1.4765349.

Edgeworth, Matt, ed. 2006. *Ethnographies of Archaeological Practice: Cultural Encounters, Material Transformations*. New York: Altamira.

Enabled Archaeology Foundation. n.d. "Our Use of Language." Accessed January 28, 2020. https://enabledarchaeologyfoundation.org/our-use-of-language/.

Fagan, Brian M., ed. 1996. *The Oxford Companion to Archaeology*. New York: Oxford.

———. 2018. *A Little History of Archaeology: An Introduction*. New Haven, CT: Yale University Press.

Feder, Kenneth L. 2020. *Frauds, Myths, and Mysteries: Science and Pseudoscience in Archaeology*. Tenth edition. New York: Oxford.

Ferris, Neal. 2003. "Between Colonial and Indigenous Archaeologies: Legal and Extra-Legal Ownership of the Archaeological Past in North America." *Canadian Journal of Archaeology* 27 (2): 154–90.

Fraser, Meredith A. 2007. "Dis/Abling Exclusion, En/Abling Access: Identifying and Removing Barriers in Archaeological Practice for Persons with (Dis)/Abilities." Ph.D. diss., American University.

Gero, Joan M. 1985. "Socio-Politics and the Woman-at-Home-Ideology." *American Antiquity* 50 (2): 342–50. https://doi.org/10.2307/280492.

Gero, Joan M., and Delores Root. 1994. "Public Presentations and Private Concerns: Archaeology in the Pages of National Geographic." In *The Politics of the Past*, edited by Peter Gathercole and David Lowenthal, 19–37. New York: Routledge.

Gilchrist, Roberta. 1994. *Gender and Material Culture: The Archaeology of Religious Women*. London: Routledge.

———. 2000. "Unsexing the Body: The Interior Sexuality of Medieval Religious Women." In *Archaeologies of Sexuality*, edited by Robert A. Schmidt and Barbara L. Voss, 89–99. London: Routledge.

Gillespie, Susan D., and Deborah L. Nichols, eds. 2003. *Archeology Is Anthropology: Archeological Papers of the American Anthropological Association no. 13*. Arlington, VA: American Anthropological Association.

Goldstein, Lynne, Barbara J. Mills, Sarah Herr, Jo Ellen Burkholder, Leslie Aiello, and Christopher Thornton. "Why Do Fewer Women than Men Apply for Grants after their Ph.D.s?" 2018. *American Antiquity* 83 (3): 367–86. https://doi.org/10.1017/aaq.2017.73.

Gonzalez, Sara L., Ian Kretzler, and Briece Edwards. 2018. "Imagining Indigenous and Archaeological Futures: Building Capacity with the Confederated Tribes of Grand Ronde." *Archaeologies: Journal of the World Archaeological Congress* 14 (1): 85–114. https://doi .org/10.1007/s11759-018-9335-0.

Gorman, Alice. 2009. "The Archaeology of Space Exploration." *The Sociological Review* 57 (1): 132–45. https://doi.org/10.1111/j.1467-954X.2009.01821.x.

———. 2019. *Dr. Space Junk vs the Universe: Archaeology and the Future*. Cambridge, MA: MIT Press.

Gould, Richard A. 2005. "Identifying Victims after a Disaster." *Anthropology News* 46 (8): 22–23. http://dx.doi.org/10.1525/an.2005.46.8.22.

———. 2007. *Disaster Archaeology*. Salt Lake City: University of Utah Press.

Graves-Brown, Paul, Rodney Harrison, and Angela Piccini, eds. 2013. *The Oxford Handbook of the Archaeology of the Contemporary World*. Oxford: Oxford University Press.

Guttmann-Bond, Erika. 2010. "Sustainability Out of the Past: How Archaeology Can Save the Planet." *World Archaeology* 42 (3): 355–66. http://dx.doi.org/10.1080/00438243 .2010.497377.

Hafner, Albert. 2012. "Archaeological Discoveries on Schnidejoch and at Other Ice Sites in the European Alps." *Arctic* 65 (1): 189–202. https://doi.org/10.14430/arctic4193.

Hastorf, Christine A. 2017. *The Social Archaeology of Food: Thinking About Eating from Prehistory to the Present*. New York: Cambridge University Press.

Handwerk, Brian. 2018. "How is Accurate is Alpha's Theory of Dog Domestication?" *Smithsonian Magazine*, August 15, 2018. https://www.smithsonianmag.com/science -nature/how-wolves-really-became-dogs-180970014/.

Haraway, Donna J. 2003. *The Companion Species Manifesto: Dogs, People, and Significant Otherness*. Chicago: Prickly Paradigm Press.

Hare, Brian, Michelle Brown, Christina Williamson, and Michael Tomasello. 2002. "The Domestication of Social Cognition in Dogs." *Science* 298 (5598): 1634–36. https://doi .org/10.1126/science.1072702.

Hare, P. Gregory, Christian D. Thomas, Timothy N. Topper, and Ruth M. Gotthardt. 2012. "The Archaeology of Yukon Ice Patches: New Artifacts, Observations, and Insights." *Arctic* 65 (1): 118–35. https://doi.org/10.14430/arctic4188.

Harris, Charles H., III, and Louis R. Sadler. 2003. *The Archaeologist Was a Spy: Sylvanus G. Morley and the Office of Naval Intelligence*. Albuquerque: University of New Mexico Press.

Harrison, Faye V. 1997. "Anthropology as an Agent of Transformation: Introductory Comments and Queries." In *Decolonizing Anthropology: Moving Further Toward an Anthropology of Liberation*, edited by Faye V. Harrison, 1–15. Arlington, VA: Association of Black Anthropologists, American Anthropological Association.

Hassan, Fekri. 1978. "Demographic Archaeology." In *Advances in Archaeological Method and Theory*, vol. 1, edited by Michael B. Schiffer, 49–103. New York: Academic Press.

Hayden, Brian. 1997. *The Pithouses of Keatley Creek: Complex Hunter-Gatherers of the Northwest Plateau*. New York: Harcourt Brace.

———. 2003. "Were Luxury Foods the First Domesticates? Ethnoarchaeological Perspectives from Southeast Asia." *World Archaeology* 34 (3): 458–69. http://dx.doi.org/10.1080 /0043824021000026459a.

Hayden, Brian, and Aubrey Cannon. 1983. "Where the Garbage Goes: Refuse Disposal in the Maya Highlands." *Journal of Anthropological Archaeology* 2 (2): 117–63.

Heath-Stout, Laura. 2019. "Diversity, Identity, and Oppression in the Production of Archaeological Knowledge." Ph.D diss., Boston University.

Hegmon, Michelle. 2003. "Setting Theoretical Egos Aside: Issues and Theory in North American Archaeology." *American Antiquity* 68 (2): 213–43. http://dx.doi.org/10.2307 /3557078.

Hester, Thomas R., Harry J. Shafer, and Kenneth L. Feder. 1997. *Field Methods in Archaeology*. Seventh edition. New York: McGraw-Hill.

Hilton, M.R. 2003. "Quantifying Postdepositional Redistribution of the Archaeological Record Produced by Freeze-Thaw and Other Mechanisms: An Experimental Approach." *Journal of Archaeological Method and Theory* 10 (3): 165–202.

Holtorf, Cornelius. 2005. *From Stonehenge to Las Vegas: Archaeology as Popular Culture*. Walnut Creek, CA: Altamira.

———. 2006. "Studying Archaeological Fieldwork in the Field: Views from Monte Polizzo." In *Ethnographies of Archaeological Practice: Cultural Encounters, Material Transformations*, edited by Matt Edgeworth, 81–94. New York: Altamira.

———. 2007. *Archaeology Is a Brand: The Meaning of Archaeology in Popular Culture*. Walnut Creek, CA: Left Coast Press.

Humes, Edward. 2012. *Garbology: Our Dirty Love Affair with Trash*. New York: Avery.

Huuki, Tuija. 2016. "Mapping Historical, Material, and Affective Entanglements in a Sámi Woman's Discriminatory Experiences in and Beyond Finnish Boarding School." *Education in the North* 23 (2): 2–23.

Hyde, E.R., D.P. Haarmann, A.M. Lynne, S.R. Bucheli, and J.F. Petrosino. 2013. "The Living Dead: Bacterial Community Structure of a Cadaver at the Onset and End of the Bloat Stage of Decomposition." *PLoS ONE* 8 (10): e77733. http://dx.doi.org/10.1371/journal.pone.0077733.

Insoll, Timothy, ed. 2011. *The Oxford Handbook of the Archaeology of Ritual and Religion*. New York: Oxford. http://dx.doi.org/10.1093/oxfordhb/9780199232444.001.0001.

Jalbert, Catherine L. 2019. Archaeology in Canada: An Analysis of Demographics and Working Conditions in the Discipline. Ph.D. diss., Memorial University of Newfoundland.

James, S.R. 1997. "Methodological Issues Concerning Screen Size Recovery Rates and Their Effects on Archaeofaunal Interpretation." *Journal of Archaeological Science* 24 (5): 385–97.

Jameson, John H., Jr., John E. Ehrenhard, and Christine A. Finn, eds. 2003. *Ancient Muses: Archaeology and the Arts*. Tuscaloosa: University of Alabama Press.

Johnson, Matthew. 2019. *Archaeological Theory: An Introduction*. Third edition. Oxford: Wiley Blackwell.

Jones, Sian. 1997. *The Archaeology of Ethnicity: Constructing Identities in the Past and Present*. New York: Routledge. http://dx.doi.org/10.4324/9780203438732.

Joyce, Rosemary. 2020. *The Future of Nuclear Waste: What Art and Archaeology Can Tell Us about Securing the World's Most Hazardous Material*. New York: Oxford University Press.

Kaminski, Juliane, Bridget M. Waller, Rui Diogo, Adam Hartstone-Rose, and Anne M. Burrons. 2019. "Evolution of Facial Muscle Anatomy in Dogs." *PNAS* 116 (29): 14677–81. https://doi.org/10.1073/pnas.1820653116.

Kaplan, M., and M. Adams. 1986. "Using the Past to Protect the Future: Marking Nuclear Waste Disposal Sites." *Archaeology* 39 (5): 107–12.

Karrow, Stuart. 2017. "Ontario's Archaeological Curation Crisis – Twenty Years Later." M.A. thesis. University of Waterloo.

Keeley, Lawrence H., and Nicholas Toth. 1981. "Microwear Polishes on Early Stone Tools from Koobi Fora, Kenya." *Nature* 293 (5832): 464–65. http://dx.doi.org/10.1038/293464a0.

Kehoe, Alice Beck. 1998. *The Land of Prehistory: A Critical History of American Archaeology*. New York: Routledge.

Kelley, Jane H., and Ronald F. Williamson. 1996. "The Positioning of Archaeology within Anthropology: A Canadian Historical Perspective." *American Antiquity* 61 (1): 5–20. http://dx.doi.org/10.2307/282294.

Kersel, Morag K. 2015. "Storage Wars: Solving the Archaeological Curation Crisis?" *Journal of Eastern Mediterranean Archaeology and Heritage Studies* 3 (1): 42–54. https://doi.org/10.5325/jeasmedarcherstu.3.1.0042.

King, Thomas F. 2005. *Doing Archaeology: A Cultural Resource Management Perspective*. Walnut Creek, CA: Left Coast Press.

Kintigh, Keith W., Jeffrey H. Altschul, Mary C. Beaudry, Robert D. Drennan, Ann P. Kinzig, Timothy A. Kohler, W. Frederick Limp, et al. 2014. "Grand Challenges for Archaeology." *American Antiquity* 79 (1): 5–24.

Kohl, Philip L. 1998. "Nationalism and Archaeology: On the Constructions of Nations and the Reconstructions of the Remote Past." *Annual Review of Anthropology* 27 (1): 223–46. http://dx.doi.org/10.1146/annurev.anthro.27.1.223.

Kohl, Philip L., and Clare Fawcett, eds. 1995. *Nationalism, Politics, and the Practice of Archaeology*. New York: Cambridge University Press.

Konefes, John L., and Michael K. McGhee. 2001. "Old Cemeteries, Arsenic, and Health Safety." In D*angerous Places: Health, Safety, and Archaeology*, edited by David A. Poirier and Kenneth L. Feder, 127–135. Westport, CT: Bergin and Garvey.

Kroeger, Alix. 2019. "The Ancient Egyptian Yeasts Being Used to Bake Modern Bread." *BBC News*, August 7, 2019. https://www.bbc.com/news/amp/world-us-canada-49262255?__twitter_impression=true.

Larsen, Clark Spencer. 1997. *Bioarchaeology: Interpreting Human Behavior from the Human Skeleton*. New York: Cambridge University Press. http://dx.doi.org/10.1017/CBO9780511802676.

Leslie, Brian. 2019. "Wildfire and Archaeology: The Good, the Bad, and the Opportunity." Time Tree Archaeology: Preserving the Past While We Build the Future, April 17, 2019. http://archaeologyblog.treetimeservices.ca/2019/04/17/wildfire-and-archaeology-the-good-the-bad-and-the-opportunity/.

Leone, Mark P., Cheryl Janifer LaRoche, and Jennifer J. Babiarz. 2005. "The Archaeology of Black Americans in Recent Times." *Annual Review of Anthropology* 34 (1): 575–98. http://dx.doi.org/10.1146/annurev.anthro.34.081804.120417.

Lesnick, Julie J. 2018. *Edible Insects and Human Evolution*. Gainesville: University Press of Florida.

Lindauer, Owen. 2009. "Individual Struggles and Institutional Goals: Small Voices from the Phoenix Indian School Track Site." In *The Archaeology of Institutional Life*, edited by April M. Beisaw and James G. Gibb, 86–104. Tuscaloosa: University of Alabama Press.

Lipe, William D. 1974. "A Conservation Model for American Archaeology." *The Kiva* 39 (3–4): 213–45. https://doi.org/10.1080/00231940.1974.11757792.

Livingston, Gretchen. 2018. "More Than One-In-Ten U.S. Parents Are Caring for an Adult." *Fact Tank: News in the Numbers*, Pew Research Center, November 29, 2018. https://www.pewresearch.org/fact-tank/2018/11/29/more-than-one-in-ten-u-s-parents-are-also-caring-for-an-adult.

Little, Barbara J., ed. 2002. *Public Benefits of Archaeology*. Gainesville: University of Florida Press.

Little, Barbara J., and Larry J. Zimmerman. 2010. "In the Public Interest: Creating a More Activist, Civically Engaged Archaeology." In *Voices in American Archaeology*, edited by Wendy Ashmore, Dorothy T. Lippert, and Barbara J. Mills, 131–59. Washington, DC: SAA Press.

Loy, Thomas H., and E. James Dixon. 1998. "Blood Residues on Fluted Points from Eastern Beringia." *American Antiquity* 63 (1): 21–46.

Lyman, R. Lee. 1994. "Quantitative Units and Terminology in Zooarchaeology." *American Antiquity* 59 (1): 36–71. http://dx.doi.org/10.2307/3085500.

Lyons, Natasha, Kisha Supernant, and John R. Welch. 2019. "What Are the Prospects for an Archaeology of Heart?" *The SAA Archaeological Record* 19 (2): 6–9.

MacFarland, Kathryn, and Arthur W. Vokes. 2016. "Dusting Off the Data: Curating and Rehabilitating Archaeological Legacy and Orphaned Collections." *Advances in Archaeological Practice* 4 (2): 161–75. https://doi.org/10.7183/2326-3768.4.2.161.

Macinnes, Lesley, and C.R. Wickham-Jones, eds. 1992. *All Natural Things: Archaeology and the Green Debate*. Oxford: Oxbow.

Marquardt, William H., Anta Montet-White, and Sandra Scholtz. 1982. "Resolving the Crisis in Archaeological Collections Curation." *Antiquity* 47 (2): 409–18. https://doi.org/10.1017/S0002731600061308.

Maschner, Herbert D.G., and Christopher Chippendale, eds. 2005. *Handbook of Archaeological Methods*, vols. 1 and 2. New York: Altamira Press.

Matisso-Smith, Elizabeth, and K. Ann Horsburgh. 2012. *DNA for Archaeologists*. Walnut Creek, CA: Left Coast Press.

McGhee, Robert. 1989. "Who Owns Prehistory? The Bering Land Bridge Dilemma." *Canadian Journal of Archaeology* 13: 59–70.

———. 2004. "Between Racism and Romanticism, Scientism and Spiritualism: The Dilemmas of New World Archaeology." In *Archaeology on the Edge: New Perspectives from the Northern Plains*, edited by Brian Kooyman and Jane Kelley, 13–22. Calgary: University of Calgary Press.

McGovern, Patrick E. 2009. *Uncorking the Past: The Quest for Wine, Beer, and Other Alcoholic Beverages*. Los Angeles: University of California Press.

Monks, Gregory G. 1981. "Seasonality Studies." In *Advances in Archaeological Method and Theory*, vol. 4, edited by Michael B. Schiffer, 177–240. New York: Academic Press.

Moore, Lawrence E. 2005. "A Forecast for American Archaeology." *SAA Archaeological Record* 5 (4): 13–16.

Moshenska, Gabriel, ed. 2017. *Key Concepts in Public Archaeology*. London: UCL Press.

Muckle, Robert. 1994. "Differential Recovery of Mollusk Shell from Archaeological Sites." *Journal of Field Archaeology* 21: 129–131.

———. 2012 . "A Bit of a Crisis in Archaeology in the Lands of Ice and Snow." *Anthropology News* 53 (6).

———. November 2014. "On Sexual Harassment and Abuse in Archaeology." *The SAA Archaeological Record* 14 (5): 32–33.

———. 2016. "Archaeology and NASA." *Anthropology News* 15(1).

———. 2018. "Archaeological Fieldwork." In *Encyclopedia of Global Archaeology*, edited by Claire Smith. Cham, Switzerland: Springer. https://doi.org/10.1007/978-3-319-51726-1.

Murray, Tim, ed. 1999. *Time and Archaeology*. New York: Routledge.

Myers, Adrian. 2010. "Camp Delta, Google Earth and the Ethics of Remote Sensing in Archaeology." *World Archaeology* 42 (3): 455–67. https://doi.org/10.1080/00438243 .2010.498640.

Nelson, Sarah Milledge. 1997. *Gender in Archaeology: Analyzing Power and Prestige*. Walnut Creek, CA: Altamira.

Nicholas, George, and Thomas D. Andrews, eds. 1997. *At a Crossroads: Archaeology and First Peoples in Canada*. Burnaby, BC: Arch Press.

O'Brien, Michael, R. Lee Lyman, and Michael Brian Schiffer. 2005. *Archaeology as Process: Processualism and Its Progeny*. Salt Lake City: University of Utah Press.

Odell, George H. 2004. *Lithic Analysis*. New York: Kluwer. http://dx.doi.org/10.1007/978-1 -4419-9009-9.

O'Leary, Beth. 2015. ""To Boldly Go Where No Man [sic] Has Gone Before:" Approaches in Space Archaeology." In *Archaeology and Heritage of Human Movement into Space: Space and Society*, edited by Beth L. O'Leary and P. Capelotti, 1–12. New York: Springer.

Orton, Clive. 2000. *Sampling in Archaeology*. New York: Cambridge University Press. http:// dx.doi.org/10.1017/CBO9781139163996.

Orton, Clive, and Michael Hughes. 2013. *Pottery in Archaeology*. 2nd ed. New York: Cambridge University Press.

Outram, Alan K., and Amy Bogaard. 2019. *Subsistence in Prehistory: New Directions in Economic Archaeology*. New York. Cambridge University Press.

Parcak, Sarah. 2019. *Archaeology from Space: How the Future Shapes Our Past*. New York. Henry Holt.

Parker Peason, Mike. 2013. *Stonehenge – A New Understanding: Solving the Mysteries of the Greatest Stone Age Monument*. New York: The Experiment.

Patrick, Linda E. 1985. "Is There an Archaeological Record?" In *Advances in Archaeological Method and Theory*, vol. 8, edited by M.B. Schiffer, 27–62. New York: Academic Press.

Patterson, Thomas C. 1999. "The Political Economy of Archaeology in the United States." *Annual Review of Anthropology* 28 (1): 155–74. http://dx.doi.org/10.1146/annurev .anthro.28.1.155.

Pearson, James L. 2002. *Shamanism and the Ancient Mind: A Cognitive Approach to Archaeology*. Walnut Creek, CA: Altamira.

Peregrine, Peter N. 2001a. *Archaeological Research: A Brief Introduction*. Upper Saddle River, NJ: Pearson Prentice Hall.

——. 2001b. "Introduction." In *Outline of Archaeological Traditions*. New Haven, CT: HRAF Press.

Peregrine, Peter N., and Melvin Ember, eds. 2001. *Encyclopedia of Prehistory*. 9 vols. New York: Kluwer.

Phillips, Tim, and Roberta Gilchrist. 2012. "Inclusive, Accessible, Archaeology: Enabling Persons with Disabilities." In *The Oxford Handbook of Public Archaeology*, edited by John Carmen and Robin Skeates, 673–93. Oxford: Oxford University Press.

Phillips, Tim, Roberta Gilchrist, Iain Hewitt, Stephanie Le Scouiller, Darren Booy, and Geoff Cook. 2007. "Inclusive, Accessible, Archaeology: Good Practice Guidelines for Including Disabled Students and Self-Evaluation in Archaeological Fieldwork Training. Higher Education Funding Council for England." Higher Education Funding Council for England, June. https://www.heacademy.ac.uk/system/files/Number5_Teaching_and_Learning _Guide_Inclusive_Accessible_Archaeology.pdf.

Poirier, David A., and Kenneth L. Feder. 2001. *Dangerous Places: Health, Safety, and Archaeology*. Westport, CT: Bergin and Garvey.

Pyburn, K. Anne, ed. 2004. *Ungendering Civilization*. New York: Routledge.

Quinlan, Angus R., and Alanah Woody. 2003. "Marks of Distinction: Rock Art and Ethnic Identification in the Great Basin." *American Antiquity* 68 (2): 372–90.

Rapp, George Jr., and Christopher L. Hill. 1998. *Geoarchaeology: The Earth Science Approach to Archaeological Interpretation*. New Haven, CT: Yale University Press.

Rathje, W.L. 2002. "Garbology: The Archaeology of Fresh Garbage." In *Public Benefits of Archaeology*, edited by Barbara J. Little, 85–100. Gainesville: University of Florida Press.

Rathje, W.L., W.W. Hughes, D.C. Wilson, M.K. Tani, G.H. Archer, R.G. Hunt, and T.W. Jones. 1992. "The Archaeology of Contemporary Landfills." *American Antiquity* 57 (3): 437–47. http://dx.doi.org/10.2307/280932.

Rathje, W.L., and C. Murphy. 1992. *Rubbish! The Archaeology of Garbage*. New York: Harper.

Reckin, Rachel. 2013. "Ice Patch Archaeology in Global Perspective: Archaeological Discoveries from Alpine Ice Patches Worldwide and Their Relationship with Paleoclimates." *Journal of World Prehistory* 26: 323–85. https://doi.org/10.1007/s10963-013-9068-3.

Reinhard, Andrew. 2018. *Archaeogaming: An Introduction to Archaeology in and of Video Games*. New York. Berghahn.

Reinhard, Karl J., and Vaughn M. Bryant, Jr. 1992. "Coprolite Analysis: A Biological Perspective on Archaeology." In *Archaeological Method and Theory*, edited by Michael B. Schiffer, 245–88. Tucson: University of Arizona Press.

Reitz, Elizabeth, and Myra Shackley. 2012. *Environmental Archaeology*. New York: Springer.

Renfrew, Colin. 1994. "The Archaeology of Religion." In *The Ancient Mind: Elements of Cognitive Archaeology*, edited by Colin Renfrew and Ezra B.W. Zubrow, 47–54. New York: Cambridge University Press. http://dx.doi.org/10.1017/CBO9780511598388.007.

——. 2000. *Loot, Legitimacy, and Ownership: The Ethical Crisis in Archaeology*. London: Duckworth.

Renfrew, Colin, and Ezra B.W. Zubrow, eds. 1994. *The Ancient Mind: Elements of Cognitive Archaeology*. New York: Cambridge University Press. http://dx.doi.org/10.1017/CBO9780511598388.

Rice, Prudence M. 1987. *Pottery Analysis: A Sourcebook*. Chicago: University of Chicago Press.

Richardson, Lorna-Jane. 2017. "I'll Give You 'Punk Archaeology,' Sunshine." *World Archaeology* 49 (3): 306–17. https://doi.org/10.1080/00438243.2017.1333036.

Roach, Mary. 2004. *Stiff: The Curious Lives of Human Cadavers*. New York: Norton.

Roper, D.C. 1979. "The Method and Theory of Site Catchment Analysis: A Review." In *Advances in Archaeological Method and Theory*, vol. 2, edited by Michael B. Schiffer, 119–40. New York: Academic Press.

Roskams, Steve. 2001. *Excavation*. New York: Cambridge University Press.

Rowan, Yorke, and Uzi Baram, eds. 2004. *Marketing Heritage: Archaeology and the Consumption of the Past*. Walnut Creek, CA: Altamira.

Russell, Miles, ed. 2002. *Digging Holes in Popular Culture: Archaeology and Science Fiction*. Oxford: Oxbow Books.

Ryan, Kevin C. 2010. "Effects of Fire on Cultural Resources." In *VI International Conference on Forest Fire Research*, edited by D.X. Viegas. https://www.fs.fed.us/rm/pubs_other/rmrs_2010_ryan_k004.pdf.

Sabloff, Jeremy A. 2008. *Archaeology Matters: Action Archaeology in the Modern World*. Walnut Creek, CA: Left Coast Press.

Salzman, Philip. 2004. "Thinking Theoretically." In *Thinking Anthropologically: A Practical Guide for Students*, edited by Philip Salzman and Patricia Rice, 29–38. Upper Saddle River, NJ: Pearson.

Scarre, Chris. 1990. "The Western World View in Archaeological Atlases." In *The Politics of the Past*, edited by Peter Gathercole and David Lowenthal, 11–17. London: Unwin Hyman.

Scarre, Chris, ed. 2013. *The Human Past: World Prehistory and the Development of Human Societies*. Third edition. New York: Thames and Hudson.

Scarre, Chris, and Brian M. Fagan. 2016. *Ancient Civilizations*. Fourth edition. New York: Routledge.

Schablitsky, Julie M., ed. 2007. *Box Office Archaeology: Refining Hollywood's Portrayals of the Past*. Walnut Creek, CA: Left Coast Press.

Schiffer, Michael B. 1987. *Formation Processes of the Archaeological Record*. Albuquerque: University of New Mexico Press.

———. 2017. *Archaeology's Footprints in the Modern World*. Salt Lake City: University of Utah Press.

Schlumbaum, Angela, Paula F. Campos, Serge Volken, Marquita Volken, Albert Hafner, and Jörge Schibler. 2010. "Ancient DNA, a Neolithic Legging from the Swiss Alps and the Early History of Goat." *Journal of Archaeological Science* 37 (6): 1247–51. https://doi.org/10.1016/j.jas.2009.12.025.

Schmidt, Robert A., and Barbara L. Voss, eds. 2000. *Archaeologies of Sexuality*. London and New York: Routledge.

Schnapp, Alain. 1996. *The Discovery of the Past*. London: British Museum Press.

Seaward, Marty R. 1999. "The Sandwich Generation Copes with Elder Care." *Benefits Quarterly* 15 (2): 41.

Shackley, Myra L. 1975. *Archaeological Sediments: A Survey of Analytical Methods*. New York: Wiley.

Shanks, Michael. 1992. *Experiencing the Past: On the Character of Archaeology*. New York: Routledge.

Shanks, Michael, and Randall H. McGuire. 1996. "The Craft of Archaeology." *American Antiquity* 61 (1): 75–88. https://doi.org/10.1017/S0002731600050046.

Shennan, Stephen J., ed. 1989. *Archaeological Approaches to Cultural Identity*. London: Unwin Hyman.

Sinopoli, Carla M. 1991. *Approaches to Archaeological Ceramics*. New York: Plenum. http://dx.doi.org/10.1007/978-1-4757-9274-4.

Skowronek, Russell K., and Charles R. Ewen, eds. 2006. *X Marks the Spot: The Archaeology of Piracy*. Gainesville: University of Florida Press.

Smith, Claire. 2004. "On Intellectual Property Rights and Archaeology." *Current Anthropology* 45 (4): 527–29. http://dx.doi.org/10.1086/423495.

Smith, Frederick. 2008. *The Archaeology of Alcohol and Drinking*. Gainseville, FL: University Press of Florida.

Smith, Laurajane. 2004. *Archaeological Theory and the Politics of Cultural Heritage*. New York: Routledge. http://dx.doi.org/10.4324/9780203307991.

Sobolik, Kristin D. 2003. *Archaeobiology*. Walnut Creek, CA: Altamira.

Starzmann, Maria Theresia. 2008. "Cultural Imperialism and Heritage Politics in the Event of Armed Conflict: Prospects for an 'Activist Archaeology.'" *Archaeologies* 4: 368–89. https://doi.org/10.1007/s11759-008-9083-7.

Stein, Julie K. 1983. "Earthworm Activity: A Source of Potential Disturbance of Archaeological Sediments." *American Antiquity* 48 (2): 277–89. http://dx.doi.org/10.2307/280451.

Stottman, M. Jay, ed. 2010. *Archaeologists as Activists: Can Archaeologists Change the World?* Tuscaloosa: University of Alabama Press.

Stringer, Chris, and Peter Andrews. 2005. *The Complete World of Human Evolution*. New York: Thames and Hudson.

Surface-Evans, Sarah L. 2016. "A Landscape of Assimilation and Resistance: The Mount Pleasant Indian Industrial Boarding School." *International Journal of Historical Archaeology* 20 (3): 574–88. https://doi.org/10.1007/s10761-016-0362-5.

Supernant, Kisha, Jane Eva Baxter, Natasha Lyons, and Sonya Atalay, eds. 2020. *Archaeologies of the Heart*. New York: Springer.

Sutton, Mark Q., and Brooke S. Arkush. 1996. *Archaeological Laboratory Methods: An Introduction*. Dubuque, IA: Kendall/Hunt Publishing Group.

Tainter, Joseph A. 2004. "Persistent Dilemmas in American Cultural Resource Management." In *A Companion to Archaeology*, edited by John Bintliff, 435–53. Oxford: Blackwell.

Tapper, James. 2019. "Dig In! Archaeologists Serve Up Ancient Menus for Modern Tables." *The Guardian*, August 11, 2019. https://www.theguardian.com/science/2019/aug/11/ancient-menus-archaeology-modern-tastes.

Thalmann, O., B. Shapiro, P. Cui, V.J. Schuenemann, S.K. Sawyer, D.L. Greenfield, M.B. Germonpré, et al. 2013. "Complete Mitochondrial Genomes of Ancient Canids Suggest a

European Origin of Domestic Dogs." *Science* 342 (6160): 871–74. https://doi.org/10.1126/science.1243650.

Thomas, David Hurst, and Robert L. Kelly. 2006. *Archaeology*. 4th ed. Belmont, CA: Wadsworth.

Trafzer, Clifford E., Jean A. Keller, and Lorene Sisquoc, eds. 2006. *Boarding School Blues: Revising American Indian Educational Experiences*. Lincoln: University of Nebraska Press.

Trigger, Bruce. 1989. *A History of Archaeological Thought*. New York: Cambridge University Press.

Tudge, Colin. 1996. *The Time Before History: 5 Million Years of Human Impact*. New York: Scribner.

Tushingham, Shannon, Tiffany Fulkerson, and Katheryn Hill. 2017. "The Peer Review Gap: A Longitudinal Case Study of Gendered Publishing and Occupational Patterns in a Female-rich Discipline, Western North America (1974–2016)." *PLoS ONE* 12 (11): e0188403. https://doi.org/10.1371/journal.pone.0188403.

Twiss, Katheryn C. 2019. *The Archaeology of Food: Identity, Politics, and Ideology in the Prehistoric and Historic Past*. New York: Cambridge University Press.

Two Bears, Davina Ruth. 2019. "Shimásáni dóó Shicheii Bi'ólta', My Grandparents' School: Navajo Survivance and Education at the Old Leupp Boarding School, 1909–1942." Ph.D. diss., Indiana University.

United States Department of Agriculture – Forest Service. 2012. "Wildland Fire in Ecosystems: Effects of Fire on Cultural Resources and Archaeology." Rocky Mountain Research Station. Central Technical Report RMRS-GTR-42-volume 3, May. https://www.fs.fed.us/rm/pubs/rmrs_gtr042_3.pdf.

VanPool, Christine S., and Todd L. VanPool. 1999. "The Scientific Nature of Postprocessualism." *American Antiquity* 64 (1): 33–53. http://dx.doi.org/10.2307/2694344.

Voss, Barbara L. 2008a. "Sexuality Studies in Archaeology." *Annual Review of Anthropology* 37: 317–36. https://doi.org/10.1146/annurev.anthro.37.081407.085238.

———. 2008b. "Domesticating Imperialism: Sexual Politics and the Archaeology of Empire." *American Anthropologist* 110 (2): 191–203. https://doi.org/10.1111/j.1548-1433.2008.00025.x.

———. 2012. "Curation as Research: A Case Study in Orphaned and Underreported Archaeological Collections." *Archaeological Dialogues* 19 (2): 145–69. https://doi.org/10.1017/S1380203812000219.

Voss, Barbara, and Megan S. Kane. 2012. "Re-Establishing Context for Orphaned Collections." *Collections: A Journal for Museum and Archives Professionals* 8(2): 87–112. https://doi.org/10.1177/155019061200800202.

Walsh, Justin St. P. 2012. "Protection of Humanity's Cultural and Historic Heritage in Space." *Space Policy* 28: 234–43. https://doi.org/10.1016/j.spacepol.2012.04.001.

Waters, Michael R., and David D. Kuehn. 1996. "The Geoarchaeology of Place: The Effect of Geological Processes on the Preservation and Interpretation of the Archaeological Record." *American Antiquity* 61 (3): 483–97. http://dx.doi.org/10.2307/281836.

Watkins, Joe E. 2001. *Indigenous Archaeologies: American Indian Values and Scientific Practice*. Walnut Creek, CA: Altamira.

———. 2003. "Beyond the Margin: American Indians, First Nations, and Archaeology in North America." *American Antiquity* 68 (2): 273–85. http://dx.doi.org/10.2307/3557080.

———. 2005. "Through Wary Eyes: Indigenous Perspectives on Archaeology." *Annual Review of Anthropology* 34 (1): 429–49. http://dx.doi.org/10.1146/annurev.anthro.34.081804.120540.

Wells, E. Christian, and Melanie N. Coughlin. 2012. "Zero Waste Archaeology." *The SAA Archaeological Record* 12 (4): 19–21.

White, Tim D., and Pieter Arend Folkens. 2000. *Human Osteology*. 2nd ed. New York: Academic Press.

Whitley, David S., ed. 1998. *Reader in Archaeological Theory: Post-Processual and Cognitive Approaches*. New York: Routledge.

Wilk, Richard R. 1985. "The Ancient Maya and the Political Present." *Journal of Anthropological Research* 41 (3): 307–26. https://doi.org/10.1086/jar.41.3.3630596.

Willey, G.R., and J.A. Sabloff. 1993. *A History of American Archaeology*. New York: Freeman.

Wood, W. Raymond, and Donald Lee Johnson. 1978. "A Survey of Disturbance Processes in Archaeological Site Formation." In *Advances in Archaeological Method and Theory*, vol. 1, edited by M.B. Schiffer, 315–81. New York: Academic Press.

Wrangham, Richard. 2009. *Catching Fire: How Cooking Made Us Human*. New York: Basic Books.

Wright, Rita P., ed. 1996. *Gender and Archaeology*. Philadelphia: University of Pennsylvania Press.

Wright, Ronald. 2004. *A Short History of Progress*. Toronto: Anansi Press.

Yalouri, Eleana. 2001. *The Acropolis: Global Fame, Local Claim*. New York: Berg.

Yoffee, Norman, and George L. Cowgill, eds. 2001. *The Collapse of Ancient States and Civilizations*. Tucson: University of Arizona Press.

Zimmerman, Larry J., Courtney Singleton, and Jessica Welch. 2010. "Activism and Creating a Translational Archaeology of Homelessness." *World Archaeology* 42 (3): 443–54. http://dx.doi.org/10.1080/00438243.2010.497400.

Zimmerman, Larry J., Karen D. Vitelli, and Julie Hollowell-Zimmer, eds. 2003. *Ethical Issues in Archaeology*. Walnut Creek, CA: Altamira.

Zimmerman, Larry J., and Jessica Welch. 2011. "Displaced and Barely Visible: Archaeology and the Material Culture of Homelessness." *Historical Archaeology* 45 (1): 67–85. https://doi.org/10.1007/BF03376821.

Zimring, Carl A., and William L. Rathje, eds. 2012. *Encyclopedia of Consumption and Waste: The Social Science of Garbage*. Thousand Oaks, CA: Sage.

Zuk, Marlene. 2013. *Paleofantasy: What Evolution Really Tells Us about Sex, Diet, and How We Live*. New York: Norton.

INDEX

Italicized page numbers indicate photographs or illustrations.

Abandoned Shipwreck Act (ASA), 64–5
abandonment of sites, 87–8
abiotic environments, reconstruction, 167
Aboriginal Peoples of Australia, 61–2
absolute (or chronometric) dating, 141, 145–8
academia, and archaeology, 10, 12–13, 35
academic archaeology, 53–4, 103, 252
acidity of sediments, 132
Acropolis of Athens, 7, *7*
action archaeology, 232–3
activist archaeology, 231–4, *232, 239*
activity area, 83
Adams, M., 23
aerial-based remote sensing, 105–7, *106*
aerial images, 105–6
aeroturbation, 94, 95
Africa, 68, 154–5
African American ethnicity, 192
agriculture, *215*
    definition and description, 174, 176
    food production, 214–17
    raised field agriculture, 232–3, 248–9
    reconstruction, 176
aliens as explanation, 221, 222, 223, 224, *225*
amateur (or avocational) archaeology, 57
Americas, first colonization of, 159
anaerobic environment, 92
analogy, reasoning by, 25–6
ancient civilizations, 161–2
ancient philosophers, 29–30
Andes region civilizations, 162
Angkor, *15,* 17
animal remains
    analysis and quantification, 130–1
    and diet, 180–1
    as ecofacts, 83
    recovery, 91
    and seasonality, 170
    skeletal remains, 116–17, 178, *178, 180*
    of twenty-first century, 253

animals
    bones, 91, 116–17, 130–1, 144
    and disturbance of sites, 94–5
    domestic *vs.* wild, 177–8
    foraging, 173–4
    and reconstruction, 167
    See also domestication of plants and animals
Anthony Island (SGaang Gwaay)/Ninstints, 69
Anthropocene, 151
anthropology, 12–13
antiquities and antiquarians, 31, 38
applied archaeology, 233
aquaturbation, 94, 95
arbitrary levels of excavation, 113–14
ArcGIS software, 247
archaeobotany (paleoethnobotany), 59
archaeological record
    definition and components, 79–84, 255
    inequality in, 160, 161, 170
    protection and ethics, 72–4
    and taphonomy, 89–90
    of twenty-first century, 253
archaeological research. *See* research
archaeological sites
    in advertising, 21
    in Britain in sixteenth century, 32
    burial of, 88, 90
    creation and processes, 84–90
    definition and types, 79–80, 82
    discovery, 99, 100, 104–11
    disturbance, 93–7
    and fire, 251
    formation processes, 85–6, 87–8
    and ice melt, 249, 250
    inventory forms, 109
    life history, 85, *85*
    markings and language, 23
    material remains as, 80, 84
    and politics, 16–18
    for population sizes, 172–3

archaeological sites (*continued*)
    and reconstruction, 166
    records review, 101
    regulations, 66
    sediments in, 88, 90
    See also destruction of sites; heritage sites
"Archaeologies of the Heart" (heart-centered
        archaeology), 230
archaeologists
    activism at work, 233
    attraction to archaeology, 6–7
    and beer, 160
    diversity in, 3, 230
    employment, 55, 76, 229–30, 252, 253
    first archaeologists, 35
    and inclusivity, 103–4
    income, 229, 230
    Indigenous Peoples as, 48–50, *49*
    as professionals, 10–11, 35
    registries, 10–11
    as spies, 18
    view and portrayal, 5–6, 20–1
    women as, 19, 44, 45, 46, *49,* 103
archaeology
    allure of, 5–7
    basic concepts, 24–6
    contemporay issues (*See* archaeology of
        today)
    contextualization, *11,* 12–22
    as craft, 11
    current state, 229–31
    definitions, 9–10, 13
    education in, 13, 53, 54, 76, 220, 229
    equity in, 103–4
    explanations in, 219–25
    future of, 251–4
    goals and role, 42, 235, 255
    history (*See* history of archaeology)
    lens of, 8–9, *47*
    in media and pop culture, 1–3, 5–6, 20–1,
        38, 54
    nature of, 3, 254
    and non-archaeologists, 252, 253
    perceptions and misconceptions, 1–3, 21
    as profession and endeavor, 2, 10–11, 35
    rationalization, 22–4
    sensationalization, 1–2
    spelling, 11
    subfields and specialties, 57–62
    support of other disciplines, 23–4
    terminology in, 230–1
    time frames, 152
    and twenty-first century, 13, 24, 46–50,
        253–4
    types, 53–7, 231, 233

See also specific topics; specific types of
        archaeology
archaeology of today
    activist archaeology, 231–4, *232,* 239
    climate change and sustainability, 248–51
    and contemporary waste, 245–6
    current state of archaeology, 229–31
    digital archaeology, 246–8
    disenfranchised, the voiceless, and invisible,
        239–43
    forensic and disaster archaeology, 243–5
    incarceration and forced removal, 235–9
archaeomagnetism, 148
archaeotourism (heritage tourism), 7, *8,* 14, 69, 70
archeology, as spelling, 11
    See also archaeology
argon/argon (Ar/Ar) dating, 148
argon dating, 147–8
armchair archaeology, 59
armed conflicts, 66, 71, 97
arsenic, 117
art
    and archaeology, 231
    cave art, 158, 220–1
    in human past, 158
    reconstruction, 200–2, *201*
    rock art, 80, 81, 193, 201
articles and journals, 54, 76, 77
artifacts
    analysis in laboratory, 123–30
    classification, 82–3, 123–4
    curation and crisis, 123, 138–9
    definition, 82–3
    and gender, 194
    and human diet, 182
    and ice melt, 249, 250
    inventory and recording, 113, 122–4
    labeling and storing, 123
    for population sizes, 172
    practice in archaeology, 3
    quantification, 130
    sorting, 122
artifact type, 123, 124
artificial selection, 226
Asia, 68, 161
Asian ethnicity, 192–3, *193*
Atalay, Sonya, 48–9
atlatls, *158*
Australia, 61–2, 68, 158–9, 238
Australopithecus, 154, 155
authenticity, 15, *16*
Aztec Empire, 190, 218

Babylon site, 97
bacteria, and decay, 87

Bahn, Paul, 221
Bamiyan Valley (Afghanistan), 84
bands, 188
Battle-Baptiste, Whitney, 45
Baumann, Timothy, 192
Baxter, Jane Eva, 195–6
Beattie, Owen, 93
beer, 160
behavioral disturbance processes (cultural
    disturbance of sites), 93–4, 96–7
behavioral (or cultural) formation processes,
    85–6, 89
Belzoni, Giovanni, 35
Beringia, 126
bias
    in archaeology, 255
    in explanations, 219–21
    gender in archaeology, 44–5, 46, 220
    and material remains, 90–3
Bible, 30, 31
bifaces, 125
Big Man (or Head Man), 189
Binford, Lewis, 42
biological anthropology, 13
biological evolution, 31, 35, 154–5
biological sex, 45
biotic environments, reconstruction, 167
bioturbation, 94
Blackley, Simon, 182
blades, 125
block excavations (horizontal excavations), 112
blood, on stone tools, 125–6
Boas, Franz, 37
Bocek, Barbara, 94
bog men, 93
bones, dating, 143
bones of animals, 91, 116–17, 130–1, 144
bones of humans
    analysis in laboratory, 132, 134–5, 136,
        138
    and diet, 180–1
    identification, 133, 136
    See also human remains; skeletons of
        humans; skulls of humans; teeth of
        humans
botanical remains, 83, 131
    See also plant remains
Bowman, Richard, 182
bp or BP ("years before present"), 147
brain (human), 154–5, 203
Braun, Sebastian Felix, 75
bread in Egypt, 182
Britain, 32, 238
Bronze Age, 29, 31, 35
burial of archaeological sites, 88, 90

burials
    arsenic in, 117
    and formation processes, 86
    as groups, 200
    in human past, 157–8
    humans together, 2
    and inequality, 186
    meaning in archaeology, 199
    mortuary practices, 199–200, 200
    for population sizes, 172
    and preservation of remains, 91–3
butchered remains, 178, 178

cache of food, 86
Cahokia Mounds, 69–70
calibrated relative dating, 142, 144
Camden, William, 31–2
Camp Delta Project, 235
campus waste audits, 246, 246
Canada
    legislation and regulations for heritage, 63, 65
    World Heritage sites, 67, 69
cannibalism, 138, 202–3
Cannon, Aubrey, 115
capa cocha ritual, 199
carbon-14 (C-14 or radiocarbon) dating, 40,
    146–7
Carnac site, 81
Carnarvon, Lord, and King Tut, 38, 41
carrying capacity, 216, 217
Carter, Benjamin P., 247
Carter, Howard, 38, 39, 41
Casella, Eleanor, 238
Çatalhöyük (Turkey), 201
catch-and-release (no-collections strategy), 139
cave art, 158, 220–1
    See also rock art
Caveman diet, 179
Central America, World Heritage Sites, 67
ceramic, 127–9, 159
    See also pottery
ceramic teawares, 234
cess, 181
Charter for the Protection and Management of
    the Archaeological Heritage (1990), 70
chemical analysis of artifacts, 125–6, 128–9
chemical weathering, 95
chemistry of deposits, 107
chert, 127
chiefdoms, 189–90
chiefs, 189
children
    of archaeologists, 103–4
    forced removal as Indigenous Peoples,
        236–7

children (*continued*)
   graffiti at plantation, *195,* 195–6
   identification in reconstruction, 194–6
   sacrifice, 199
Chilkoot Trail (Canada/US), 84
china, 127
China, and origins of archaeology, 30
chipping (flaking) of stone, 124–5, 126
Christensen, Kim, 233–4
chronological sequencing, 141–4
chronometric (absolute) dating, 141, 145–8
civilizations
   ancient, 161–2
   classical, 31
   collapse, 217–19, *219,* 221
Clancy, Kathryn, et al., 46
clans, 193–4
Clark, Geoffrey, 229
Clarke, David, 42
class, 186
classical civilizations, 31
clay, 91, 127–8
climate change, 248–9, 250–1
Coastal Heritage at Risk Project (SCHARP)
     project, 240–1
Coca-Cola advertising, 21
cognitive archaeology, 197
collaborative archaeology, 233
collapse of civilizations, 217–19, *219,* 221
collections (archaeological), 138–9
color of sediments, 132
Colwell, Chip, 75
commercial archaeology. *See* CRM
commercialization, and ethics, 74
commercial sites, 82
community archaeology, 233
complex (or specialized) foraging, 174
conceptual frameworks
   in archaeology, 211–14
   bias in, 219
   description and role, 22, 211
Confederated Tribes of Grand Ronde, 49–50
conferences and presentations, 77, 248
conflict, 66, 71, 97, 218, 234
Conkey, Margaret, 44
constructed features, 83
construction, and destruction of sites, 96
consultation of people, 101, 104–5
Convention for the Protection of Cultural
     Property in the Event of Armed Conflict
     (Hague Convention) (1954), 66
Convention on the Protection of the Underwater
     Cultural Heritage (2001), 70
cooking hypothesis, 157

coprolites, 137, 181
Cordain, Loren, 179
core tools, 125
Crandall, Brian D., 116–17
cranial sutures, *134,* 134–5
cranium of humans. *See* skulls of humans
Crass, Barbara, 199
critical thinking skills, 221
CRM (cultural resource management or industry
     and archaeology or commercial archaeology)
   description, 14–15, 54–5
   digging decisions, 111–12
   employment in, 55, 230
   fieldwork and excavations, 99, 100
   future of, 252–3
   logistics, 102
   profit aspect, 75
   report of research, 103
   research in, 100, 101, 103
Cro-Magnon, and cave art, 158
cross-dating (dating by association), 142, 144
cryoturbation, 94, 95
C-transforms (cultural disturbance of sites),
     93–4, 96–7
"cult of domesticity", 234
cultural anthropology, 13, 116
cultural disturbance of sites, 93–4, 96–7
cultural ecology, 165, 211, 212, 213
cultural evolution, 35–7
cultural formation processes, 85–6, 89
cultural landscapes, 84
cultural materialism, 211, 212, 213
cultural remains and materials, ground-based
     techniques, 107, 108
cultural resource management (CRM). *See*
   CRM
culture and cultures
   and adaptation, 38, 165
   choronogical development, 37–9
   definition and concept, 24–5
   and environment, 165–6
   nature of, 42
   social and ideological reconstruction (*See*
     social and ideological aspects
     reconstruction)
   spheres, 25
culture change
   conceptual frameworks, 211–14
   mechanisms, 209–11
culture-historical period, 37–8
culture history
   in new archaeology, 42
   in traditional archaeology, 37–8, 39–40, 42
culture history reconstruction

of ancient civilizations, 161–2
dating, 141–8
at regional level, 152–3
stratigraphy example, *149*
and time conceptualization, 150–3
of world prehistory, 153–61
culture process, 42
culture reconstruction, 42
cumulative features, 83
curation crisis, 138–9
curation of artifacts, 123, 138–9
curatorial standards, 139
Curse of King Tut, 38, 41
customs, 24

Dakota Access pipeline (DAPL), 74–6
Darwin, Charles, 35
data, in digital archaeology, 247–8
data collection, 101–3
dating
    absolute dating, 141, 145–8
    methods and techniques, 141–8, *149*
    relative dating, 141–5
    technologies development, 40
dating by association (cross-dating), 142, 144
Dawdy, Shannon, 89
debitage (detritus), 125
Declaration Concerning the Intentional
    Destruction of Cultural Heritage (2003),
    64, 70–1
decolonization of archaeology, 47–50
deep time, 25, 34, 150
De León, Jason, 241, 242–3
Deloria, Vine, Jr., 56
dendrochronology (tree-ring dating), 146
dentition of humans, 132, 134, 135, 181
    See also human remains
descendant communities, 105
descent groups, 193–4
descriptive typology, 123
destruction of sites
    and conflict, 97
    from construction and development, 43, 96,
        255
    regulations, 43, 64, 70–1
    types and examples, 18
detritus (debitage), 125
development projects, 43, 55, 74–5
diachronic change, 209–10
diet, reconstruction, 179–82
    See also food
diffusion, 38, 210
Digital Archaeological Record (tDAR), 248
digital archaeology, 246–8

disabilities, people with, 104
disaster archaeology, 243, 244–5
discovery of archaeological sites
    aerial-based remote sensing, 105–7, *106*
    fortuitous discovery, 104, 105
    ground-based remote sensing, 105, 107, *109*
    monetary value, 1–2
    predictive modeling and consultation, 104–5
    research stages, 99, 100
    by samples use, 105, 109–11
    surface survey, 105, *108*, 108–9
disease, and human remains, 136
disenfranchised, the voiceless, and invisible, 239–
    43
disturbance processes of sites
    cultural disturbance, 93–4, 96–7
    natural disturbance, 93–5
diversity in archaeologists, 3, 230
DNA, 138
dogs, domestication, 225–6
Doig, Federico Kauffmann, 22
domestication, definition, 226
domestication of plants and animals
    definition and attributes, 176, 177
    dogs, 225–6
    and food production, 214, 215, 217
    in human past, 159–61
    in reconstruction, 175, 176–9
drones, 106, *106*

early humans, discoveries, 39
earth, origin and age, 31, 34
earthen mounds, excavations, 32
earthenware, 127
earthwork, as site, 80, 81
earthworms, 94
Easter Island/Rapa Nui, *225*
ecofacts, 83–4, 113, 130–2
ecological adaptations reconstruction
    diet, 179–82
    and domestication, 176–9
    of paleoenvironments, 165–8
    settlement patterns, 168–73
    subsistence strategies, 173–6
    as work, 185
ecological archaeology, 165
ecological frameworks, 211, 213, 217–18, 219
ecological information, for population sizes, 172
ecological sphere, 25
education in archaeology, 13, 53, 54, 76, 220,
    229
egalitarian groups, 186
Egypt
    agriculture, *215*

Egypt (*continued*)
   as civilization, 161, *162*
   discovery and excavations, 34, 38
   foodways, 182
elders care, by archaeologists, 103
empires, 190–1
employment of archaeologists, 55, 76, 229–30,
   252, 253
Energy Transfer company, 75–6
Enlightenment, 30–2
environmental conditions, 91–3, 165–6
environmental movement, 19
equity in archaeology, 103–4
erosion, and remains, 95
espionage by archaeologists, 18
ethics
   by archaeological association, 72
   and archaeology, 46, 72–6
   and legislation, 74–6
ethnic group, 192
ethnic identity, reconstruction, 192–3
ethnic markers, 192–3, *193*
ethnoarchaeology, 26, 86, 115–16
ethnographic analogy, 26
Eurocentrism, 220, 225, 230–1
Europe, 32, 68
evolution
   concept, 25
   development, 31, 35–6
   human, 154–5
   in situ, 209–10
excavations
   digging decisions, 111–14
   example, *114*
   and fieldwork, 99, 111–14
   first in archaeology, 32
   methods and tools, 37, 112–13, *114*
   for museums, 35
   recording and notes, 113–14
   research stages, 99, 100
exoarchaeology (space archaeology), *60,* 61–2, 71
experimental archaeology, 26, 116–17
explanations in archaeology
   bias in, 219–21
   competing explanations evaluation, 221–5
explanatory power of the hypothesis, 222
extraterrestrial explanations, 221, 222, 223, 224,
   225

fabric of ceramic, 127
families, and houses, 169–70
fatalism, 218
faunal remains, 83
   See also animal remains

features, description, 83
feces (human), 137, 181
Feder, Kenneth, 118
feminism, 19
feminist archaeology, 44–6, 247
field experiments, 116
field laboratories, 115, 121
"Field Methods in Indigenous Archaeology"
   (FMIA) project, 49–50
field schools, 54
field walking (surface survey), 105, *108,* 108–9
fieldwork
   archaeologists in, 103–4
   data collection, 101–3
   discovery of sites, 99, 104–11
   example, *113*
   excavation of sites, 99, 111–14
   foundations, 37
   hazards, 117–18
   vs. laboratory work, 139
   logistics, 102
   research design, 99–103, 115–16
Finland, forced removals, 236–7
fire archaeology, 250, 251
fire use, 156–7
First Nations, 18
   See also Indigenous Peoples
first-wave feminist archaeology, 44–5
flakes, *125*
flake tools, 125
flaking (chipping) of stone, 124–5, 126
flintknapping, 125, *125*
fluorine, uranium, nitrogen technique, 143–4
food, 159–61, 203, 217
   See also subsistence strategies
food production, transition to, 214–17
foodways, reconstruction, 182
foraging, 173–4, 215, 216
forced removal, 236–8
forensic archaeology and anthropology, 59, 243
forensics, archaeologists in, 22
fortuitous discovery of sites, 104, 105
frameworks
   role in archaeology, 8, 22, 26, *47*
   science as, 30–1, 34
   See also conceptual frameworks; specific
     frameworks
Franklin Expedition burials, 92–3
frequency seriation, 142, 143
functional typology, 123
funding
   and digital data, 247–8
   in future archaeology, 252
   by government, 20, 54

by media, 21
for research, 13, 54
in US, 44

Gage, Matilda Joslyn, 233–4
garbage, 59–60, 61, 85, 245–6, *246*
Garbage Project, 60, 62
garbology, 59–60, 62
gender
    in archaeologists, 229
    biases in archaeology, 44–5, 46, 220
    description, 194
    in feminist archaeology, 45
    reconstruction, 194
generalized foraging, 173–4
general theory (high-level research), 208–9
geochemical ground-based techniques, 107
geographers, consultation, 105
geographic information systems (GIS), 104
geological epochs, 150–1
geologists, consultation, 105
geophysical ground-based techniques, 107
Germany, 17
Gero, Joan, 44
Gilchrist, Roberta, 45
glaciers and glacial ice, 168, 249
glass and metal artifacts, analysis, 129–30
GlobalXplorer program, 252
glossary, 257–72
glyphs in Nazca desert, 222–4, *224*
goddess figurine, *201*
god(s), in explanations, 221, 222
Goldstein, Lynne, et al., 46
Gonzalez, Sara, 49
Gorman, Alice, 61–2
Gould, Richard, 245
government, funding by, 20, 54
grand theory, 208, 211
grave goods, 186, 199
graviturbation (mass wasting), 94, 95
gray literature, 55, 77
Great Britain. *See* Britain
Great Zimbabwe site, 17
ground-based remote sensing, 105, 107, *109*
ground reconnaissance (surface survey), 105, *108*, 108–9
groups, 186–7
Guantánamo Bay detention camp, 235–6, *236*
Guttmann-Bond, Erika, 248–9

habitation, description as site, 80, 82
Hague Convention (Convention for the Protection of Cultural Property in the Event of Armed Conflict) (1954), 66

hand axes, 156
Haraway, Donna J., 225–6
Hayden, Brian, 115
hazards, in fieldwork, 117–18
Head Man (or Big Man), 189
Head-Smashed-In Buffalo Jump, 69
heart-centered archaeology ("Archaeologies of the Heart"), 230
Herculaneum, 32
heritage
    definition, 75
    framework for, 22
    presentation of, 15
    regulations and legislation, 62–5
heritage industry, 14–15, 23
heritage management, 62, 64–6, 69–71
heritage sites
    and archaeology, 14–15
    assessment of significance, 23
    and land-altering projects, 55
    and national identity, 16–17
    protection and investigation, 18
    See also archaeological sites
heritage tourism (archaeotourism), 7, *8,* 14, 69, 70
heuristic theory, 211
    See also conceptual frameworks
hieroglyphics, deciphering, *33,* 34
high-level research (general theory), 208–9
Hilton, M.R., 95
historical particularism, 37
historic archaeology (text-aided archaeology), 57, 59
historic sites, description and subtypes, 80, 82
history of archaeology
    ancients to eighteenth century, 29–34
    description as focus, 37–9
    diversification and critical aspects in archaeology, 42–4, 46
    and fascination by public, 38–9
    in nineteenth century, 34–7
    origins, 29–31
    in twentieth century, 37–44
    in twenty-first century, 13, 24, 46–50, 253–4
    See also archaeology of today
Hodder, Ian, 43, 44
holism, 25
Holtorf, Cornelius, 21
homelessness, 240, *241*
Homininae family, 154
Homo erectus and *Homo ergaster,* 154–5, 156
Homo genus, 10, 154–5
Homo habilis, 154
Homo sapiens, 157–8, *159*

horizon, as time unit, 153
horizontal excavations (block excavations), 112
horticulture, 174, 175–6
household archaeology, 169
houses (individual), *169, 171*
   and inequality, 186–7
   for population sizes, 172–3
   as settlement pattern, 168, 169–70
human, definition, 10
human burials, 86
human-controlled fires, 156–7
human feces, 137, 181
human past
   and frameworks, 8
   interest in, 6–7, 8
   outline, 153–61
   ownership and ethics, 72–3
human remains
   age at death, 134–5
   analysis in laboratory, 132, 134–8
   decay, 87
   positioning of body, 199
   practice in archaeology, 2
   as prehistoric site, 80, 81
   preservation, 92–3
   regulations, 71
   sex and other determinations, 136, 138
   of twenty-first century, 254
   See also bones of humans; skeletons of
       humans; skulls of humans; teeth of
       humans
humans
   in archaeology's definition, 9–10
   biological evolution, 154–5
   global expansion, *159*
   and lens of archaeology, 8–9
   sexual dimorphism, 136
   and tool use, 155–6
human soft tissue, 181
Humes, Edward, 245
hunters and gatherers, 174
hunting, in human past, 156
Hurricane Katrina, *89,* 89–90
Hutton, James, 34
Hyde, E.R., et al., 87
hypotheses, 101, 221–4

ice melting, 249
ice patch archaeology, 249, 250
ICOMOS (International Council on Monuments
   and Sites), heritage regulations, 63, 70
ideal data, 101, 102
ideal methods, 102
ideas, 22, 38, 210

identity
   and feminist archaeology, 45
   kinds and evidence, 191–2
   national identity, 16–17
   reconstruction, 191–4, 196
ideological frameworks, 213–14, 217, 218
ideological sphere, 25
ideology, reconstruction, 197–204
impoverished people, and frameworks, 213
incarceration, 235–6, 238–9
income of archaeologists, 229, 230
Indigenous archaeology, 56–7
Indigenous empowerment, 19, 56
Indigenous Peoples
   as archaeologists, 48–50, *49*
   and archaeology in North America, 56
   boarding schools in US, 237–8
   claims to rights and territories, 18, 22
   decolonization of archaeology, 48–50
   and development of archaeology, 37
   earthen mounds, 32
   food production, 216
   forced removal of children, 236–7
   heritage definition, 75
   power relationships, 56
   and space archaeology, 61–2
   statues on Rapa Nui, *225*
   and terminology, 230–1
   traditional territories, 171
individual houses. *See* houses
individuals, identification, 196
industrial sites, 82
industry and archaeology. *See* CRM
inequality
   in archaeology record, 160, 161, 170
   reconstruction, 186–7
information sharing, 76–7
Inka Empire, 190–1
Inka ritual, 199
innovation, 210
inorganic materials/remains, 91
in situ evolution, 209–10
intellectual property rights, 74
intelligence of humans, 3, 255
International Space Station (ISS), 61
Internet, 77
interviews and questions, as method, 116
Inuit, burials, 199
invention, 210
inventory of artifacts, 113, 122–4
Iraq, 17
Iron Age, 29, 31, 35
isolated finds, 82, 86
isotopes, and diet, 180–1

Jalbert, Catherine, 45
Japanese American porcelain, *128*
Jefferson, Thomas, 32
Johnson, Matthew, 207–8
journals and articles, 54, 76, 77
Joyce, Rosemary, 247
judgmental sampling (non-probabilistic sampling), 109–10, 112

Kakadu (Australia), *82*
Kaplan, M., 23
Keatley Creek (Canada), 170, 186
Keeley, Lawrence, 126
King Tut's tomb, 38, *39,* 41
Koobi Fora (Kenya), 126
Kwayday Dan Ts'inchi, 249

laboratories, role and types, 121–2
laboratory work, *137*
    artifact analysis, 123–30
    ecofact analysis, 130–2
    vs. fieldwork, 139
    human remains analysis, 132, 134–8
    processes, *122,* 122–3
    role, 121
land-altering projects, 55
landforms, dating of, 144
L'Anse aux Meadows site, 69, 193
law of superposition (stratigraphic dating), 31, 142
leadership, in societies, 189, 190
Leakey, Louis, 39, *40*
Leakey, Mary, 39
Leakey, Richard, 39
Leakey family, as archaeologists, 39, 40
legislation
    and archaeology in industry, 55
    and development of sites, 43, 75–6
    and ethics, 74–6
    and heritage, 62–5
    of sites, 18
    underwater objects, 70
lens of archaeology, 8–9, *47*
level notes, 113
Lewis, Tiana, *49*
LIDAR (Light Detection and Ranging), 107
lineages, 193
linguistic anthropology, 13
literature reviews, 100–1
lithic artifacts, analysis, 124–7
lithic scatter, 81, 83
lithic technology, *125*
living museums, 15, *16*
looters and looting, 57, 65, 74, 96–7

lost artifacts, 86
Lothrop, Samuel, 18
Love, Serena, 182
lovers entangled in death, 2
low-level (low-range) research, 207–8
Lyell, Charles, 34
Lyons, Natasha, et al., 230

Maasai village, 170, *171*
Macchu Pichu (Peru), 7, *8,* 21–2
magnetometers, *109*
male bias, 220
manual ground-based techniques, 107
mass wasting (graviturbation), 94, 95
material remains
    as archaeological sites, 80, 84
    in archaeology's definition, 9–10
    bias in preservation, 90–3
    and children, 194–6
    description, 10
    and inequality, 187
    in origins and development of archaeology, 29–30, 31–6
    radiocarbon dating, 40
    See also animal remains; plant remains
matrix, 84, 113–14
    See also sediments
matrix chemistry, 93
Maya, 115, 221
Mayan sites, 16, *219*
media, 1–3, 5–6, 20–1, 38, 54
Mediterranean civilizations, 161
megaliths, 80, *81*
men, 44–5, 220
    See also gender
Mesa Verde (Colorado), *69,* 70
Mesoamerica, 152, 161
Mesopotamia, 161
metal and glass artifacts, analysis, 129–30
metals, 91
Mexico, 241–2
microwear, 126
middens, 80
Middle Ages, 30
middle-level (middle-range) research, 43, 208
migration, 210–11, 241–3, *242*
minimum number of individuals (MNI), 131
MNI as acronym, 130, 131
monuments (or monumental) architecture, 189, 190
Morgan, Lewis Henry, 36–7
Morley, Sylvanus, 18
mortuary archaeology, *200*

mortuary practices, 199–200, *200*
Moshenska, Gabe, 239, *240*
mounds, excavations, 32
mummies and mummification, 93
Munsell system, 132
museums, 30, 34–5
Myers, Adrian, 235, 236

Nabonidus, and origins of archaeology, 30
Napoleon Bonaparte, 34
National Geographic, 17
National Historic Preservation Act (NHPA), 64, 75
national identity, and heritage sites, 16–17
Native American Graves Protection and Repatriation Act (NAGPRA), 56, 65
Native Americans. *See* Indigenous Peoples
natural disturbance of sites, 93–5
natural formation processes, 85–6, 89
natural levels of excavation, 113–14
Nazca desert hummingbird, 222–4, *224*
Neandertals, burials, 157–8
Near East, 161
Neolithic houses reconstruction, *16*
new archaeology (processual archaeology), 42–3, 185
New Orleans, 89–90
New World archaeology, 59
Ninstints (Nans Dins), 69
no-collections strategy (catch-and-release), 139
non-archaeologists, 252, 253
non-cultural disturbance processes (natural disturbance of sites), 93–5
non-cultural (or natural) formation processes, 85–6, 89
non-probabilistic sampling (judgmental sampling), 109–10, 112
notes and sketches, 113–14
N-transforms (natural disturbance of sites), 93–5
nuclear waste, 23, 24
number of identified specimens (NISP), 131

Obama, Barack, 235–6
obsidian hydration, 144
obsidian trade, 210
Occam's Razor (or Occam's Rule), 222, 224
Olduvai Gorge (Tanzania), 39
Old World archaeology, 59
organic artifacts, analysis, 129
organic materials/remains, 91–2
orphaned collections, 138, 139
Otzi the Iceman, 92, 249
ownership of archaeological resources, 65

paleodiet, 179
paleoenvironments, reconstruction, 165–8
paleoethnobotany (archaeobotany), 59
paleofantasies, 6, 179
paradigm. *See* conceptual frameworks
Paranthropus, 154
Parcak, Sarah, 252
participant observation, 115–16
past. *See* human past
pastoralism, 174, 175, *175*
Pearson, James, 217
peat bogs, 93
pelvis identification, 136, *136*
Peregrine, Peter, 152–3
permits and permissions, 102
Persia, 30
Peru, 55
petroform, description as site, 80–1
petroglyphs, 81, 200–1
pharmaceuticals, 217
phases, description as time unit, 153
pH of sediments, 132
phosphorus, 107
physical weathering, 95
pictographs, 81, 200–1
Piltdown Man, 143–4
pirates, identification, 196–7
pithouses, 186
Pitt Rivers, Henry Lane-Fox, 37
place, as bias, 220–1
plant remains, 91, 170–1, 180–1, 253
plants
    and disturbance of sites, 94
    domestic *vs.* wild, 176, 177
    foraging, 173–4
    as pharmaceuticals, 217
    and reconstruction, 167
    See also domestication of plants and animals
Plateau Pithouse Tradition, 153
pointing trowels, 112
Poirier, David, 118
politics, and archaeology, 16–18
Polly Hill Plantation graffiti, *195,* 195–6
Pompeii, 32, 88, *88,* 90
pop culture
    archaeology and archaeologists, 1–3, 5–6, 19–22
    and King Tut, 38, 41
population pressure, and food production, 216, 217
population sizes, 172–3
porcelain, 127
porcelain bowl, *128*
post-depositional disturbance processes, 93–7

post-processual archaeology, 43–4, 185
potassium/argon dating (K/Ar), 147–8
pothunters and pothunting. *See* looters and
    looting
pottery, 127–9, 159
    See also ceramic
predictive modeling, 104–5
prehistoric archaeology, 57
prehistoric sites, description and subtypes, 80–2
prehistory
    population sizes, 173
    sequence of events, 153–61
    as term, 231
    time units, 151–3
prestige goods, 187
primary refuse, 85–6
prisoners, study of, 238–9
probabilistic sampling (statistical sampling), 110–
    11, 112
processual (new) archaeology, 42–3, 185
projectile points, dating, 143
protection of sites, 18
provenience, 113
pseudoarchaeology, 57, 223
public archaeology, 233, 234, 239–41
    definition, 239, *240*
Pueblo de Taos and Chaco Canyon (New
    Mexico), 70
pyramids, *162*

race and racism, 45
radiocarbon dating, 40, 146–7
raised field agriculture, 232–3, 248–9
ranked groups, 186
Rapa Nui/Easter Island, *225*
Rathje, William L., 60, 61
reasoning by analogy, 25–6
reconstruction. *See* culture history reconstruction;
    ecological adaptations reconstruction; social
    and ideological aspects reconstruction
record. *See* archaeological record
recycling of material remains, 96
refuse, 85–6, 115
    See also trash
regions, 152–3, 168, 172, 173
Register of Professional Archaeologists (RPA), 11
registries for archaeologists, 10–11
regular laboratories, 121–2
regulations, for heritage, 63–4
relative dating, 141–5
religion, 197, 218
religious ritual, reconstruction, 197–9
remote sensing
    aerial-based, 105–7, *106*

    ground-based, 105, 107, *109*
Renaissance, 30–1
Renfrew, Colin, 197
research
    in archaeology, 13, 53, 54
    background research, 100–1
    design of fieldwork, 99–103, 115–16
    frameworks, 214
    funding, 13, 54
    in future archaeology, 251
    hypotheses, 101, 221–4
    information sharing, 76–7
    levels, 207–9
    and national identity, 16–17
    need for, 100
    report of research, 103
    stages, 99, 100–3
resource utilization, as site, 80, 81
responsibilities to various groups, 74–6
reuse of sites, 96
ritual, 157, 197–9
Roach, Mary, 87
rock art, 80, 81, 193, 201
    See also cave art
rodents, 94
Roman Coliseum, *191*
Roman Empire, 191
Rosetta Stone, *33, 34*
rubbish, 85

Sabloff, Jeremy, 232, 233
sacred sites, reconstruction, 197–9
Salzman, Philip, 211
Sámi children, 236–7
samples and sampling, in discovery of sites, 105,
    109–11
San Salvador (Bahamas), 195–6
saprophytic organisms and activity, 92
savagery, barbarism, and civilization (unilinear
    theory), 36–7, 38, 188
Scarre, Chris, 220
Schliemann, Heinrich, 105
Schnidejoch mountain ridge/pass, 250
science, 30–1, 34, 223
Scotland, 240–1
screens and screen size, 112
sculptures, 202
seasonality studies, 170
secondary refuse, 85–6
second-wave feminist archaeology, 45
sedentism, 160–1, 215–16
sediments (natural)
    analysis in laboratory, 131–2
    and archaeological sites, 88, 90

sediments (natural) (*continued*)
  as ecofacts, 83–4
  and formation processes, 83, 85
  ground-based techniques, 107
  and reconstruction, 167–8
  sieving, 112
  of twenty-first century, 254
segmentary societies (tribes), 188–9
selective breeding, 226
seriation, 142–3
settlement patterns, reconstruction, 168–73
settlements, 172–3, 186–7, 254
sex and gender, reconstruction, 194
sexual discrimination, 46
shamans and shamanism, 188, 200–1, 217
shell middens, 80
shells, and trade, 210
ship iconography, 195–6
shoring of walls, 118
shrew eating experiment, 116–17
Shroud of Turin, dating, 147
sieving and sifting, 112, *114,* 131
simple random sampling, 110
single settlements, as pattern, 168, 170–1
site catchment analysis, 171
site exploitation territory, 171
site formation processes, 85–6, 87–8
sites. *See* archaeological sites; heritage sites
skeletal remains of animals, 116–17, 130–1, 178, *178, 180*
skeletons of humans
  and diet, 180–1
  identification, *133, 136*
  and inequality, 186
  practice in archaeology, 2
  See also bones of humans; human remains
Skellig Michael (Ireland) site, *20*
skulls of humans
  analysis, 134–5, 136
  cranial sutures, *134,* 134–5
  trepanation, 138, 203–4, *204*
  See also human remains
slaves, 195–6
social activism, 233–4
social and ideological aspects reconstruction
  identity, 191–4, 196
  ideology, 197–204
  inequality, 186–7
  overview, 185
  society types, 187–91
social frameworks, 213, 218
social inequality, in archaeological record, 160, 161, 170
social movements, 6, 19

social sphere, 25
society
  categories and models, 187–8
  vs. culture, 25
  evidence used, 187
  and food production, 216–17
  reconstruction, 187–91
Society for American Archaeology (SAA), 72, 248
software, 247
soil(s)
  in discovery of sites, 106, 107, 108
  texture and color analysis, 131–2
South America, World Heritage Sites, 67–8
space archaeology (exoarchaeology), *60,* 61–2, 71
space race, 61
spear-throwers, *158*
specialized (or complex) foraging, 174
Stahl, Peter W., 116–17
Standing Rock Sioux Reservation, 75
Starzmann, Maria Theresia, 234
State Historic Preservation Offices, 248
states, as society, 190
statistical sampling (probabilistic sampling), 110–11, 112
Stein, Julie, 94
stone, 91
Stone Age, 29, 31, 35
Stonehenge (Great Britain), *73,* 73–4
stones, types and uses, 126–7
stone tools, 124–6, *125,* 155
stoneware, 127
Stottman, M. Jay, 231, 232
stratified groups, 186
stratified random sampling, 110
stratigraphic dating (law of superposition), 31, 142
stratigraphy, *149,* 254
stylistic seriation, 142–3
subsistence strategies, 173–6
surface survey, 105, *108,* 108–9
sustainability, 249
Swiss Alps, 250
synchronic change, 209
systematic sampling, 111

Taliban regime, 18, 84
taphonomy, 89–90, 91
Tasmania, female prisoners, 238
taxonomic identification, 130–1
technological change and diffusion, 210
technology, 246–7, 251
teeth of humans, 132, 134, 135, 181
  See also human remains
tell, 80
terminus ante quem (TAQ), 145

terminus post quem (TPQ), 145
terminus quem dating, 142, 145
terra cotta, 127
terra cotta warriors of Xi'an, *71*
text-aided (historic) archaeology, 57, 59
texture of sediments, 131–2
thermoluminescence, 148
third-wave feminist archaeology, 45–6
Thomsen, Christian, 35
three-age system, 29, 31, 35
Tikal (Guatemala), *219*
time
    as bias, 220–1
    conceptualization, 150–3
    dating techniques, 141–8
    at regional level, 152–3
    time frames in archaeology, 151–2
Titanic, 2
today, archaeology of. *See* archaeology of today
tomb of Tutankhamen, 38, *39,* 41
tools, 124–6, *125,* 155–6
    See also stone tools
Toth, Nick, 126
tourism to ancient sites and ruins, 7, *8,* 14, 69, 70
toxic substances in fieldwork, 117
trace-element analysis, 210
trade, inferences about, 210
tradition, as time unit, 152–3
traditional territory, 168, 171, 173
trampling by humans, 96
transegalitarian groups, 186
trash, 59–60, 62, 61, 85, 245–6, *246*
treasures in discoveries, 2, 20
tree-ring dating (dendrochronology), 146
trepanation (trephination), 138, 203–4, *204*
tribes, 188–9
Tringham, Ruth, 247
trowels, 112
Trump, Donald, 236
Turkana pastoralism, *175*
Turkana village, *169*
Tushingham, Shannon, et al., 46
Tutankhamen tomb, 38, *39,* 41
Tylor, Edward, 36
typology, 123

UN (United Nations), heritage regulations, 64
underwater objects, legislation, 70
underwater wrecks, 2
undocumented migration and border crossings, 241–3, *242*
Undocumented Migration Project, 241–3
UNESCO (United Nations Educational,

Scientific, and Cultural Organization), heritage regulations, 63–4, 66, 70–1
UNESCO Convention Concerning the Protection of the World Cultural and Natural Heritage (1972), 66
UNESCO Convention on the Means of Prohibiting and Preventing the Illicit Import, Export, and Transfer of Ownership of Cultural Property (1970), 66
UNESCO Recommendations on International Principles Applicable to Archaeological Excavations (1956), 66
UNIDROIT Convention on Stolen and Illegally Exported Cultural Objects, 66
unifaces, 125
uniformitarianism, 34
unilinear theory of cultural evolution, 36–7, 38, 188
United Nations Outer Space Treaty (1967), 71
United States
    activism at work, 233
    bias from, 221
    boarding schools for Indigenous Peoples, 237–8
    data storage, 247–8
    first excavations, 32
    heritage and ideology, 17
    incarcerations and prisoners, 235–6, 239
    legislation and regulations for heritage, 63, 64–5, 75–6
    looting of sites, 65
    nuclear waste, 23, 24
    trash, 245
    undocumented border crossing, 241–2
    World Heritage sites, 67, 69–70
universities, waste audits, 246, *246*
Unpiloted Aerial Vehicles (UAVs), 106, *106*
use-wear studies, 243
Ussher, James, 31

vegetation, in discovery of sites, 106, 108
Venus figurines, 202
Vermillion Accord on Human Remains (1989), 71
Vick, Amanda, *49*
Vikings, 193
volcanic sediments, dating, 147–8
von Daniken, Erich, 223
Voss, Barbara, 45, 139

WAC (World Archaeology Congress), heritage regulations, 64, 71
Walsh, Justin St. P., 61
war. *See* conflict
waste. *See* trash

waste reduction, 249
water, and preservation of remains, 93
waterways, and reconstruction, 166, 167–8
weathering of remains, 95
websites, 77
Wilk, Richard, 221
wind, 167, 168
wolves, 225, 226
women
    as archaeologists, 19, 44, 45, 46, *49,* 103
    and domesticity, 234
    in figurines, *201,* 202
    as prisoners, 238
    in reconstruction, 194
    See also gender

Woomera rocket range, 61–2
World Heritage List, 66
World Heritage Sites, 66–8, 234
Worsaae, Jacob Jens, 35
Wrangham, Richard, 157
writing systems, 190
written record, of twenty-first century, 253–4

Xi'an (China), and terra cotta warriors, *71*

"years before present," 147
youth violence, and frameworks, 213–14
Yukon Ice Patches, 250

Zimmerman, Larry, 240